The Funding of School Education

CONNECTING RESOURCES AND LEARNING

OECD

BETTER POLICIES FOR BETTER LIVES

This work is published on the responsibility of the Secretary-General of the OECD. The opinions expressed and arguments employed herein do not necessarily reflect the official views of the Organisation or of the governments of its member countries.

This document and any map included herein are without prejudice to the status of or sovereignty over any territory, to the delimitation of international frontiers and boundaries and to the name of any territory, city or area.

Please cite this publication as:
OECD (2017), *The Funding of School Education: Connecting Resources and Learning*, OECD Publishing, Paris.
http://dx.doi.org/10.1787/9789264276147-en

ISBN 978-92-64-27613-0 (print)
ISBN 978-92-64-27614-7 (PDF)
ISBN 978-92-64-27618-5 (epub)

Series: OECD Reviews of School Resources
ISSN 2413-4333 (print)
ISSN 2413-3841 (online)

The statistical data for Israel are supplied by and under the responsibility of the relevant Israeli authorities. The use of such data by the OECD is without prejudice to the status of the Golan Heights, East Jerusalem and Israeli settlements in the West Bank under the terms of international law.

Photo credits: Cover © VLADGRIN/Shutterstock.com.

Foreword

School systems have limited financial resources with which to pursue their objectives and the design of school funding policies plays a key role in ensuring that resources are directed to where they can make the most difference. This report seeks to assist governments in achieving their education policy objectives through the efficient and equitable use of financial resources. It provides a systematic analysis of school funding policies by looking into the organisation of responsibilities for raising and spending school funds, the design of mechanisms to distribute funding to schools, the procedures for planning education budgets, and the practices for monitoring, evaluating and reporting how funding has been used. Eighteen school systems were actively engaged in the preparation of this report. In addition, the analysis considers the broader research and policy literature on school funding approaches in other OECD and partner countries.

This report is the first in a series of thematic comparative reports which bring together the findings of a major OECD project on the effective use of school resources, the OECD Review of Policies to Improve the Effectiveness of Resource Use in Schools (School Resources Review). Forthcoming reports will focus on the organisation of the school offer and on the management of human resources in school education. The School Resources Review was launched in 2013 to help countries exchange best practices and learn from one another, and to gather and disseminate evidence of what works in school resource policies. The project highlights issues and explores ideas for policy development that may be difficult to raise in national debates. It seeks to inform discussions among stakeholders with new and different perspectives that are based on research and evidence from different countries. This ambition also underpins the idea of the thematic comparative reports and the work behind them.

This report was co-authored by Luka Boeskens, Gonçalo Lima, Deborah Nusche (co-ordinator), Thomas Radinger and Claire Shewbridge from the OECD Directorate for Education and Skills. The work on this report was led by project managers Deborah Nusche (since December 2016) and Paulo Santiago (January to July 2016). Paulo Santiago co-ordinated the initial structure and extended outline of this report. Joris Ranchin led the initial stages of the qualitative data collection on countries' approaches to school funding. Eleonore Morena was responsible for the production and layout of the report and contributed to editing and proofreading. Meral Gedik, Florence Guerinot and Anne-Lise Prigent provided valuable advice on the production of the report. Cassandra Davis advised on communication and dissemination activities.

Acknowledgements

This report would not have been possible without the support of the 18 education systems actively engaged in the School Resources Review. Participating countries committed substantial resources and opened their school resource policies to review and debate. National co-ordinators (listed in Annex D) played a key role in this exchange, enriching discussions with their insights from particular contexts and co-ordinating their country's participation in the project.

The OECD Education Policy Committee and Group of National Experts (GNE) on School Resources, as well as the individual delegates to these bodies, provided essential support and analytical guidance since the inception of the project, and offered useful feedback on drafts of this report. At the time of publication of this report, the Group of National Experts was chaired by Mr Jørn Skovsgaard, Senior Advisor of the Danish Ministry of Education; and had as vice-chairs Ms Marie-Anne Persoons, Advisor International Policy in the Strategic Policy Support Division of the Flemish Ministry of Education and Training and Mr Matej Šiškovič, Director of the Educational Policy Institute at the Slovak Ministry of Education, Science, Research and Sports. Ms Shelley Robertson, Chief Advisor International Education, New Zealand Ministry of Education, served as vice-chair for the GNE from May 2014 to May 2015 and chaired its 1st meeting. The dedication and leadership of the chair and vice-chairs is gratefully acknowledged.

The School Resources Review and this report also benefited substantially from the active involvement of different stakeholders with an interest in education. The Business and Industry Advisory Committee to the OECD (BIAC) and the Trade Union Advisory Committee to the OECD (TUAC) participated in meetings of the Group of National Experts on School Resources as permanent observers and commented on drafts of this report. During individual country reviews, students, parents, teachers, school leaders, researchers and employers made their time available to meet with review teams and to provide their perspective of school resource policy issues.

Within a broader framework of collaboration, a partnership with the European Commission (EC) was established for the OECD School Resources Review, as part of which this report was prepared. The support of the EC covers part of the participation costs of countries which are part of the European Union Erasmus+ programme and contributes significantly to the preparation of the series of thematic comparative reports, including this report on school funding. The support of the European Commission for the School Resources Review is gratefully acknowledged. The review team would like to thank in particular current and former colleagues at the EC Directorate-General for Education and Culture, *Unit A.2: Education and Training in Europe 2020* under the leadership of Michael Teutsch (until December 2016) and Denis Crowley (since January 2017) and deputy leadership of Mónika Képe-Holmberg, and *Unit B.2: Schools and Multilingualism* under the leadership of Sophie Beernaerts (until December 2016) and Michael Teutsch (since January 2017) and deputy leadership of Diana Jablonska. Unit A.2 co-ordinated the collaboration at the EC and contributed to the individual country reviews (see Annex D).

In addition, collaboration with Eurydice, the Inter-American Development Bank (IDB), the Organising Bureau of European School Student Unions (OBESSU), the Standing International Conference of Inspectorates (SICI), the United Nations Educational, Scientific and Cultural Organization (UNESCO), the UNESCO International Institute for Educational Planning (IIEP-UNESCO) and the World Bank, ensured synergies between the work undertaken by different organisations and provided valuable input into the project and this report.

The review is indebted to the many individual experts who contributed to the country review visits and the resulting country review reports that are part of the publication series *OECD Reviews of School Resources* (for the composition of the country review teams, see Annex D). Their expertise, analytical contributions to the country-specific reports and professional exchanges with OECD Secretariat members provided the foundation for analysing school funding from a comparative perspective in this report. The country background reports prepared by participating countries provided a further important source of information and thanks are due to all those who contributed to these reports. In addition to this publication, by June 2017, the review had generated 16 reports by participating countries, 10 reports by external review teams and several research papers (all available on the OECD website at *www.oecd.org/education/schoolresourcesreview.htm*).

Within the OECD Directorate for Education and Skills, from its inception until the publication of this report, the review was carried out by the Early Childhood and Schools Division under the leadership of Michael Davidson (from January 2013 to September 2014) and Yuri Belfali (from October 2014 to July 2016) and by the Policy Advice and Implementation Division under the leadership of Paulo Santiago (since August 2016). Deborah Nusche (co-ordinator since December 2016), Thomas Radinger, Paulo Santiago (co-ordinator between January 2013 and July 2016) and Claire Shewbridge were responsible for the review, assuming leadership for the analytical work and individual country reviews. Important analytical contributions to the project were made by Anna Pons (who led the review of Kazakhstan) and Tracey Burns (who participated in the review of Uruguay). Eleonore Morena (since November 2014), Elizabeth Zachary (from October 2013 to December 2014) and Heike-Daniela Herzog (from January 2013 to September 2013) took responsibility for the administrative work within the review, the organisation of meetings and communication with the countries.

Gratitude is also extended to current and former team members who supported the work of the project at different stages. Macarena Ares Abalde, Francesc Masdeu Navarro and Alette Schreiner provided substantial input into the project's knowledge base. Luka Boeskens, Tala Fakharzadeh, Anna Gromada, Gonçalo Lima, Kerstin Schophol, Oliver Sieweke and Antoine Papalia provided research assistance and summarised key areas of the literature on school resources during their internships with the review. The Jaume Bofill Foundation sponsored the secondment of Macarena Ares Abalde (March to August 2013) and Francesc Masdeu Navarro (November 2013 to November 2014), and the Ministry of Education and Research of Norway sponsored the secondment of Alette Schreiner (September to December 2013) with the OECD Secretariat. The German Academic Exchange Service (*Deutscher Akademischer Austauschdienst*, DAAD) and the German National Academic Foundation sponsored Luka Boeskens' appointment with the OECD Secretariat as a Fellow of the Carlo Schmid Programme.

A larger group of colleagues within the OECD provided advice at key stages. In particular, collaboration was established with the Programme for International Student Assessment (PISA), the Teaching and Learning International Survey (TALIS), the INES Network for the Collection and the Adjudication of System-Level Descriptive Information on Educational Structures, Policies and Practices (NESLI), the Centre for Educational Research and Innovation's (CERI) work on Governing Complex Education Systems, the Learning Environments Evaluation Programme (LEEP), the Fiscal Network in the Economics Department and the Budgeting and Public Expenditures and Public Sector Integrity Divisions in the Directorate for Public Governance and Territorial Development.

Table of contents

Tables

Figures

Follow OECD Publications on:

 http://twitter.com/OECD_Pubs

 http://www.facebook.com/OECDPublications

 http://www.linkedin.com/groups/OECD-Publications-4645871

 http://www.youtube.com/oecdilibrary

 http://www.oecd.org/oecddirect/

Abbreviations and acronyms

CBA	Central Budget Authority
CBR	Country Background Report
EC	European Commission
ECEC	Early Childhood Education and Care
ERDF	European Regional Development Fund
ESF	European Social Fund
EU	European Union
GDP	Gross Domestic Product
GNE	Group of National Experts
ICT	Information and Communication Technology
IDB	Inter-American Development Bank
IIEP-UNESCO	UNESCO International Institute for Educational Planning
ISCED	UNESCO International Standard Classification of Education
MTEF	Medium-Term Expenditure Framework
OECD	Organisation for Economic Co-operation and Development
PISA	OECD Programme for International Student Assessment
PPP	Purchasing Power Parity
SEN	Special Educational Needs
TALIS	OECD Teaching and Learning International Survey
UNESCO	United Nations Educational, Scientific and Cultural Organization
VET	Vocational Education and Training

Executive summary

This report constitutes the first in a series of thematic comparative reports bringing together the findings of the *OECD Review of Policies to Improve the Effectiveness of Resource Use in Schools (School Resources Review)*. It provides analysis and policy options to assist governments in achieving their education policy objectives through the efficient and equitable use of financial resources. Following an introductory chapter explaining the importance of school funding policies, the report's remaining chapters focus on the following thematic areas:

- How responsibilities for raising and spending school funds can be effectively organised in increasingly complex education systems.
- How mechanisms for the distribution of funding to schools can be designed to efficiently support student learning, equity and related policy objectives.
- How planning procedures can inform the preparation of education budgets to ensure their long-term sustainability and alignment with policy priorities.
- How the effective use of school funding can be enhanced through monitoring, evaluation and reporting practices.

Chapter 1, *Why Look at School Funding Policies?*, sets the context for this report. It outlines the importance of school funding policies, describes major contextual developments that shape the funding of school education and explains the terms and concepts used throughout the report. Well-designed school funding policies are crucial to achieve quality, equity and efficiency objectives in school education. While the overall level of school funding matters, the strategies used to allocate it are at least as important. As countries seek to enhance the performance of all students while also providing more equitable learning opportunities for different groups, there has been greater focus on ensuring that resources are directed to the areas where improvements in teaching and learning outcomes can best be achieved. Developing an equitable distribution of school funding requires countries to take into account both horizontal equity (allocating similar levels of resources to similar types of provision) and vertical equity (allocating different levels of resources to student groups with different needs). It is also important to recognise that the pursuit of efficiency and equity can go hand in hand when it comes to the allocation of resources. Ensuring that students with different needs and from different backgrounds have access to high quality education from an early age, for example, can be an effective means to reduce systemic inefficiencies.

Chapter 2, *Governing School Funding*, describes the different bodies involved in raising, managing and allocating school funds across OECD review countries and analyses how the relationships between these bodies are organised. As school systems have become more complex and characterised by multi-level governance, a growing set of actors including different levels of the school administration, schools themselves and private providers are involved in school funding. While on average across OECD countries, central governments continue to provide the majority of financial resources for schools, the responsibility for spending these funds is shared among an increasingly wide range of actors. In many countries, the governance of school funding is characterised by increasing fiscal decentralisation, considerable responsibility of schools over budgetary matters and growing public funding of private school providers. These developments generate new opportunities and challenges for school funding policies and need to be accompanied by adequate institutional arrangements. To support effective school funding and avoid adverse effects on equity in changing governance contexts, the chapter recommends that reforms should seek to: ensure that roles and responsibilities in decentralised funding systems are well aligned; provide the necessary conditions for effective budget management at the school level; and develop adequate regulatory frameworks for the public funding of private providers.

Chapter 3, *Distributing School Funding*, presents an overview of how OECD review countries distribute school funding between different levels of administration and to individual schools, focussing on the design of effective allocation mechanisms for the funding of both current and capital expenditure. The chapter discusses fundamental questions that need to be addressed when designing a funding allocation model. It finds that well-designed funding formulas are a particularly effective means to distribute funding for current expenditure in a transparent and efficient way. By including weights to distribute additional funds to particular categories, funding formulas can also play a critical role in aligning the distribution of resources with educational priorities such as promoting greater equity. Regardless of the allocation mechanism, the method used to identify differential resource needs should be subject to periodical reviews and based on national research, reliable data and transparent criteria. The chapter recommends that governments: ensure a stable and publicly known system to allocate public funding to schools; follow a set of guiding principles when designing funding formulas to distribute resources; and seek efficient ways to support the achievement of equity objectives through school funding mechanisms.

Chapter 4, *Planning the Use of School Funding*, examines the practices and procedures involved in planning the use of school funding in OECD review countries. It analyses how effective planning and budgeting can contribute to greater resource efficiency and the alignment of spending with policy objectives. The preparation of education budgets is increasingly embedded in multi-annual planning processes, which can assist spending authorities in making informed and sustainable budgeting choices and which provide them with additional security when engaging in longer-term investments. However, the chapter finds that multi-annual expenditure plans are not always sufficiently linked to strategic targets and priorities. From the central to the school level, the planning of education resources should be informed by research and evaluation results as well as strategic objectives to guide the planning process and employ resources as effectively and equitably as possible. Increasing the capacity to mobilise evaluation, monitoring and research results during the budget planning process is therefore central to promoting effective spending on education. The planning of education budgets should also be flexible enough to respond to new priorities and unforeseen circumstances as well as providing incentives for efficiency, for example through the transparent regulation of carry-over rights for unspent resources.

Chapter 5, *Evaluating the Use of School Funding*, analyses how the evaluation and monitoring of school funding can serve to hold decision makers accountable, make the use of resources transparent and ensure that available resources are used efficiently and equitably. Practices to evaluate the use of school funding include accounting, financial reporting, internal management and control, external audits and individual performance management. The effectiveness of these activities depends on reliable data and information management as well as adequate indicator frameworks and benchmarking systems. Rather than focussing on compliance alone, systems should also develop capacity to relate inputs to associated educational processes and outcomes while bearing in mind the challenges involved in evaluating efficiency and outcomes in the area of education. Policies and programmes should be subject to impact evaluations and their results should be used to inform strategic budget planning processes. Another concern in increasingly complex governance systems is to ensure adequate accountability and transparency and to balance accountability with trust. Particularly at the local and school level, measures to provide information about the use of funding should be accompanied by steps to mitigate the administrative burden this entails. Complementing the vertical accountability generated through reporting and evaluation with horizontal and bottom-up forms of accountability through stakeholder involvement can be a successful strategy to address this challenge. The chapter also highlights the need to make inequities in the use of resources transparent and to monitor how they affect the educational outcomes of disadvantaged students.

The funding of school education: Main findings and policy pointers

The importance of school funding policies

This study on school funding policies was conducted for a number of reasons:

- The mechanisms through which school funding is governed, distributed and monitored play a key role in ensuring that resources are directed to where they can make the most difference. While the overall level of funding matters, the strategies used to allocate and match resources to learner needs are at least as important.

- As most school funding comes from public budgets, developing effective mechanisms to allocate this funding among competing priorities is an important policy concern for governments. School systems have limited resources with which to pursue their objectives and using these resources efficiently is a key aim for their activities.

- Efficiency alone is not the main concern of school systems but needs to be achieved alongside the quality and equity objectives that are at the heart of schooling. The report focuses on how school funding policies can best be designed so that available resources are directed to supporting high quality teaching and providing equitable learning opportunities for all students.

- As efficiency in school education has traditionally been considered from an economic perspective, this study aims to look at school funding questions from a more educational angle. It analyses school funding policies taking into account the complexity of educational processes, the diversity of educational goals, the range of different governance contexts across school systems and the importance of social and institutional arrangements in developing adequate school funding policies.

The report was prepared as part of a major OECD study on the effective use of school resources resulting in the publication series *OECD Reviews of School Resources*. Eighteen school systems (referred to as the "OECD review countries") were actively engaged in the preparation of this report through participation in a qualitative data collection, preparation of detailed country background reports and/or participation in OECD-led country reviews. In addition, the analysis considers the broader research and policy literature bringing together findings from as many OECD and partner countries as possible.

Governing school funding

The governance of school funding across OECD review countries is characterised by complex relationships between the various actors involved in raising and spending funds for schooling.

While the majority of school funding originates at the central government level, other actors also increasingly contribute to raising funds for school services. Sub-central governments typically complement central school funding from their own revenues and private spending on schools has increased considerably in recent years. International funding provides an important complement to national sources of school funding in a range of countries.

As the sources of funding are becoming more diverse, an increasing set of actors in the school system are also gaining influence on spending decisions. In many countries, sub-central governments have emerged as important actors in the allocation and management of school funding, individual schools have obtained greater responsibility over budgetary matters and private school providers have become important end users of public spending. In more centralised school systems, a range of different central-level agencies may contribute to managing and allocating funds for schooling.

Pointers for policy: Trends towards multi-level and multi-actor governance of school funding need to be accompanied by adequate institutional and regulatory frameworks to optimise the role of each actor in ensuring an effective and equitable allocation of funds. In designing these framework conditions, school systems need to take into account the important role of key stakeholder groups such as school boards, teacher and school leader professional organisations, student and parent associations, community organisations and employers. This report discusses three key governance aspects that have shaped school funding policies in many OECD countries: fiscal decentralisation, school autonomy over budgetary matters and the use of public funding by private providers. The related opportunities, challenges and policy pointers are explored below.

Clarifying roles and responsibilities in decentralised school funding systems

Across OECD countries, sub-central governments are responsible for distributing the largest share of public funding – almost 60% of final funds – among individual schools. They typically complement central school funding from their own revenues while also acting as an intermediary distributing central government funding to schools. While motivations vary across countries, fiscal decentralisation is typically expected to increase responsiveness to the demands of local communities, raise the potential for innovation and adapt resource management to local conditions. But achieving equitable expenditure outputs for students in decentralised funding systems requires well-designed fiscal relations, adequate coordination and capacity building across different levels of government.

If sub-central governments are responsible for funding school education mostly from their own revenues, there is a risk that the different spending capacities of richer and poorer jurisdictions exacerbate inequality of opportunity for students in different parts of a country. In such contexts, areas with more disadvantaged students are likely to have fewer resources available to meet student needs. Fiscal transfers are widely used across OECD countries to help provide adequate sub-central revenue levels and equalise spending capacity across jurisdictions, but there is a risk that strong reliance on such transfers may generate inefficiencies, mistrust and reduced accountability due to the split between funding and spending responsibilities between different levels of the system. Even where sub-central authorities have similar revenue levels, expenditure for students with similar needs may vary across jurisdictions due to differences in sub-central priorities and funding allocation mechanisms.

While fiscal decentralisation offers the potential for sub-central governments to adapt school funding to local needs, it also increases the complexity of education governance and funding arrangements. In a multi-level school funding approach, the roles and responsibilities of different administration levels need to be well aligned to avoid inefficiencies due to duplication of roles, overlapping responsibilities, competition between different tiers of government or a lack of transparency in resource flows. Fiscal decentralisation may also raise capacity challenges, especially in small jurisdictions which may have limited staff and expertise to support schools in managing funds strategically.

Pointers for policy: In decentralised school funding systems, sub-central authorities need to have both adequate revenues to meet the needs of their students and relevant capacity to fulfil their funding responsibilities. In addition, it is key to ensure a clear distribution of roles and responsibilities across different levels of government and to develop well-defined lines of accountability. Sub-central responsibility for spending should be adequately aligned to responsibility for raising funds. Reliance on own tax revenue has a number of advantages in terms of local autonomy, accountability and responsiveness to local preferences. But it needs be complemented by well-designed equalisation systems to provide sub-central authorities with the necessary revenue to offer equal opportunities for their students and capacity building to support effective local education management. Developing a whole-of-system approach to school funding that aligns roles and balances tensions should involve reflection about both governance structures (e.g. the most efficient number of governance levels involved in school funding) and governance processes (e.g. stakeholder involvement, open dialogue and use of evidence and research).

Supporting schools with their budgetary responsibilities

Since the 1980s, many school systems have granted school-level professionals greater responsibility for budgetary matters. Experience in some of the OECD review countries indicates that an absence of resource autonomy at the school level risks constraining schools' room for manoeuvre in developing and shaping their own profiles and may create inefficiencies in resource management. School autonomy over budgetary matters can provide schools with needed flexibility to use allocated resources in line with local needs and priorities. But it also needs to be accompanied with adequate transparency, leadership capacity and support, and mechanisms to avoid widening inequities.

While school autonomy in generating funds can help promote local efforts to complement school revenues, there are concerns about the inequities this creates. Schools in challenging socio-economic circumstances will be less able to complement their budget with parental or other local contributions. In some countries insufficient monitoring of school income leads to a lack of transparency regarding the real resource levels of individual schools, which makes it difficult to achieve equitable resource levels through school funding mechanisms.

Budget management responsibilities offer potential for more strategic management at the school level, but the effective use of funds requires well-functioning school leadership and management structures. Greater autonomy over funding decisions might increase existing inequities between schools, with some schools facing greater challenges in linking spending choices to improvement priorities. Administering and allocating funds effectively requires time, administrative capacity and adequate preparation of school leadership teams. Experience in OECD review countries indicates that delegating budgetary responsibilities to schools may create tensions between pedagogical and administrative school leadership. While budgetary autonomy allows aligning budget planning with pedagogical needs of schools, it may also place considerable administrative, managerial and accounting burdens on leaders, reducing their time for pedagogical leadership.

Pointers for policy: The effect of schools' budgetary autonomy on school processes and outcomes depends on their ability to make use of this autonomy in a constructive way and thus requires a strengthening of school leadership and management, as well as support for school leaders with budgeting tasks. Professional preparation and development programmes for school leaders should prepare them for their resource management responsibilities within a framework of pedagogical leadership. Furthermore, autonomous schools need to be embedded in adequate institutional frameworks in order to avoid that increased autonomy results in widening inequities across schools. When school autonomy, school evaluation, accountability and support are intelligently combined, they have greater leverage to impact positively on teaching and learning. Considerations about schools' responsibility for budgetary matters should also go together with discussions about school size and school network policies. Providing the structures and support to help schools group together and share resources can help achieve economies of scale and a more effective use of funding.

Developing regulatory frameworks for the public funding of private schools

Over the past three decades, the public funding of private school providers has become more common across OECD countries. The public funding of private schools is typically combined with parental choice systems that are intended to encourage greater diversity and quality in the educational offer. However, a number of risks for equity need to be taken into account.

In some countries, publicly funded private schools do not only enjoy greater pedagogical freedom than public schools but also greater autonomy in admission and tuition fee policies. However, if publicly funded private schools are allowed to select students based on performance, there are risks that they "cream skim" high-ability students from the public sector, particularly if their public counterparts are required to operate open enrolment or use only non-academic criteria to select students. Further, if publicly funded private schools can demand parental contributions in addition to the public funds they receive, this risks reinforcing segregation along socio-economic lines, with students from more advantaged socio-economic backgrounds having more options to enrol in private schools.

This may lead to a situation where both high-ability and socio-economically advantaged students opt out of the public school system. In such contexts, diminished peer effects and greater resource needs of disadvantaged students are likely to make it ever more difficult for public schools to retain both students and funding. Research also indicates that even where private schools cannot select students or raise fees, families from disadvantaged backgrounds are less likely to make use of school choice and less frequently consider academic quality criteria when deciding which schools to attend.

Pointers for policy: To counteract adverse effects on equity related to the public funding of private schools, school systems should consider requiring all publicly funded providers to adhere to the same regulations regarding tuition and admission policies, and ensure that compliance with such regulations is effectively monitored. Admission procedures for oversubscribed schools should be homogenous and transparent. It is also important to ensure transparency and accountability for the use of public funding by private providers, and to provide families with adequate access to information and support so that they can make informed choices for their children.

Distributing school funding

School systems need to consider a series of guiding questions to design a funding model that best fits the established governance structure. These include the following:

● *Who is responsible for the final allocation of funding to schools?*

In many systems, there is a complex mix of responsibilities for funding allocations to schools. But the balance of these responsibilities is not set in stone and can be changed alongside the introduction of new funding allocation mechanisms, as has been the case in several OECD countries.

● *Which resource categories does this apply to?*

Different authorities may be responsible for current expenditures (staff, operational costs), capital expenditures (infrastructure) or a mix of these. It needs to clear which authority is responsible for allocating which category. The type of allocation mechanism that is most suitable will depend on the resource category that is considered.

● *What conditions (if any) should be set for the funding allocation?*

Even if a sub-central authority is responsible for the final allocation to schools, central authorities may specify for what purpose the money should be spent. Equally, different conditions can be set by sub-central authorities when allocating final funds to individual schools. The various restrictions associated with transferred funds provide a good indication of the room for manoeuvre given to sub-central authorities and schools in a system.

● *How much of the funding will be distributed via the main allocation mechanism and how much via other mechanisms (such as targeted funds)?*

There is an argument that efficiency is improved if a greater share of funding is included in the main allocation mechanism. At the same time, there is a case for retaining a proportion of funding at the central level, e.g. for emergency expenditures or priority areas where it is judged that schools would not make adequate provision.

● *What basis will be used to fix the amount of funding allocated to schools?*

Broadly, among OECD review countries, there are four major bases for determining funding. These main types of funding allocation mechanisms are described in Box 1.

Box 1. **How are the amounts allocated to schools determined?**

Administrative discretion is based on an individual assessment of the resources that each school needs and **incremental costs** consider historical expenditure to calculate the allocation for the following year. These two approaches are often combined, and usually they are used in centralised systems.

Bidding and bargaining involve schools responding to open competitions for additional funding offered via a particular programme or making a case for additional resources.

Formula funding involves the use of objective criteria with a universally applied rule to establish the amount of resources each school is entitled to.

Pointers for policy: A general principle for a more effective funding distribution is to ensure that funds are allocated in a transparent and predictable way. Ensuring a stable and publicly known system to allocate public funding allows schools to plan their development in the coming years. This requires stability in the principles and technical details of the funding distribution system. Managing the effective implementation of new funding mechanisms is also key. When a decision is made to introduce a new funding allocation mechanism, an excellent design of the mechanism is not enough. It is important to have a realistic estimate of the implementation costs involved, to consult and bring on board the system's key stakeholder groups and to manage effectively the political economy of funding reform. Adequate stakeholder consultation is important to increase the perceived fairness of an allocation system and can help ensure that funding mechanisms respond to challenges that were not anticipated. The OECD review has also highlighted the importance of conducting periodic reviews of funding allocation mechanisms to ensure they remain optimal.

Providing equity funding to schools

A key concern in designing funding allocation mechanisms is to ensure that funding is allocated equitably to schools that are most in need of additional resources. The following challenges and trade-offs need to be considered when choosing an allocation mechanism for equity funding.

There are two broad approaches when designing mechanisms to allocate funding that recognises different needs across schools: the inclusion of additional funding in the main allocation mechanisms for particular schools (e.g. by including weightings in the funding formula to systematically allocate additional resources to certain categories); or the provision of targeted funding in one or a series of different grants external to the main allocation mechanism. Typically, a mix of these funding mechanisms is found in many systems.

Targeted programmes will provide funding to be used by schools for specific purposes and thereby ensure responsiveness to emerging priorities and the identified needs of particular groups. However some countries have multiplied targeted programmes over time generating overlap, excessive bureaucracy and a lack of long-term sustainability for schools. Many countries provide targeted additional resources in kind, most typically additional teaching hours or positions. Another form of in-kind allocation is the provision of professional development opportunities for staff.

Other countries give more discretion to the school level in how to use equity funding. This gives school professionals more flexibility in allocating funds to address particular local challenges. In a context where schools have large discretion over the use of equity funding, strong accountability at the school level including with scrutiny by school boards on educational provision for different student needs and its impact on learning will play a key role. Funding mechanisms will need to manage tension between flexibility in using funds based on local judgements and accountability to maintain public confidence in the use of equity funds to the benefit of target groups. Accountability requirements need to be well-designed to avoid excessive administrative and reporting burdens on schools and other potential adverse effects.

Systems vary in whether they channel equity funding to certain geographical areas or to the actual population in each school. While allocating funding to the actual population allows better reaching the entire target group, such approaches do not account for the additional challenges created by a high concentration of disadvantage in a particular area. Area-based funding aims to address the additional negative effects that socio-economic disadvantage has when it is concentrated in a particular area. However, such approaches risk leaving out a proportion of the disadvantaged population in a system and include many individuals who are not disadvantaged. There is also evidence that the "target area" label can be stigmatising and encourage flight of middle class families from these areas.

Another major challenge in providing equity funding lies in estimating the different costs involved in providing adequate school education to student groups with different educational needs. Improving the financial distribution across students and schools requires regular and detailed analysis of the adequacy of funding and its effects on the quality of teaching, the efficiency of schools and the equity of educational opportunities. Evaluations of the actual costs should be based on evidence from regular audit work and academic research. Comprehensive and compelling analysis and empirical evidence on the exact cost differences would strengthen the basis for policy decisions to review or adjust parameters included in funding mechanisms.

Pointers for policy: Beyond a certain level of investment what matters most is how funding is allocated to schools and students that are most in need of additional resources. The OECD review has highlighted the importance in striking a balance between targeted and regular funding to more efficiently support greater equity within a school system. While the use of targeted programmes allows better steering and monitoring the use of public resources for equity purposes at the school level, there are risks that a multiplication of targeted programmes leads to piece-meal re-centralisation, a lack of co-ordination between different programmes, inefficiencies due to imposed restrictions on schools and greater administrative costs. There are, therefore, arguments to reduce transaction costs by limiting the number of different targeted programmes and including adjustments for equity within the major part of funding allocation via a formula. This can simplify the funding system overall, although it needs to be accompanied by adequate accountability for the use of equity funds to the benefit of identified target groups. Reliable evidence should be gathered on the adequacy of funding in general, and on specific elements that funding mechanisms aim to address, e.g. equity problems related to socio-economic disadvantages, concerns for a more equitable distribution of funding in rural locations and the education of students with special educational needs.

Choosing indicators to design funding allocation mechanisms

In designing funding allocation mechanisms, systems need to pay adequate attention to data requirements and the choice of indicators. For all indicators, there is a trade-off between simplicity and transparency on the one hand and accuracy and fairness on the other. Relatively simple indicators are likely to leave out some parts of the target population. For more precise targeting to local contexts, more complicated indicators need to be established, although a higher degree of complexity makes these less transparent and understandable to a wider public. In many countries there is an ongoing debate as to how many indicators of need can be included in funding allocation mechanisms. There are also examples where the use of simpler indicators did not make a large difference to schools' funding levels.

The availability and quality of data is a key concern when compiling indicators. In general, area-based measures may rely on data that is less up-to-date or sample-based, thus limiting the accuracy for targeting smaller areas. In recent years, many OECD countries have implemented electronic reporting systems for schools, which offer a wealth of data for indicators and can allow more accurate targeting of resources. However, there may be concerns about the reliability of school reports when there is incentive to inflate or deflate numbers in order to benefit from additional resources. For example, when funding is directly linked to the identification of individual students as having particular characteristics of disadvantage or special educational needs, this may lead to excessive labelling of students which is stigmatising for individuals and can lead to considerable cost inflation. A further problem is the misclassification and missing data on part of schools or students.

Pointers for policy: The OECD review has revealed that a wide range of different indicators are used across countries to distribute funding to schools. There is evidence of considerable refinement in indicators used over recent years and a policy consensus to use indices comprising multiple indicators in order to improve the targeting to socio-economic disadvantage. While the use of census-based data has been criticised in some systems for being out-of-date, it has the advantage that it cannot be manipulated by schools thus giving greater integrity to the funding allocation. Using census-based data as a proxy for data on individual student characteristics would be less accurate in targeting individual students, but authoritative national research can be used to choose the best proxy indicator or combination of indicators. This also holds the advantage of reducing reporting burden on schools. In seeking a good balance between census-based and school-based indicators, one option is to use individually targeted funding for students with more severe special educational needs, complemented by a census-based funding approach for students with milder special educational needs or those linked to socio-economic disadvantage.

Designing funding formulas for current expenditure

The use of formula funding is well suited to the distribution of current expenditure and many countries have introduced this. There are three broad functions that funding formulas can aim to support. First, one of the most important functions of a funding formula is to promote equity by ensuring that similar funding levels are allocated to similar types of provision (horizontal equity) and that differential amounts can be added to the basic allocation according to the assessed degree of educational need (vertical equity). Second, funding formulas can have a directive function aiming to promote certain behaviour in funding recipients or to promote certain policies (for example, an additional amount can be added to the basic allocation to support schools with lower enrolment levels). Third, some countries use funding formulas to introduce market regulation or support broader school choice policies (see above). The greater the proportion of funding that is allocated on a simple per student basis, the more this function will be emphasised. While countries will emphasise these three functions to differing degrees, a major benefit of a funding formula is the transparency that it provides. The presentation of clear criteria that can be scrutinised and negotiated can help stimulate public debate and build general acceptance of a formula by major stakeholders as a fair method for school funding.

Within a funding formula, coefficients should adequately reflect different per student costs. This requires the introduction of different adjustment components. A balance needs to be struck between a simple formula, which might fail to capture school needs with full accuracy, and a sophisticated formula, which may be difficult to understand and discuss. As a guide for designing formulas to better meet differing needs, research has identified four main components: i) a basic allocation per student or per class that is differentiated according to the school year or stage of schooling; ii) an allocation for specific educational profiles or curriculum programmes, such as a focus on the arts, sports, different vocational fields or special educational needs programmes; iii) an allocation for students with supplementary educational needs adjusting for different student characteristics or elements of disadvantage; and iv) an allocation for specific needs related to school site and location, adjusting for structural differences in operational costs, such as for rural areas with lower class size.

In countries where sub-central authorities have responsibility for funding allocation, there is a great opportunity for system learning. While central authorities cannot directly influence funding allocation, more attention can be devoted to improving efficiency in different approaches used within the country. There will be many different funding formulas developed at the regional or local levels to distribute funding to schools. Many of these will share the aim of providing a more equitable funding allocation. There is, therefore, much potential for local authorities to learn from each other regarding the effective design of funding formulas. Some larger authorities with greater capacity may have developed funding formula with external expertise. Sharing knowledge across authorities can help to avoid duplication of efforts. At the central level there is room to identify and promote best practices in funding allocation.

Pointers for policy: Funding formulas are widely used for distributing current expenditure to schools. The introduction of a funding formula can help provide a clear framework for debates on the sufficiency and proper allocation of funding. Different parameters within the formula may be debated, which can help stakeholders to express their position clearly and make agreements that can be monitored. A well-designed funding formula can provide an efficient, equitable, stable and transparent method of distributing funding for current expenditures to schools. However, inadequate formulas may exacerbate inequities and also inefficiencies. While there is no single best practice funding formula, there are a set of guiding principles that can help design effective formulas. These include: aligning formulas with school system priorities and establishing evaluation criteria accordingly; adequately reflecting different per student costs of providing education; promoting budgetary discipline; and ensuring the periodical review of formulas to assess the need for adjustments.

Planning the use of school funding

The process leading up to the formulation and implementation of funding plans is a key stage of the budgeting cycle. It provides an opportunity to reflect upon previous expenditure and future resource needs in order to develop financially sustainable budgets that support the provision of high quality education and effectively address policy priorities.

Linking budget planning to educational objectives

As policy objectives evolve, countries need to adapt their budget plans to best support these objectives. Developing linkages between budget and strategy frameworks can provide governments with a clearer picture of where public funding is spent, facilitate the allocation of funding according to policy priorities and make it easier to track spending against the achievement of policy objectives.

But this process is not always straightforward. Many countries face challenges in establishing a shared understanding of educational quality and priorities that would be suitable to guide the budgeting process. Even where goal-oriented budget planning procedures are in place at the central level, these are not always adopted at sub-central levels of the administration. Decentralising resource management responsibilities requires capacity building for strategic budget planning at levels of the system.

The effective planning of school funding strategies and reform initiatives also requires systematic mobilisation of knowledge generated through research, evaluation, monitoring and audit activities (more on this below). Evaluation results can be used to inform decisions throughout the budgeting cycle and serve as a basis for professional discussion among stakeholders concerning future reform initiatives. However, many countries lack effective mechanisms to strategically integrate data and educational research into a process of evidence-based resource planning.

Pointers for policy: Aligning funding strategies with policy objectives is crucial to ensure that school funding is effectively used to support educational improvement and reforms. Building a shared understanding of a country's strategic vision for educational improvement among stakeholder groups and levels of authority can increase the coherence of budget planning activities across the education system. In addition, evidence on the effectiveness of past spending decisions should be used to inform discussions among stakeholders and help responsible authorities in making informed decisions throughout the budget preparation process. To effectively inform evidence-based budget planning, the data generated by evaluation activities should focus on assessing the impact of programmes and policy initiatives, ideally relating it to previously established objectives and expenditure information. Education systems should also promote the creation of fora that foster co-operation between researchers, stakeholders, policy makers and institutions that can act as knowledge brokers in order to consolidate evidence and facilitate its integration into the budgeting processes.

Striking a balance between predictability and flexibility in budget planning

Strategic thinking and long-term planning are central to the successful governance of complex education systems. Forecasts and projections of future resource needs can be used throughout the different stages of the budgeting process, ensure the education system's long-term fiscal sustainability and develop clear implementation paths for educational reforms. Forecasting resource needs in the education sector involves anticipating developments in the demand for services across different education levels and sectors as well as their implications for human, pedagogical, physical and financial resource needs. At the central level, baseline data on demographic changes in the school-age population and information on previous budget allocations may be combined with additional parameters of varying complexity, for example projected enrolment rates and student flows, different modalities of resource utilisation and macroeconomic or budgetary indicators.

Over the past decades, a growing number of OECD countries have adopted medium-term expenditure frameworks to carry out the budgeting process with a multi-year perspective. Such frameworks can help ensure that policy proposals and programmes are backed by a medium-term budget and that costs at different stages of their implementation are adequately accounted for. At the same time, the nature of the budget preparation schedule is often such that educational resource needs, particularly at the local level, are only imperfectly known by the time at which budgets need to be approved. A whole-of-system approach to education planning therefore needs to reconcile the importance of longer-term budgetary frameworks and the predictability they afford with a sufficient degree of flexibility to respond to changing conditions in the short term.

Since budgets are typically granted for a given fiscal year, carry-over rules regulate the extent to which actors at different levels of the education system can use unspent financial resources beyond this point. Prohibiting providers from retaining savings between budget years may lead to inefficient spending patterns towards the end of the fiscal year and rigid restrictions on carry-over practices can compound other sources of inefficiency such as shortcomings in national planning procedures. On the other hand, unrestricted carry-over rights may reduce transparency in the timing of expenditures and lead schools to accumulate excessive surpluses. This can cause spending fluctuations and the allocation of resources to student cohorts for whom they were not originally intended.

Pointers for policy: Adopting a multi-annual budgeting process can provide actors across a school system with a means to strategically plan their operations and to take into account potential trade-offs between alternative spending options as well as their longer-term expenditure implications. The development of multi-annual budgets should be guided by high-quality forecasting mechanisms to create the conditions necessary to commit to longer-term allocations. At the same time, introducing an appropriate degree of flexibility into the budgeting process will improve responsiveness to unforeseen circumstances and promote more efficient spending decisions at the sub-central level. Schools and local authorities should also be provided with some room to carry unused appropriations forward from one budget year to the next. This can discourage inefficient expenditures towards the end of the budget cycle and provide schools and local authorities with incentives to mobilise additional revenue or improve the efficiency of their operations, although regulations should prevent the accumulation of excessive surpluses.

Evaluating the use of school funding

Evaluation provides information on what a planned budget actually delivers beyond the intentions for the use of resources expressed in the budget allocation. An approach to the evaluation of funding that sets inputs in relation to the processes and outcomes of a school system will provide helpful information to improve decision making and make the use of resources more effective. However, evaluating the effectiveness of resource use is challenging due to the complex nature of education. Some countries do not have standardised national measures of student outcomes at all or only for particular stages of education or in discrete skill areas. Also, while national education goals are typically comprehensive and broad, evaluation systems are more limited in the information they can offer. In addition, as investments may take time to have an effect and many other factors also shape outcomes, conclusions are difficult to draw even where both costs and outcomes can be realistically assessed.

In many systems, the important role played by sub-central and school level actors in using school funds introduces further complexities to evaluating the use of funding. There may be disagreements across actors on objectives, targets and indicators to be used in the evaluation of school funding as well as co-ordination challenges related to timely reporting and sharing of information. School evaluation approaches across OECD review countries consider the use of funding by schools to varying degrees and links between resource use and achievement of strategic goals of a school are not always established. In some contexts, evaluation of budgetary matters may be limited to monitoring compliance instead of a focus on the effective use of funding for improvements.

Pointers for policy: An approach to school system evaluation which involves analysis of both financial and educational data and aims to identify effective investments can help improve the future use of public funding in the school sector. To improve the information basis, system evaluation policies should seek to: develop indicator frameworks for the systematic mapping of available information against education system goals; design national strategies to monitor student learning standards; and collect qualitative information on the school system. It is also important to integrate existing databases and information systems which are often split across different levels of governance and different institutions. In contexts of school autonomy, approaches to school evaluation should consider how schools use their funds to promote the general goals of the school system, implement their school development plans and ultimately improve teaching and learning for all students based on a common vision of a good school. School evaluation should bring together both pedagogical and financial aspects of school operation, and review how resource use affects the achievement of strategic goals and the quality of teaching and learning. This requires building the evaluation capacity of external evaluators, school leaders and school boards so that they are able to collect and use data and information for improvement.

Evaluating the equity outcomes of school funding

Many countries invest considerable resources to improve the educational opportunities and outcomes for student groups at risk of underperformance. But this financial commitment is not always matched with a strategy for monitoring the progress and outcomes of these groups. Monitoring equity can inform school funding decisions to the benefit of disadvantaged groups, help to target financial support more effectively, and increase the overall focus on equity in resource use decisions across the system, including at the level of sub-central authorities and schools.

Monitoring the impact of school funding on priority groups is particularly important in complex governance systems where resources intended for disadvantaged groups are channelled through several authorities or providers. Local or school autonomy in spending decisions may mean that central equity funding strategies may be undermined at the local or school level if equity funding is shifted towards other student groups or allocated to purposes that have little effect on target groups. It is therefore crucial to ensure transparency about the distribution and use of funding and the actual expenditure outputs (the real cost of educating a student as opposed to the planned funding per student) within schools. At the same time, it is important to note that there is a tension between the benefits of transparency and reporting and the administrative burden this may entail at the local and school level.

Pointers for policy: Many countries show a considerable financial commitment to supporting students at risk of underperformance, and this focus on additional inputs needs to be matched with sufficient attention to monitoring the outcomes of different student groups. This would help to determine the extent to which the school system meets their needs. Countries should set clear equity goals for the system and develop related indicators to monitor their achievement. This should entail the collection and analysis of data on the demographic characteristics of schools and students and the learning and other outcomes of groups at risk of underperformance. Key data on learning outcomes should be sufficiently broken down for different student groups to facilitate analysis of the challenges they face. Disaggregated data can also help to facilitate peer-learning among schools with a similar student intake and similar challenges. Commissioning thematic studies on the use of resources for equity is another option for monitoring the equity of the school system.

Where multiple equity programmes serving similar goals are in place, it is important to approach evaluation from a whole-of-government perspective and avoid inefficiencies through regular monitoring, sharing of relevant data, co-ordination and potential consolidation of programmes.

Promoting transparency in the use of school funding

Evaluating the use of school funding gives a fuller picture of the educational experience that is actually provided to students in relation to what was planned. In practice, budgets are rarely implemented exactly as approved. This can be for legitimate reasons, such as adjustments in policies in response to emerging challenges. But the effective implementation and execution of a budget may also be hindered by a lack of capacity, mismanagement or unauthorised expenditures. Ensuring integrity has gained increasing relevance in a context in which levels of public trust in government have decreased in the wake of the financial and economic crisis in many countries. Budget transparency, i.e. the disclosure of relevant fiscal information in a timely and systematic manner, is important for accountability and participation throughout the budgeting process.

In some countries, there has been a trend towards more explicit multiple accountability designs that involve a broad range of stakeholders in decision making and accountability. School boards, which usually comprise representatives of parents, teachers, the local community and sometimes students, can play a key role in monitoring the use of funding at the school level and in providing horizontal accountability of school-based resource management. Bottom-up accountability through the direct engagement of citizens can play an important role in complementing vertical and horizontal accountability of public authorities, although it also increases the complexity of education governance. Multiple accountability is still a fairly new concept and the amount of available research on how to make it work is modest. While it provides opportunities, such as new sources of information to learn, improve and steer, it also carries a risk of information overload, and it can be difficult to involve less powerful voices in multiple accountability processes.

Pointers for policy: Budgetary reporting can provide decision makers and stakeholders with clear information about resource use and enhance the quality of policy decisions via robust analysis of financial and non-financial data. To this end, budgetary reporting should be presented alongside reporting about the quality and equity of a school system in relation to established policy objectives and targets. This can help communicate the goals of investments in the school system and build social consensus about fiscal efforts for schooling. Countries with a large degree of school autonomy should also encourage the dissemination of information about school budgets together with information about school development plans and other activities at the school. But reporting of school-level information needs to be weighed against the administrative burden involved and it needs to be ensured that schools have sufficient administrative support and access to national data sufficiently disaggregated for use at the school level. Broader strategies to build evaluation capacity in school systems should also focus on skills to use the resulting information for improvement. Education authorities can support school boards by providing guidance and relevant information for them to play a key role in monitoring schools' use of funds. Accountability measures that involve multiple stakeholders can usefully complement traditional measures of vertical accountability.

Chapter 1

Why look at school funding policies?

This report is concerned with school funding policies that can help countries achieve their educational goals and student learning objectives. This chapter sets the context for the subsequent analysis. First, it highlights the importance of well-designed school funding strategies for achieving quality, equity and efficiency objectives in schooling. Second, it explores major contextual developments shaping the funding of school education across different countries. Third, it explains how this report looks at school funding and the evidence base that it draws from. The annex to this chapter provides detailed definitions and discussion of the concepts of effectiveness, efficiency and equity that will be used throughout the report.

The statistical data for Israel are supplied by and under the responsibility of the relevant Israeli authorities. The use of such data by the OECD is without prejudice to the status of the Golan Heights, East Jerusalem and Israeli settlements in the West Bank under the terms of international law.

Why school funding policies are important

Directing school funding to where it matters

The overall level of school funding matters, but funding allocation strategies are at least as important. While the ability to provide quality education for all and to respond to new priorities depends on the availability of adequate funding for education, the mechanisms through which school funding is governed, distributed and monitored play a key role in ensuring that resources are directed to where they can make the most difference.

Previous OECD (2016a) work found that while larger education budgets are no guarantee of better student results, a minimum level of spending is necessary for ensuring good quality education provision. A school system that lacks quality teachers and school leaders, adequate infrastructure and textbooks will have more difficulties to promote quality education. At the same time, the overall level of school funding does not seem to be a key factor for the success of high-performing school systems (OECD, 2016a).

Indeed, Figure 1.1 shows that among the countries with lower overall levels of school funding (falling below a cumulative spending per student threshold of roughly USD 50 000 in purchasing power parity [PPP] terms), there is an observed positive correlation between cumulative spending per student and students' performance in the OECD Programme for

Figure 1.1. **Cumulative spending per student from age 6 to 15 and science performance, 2015**

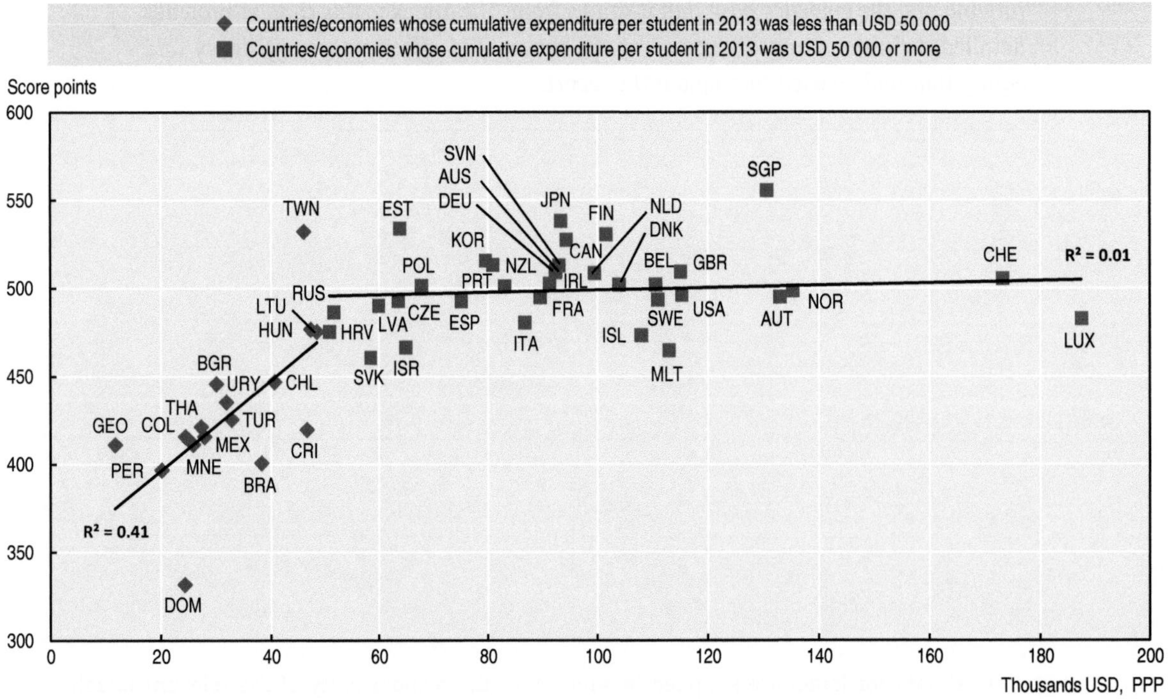

Source: OECD (n.d.), PISA 2015 Database, www.oecd.org/pisa/data/2015database/, Tables I.2.3 and II.6.58.

International Student Assessment (PISA). Among the countries with higher overall levels of school funding, there is no observed relationship between cumulative spending per student and students' performance. This suggests that beyond a certain level of investment what matters more is not the aggregate level of expenditure, but rather the design of education policies, the mechanisms through which funds are allocated and how these determine where additional resources are channelled.

Even in countries where the overall level of funding for schools is comparatively high, there may be underinvestment in certain parts of the school system, which can result in serious educational inequalities, as resource challenges tend to concentrate in certain disadvantaged areas or schools (OECD, 2012a). Research in the United States has shown that finance reforms directed to guarantee an adequate provision of resources in low-income schools were crucial to reduce overall achievement gaps between high- and low-income school districts (Lafortune et al., 2016), increased the likelihood of high-school graduation and educational attainment for children from poor families, and diminished their socio-economic disadvantage in terms of earnings and income later in life (Kirabo Jackson et al., 2014).

Making the best use of limited resources

School systems have limited resources with which to pursue their objectives. As most school funding in OECD countries comes from public budgets, the best allocation of this funding among competing priorities is a relevant policy concern.

School education is costly and getting more so (Baumol, 2012; Wolff et al., 2014; Wolff, 2015). The long-term pattern of education spending largely reflects a continuous increase in the cost of human resources. Since public sector services and education in particular have limited ability to substitute human resources by less costly productive capital, such as machines, it is expected that the public costs of education will continue to rise (Baumol, 2012). Since long-run education expenditure has been increasing among OECD countries and education services have become relatively more expensive than other goods (De Witte and López-Torres, 2017), ensuring an efficient allocation of school funding is a key concern for OECD governments.

Policies aimed at reshaping the organisational structures and changing institutional habits in school systems are typically not easily accepted by public opinion and need to be carefully developed and implemented in collaboration with key stakeholder groups, such as social partners and parents. A recognition of the fact that the costs of education tend to increase in the long run helps to justify a focus on achieving greater efficiency by minimising expenditures that do not contribute to the quality and equity of education. Otherwise the pressure on resources and limited available funding could eventually crowd out the most talented human resources in the school sector. In order to build momentum for change and engage stakeholders in designing a more efficient provision of education, it is important not to focus merely on cost savings but to ensure that strategies to achieve greater efficiency in a school system go in line with a focus on improving quality and equity.

While the effective use of resources is a general aim of all public activity, in times of economic downturn, expectations for an efficient use of public resources are typically even stronger: the allocation of public resources is more scrutinised and political choices are increasingly based on efficiency arguments. Despite the long-term continuous increase in educational expenditures as a share of gross domestic product (GDP), public spending on education across the OECD has lagged behind the growth of GDP since 2010 (OECD, 2016b).

The recent pattern in education expenditures also reflects a prioritisation of public expenditures between education and other public services. Figure 1.2 shows this trend, although also including expenditure in tertiary education. In such contexts, governments willing to further invest in education may justify their choices based on reforms targeted to increase the external efficiency of school systems, that is to show how the costs of providing quality education translate into better social and economic outcomes (for detailed definitions of efficiency and equity, see Annex 1.A1).

Figure 1.2. Change in public expenditure on education as a percentage of total public expenditure, 2008 and 2013

Primary to tertiary education (2008 = 100, 2013 constant prices)

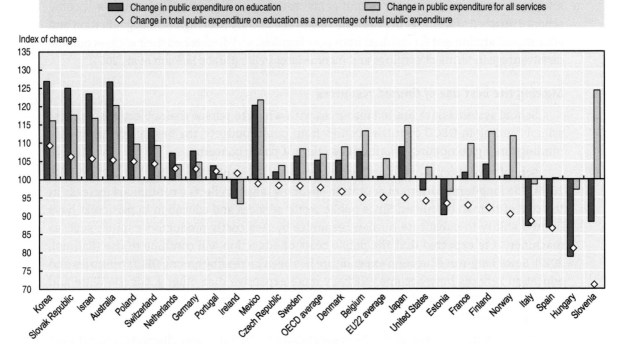

Source: OECD (2016b), *Education at a Glance 2016: OECD Indicators*, *http://dx.doi.org/10.1787/eag-2016-en*, Figure B4.2.

Looking at school funding from an educational perspective

Educational efficiency is typically conceptualised as the ability of fulfilling maximum educational potential at the lowest possible cost. In this context, improving the efficiency of a school or school system can be attained in two ways: either by maintaining identical levels of outcomes while lowering the amount of school funding, or by attaining better outcomes with the same level of funding (for a detailed discussion and definitions of efficiency see Annex 1.A1). However, as described in Box 1.1 there are limitations to efficiency analyses in the education sector. Recognising these limitations is important to frame the analysis provided in this report.

The purpose of this report is to look at the use of school funding from an educational perspective by taking into account the complexity of educational processes; the breadth and diversity of educational goals across OECD countries; the synergetic relationships between resources invested at different levels of a school system; the organisational and governance contexts of schooling in different countries; and the importance of social and

Box 1.1. **Limitations to efficiency analyses in education**

Annex 1.A1 provides a brief summary of the main methods used for quantifying effectiveness and efficiency in the use of school resources as well as their main advantages and drawbacks. Analyses of effectiveness and efficiency are sometimes used for school benchmarking, increased accountability, local and school capacity building, as well as for cross-country comparisons and peer learning among countries. However, quantitative analyses of educational efficiency are subject to several conceptual and measurement concerns and it is important to keep these limitations in mind when using such analyses as a source of expertise for educational policymaking. Due to the limitations explored below, the use of this type of studies generally provides an incomplete picture for policy. The use of qualitative and mixed-methods provides more room to take into account specific governance contexts.

Conceptual limitations

- It is not possible to have an absolute account of efficiency. In this sense, no abstract school or school system can be conceived as perfectly efficient. Absolute efficiency would imply knowing the limits of the educational process; however, it is both intuitively and empirically challenging to have a notion of these limits. These difficulties not only stem from the multiple inputs and objectives of the educational process, but mainly from the uncertainty underlying the educational process itself. Teaching and learning are complex rather than mechanical processes, which complicates the task of finding a single best way of guaranteeing efficiency. The mechanisms by which given combinations of resources are turned into desired outcomes are not clear and feed into one another, implying that no benchmark system can be established from these fundamental relations. Educational efficiency evaluations are thus always relative to an existing standard, either in the past or in other educational systems.

- For comparisons to be valid and the use of educational efficiency to be politically useful, the educational resources and outcomes must be considered in a sufficiently standardised way. The conditions of educational provision in the systems compared in the analysis must be sufficiently similar (Wolter, 2010). Identifying the context and main features of each school system is thus crucial for establishing both the main similarities and differences, helping to frame general recommendations. However, even if conditions are sufficiently comparable, the relative importance to different educational objectives may vary across countries. This means that the comparative work should mostly refer to the stated general educational goals set by the countries, and not to objectives discretionarily chosen during the analysis.

- Efficiency analyses, as defined in Annex 1.A1, are generally strictly focused on the quantitative relation between inputs and outcomes. Therefore, there is a risk that comparative analysis fails to capture the synergetic relations between school resources across the different levels of a school system. Such approaches might disregard the organisation and governance features of schools, local authorities and the school system as a whole. Beyond the right allocation of educational resources, designing adequate organisational structures is essential for fulfilling the potential of school systems with given financial resources.

- Efficiency analyses do not always adequately take social considerations into account. However, education officials are often more interested in the allocation of resources that is more efficient from a societal perspective, and guarantees a distribution of resources complying with a given degree of fairness. An excessive focus on allocations which are strictly efficient at the school and system level can lead to outcomes which are nevertheless

> ### Box 1.1. **Limitations to efficiency analyses in education** (*cont.*)
>
> insensitive to prevailing social and institutional arrangements. Therefore, it is important to account for decisive components of educational policy reality, including persistent institutional habits and unwillingness or resistance to change, but also the importance attributed by school systems to providing adequate educational opportunities to all students.
>
> **Methodological limitations**
>
> ● Despite consistent methodological improvements, efficiency evaluations are still particularly sensitive to the choice of the methods employed in the analyses. Therefore, the selection of the most suitable model for efficiency analyses needs to consider a number of criteria such as acceptability, applicability or understandibility (Huguenin, 2015). Educational policies aimed at reforming resource allocation patterns should thus consider multiple approaches (Grosskopf et al., 2014).
>
> ● Efficiency is significantly influenced by factors which are not exclusively under the discretion of educational authorities, such as parental background, the acquired skills and characteristics of children when entering school or the average wealth of the citizens of a country, as measured by GDP per capita. Policies aimed at increasing efficiency in the use of school resources should thus take the importance of these factors into account.
>
> *Source:* Grosskopf, S. et al. (2014), "Efficiency in education: Research and implications", *EdPolicyWork Working Papers Series*, *http://dx.doi.org/10.1093/aepp/ppu007*; Huguenin, J.-M. (2015), "Data Envelopment Analysis and non-discretionary inputs: How to select the most suitable model using multi-criteria decision analysis", *Expert Systems with Applications*, *http://dx.doi.org/10.1016/j.eswa.2014.11.004*; Wolter, S.C. (2010), "Efficiency in education: 20 years of talk and no progress?", in S.M. Stoney (ed.), *Beyond Lisbon 2010: Perspectives from Research and Development for Education Policy in Europe*, National Foundation for Educational Research (NFER), Slough.

institutional arrangements in reform negotiation and change processes. Economic and financial perspectives will be considered in light of broader objectives for schooling and with a focus on the extent to which they promote quality, equity and desired long-term impacts of schooling.

Achieving efficiency and equity objectives together

Equity and efficiency are sometimes seen as competing goals as a focus on equity in education often entails higher investment for disadvantaged student groups and this additional funding may not proportionally translate into overall higher achievement at the aggregate level. This could lead to lower efficiency and thus a potential trade-off between the two objectives. However, the relationship between efficiency and equity is not that clear-cut, and education officials are not necessarily faced with a choice between the two goals.

Admitting that efficiency and equity can be complements to one another changes the focus in policy debates from a matter of political preference for one or the other objective towards seeking organisational design features that best favour synergies between equitable education, better results, and the best use of the available resources. If schools manage to support all students in achieving their full potential, an efficient school system can also be equitable at the same time (Wößmann, 2008).

As countries seek to enhance the performance of all students while also providing more equitable learning opportunities for different groups, there has been greater focus on ensuring that resources are directed to the areas where improvements in teaching and learning outcomes can best be achieved. Research has revealed a number of policy directions which appear to support both equity and efficiency objectives and which, therefore, warrant attention from policy makers when considering where to invest resources. Some examples are explored below.

Supporting high quality early childhood education and care

Education is a self-reinforcing process, in which new knowledge and skills are attained building on a previous solid basis of both those factors. In other words, early cognitive and non-cognitive development makes it easier to acquire skills and knowledge later in life. Therefore, policies directed to providing better early childhood education and care (ECEC) have a multiplicative effect over an individual's life cycle. Research indicates that offering high quality early childhood education and care for all children increases student achievement in later stages of the schooling process and reduces the impact of socio-economic background on future academic performance (Cunha et al., 2006; Heckman, 2006; Schütz et al., 2008; Wößmann, 2008; Blankenau and Youderian, 2015). It also supports early social and emotional development, which has positive effects on the continued development of non-cognitive skills (Kautz et al., 2015).

Conversely, failing to provide the adequate level of resources to sustain high ECEC is likely to result in increased expenditure needs at later stages of the schooling process. Allocating funding to high quality ECEC, while targeting it particularly to disadvantaged children, is therefore a fundamental policy lever for attaining both efficiency and equity in education. However, as for all levels of education, not only the amount of funding is important, but more particularly the way in which these additional resources translate into high quality education and care. Ensuring adequate levels of funding should allow for recruiting, developing and supporting qualified staff to foster the development of children's cognition, socio-emotional capacities and attitudes towards learning.

Reducing educational failure

Educational failure, that is when students do not progress through the system as expected and exit with insufficient knowledge, skills and competencies, has a high cost for school systems and individuals, and is an important source of inefficiency in many OECD review countries. Students at risk of dropping out are often those with the lowest skills, and thus the least prepared for leaving the education system to enter the labour market. Failure to guarantee students a minimum level of skills and achievements before they leave the school system is an important challenge across OECD countries (OECD, 2012b).

Educational failure may be linked to the fact that some school systems allocate resources in a traditional pattern in which students who progress through to the end of secondary education are treated from a funding angle as requiring higher spending, while students who are struggling at the primary or lower secondary levels receive fewer resources. Despite the demonstrated importance of the early years of schooling, in several countries more school resources are still allocated to higher levels of education. There is a case to be made for seeking greater balance in funding across educational levels. A major reduction in under-achievement in primary school could help increase the flow of students into cognitively demanding secondary school programmes and reduce levels of dropout as well as unemployment on leaving school.

Addressing inadequate approaches to distributing students across schools and programmes can also help reducing educational failure and increase both equity and efficiency. Grouping students by ability may allow offering the optimal pace and level of instruction to each group. But this needs to be weighed against the serious risks for equity and student motivation when labelling certain students as "low-ability" students and providing less stimulating academic environments to them, especially when this happens at a relatively early stage of schooling. There is evidence from different countries that the grouping of students is often biased with other criteria than student ability influencing the grouping process and students being ineffectively allocated to groups (Resh, 1998; Prenzel et al., 2005; Schofield, 2005; Strand, 2007). Several cross-country studies find that, after controlling for a range of other factors, early tracking of students into different programmes into is associated with greater inequality of results across students, with no discernible effect on overall performance (Schütz et al., 2007; Hanushek and Wößmann, 2006; Meier and Schütz, 2007).

Another related practice raising challenges for equity and efficiency in some countries is year repetition in response to underperformance by individual students. A vast body of literature reports that the slight academic benefits of year repetition are short-lived, while it holds high individual and social costs (OECD, 2012b). The direct costs of year repetition for school systems are high as the retention of students in the system increases the number of enrolled students and thus the level of funding required, besides delaying entry to the labour market.

Investing in teacher quality

Attracting and retaining an adequate teaching workforce is a policy imperative. Teachers are the most important resource in schools and the quality and effectiveness of their teaching is essential for student learning (Rockoff, 2004; OECD, 2005). Investing insufficiently in the teaching workforce might generate ineffectiveness through the crowding out of the best and most qualified human resources. Spending reforms driven by reductions in teachers' salaries, initial education and professional training may entail a loss of attractiveness of the profession and create challenges to quality, equity and efficiency in the long run.

Teachers' compensation levels play a role in determining who comes to the profession, who remains and for how long (OECD, 2005; Dolton and Marcenaro-Gutierrez, 2011). But not only the compensation levels are important, but working conditions in general, including recruitment, management, professional autonomy, collaboration and support. The OECD (2016d) report prepared for the 2016 International Summit on the Teaching Profession highlights the importance of effective and continuous teacher professional development and the policies underpinning it. Given the importance of teaching workforce policies for high quality schooling, a dedicated comparative thematic report will be prepared as part of the School Resources Review to analyse country policies for managing human resources in school education (OECD, forthcoming).

In this context, teacher-student ratios and class size are much debated topics in education policy. Strategies targeted at reducing class size are generally supported by arguments related to closer ties between teachers and students, increased time on task, and the potential to foster better learning environments with more individualised attention to students. The potential benefits of small classes need to be weighed against other potential investments such as the improvement of teacher education, professional development and employment conditions or more widespread use of assistant teachers and other professionals who can support qualified teachers. In other words, there may be a policy trade-off between investing in *more* human resources by maintaining small classes, and investing in *better* human resources and new approaches to teaching and learning (Dolton and Marcenaro-Gutierrez, 2011; Bietenbeck et al., 2015). Given the high cost of class size reduction policies, these appear comparatively less efficient than other interventions to support student learning (Rivkin et al., 2005; Hattie, 2009; Hanushek, 2011).

Despite the existence of a polarised debate over the effects of class size on students' achievement (for a review, see for example Santiago, 2002), there is considerable consensus in the research literature that small classes have a strong positive effect on the learning of particular student groups such as those in the earlier years of education and from disadvantaged socio-economic backgrounds (Robinson and Wittebols, 1986; Mosteller, 1995; Krueger, 1999; Angrist and Lavy, 1999; Molnar et al., 2001 Lindahl, 2001; Björklund et al., 2005; Andersson, 2007; Chetty et al., 2011; Dynarski et al., 2011). This indicates that additional available teacher resources would be optimally allocated if they were targeted at those who are likely to benefit the most, i.e. disadvantaged groups and students in pre-primary and primary schools.

Matching the school offer to changing demand

Several OECD review countries face an important decline in the student population, especially in rural areas. This raises the unit cost of education in these areas, as the fixed costs for organising schools (e.g. buildings, materials, staff) do not decrease proportionally to the decline in student numbers. In countries with many small schools, underutilisation (i.e. large spaces and high staff numbers for few students) is very likely to occur. Small rural schools also often face difficulties in recruiting qualified teachers and may face shortages, high attrition rates and limited opportunities for teacher professional development (Ares Abalde, 2014). As the cost of maintaining small schools with sharply decreasing enrolment is high, if there is evidence of a loss of quality keeping these schools open may represent an expensive inefficiency for the school system.

Policies to maintain small rural schools are often related to broader rural development strategies, recognising the important role of schools for local communities. In addition, many countries aim to provide schooling for young children at a reasonable distance from home as the benefits from small schools appear highest for students at a young age (e.g. close relationships between students, teachers, families and communities). But at later stages of schooling, larger schools can provide a range of advantages for students which are likely to outweigh the burden and cost of transportation (e.g. a more diverse programme and course offer, more specialised teachers who are better connected to a professional community, a larger choice of extracurricular activities and greater possibilities to organise comprehensive schooling or full-day provision [for a review of the respective benefits and drawbacks related to maintaining or consolidating small schools, see Ares Abalde, 2014]).

When considering consolidation policies, attention to local contexts is essential. In some cases there are few possibilities to consolidate the organisation of the school offer due to geographic and demographic conditions. In other cases policies to provide incentives and support for schools to operate on a larger scale by merging or clustering providers can help address some of the challenges faced by small schools. However, policy makers need to ensure that consolidation agendas are not just driven by a focus on cost savings but linked to school improvement strategies. This requires developing a vision with local authorities, schools and parents and ensuring a strong focus on the quality and equity of educational opportunities provided in the consolidated schools or school clusters.

The respective needs of rural versus urban areas also need to be kept in mind. In countries with changing demographic patters, the higher per-student cost in rural areas might direct resources away from other priorities, such as investing in urban schools which typically face their own set of equity challenges linked to greater student diversity and socio-economic disadvantage. Given the importance of matching the supply of schooling to changing demand across school systems, a dedicated comparative thematic report will be prepared as part of the School Resources Review to analyse country policies for organising the school offer (OECD, forthcoming).

Contextual developments shaping school funding policies

School funding policies do not take place in a vacuum but they are closely interlinked with wider developments in school governance contexts. In recent years, the organisation of OECD school systems has become increasingly complex and characterised by multi-level governance where the links between multiple actors operating at different levels are more fluid and open to negotiation (Burns and Köster, 2016). Although country contexts vary, in many countries there have been trends towards decentralisation across different levels of the school administration, enhanced school autonomy, and an increasing reliance on market-type mechanisms and incentive schemes. A large set of actors including regions, municipalities, different central and sub-central agencies, schools and private actors have gained responsibilities for managing budgets, recruiting staff and providing accountability information on the use of funding. In addition, key stakeholder groups such as school boards, parents associations, teacher unions and professional organisations and employers are recognised as important partners in school systems. These groups participate increasingly in negotiation and dialogue to influence the design of school funding mechanisms (Chapter 3) and in holding different actors accountable for the use of school funding (Chapter 5). The funding of school education has been affected by these broader governance trends and they influence the set of policy options available to countries. These contextual developments are briefly described in this section.

The decentralisation and devolution of education and other public services is expected to increase responsiveness to the demands of local communities, raise the potential for innovation, adapt financial and human resource management to local conditions and generate trust, commitment and professionalism. The arguments towards greater decentralisation and school autonomy are generally framed within the set of relations between schools and the environment in which these operate. These relations are of mutual influence: the context in which schools operate impacts on the level of resources available for their activities, and the schools themselves also contribute to shaping the communities in which they are integrated (Scheerens et al., 2011). More autonomous schools and local administrations have the potential to use the available resources more effectively as they are better able to adapt these to their local conditions and influence the operating environment (Scheerens, 2004).

On the other hand, governance arrangements that devolve responsibilities to a broad range of actors may raise concerns about the lack of systematic application of central directions, inconsistency of practices, ineffective or inequitable use of resources, and/or insufficient capacity for developing effective funding schemes at the local or school level. These concerns might be amplified by weak articulations between the different decision-making levels and limited collaboration between the actors involved. Excessively complex governance arrangements can lead to inefficient school funding structures if roles are duplicated, responsibilities overlap, actors compete and resources flows through the system lack transparency (Chapter 2). The measure of success of fiscal decentralisation and school autonomy in funding decisions will be how these translate into enhanced learning environments and contribute to better teaching and learning outcomes by matching resources to where they are most needed.

The above-mentioned governance trends have taken place across OECD countries to varying degrees over the past decades and it is important to keep in mind that countries have different points of departure regarding the level of decentralisation and devolution in their school systems (Burns and Köster, 2016). Federal countries such as Australia, Austria, Canada, Germany or the United States have a long history of decision-making powers being shared between central and state levels. Other countries such as Finland and the United Kingdom have strong traditions of decentralisation with the local level in charge of most schooling decisions. Yet another group of countries, such as Belgium and the Netherlands, have well-established practices of free school choice and a long tradition of publicly funding private schools (Burns and Köster, 2016). These institutional traditions have an important impact on school funding arrangements in each country and the range of policy options that are available in further developing school funding strategies.

It is also important to note that countries emphasise sub-central and school-based decision making to varying degrees and that decentralisation and school autonomy are not necessarily pursued as parallel strategies. For example, some countries where sub-central authorities have high levels of decision-making power (e.g. federal countries) may grant less autonomy to schools, whereas countries with high levels of school autonomy may retain a higher share of decision making at the central rather than at regional and local levels. OECD (2014) suggests that different driving factors may be behind the trends towards decentralisation and school autonomy: decentralisation of educational decision making to different levels of government might be more frequently part of broader public sector reform, whereas enhanced school autonomy might be prompted by more education-specific concerns about school management and performance.

In most countries, increased autonomy has been balanced by the strengthening of accountability requirements for local education authorities and schools. While further autonomy is given to the local level in many countries, other responsibilities are generally retained by central authorities (Levačic et al., 2000). These responsibilities are of a different kind, but still essential for ensuring efficient allocations of school resources. Strategic steering, standard setting, support and capacity development are all activities which are typically performed at a central level. This allows benefiting from positive externalities at the system level and addressing co-ordination problems across different levels of decision making. Nevertheless, these developments require the elaboration of more sophisticated school funding strategies, including in terms of designing allocation mechanisms that fit with school governance contexts (Chapter 3) and monitoring of the use of funds at the local and school level (Chapter 5).

Education services are usually framed within a set of public regulatory instruments, which means that funding is generally determined at a political level, rather than based on market incentives. However, some countries have introduced a range of market-type mechanisms in education, such as a free parental choice of schools, increased budgetary and management autonomy for school agents, greater emphasis on centrally determined objectives and the promotion of school competition through increased accountability and benchmarking. The use of such mechanisms generally aims to provide incentive systems for different actors in school systems. However, country experience indicates that there are a broad range of challenges regarding the use of market mechanisms. These are related to the unintended consequences of high-stakes accountability (for an in-depth analysis, see OECD, 2013b), the limited ability of demand and supply in the school sector to adapt to changing situations, and equity concerns related the unequal distribution of choice opportunities, with more affluent parents exercising choice more often (Blanchenay and Burns, 2016; see also Chapter 2).

How this report looks at the funding of school education

This report was prepared as part of a major OECD study on the effective use of school resources resulting in the publication series *OECD Reviews of School Resources*. This publication series will include thematic comparative reports on the different types of resources considered in the review including: i) the funding of school education (the present report); ii) the organisation of the school offer (forthcoming); and iii) the management of human resources in school education (forthcoming). Box 1.2 and Annex C provide more information on the main features of the OECD review.

Box 1.2. **The OECD School Resources Review**

The *OECD Review of Policies to Improve the Effectiveness of Resource Use in Schools* (also known as the *School Resources Review*) was launched in 2013. This review is conducted in collaboration with countries and under the guidance of the OECD Group of National Experts (GNE) on School Resources, comprising representatives from all participating countries, plus other OECD countries. The review is designed to respond to the strong interest in the effective use of school resources evident at national and international levels. It provides analysis and policy advice on the use of school resources to help governments achieve quality, efficiency and equity objectives in education. It focuses on primary and secondary school education, although links to other levels of education are also established where relevant.

Key issues for analysis

There are a broad range of resources used in school systems. This review concentrates mainly on three interlinked types of resources:

- **Financial resources** (e.g. expenditures on education, funding mechanisms, school budget).
- **Physical resources** (e.g. school size and location, school buildings, equipment).
- **Human resources** (e.g. teachers, school leaders, education administrators).

The overarching policy question is "What policies best ensure that school resources are effectively used to improve student outcomes?". In considering policies to ensure that these resources are effectively used to improve student outcomes, the review focuses on four key issues for analysis: governance of resource use (how to govern, plan and implement resource use); resource distribution (how to distribute resources across levels, sectors and student groups); resource management (how to manage evaluate and follow up on resource use); and resource utilisation (how to utilise resources for different programmes and priorities).

Review objectives and methodology

The analysis developed by the project is designed to support the development of effective national education policy. In particular, the project proposes policy options that best ensure that school resources are effectively and equitably used to improve student outcomes.

Box 1.2. **The OECD School Resources Review** (cont.)

The project provides opportunities for exchanges of best practices, mutual learning, gathering and dissemination of information and evidence of what works. It is also expected that, through the wide public dissemination of its results, the project will inform national policy debates on school resource among the relevant stakeholders.

The project involves a reflection about the policy implications of the currently available evidence on resource use in schools in a wide range of national settings. Evidence analysed includes the relevant academic and policy papers published in peer-reviewed journals, detailed information provided by countries on their school resource use policies, and views and perspectives collected from a wide range of stakeholders in a variety of countries. The work is undertaken through a combination of desk-based analysis, country reviews and periodic meetings of the Group of National Experts (GNE) on School Resources to provide feedback on substantive documents and determine priorities for further analytical work. The work involves three major strands:

- **An analytical strand** to draw together evidence-based policy lessons from international data, research and analysis. The analytical strand uses several means – literature reviews, country background reports (CBRs) and data analyses – to analyse the factors that shape resource use in school systems. The CBRs use a common framework to facilitate comparative analysis and maximise the opportunities for countries to learn from each other.

- **A country review strand** to provide policy advice to individual countries tailored to the issues of interest in those countries, on the basis of the international evidence base, combined with evidence obtained by a team of experts visiting the country. For each country review, a team of up to five reviewers (including at least two OECD Secretariat members) analyses the CBR and subsequently undertakes an intensive case study visit of about eight days in length. Each study visit aims to provide the review team with a variety of perspectives on school resource policies and includes meetings with a wide variety of stakeholders. Country review reports are published in the series OECD *Reviews of School Resources*.

- **A synthesis strand** with the preparation of a series of thematic comparative reports. These blend analytical and review evidence and provide overall policy conclusions on specific themes.

Collaborations

The project is conducted in co-operation with a range of international organisations to reduce duplication and develop synergies. In particular, within a broader framework of collaboration, a partnership with the European Commission (EC) is established for this project. The support of the EC covers part of the participation costs of countries which are part of the European Union Erasmus+ programme and contributes to the preparation of the series of thematic comparative reports. In addition, the review of Kazakhstan was undertaken in co-operation with the World Bank. Other international agencies collaborating with the project include Eurydice, the Inter-American Development Bank (IDB), the Organising Bureau of European School Student Unions (OBESSU), the Standing International Conference of Inspectorates (SICI) and the United Nations Educational, Scientific and Cultural Organization (UNESCO). Social partners are also involved through the contribution of Trade Union Advisory Committee to the OECD (TUAC) and the Business and Industry Advisory Committee to the OECD (BIAC), which participated in the GNE as Permanent Observers.

Aims of this report

This report on the funding of school education is the first in a series of thematic comparative reports. Figure 1.3 presents an overview of the main themes and guiding questions addressed by the report. It is intended to add value to the wide range of materials produced through the OECD review (Box 1.2) in the area of school funding by drawing out its key findings and policy messages. This report seeks to:

- Provide an international comparative analysis of funding policies in school education.
- Provide a stock-take of current school funding policies and practices in countries.
- Develop a comprehensive framework to guide the development of school funding policies.
- Propose policy options for the development of school funding policies in different contexts.
- Identify priorities for follow-up work.

Figure 1.3. **The funding of school education: Main themes and guiding questions for the report**

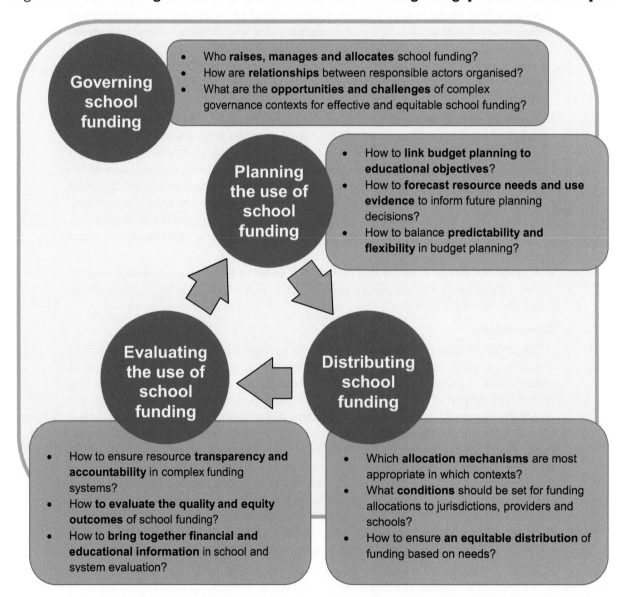

Country participation and sources of information

Eighteen school systems were actively engaged in the preparation of this report. These are referred to as the "OECD review countries" throughout the report. These 18 school systems cover a wide range of economic and social contexts, and among them they illustrate quite different approaches to school funding. This allows a comparative perspective on key policy issues. In addition, this report seeks to go beyond information collected from the 18 participating countries by considering cross-country data available from broader OECD and other data collections as well as the relevant international research literature.

Most of the OECD review countries took part in a collection of qualitative data on the main features of their school funding approaches and prepared a detailed background report, following a standard set of guidelines. In addition, ten of these school systems also opted for a detailed country review, undertaken by a review team consisting of members of the OECD Secretariat and external experts. Country reviews provide an independent analysis by the review team of identified strengths and challenges in the use of resources in these countries. In their analyses, the review teams have drawn on information gathered in interviews with a broad range of stakeholders, including social partners, during a main country review visit.

This report draws on four main sources of information:

- A range of literature reviews bringing together research findings on relevant issues from as many school systems as possible beyond the OECD review countries. These literature reviews include OECD working papers on budgeting and accounting in OECD education systems; the public funding of private schools; conceptualising and measuring efficiency and equity in the use of school resources; the funding of vocational education and training; the funding of special educational needs provision; and targeted funding schemes. Annex C provides an overview and links to published literature reviews.

- Seventeen responses to a qualitative data collection on national approaches to school funding provided by the following school systems: Austria, Belgium (Flemish Community), Belgium (French Community), Chile, the Czech Republic, Denmark, Estonia, Iceland, Israel, Kazakhstan, Lithuania, Portugal, the Slovak Republic, Slovenia, Spain, Sweden and Uruguay. The information collected is summarised in comparative tables included in the annexes to individual chapters of this report.

- Sixteen country background reports prepared by the following school systems: Austria, Belgium (Flemish Community), Belgium (French Community), Chile, the Czech Republic, Denmark, Estonia, Iceland, Kazakhstan, Lithuania, Luxembourg, the Slovak Republic, Slovenia, Spain, Sweden and Uruguay.

- Ten country review reports prepared by OECD-led review teams for the following school systems: Austria, Belgium (Flemish Community), Chile, the Czech Republic, Denmark, Estonia, Kazakhstan, Lithuania, the Slovak Republic and Uruguay.

This thematic synthesis report provides examples of country initiatives in funding school education (available also in specific boxes). These country examples do not constitute best practices or recommendations of a particular approach and have not necessarily been evaluated through a programme evaluation, but rather help to illustrate points made in the analysis and show different approaches. It should be noted that country-specific information given in this report with no associated source or reference is taken from country background reports and country review reports produced through the review. All documents produced through the review are available from *www.oecd.org/education/schoolresourcesreview.htm*.

The importance of context

When reading this report, it is important to keep in mind that the contexts within which school funding policy making operates can vary markedly across countries depending on their historical traditions, educational cultures and economic and social conditions. Policy initiatives that work well in one national context are not necessarily transferable. The review has attempted to be sensitive to this through an approach that analyses school funding policies in relation to the values, vision and organisation of school systems in different countries as well as the broader economic, social and political contexts in which they operate. It is important to note that not all policy directions apply equally across countries. In a number of cases the policy suggestions are already in place, while for other countries they may have less relevance because of different social, economic and educational structures and traditions. The implications also need to be treated cautiously because in some instances there is not a strong enough research base across a sufficient number of countries to be confident about successful implementation. Rather, the discussion attempts to distil potentially useful ideas and lessons from the experiences of countries that have been searching for better ways to govern, distribute and manage school funding.

The structure of this report

The report has five chapters. Following Chapter 1 which explains the importance of school funding, Chapters 2-5 are concerned with the key substantive issues involved in school funding policies: *Governing School Funding* (Chapter 2); *Distributing School Funding* (Chapter 3); *Planning the Use of School Funding* (Chapter 4); and *Evaluating the Use of School Funding* (Chapter 5). The chapters provide a description of school funding frameworks in countries; analyse strengths and weaknesses of different school funding approaches; and provide recommendations for the improvement of funding strategies.

References

Ammermüller, A. (2005), "Educational opportunities and the role of institutions", *ZEW Discussion Paper*, No. 05-44, *http://dx.doi.org/10.2139/ssrn.753366*.

Andersson, C. (2007), "Teacher density and student achievement in Swedish compulsory schools", *Working Paper 2007:4*, Institute for Labour Market Policy Evaluation (IFAU), Uppsala.

Angrist, J. and V. Lavy (1999), "Using Maimonides' rule to estimate the effect of class size on scholastic achievement", *The Quarterly Journal of Economics*, Vol. 114/ 2, The MIT Press, pp. 533-575.

Ares Abalde, M. (2014), "School Size Policies: A Literature Review", *OECD Education Working Papers*, No. 106, OECD Publishing, Paris, *http://dx.doi.org/10.1787/5jxt472ddkjl-en*.

Bascia, N. and B. Faubert (2012), "Primary class size reduction: How policy space, physical space, and spatiality shape what happens in real schools", *Leadership and Policy in Schools*, Vol. 11/3, Taylor and Francis, pp. 344-364, *http://dx.doi.org/10.1080/15700763.2012.692430*.

Baumol, W.J. (2012), *The Cost Disease: Why Computers Get Cheaper and Health Care Doesn't*, Yale University Press, London.

Berne, R. and L. Stiefel (1999), "Concepts of school finance equity: 1970 to the present", in H.F. Ladd, R. Chalk, and J.S. Hansen (eds.), *Equity and Adequacy in Education Finance: Issues and Perspectives*, National Academy Press, Washington, DC.

Bietenbeck, J., M. Piopiunik and S. Wiederhold (2015), "Africa's skill tragedy : Does teachers' lack of knowledge lead to low student performance?", *CESifo Working Paper 5470*, CESifo Group Munich.

Björklund, A. et al. (2004), "Education, Equality and Efficiency – An Analysis of Swedish School Reforms during the 1990s", *IFAU report 2004: 1*, Institute for Labour Market Policy Evaluations, Uppsala.

Blanchenay, P. and T. Burns (2016), "Policy experimentation in complex education systems", in T. Burns and F. Koester (eds.) (2016), *Governing Education in a Complex World*, OECD Publishing, Paris, *http://dx.doi.org/10.1787/9789264255364-10-en*.

Blankenau, W. and X. Youderian (2015), "Early childhood education expenditures and the intergenerational persistence of income", *Review of Economic Dynamics*, Vol. 18/2, Elsevier Inc., pp. 334-349, *http://dx.doi.org/10.1016/j.red.2014.06.001*.

Burns, T. and F. Köster (eds.) (2016), *Governing Education in a Complex World*, Educational Research and Innovation, OECD Publishing, Paris, *http://dx.doi.org/10.1787/9789264255364-en*.

Busemeyer, M. (2008), "The impact of fiscal decentralisation on education and other types of spending", *Swiss Political Science Review*, Vol. 14/3, Wiley-Blackwell.

Castelli, L., S. Ragazzi and A. Crescentini (2012), "Equity in education: A general overview", *Procedia – Social and Behavioral Sciences*, Vol. 69, Elsevier B.V., pp. 2243-2250, *http://dx.doi.org/10.1016/j.sbspro.2012.12.194*.

Chmielewski, A.K. (2014), "An international comparison of achievement inequality in within- and between-school tracking systems", *American Journal of Education*, Vol. 120/3, University of Chicago Press, pp. 293-324.

Cunha, F. et al. (2006), "Interpreting the evidence on life cycle skill formation", in E.A. Hanushek and F. Welch (eds.), *Handbook of the Economics of Education*, Vol. 1, North-Holland, Amsterdam.

De Witte, K. and L. López-Torres (2017), "Efficiency in education: A review of literature and a way forward", *Journal of the Operational Research Society*, Vol. 68/4, pp. 339-363, *http://dx.doi.org/10.1057/jors.2015.92*.

Dolton, P. and O.D. Marcenaro-Gutierrez (2011), "If you pay peanuts do you get monkeys? A cross-country analysis of teacher pay and pupil performance", *Economic Policy*, Vol. 26/65, Oxford University Press, pp. 5-55.

Fakharzadeh, T. (2016), "Budgeting and Accounting in OECD Education Systems: A Literature Review", *OECD Education Working Papers*, No. 128, OECD Publishing, Paris, *http://dx.doi.org/10.1787/5jm3xgsz03kh-en*.

Fazekas, M. (2012), "School Funding Formulas: Review of Main Characteristics and Impacts", *OECD Education Working Papers*, No. 74, OECD Publishing, Paris, *http://dx.doi.org/10.1787/5k993xw27cd3-en*.

Field, S., M. Kuczera and B. Pont (2007), *No More Failures: Ten Steps to Equity in Education*, OECD Publishing, Paris, *http://dx.doi.org/10.1787/9789264032606-en*.

Finn, J.D and C.M. Achilles (1990), "Answers and questions about class size: A state-wide experiment", *American Educational Research Journal*, Vol. 27, Sage, pp. 557-575.

Fischer, N. and E. Klieme (2013), "Quality and effectiveness of German all-day schools: Results of the study on the development of all-day schools", in J. Ecarius et al. (eds.), *Extended Education – an International Perspective*, Barbara Budrich Publishers, Opladen, pp. 27-52.

Gibbs, C (2014), "Experimental evidence on early intervention: The impact of full-day kindergarten", *EdPolicyWork Working Papers Series*, Vol. 34, University of Virginia, *http://curry.virginia.edu/uploads/resourceLibrary/34_Full_Day_KG_Impact.pdf*.

Grosskopf, S., K.J. Hayes and L.L. Taylor (2014), "Efficiency in education: Research and implications", *Applied Economic Perspectives and Policy*, Vol. 36/2, Oxford University Press, pp. 175-210, *http://dx.doi.org/10.1093/aepp/ppu007*.

Hanushek, E.A. (2011), "The economic value of higher teacher quality", *Economics of Education Review*, Vol. 30, Elsevier, pp 466-479.

Hanushek, E.A. (2006), "School resources", in E.A. Hanushek and F. Welch (eds.), *Handbook of the Economics of Education*, Elsevier B.V.

Hanushek, E.A. and L. Wößmann (2006), "Does educational tracking affect performance and inequality? Differences-in-differences evidence across countries", *The Economic Journal*, Vol. 116/510, Wiley-Blackwell, pp. C63-C76.

Hattie, J. (2009), *Visible learning: A Synthesis of over 800 Meta-analyses Relating to Achievement*, Routledge, London.

Heckman, J. (2006), "Skill formation and the economics of investing in disadvantaged children", *Science*, Vol. 312, American Association for the Advancement of Science, pp. 1900-1902.

Huguenin, J.-M. (2015), "Data Envelopment Analysis and non-discretionary inputs: How to select the most suitable model using multi-criteria decision analysis", *Expert Systems with Applications*, Vol. 2/5, Elsevier Ltd, pp. 2570-2581, *http://dx.doi.org/10.1016/j.eswa.2014.11.004*.

Kautz, T. et al. (2015), "Fostering and Measuring Skills: Improving Cognitive and Non-cognitive Skills to Promote Lifetime Success", *OECD Education Working Papers*, No. 110, OECD Publishing, Paris, *http://dx.doi.org/10.1787/5jxsr7vr78f7-en*.

Kirabo Jackson, C., R. Johnson and C. Persico (2014), "The effect of school finance reforms on the distribution of spending, academic achievement and adult outcomes", NBER *Working Paper Series, Working Paper* 20118, National Bureau of Economic Research, Cambridge MA, *www.nber.org/papers/w20118*.

Krueger, A. (1999), "Experimental estimates of education production functions", *The Quarterly Journal of Economics*, Vol. 114/ 2, Oxford University Press, pp. 497-532.

Lafortune, J., J. Rothstein and D. Whitmore Schanzenbach (2016), "School finance reform and the distribution of student achievement", *Northwestern Institute for Policy Research Working Paper Series*, WP-16-04, Northwestern University, *www.ipr.northwestern.edu/publications/papers/2016/WP-16-04.html*.

Levačic, R. (2008), "Financing schools: Evolving patterns of autonomy and control", *Educational Management Administration and Leadership*, Vol. 36/2, Sage Publications, pp. 221-234, *http://dx.doi.org/10.1177/1741143207087774*.

Levačic, R. et al. (2000), "Funding schools by formula: comparing practice in five countries", *Journal of Education Finance*, Vol. 25/4, University of Illinois Press, pp. 489-515.

Levin, B. (2003), *Approaches to Equity in Policy for Lifelong Learning*, Paper commissioned by the OECD Education and Training Policy Division for the Equity in Education Thematic Review, *www.oecd.org/education/school/38692676.pdf*.

Levin, H.M. (2015), "Issues in educational privatisation", in H.F. Ladd and M.E. Goertz (eds.), *Handbook of Research in Education Finance and Policy*, Routledge, New York.

Lindahl, M. (2001), "Home versus school learning: A new approach to estimating the effect of class size on achievement", *IZA Discussion Papers*, No. 261, Institute for the Study of Labor (IZA), Bonn.

Lockheed, M.E. and E. Hanushek (1994), "Concepts of educational efficiency and effectiveness", *Human Resources Development and Operations Policy Working Paper*, No. HRO 24, World Bank, Washington, DC.

Meier, V. and G. Schütz (2007), "The economics of tracking and non-tracking", *Ifo Working Paper* No. 50, CESifo, Munich.

Molnar, A. et al. (2001), *2000-2001 Evaluation Results of the Student Achievement Guarantee in Education (SAGE) Program*, Center for Education Research, Analysis and Innovation (CERAI), University of Wisconsin-Milwaukee.

Mosteller, F. (1995), "The Tennessee study of size in the class grades", *The Future of Children*, Vol. 5/2, Princeton University, pp. 113-127, *http://dx.doi.org/10.2307/1602360*.

OECD (forthcoming), *The Management of Human Resources in School Education* [Working Title], OECD Reviews of School Resources, OECD Publishing, Paris.

OECD (forthcoming), *The Organisation of the School Offer* [Working Title], OECD Reviews of School Resources, OECD Publishing, Paris.

OECD (2016a), *PISA 2015 Results (Volume I): Excellence and Equity in Education*, OECD Publishing, Paris, *http://dx.doi.org/10.1787/9789264266490-en*.

OECD (2016b), *Education at a Glance 2016: OECD Indicators*, OECD Publishing, Paris, *http://dx.doi.org/10.1787/eag-2016-en*.

OECD (2016c), *PISA 2015 Results (Volume II): Policies and Practices for Successful Schools*, OECD Publishing, Paris, *http://dx.doi.org/10.1787/9789264267510-en*.

OECD (2016d), *Teaching Excellence through Professional Learning and Policy Reform: Lessons from around the World*, OECD Publishing, Paris, *http://dx.doi.org/10.1787/9789264252059-en*.

OECD (2016e), *Low-Performing Students: Why They Fall Behind and How to Help Them Succeed*, OECD Publishing, Paris, *http://dx.doi.org/10.1787/9789264250246-en*.

OECD (2015a), *Education at a Glance 2015: OECD Indicators*, OECD Publishing, Paris, *http://dx.doi.org/10.1787/eag-2015-en*.

OECD (2014), *Fiscal Federalism 2014: Making Decentralisation Work*, OECD Publishing, Paris, *http://dx.doi.org/10.1787/9789264204577-en*.

OECD (2013a), *PISA 2012 Results: What Makes Schools Successful (Volume IV): Resources, Policies and Practices*, OECD Publishing, Paris, *http://dx.doi.org/10.1787/9789264201156-en*.

OECD (2013b), *Synergies for Better Learning: An International Perspective on Evaluation and Assessment*, OECD Publishing, Paris, *http://dx.doi.org/10.1787/9789264190658-en*.

OECD (2012a), "Does Money Buy Strong Performance in PISA?", *PISA in Focus*, No. 13, OECD Publishing, Paris, *http://dx.doi.org/10.1787/5k9fhmfzc4xx-en*.

OECD (2012b), *Equity and Quality in Education: Supporting Disadvantaged Students and Schools*, OECD Publishing, Paris, *http://dx.doi.org/10.1787/9789264130852-en*.

OECD (2005), *Teachers Matter: Attracting, Developing and Retaining Effective Teachers*, OECD Publishing, Paris, *http://dx.doi.org/10.1787/9789264018044-en*.

OECD (n.d.), *PISA 2015 Database*, *www.oecd.org/pisa/data/2015database/*.

Prenzel, M. et al. (eds.) (2005), *PISA 2003: Ergebnisse des Zweiten Ländervergleichs Zusammenfassung [PISA 2003: Results of the Second Inter-state Comparison, Summary]*, PISA-Konsortium Deutschland.

Resh, N. (1998), "Track placement: How the 'sorting machine' works in Israel", *American Journal of Education*, Vol. 106/ 3, University of Chicago Press, pp. 416-438.

Rivkin, S.G., E.A. Hanushek and J.F. Kain (2005), "Teachers, schools and academic achievement", *Econometrica*, 73:2, Wiley-Blackwell Publishing Inc., pp. 417-458.

Robinson, G.E. and J.H. Wittebols (1986), *Class Size Research: A Related Cluster Analysis for Decision-Making*, Education Research Service, Arlington, VA.

Rockoff, J. (2004), "Impact of teachers on student achievement: Evidence from panel data", *American Economic Review*, Vol. 94/2, American Economic Mission, pp. 247-252, *http://dx.doi.org/10.1257/0002828041302244*.

Santiago, P. (2002), "Teacher Demand and Supply: Improving Teaching Quality and Addressing Teacher Shortages", *OECD Education Working Papers*, No. 1, OECD Publishing, Paris, *http://dx.doi.org/10.1787/232506301033*.

Scheerens, J. (2004), "Perspectives on education quality, education indicators and benchmarking", *European Educational Research Journal*, Vol. 3/1, Sage, pp. 115-138, *http://dx.doi.org/10.2304/eerj.2004.3.1.3*.

Scheerens, J., H. Luyten and J. Ravens (2011), *Measuring Educational Quality by Means of Indicators*, Spriner Netherlands, *http://dx.doi.org/10.1007/978-94-007-0926-3_1*.

Schofield, J.W. et al. (2006), "Migration background, minority-group membership and academic achievement: Research evidence from social, educational, and developmental psychology", *AKI Research Review 5*, Programme on Intercultural Conflicts and Societal Integration (AKI), Social Science Research Center, Berlin.

Schütz, G., H.W. Ursprung and L. Wößmann (2008), "Education policy and equality of opportunity", *Kyklos*, Vol. 61/2, Wiley-Blackwell, pp. 279-308.

Shavit, Y. and W. Müller (2006), "Vocational secondary education, tracking, and social stratification", in M.T. Hallinan (ed.), *Handbook of the Sociology of Education*, Springer US, *http://link.springer.com/chapter/10.1007/0-387-36424-2_20*.

Strand, S. (2007), *Minority Ethnic Pupils in the Longitudinal Study of Young People in England (LSYPE)*, Centre for Educational Development Appraisal and Research, University of Warwick and Department for Children, Schools and Families, London.

Waslander, S., C. Pater and M. van der Weide (2010), "Markets in Education: An Analytical Review of Empirical Research on Market Mechanisms in Education", *OECD Education Working Papers*, No. 52, OECD Publishing, Paris, *http://dx.doi.org/10.1787/5km4pskmkr27-en*.

Wolff, E.N. (2015), "Educational expenditures and student performance among OECD countries", *Structural Change and Economic Dynamics*, Vol. 33, Elsevier B.V., pp. 37-57, *http://dx.doi.org/10.1016/j.strueco.2015.02.003*.

Wolff, E.N., W.J. Baumol and A.N. Saini (2014), "A comparative analysis of education costs and outcomes: The United States vs. other OECD countries", *Economics of Education Review*, Vol. 39, Elsevier Ltd, pp. 1-21, *http://dx.doi.org/10.1016/j.econedurev.2013.12.002*.

Wolter, S.C. (2010), "Efficiency in education: 20 years of talk and no progress?", in S.M. Stoney (ed.), *Beyond Lisbon 2010: Perspectives from Research and Development for Education Policy in Europe*, National Foundation for Educational Research (NFER), Slough.

Wößmann, L. (2016), "The importance of school systems: Evidence from international differences in student achievement", *Journal of Economic Perspectives*, Vol. 30/3, American Economic Association, pp. 3-32.

Wößmann, L. (2008), "Efficiency and equity of European education and training policies", *International Tax and Public Finance*, Vol. 15/2, Springer US, pp. 199-230, *http://dx.doi.org/10.1007/s10797-008-9064-1*.

ANNEX 1.A1

Key terms and concepts

Effectiveness, efficiency and equity

In the economic literature, education is typically conceptualised as a process turning a given set of resources into a given set of outcomes. Schooling is thus the transformation of resources (e.g. students' and teachers' characteristics, classroom size, or schools' facilities) into individual (e.g. improved cognitive skills, successful integration in the labour market or individual wellbeing) and social outcomes (e.g. increased democratic participation, intergenerational mobility or social cohesion). This process is mediated by the institutional factors shaped by educational policy (e.g. decentralisation of school funding, higher school autonomy or benchmarking between schools) and broader national policies and governance structures.

Contextual factors also affect the success of the school system and the effectiveness of political reforms. The socio-economic background of students, the characteristics of the students' neighbourhood and peers and the location of schools all influence the capacity to make the most out of the available resources. Therefore, there has been a greater focus on ensuring that resources are directed to those areas where improvements in teaching and learning can best be achieved and where funding is most needed. In this context, devising funding strategies promoting an *effective*, *efficient* and *equitable* use of resources is of key importance.

Effectiveness

Educational effectiveness refers to the potential of a particular combination of school resources to provide desired outcomes. Effective schools or school systems are those able to adequately accomplish stated education objectives, producing the maximum possible outcomes by using available human and physical resources. Studies of educational effectiveness analyse whether specific resources have positive effects on different outcomes, and if so, how large these effects are (Lockheed and Hanushek, 1994). In contrast to studies of efficiency (see below), effectiveness analyses are not necessarily concerned with the cost of different resources, but rather with which minimum combination of resources provides a desired level of school quality or longer-term social and economic outcomes.

Effectiveness can be internal or external, depending on the nature of the outcomes being considered. Internal effectiveness analyses assess the extent to which the potential for providing quality education is being fulfilled to achieve outcomes that directly accrue to the education system such as student achievement or literacy and numeracy levels. Educational policies targeted at increasing internal effectiveness are dependent on an evaluation of alternative uses of resources *within* the school system. External effectiveness, on the other hand, addresses how that educational potential is being fulfilled in terms of private and social financial outcomes. This type of analysis focuses on the ways in which particular combinations of non-financial resources, such as different teachers' characteristics or different educational curricula, influence longer-term outcomes in the labour market. However, external effectiveness evaluations are of little value to provide guidance to educational policy since the financial effort invested in providing the human and physical resources is not quantified. Hence, the concept is normally used as a first stage of a cost-benefit analysis (Lockheed and Hanushek, 1994).

Improving internal or external effectiveness can be attained through two different approaches: either by maintaining identical levels of outcomes while lowering the intensity of resources in the system, or by attaining better outcomes with the same level of resources employed. The choice of the approach has important implications for policy makers and will depend on contextual factors. The best way for seeking more effective school systems is always dependent on the political, cultural and economic constraints faced by education officials. In times of economic growth, an orientation towards increasing student performance, with a controlled increase or constant allocation of school resources used may more easily earn political traction while in times of severe budget constraints the overuse of public resources becomes more salient and there is greater pressure for reallocation to other uses. In any case, even with favourable political and economic conditions, having a more effective school system overall means a better adequacy between school resources and educational outcomes – which does not mean that *more* resources necessarily lead to better results.

Efficiency

Educational efficiency, in turn, refers to the ability of fulfilling the maximum educational potential at *the lowest possible cost*. It thus adds a financial cost component to effectiveness analyses. This means that it does not only matter, for instance, how many teachers per student or computers per school an educational system needs in order to provide quality education, but rather how the intensity of those resources translates into financial investment needs weighs on budgetary decisions. Thus, in order to analyse efficiency, it is necessary to have information regarding the cost of human and physical resources.

From these definitions, it follows that a school system can be effective without being efficient, but cannot be efficient without being effective. From a political perspective, this implies that there is no logical support for seeking cost reducing policies based on an efficiency argument, if a neutral or positive impact on effectiveness is not guaranteed in the first place. Thus, a policy reform can only reveal itself truly efficient if, from its proceedings, internal and external effectiveness remain at least unchanged.

Efficiency can also be internal or external depending on the nature of the outcomes considered. Internal efficiency focuses on the relationship between financial resources and outcomes which directly accrue to the school system, like student achievement or literacy and numeracy levels. In the context of education policies, evaluations of internal efficiency are targeted at assessing how the available funds can be best allocated *within* the system. The use of these analyses can provide guidance on which school funding policies should be pursued. External efficiency, on the other hand, focuses on comparing the benefits from investing in the school system with the benefits from investing comparable amounts in alternative priorities. As a condition, the outcomes of the different priorities must be comparable, which normally implies that these are measured as financial returns, normally in the labour market context. Thus, these evaluations help to understand how many funds should be allocated *to* or *from* the system. They also provide the justification for long-term trends in education expenditures by showcasing how the economic costs of providing quality education can continuously translate into improved social and economic outcomes. Analyses of external efficiency are beyond the scope of this report.

As in the case of effectiveness, efficiency improvements can be obtained either through an input or output perspective. School systems can become more efficient either by consuming less financial resources with no change in the outcomes, or by improving their outcomes with no change in the level of financial investment.

Equity

Educational equity is a broad and not easily definable concept. Studies of educational equity are concerned not only with issues internal to the school system, but typically also explore broader phenomena such as housing segregation, social discrimination and integration of immigrants and minorities (Levin, 2003).

The pursuit of equity in education usually takes into account three different possible strategies underpinning policymaking: seeking equal opportunities, equal treatment or equal results across students and schools (Castelli et al., 2012). Equity is not, in every circumstance, synonym of equality: it is open to the unequal treatment of those who come from different starting points. Striving for equal results across students with different characteristics allows for differences in funding that take into account the differential costs of providing similar educational experiences to different student groups. The different approaches also reveal a different relevance given to the phases of the educational process. While the concern with equal opportunities entails the provision of sufficiently differentiated levels of resources to ensure identical levels of quality, the focus on equity as an achievement equaliser turns the debate towards the best policies to ensure an even distribution of educational outcomes.

There are two main ways of operationalising equity in education: horizontally and vertically. While horizontal equity considers the overall provision of resources to each part of the school system, vertical equity justifies policy options targeted to ensure disadvantaged groups of students or schools have access to additional funds. As will be explained below, horizontal and vertical equity can be complementary goals. While horizontal equity is assessed by minimum variability in the distribution of resources for similar students, vertical equity focuses on providing differential funding for different student groups based on their needs. In order to minimise an apparent tension between these concepts, the analyses must be clearly identified and be correctly conditioned to the relevant factors for differentiation. The next sections will better address these concerns.

Horizontal equity

Horizontal equity is usually defined as the equal treatment of equals. It closely reflects the principle of equality in resource distribution, such that the same amount of school resources is allocated for similar types of provision. For the case of horizontal equity, the differences in educational opportunities are analysed within each subpopulation of students or schools to be targeted. It is, then, a useful concept when applied to intra-group equality, if the relevant subpopulations are well identified and separately analysed (Berne and Stiefel, 1999). Horizontally equitable funding schemes are set such that there is a minimum dispersion of access to resources within the relevant subpopulations of students or groups of schools.

Vertical equity

Vertical equity is typically defined as the unequal treatment of unequals. In other words, students or schools with different characteristics should be given access to different levels of funding. These differences in funding reflect the additional costs of providing similar educational experiences across students with different characteristics. It is thus the concept that most closely reflects the principle of equal educational opportunity. At the student level, it implies that funding should be allocated according to the specific needs of each subpopulation of student, identified by its relevant characteristics. Previous analyses of PISA data indicate that the risk of low performance is significantly different and systematically increases for students with key identified characteristics (OECD, 2016c; OECD 2016e). These characteristics are normally those of family and cultural background, gender, ethnicity, immigrant status or specific special educational needs. At the school and regional levels the usual characteristics considered are related with the level of urbanisation of the municipality or region, its size and the capacity to raise additional revenues. Funding strategies for education must take this into account if equity across different groups of students is to be achieved. Vertically equitable funding schemes are set such that all students have an equal opportunity to achieve their full potential, independently of circumstances which are out of their direct control.

At first sight, the definitions of the concepts of vertical and horizontal equity may seem to imply a trade-off. Allocation of differential funding to comply with vertical equity objectives leads to overall variability in funding across regions and schools which could hinder horizontal equity. However, a clear conceptual distinction and assessment reveals no such concern, as horizontal equity can be pursued with no prejudice of vertical concerns. It is possible to both provide differential funding across subpopulations of students, while guaranteeing minimum variability of access to resources within those subpopulations. So, while a funding scheme can allocate additional funding for schools with a higher proportion of students from disadvantaged socio-economic backgrounds, horizontal equity can be attained by guaranteeing that such additional funding is identical for those groups of students or schools with similar characteristics.

Research in the area of educational economics has provided evidence supporting well designed and transparent *funding formulas* as the best way to combine horizontal and vertical equity, while incentivising the efficient use of school resources at the different levels of the system (Levačic, 2008). A funding formula is a set of agreed funding criteria which are impartially applied to each school, normally through a mathematical formula making the coefficients attached to each criterion explicit (Levačic et al., 2000; Fazekas, 2012). Through funding formulas, the equity and efficiency objectives are made explicit and the coefficients yield the potential to better address specific school priorities. Chapter 3 includes a more thorough discussion of funding formulas and other funding mechanisms used by the countries analyses in this report.

Measuring efficiency

Efficiency as a normative concept

Efficiency is different from productivity due to its normative nature. Productivity stands for the ratio between the outputs and inputs involved in a given production process.

Conceptualising the education process as production, a measure of productivity in this sense would be given by the simple ratio between educational outcomes, such as student achievement, and a measure of resources invested in that education process. On the other hand, technical efficiency measures attempt to capture the distance between the *observed* productivity and the productivity that would be *maximally attainable* given the same level of resources invested (input-oriented approach) or the same level of outputs (output-oriented approach). In the case of education, and taking an input-oriented approach at the school-level, the degree of technical inefficiency can be measured as the proportion of resources that could be saved for a given level of student achievement, if the school would be operating optimally. Therefore, technical efficiency is a normative concept since it presumes the existence of an optimal relation between the resources invested and the outcomes of that investment. The existence of this optimal point sets a benchmark for performance, as it is assumed that schools and school systems can seek to operate at this level.

When not only the quantity but also the prices of inputs are taken into account, there is also an optimal relation to be considered. In that case, the concept of allocative efficiency is taken into account. However, in the case of education, it is harder to obtain a reliable measure of allocative efficiency as the prices of relevant inputs in the education process are generally not available and are not separable from the price of other inputs. For instance, while specific teaching skills are shown to have higher impact on students' success than others, the pricing of those skills is not separable from the full cost of hiring a teacher. Furthermore, teachers' salaries are generally influenced by institutional factors that might be detached from the strict teaching and learning processes occurring at the classroom-level. The priorities for the organisation of the educational process are still relatively more influenced by discretionary budgetary decisions of school leaders and other educational officials combined with some influence of market mechanisms, rather than the strict reliance on the adjustment between input supply and demand. For international comparisons of allocative efficiency it adds the difficulty in having internationally comparable sets of financial resources. Differences in teachers' salaries across countries are strongly influenced by institutional differences in labour market legislation and the average labour productivity of each economy. These are factors external to school systems themselves, and should not contaminate evaluations of educational efficiency. Although these differences can be partially controlled for, a substantial part of the literature in efficiency measurement has thus been focusing on measuring technical efficiency instead of allocative efficiency. However, there is no divergence in qualitative conclusions as the former is a necessary condition for the latter. Policies conducive to the effective use of resources are necessary to promote an efficient use of resources.

Efficiency as a relative concept

The theoretical existence of a benchmark to which the observed productivity can be compared to immediately poses a practical question, namely that of knowing how to empirically determine this benchmark. Empirical studies assume that the potential to reach a given level of productivity can be inferred from the sample of observed productivities used in the comparative evaluation. Therefore, efficiency is seen as a relative concept. For instance, the potential of a specific school to reach given results can be inferred from the set of schools that have an identical intensiveness of resources. Schools that have better results using the same amount of resources as schools with lower results are said to be more technically efficient from an output-oriented perspective.

However, the ability to use school resources effectively also depends on contextual and institutional factors not directly related to school management or educational policy. Efficiency measures not taking these factors into account tend to capture the harshness of the conditions in which schools operate rather than the strict ability of school management to turn resources into results. The way inputs which are or not under the discretion of education officials are considered in the analyses is therefore fundamental, as different approaches change the efficiency estimates.

Efficiency as a measurable concept

Efficiency measurement studies can be a useful tool in diagnosing where efficiency problems might be occurring and where resources might be used more effectively. Box 1.A1.1 provides a brief summary of the main methods used in efficiency measurement.

However, from a policy perspective, cautions should be taken when using efficiency measurement studies to change the allocation of school resources. The conclusions are mainly based on correlational evidence, not providing a clear direction of causality. School systems are characterised by complex behaviours of the agents involved, and the true causality relation is not easily discernible exclusively by measurement studies, at least with the research tools available today. Furthermore, the efficiency estimates are sensitive to factors at the discretion of the analyst: the choice of inputs and outputs to include in the analyses, the choice of factors which the analyses are conditioned to, the methods employed and the assumptions behind those methods. Studies that apply multiple approaches, with sensitivity and robustness analyses are more reliable for their empirical credibility. Mixed-methods approaches, including qualitative assessments can provide the greatest insights to policy (Grosskopf et al., 2014).

Box 1.A1.1. **Main approaches to efficiency measurement in education**

The literature in efficiency measurement can be divided in parametric and non-parametric methods. Parametric approaches assume that the process by which inputs are turned into outputs can be represented by a mathematical function. If the assumptions are correct then parametric methods are the best way to estimate the efficiency scores. Parametric methods are valuable due to their statistical properties. Confidence intervals can be easily constructed from the standard errors and the assumed functional form enables to easily quantify the marginal effect of given variables over efficiency estimates and their statistical significance. Furthermore, parametric methods can also be stochastic, meaning that the efficiency estimates can be separated from unexplained variation.

On the other hand, non-parametric techniques rely on a set of less stringent assumptions about the production process. The way by which inputs are turned into outputs is not assumed, meaning that the observed productivities are completely inferred from the data. This has some limitations. First, no standard significance tests and marginal effects can be directly computed. Second, non-parametric estimates are generally deterministic, meaning that these can be easily contaminated by unexplained variation in the data, making it more sensitive to measurement errors and outliers. However, recent developments in non-parametric methods have been able to overcome or at least limit most of these drawbacks, making them more robust. As such, different re-sampling methods have been bridging the gap between parametric and non-parametric literatures by incorporating statistical properties in the measurement process. These allow for more robust efficiency estimates.

Box 1.A1.1. **Main approaches to efficiency measurement in education** (*cont.*)

Non-parametric methods have been the most applied in educational efficiency measurement studies (De Witte and López-Torres, 2017). Two justifications for this relate to the nature of the educational process. First, the process by which educational inputs are turned into educational outcomes is generally unknown and difficult to translate in a mathematical function. Therefore, non-parametric methods, by not requiring a specific functional form, seem like a natural choice, as the relative importance of each input for the educational process is directly inferred from the data. Second, school systems and schools seek to fulfil multiple goals, and non-parametric methods more easily deal with multiple outputs than parametric ones.

Source: De Witte, K. and L. López-Torres (2017), "Efficiency in education: a review of literature and a way forward", *Journal of the Operational Research Society, http://dx.doi.org/10.1057/jors.2015.92.*

Chapter 2

Governing school funding

This chapter describes the different actors involved in raising, managing and allocating school funds across countries and analyses how the relationships between these actors are organised. It looks at both the sources of school funding (who raises funds for school education?) and the responsibilities for spending these funds (who manages and allocates funds for school education?). As OECD school systems have become more complex and characterised by multi-level governance, a growing set of actors including different levels of the school administration, schools themselves and private providers are increasingly involved in financial decision making. The chapter analyses the opportunities and challenges for effective school funding in such multi-level governance contexts and explores a range of policy options to reap the potential benefits of fiscal decentralisation, school autonomy over budgetary matters and involvement of private school providers in the use of public funds.

Public governance refers to the formal and informal arrangements that determine how public decisions are made and how public actions are carried out (OECD, 2011a). In the context of school funding, governance questions are ultimately concerned with who makes, implements and monitors the decisions about how funding is spent. Where the decision-making power on school funding is located is closely related to where such funding is raised, i.e. in school systems where a large part of school funding originates from the local government, the local level is likely to have a greater say in steering its schools and making funding allocation decisions. This chapter describes the different actors involved in raising, allocating and managing school funding and it analyses how the relationships between these actors are organised in different OECD and partner countries. Following this short introduction, it looks at i) the sources of school funding (who raises funds for school education?) and ii) the responsibilities for spending these funds (who manages and allocates funds for school education?).

Sources of school funding

This section provides an overview of the main actors involved in providing funds for school education. It finds that while the majority of school funding originates at the central government level, other actors also increasingly contribute to raising funds for school services. Sub-central governments typically complement central school funding from their own revenues while also acting as an intermediary distributing central government funding to schools. In addition, private spending on schools – which may originate from households, employers or communities – has increased considerably in recent years. Finally, international funding also provides an important complement to national sources of school funding in a range of countries.

The vast majority of school funding comes from public sources

In most OECD countries, governments provide by far the largest proportion of education investment. Governments subsidise education mostly through tax revenues (e.g. taxation upon earnings, property, retail sales, general consumption) collected at the different administration levels. On average across the OECD, almost 91% of the funds for schooling come from public sources (OECD, 2016a). Chile is the only OECD country where the share of public funds in overall expenditure on schooling was below 80% in 2013 (OECD, 2016a). In providing public funding for schooling, governments guarantee universal access to basic education by ensuring free provision or reducing the financial contributions of parents to a minimum.

Investing in an accessible, high-quality education system is a crucial means to provide people with the knowledge and skills they need to succeed in the labour market and to foster individual wellbeing as well as social cohesion and mobility. There is also a clear economic rationale for the public funding of education. According to OECD analyses, the benefits of educational investments not only accrue to the individuals receiving it, but also to society at large, providing strong economic incentives for governments to engage in the public funding of education. More highly educated individuals require less public expenditure on social welfare programmes and generate higher public revenues through the taxes paid once they enter the labour market. Figure 2.1 shows the public costs and benefits associated with an average person attaining tertiary education across OECD countries (OECD, 2016a).

Figure 2.1. **Public costs and benefits of education on attaining tertiary education, by gender, 2012**

In equivalent USD converted using PPPs for GDP

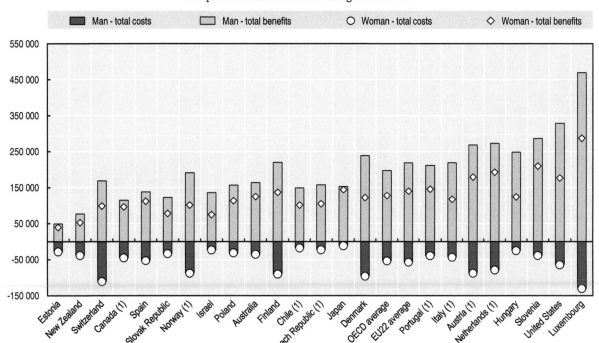

1. Year of reference differs from 2012, Please see OECD (2016a), Tables A7.4a and A7.4b for further details.
Note: Countries are ranked in ascending order of net financial public returns for a man.
Source: OECD (2016a), *Education at a Glance 2016: OECD Indicators, http://dx.doi.org/10.1787/eag-2016-en,* Tables A7.4a and A7.4b; see Annex 3 for notes (*www.oecd.org/education/education-at-a-glance-19991487.htm*).

Most systems rely on a mix of central and sub-central funding for schools

The governance of school funding varies between countries, with a few countries such as New Zealand (100%), the Netherlands (89%), Hungary (88%) and Slovenia (88%) funding schools mostly from central budgets, while most expect sub-central governments to contribute significantly to raising funds for school education. On average across the OECD, 55% of initial public funds for schooling originate at the central government level, while regional and local governments contribute about 22% of initial funds each (OECD, 2016a). Across the OECD review countries, the responsibilities for raising funds for schooling are typically distributed between two or three levels of governance, with the exceptions of Belgium (where four levels of governance are involved) and Uruguay (where the central level is the only source of school funding) (Table 2.A1.1).

Regarding the composition of final funds allocated to schools, central government funding of public services depends mainly on taxes, while the sub-central revenue mix includes both taxes (whether own taxes or those shared with other tiers of government) and transfers from higher levels of government. Sub-central governments may also rely on user fees, although these typically represent a small proportion of their revenue. Figure 2.2 shows the composition of sub-central government revenues across OECD countries. On average across the OECD, almost equal parts of overall sub-central government revenue came from taxes (42%) and from transfers (44%) in 2013. Fourteen percent came from user fees (OECD/KIPF, 2016).

Figure 2.2. **Revenue composition of sub-central governments, 2013**

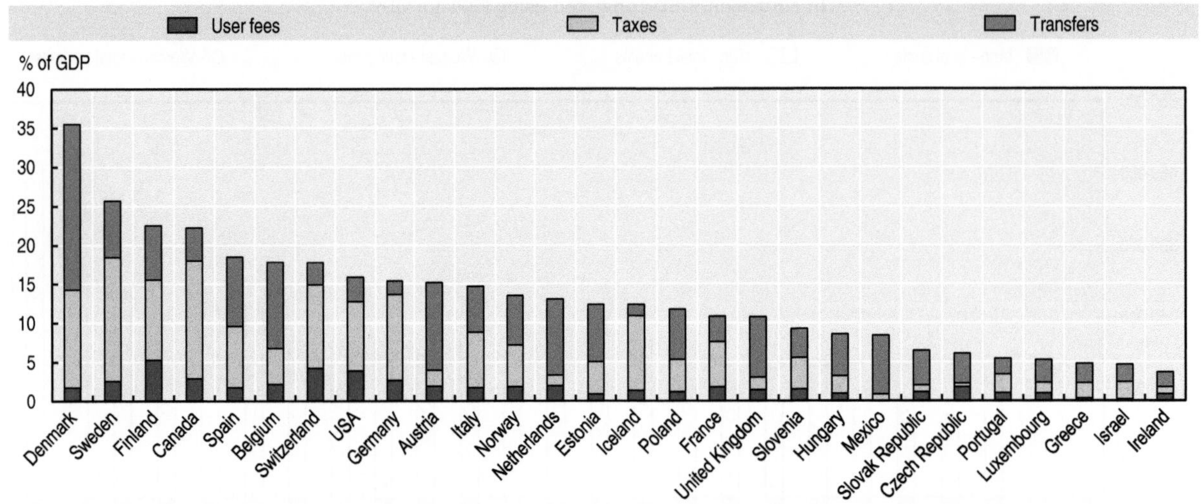

Source: OECD/KIPF (2016): Fiscal Federalism 2016: Making Decentralisation Work, http://dx.doi.org/10.1787/9789264254053-en.

Across OECD countries, sub-central entities have varying degrees of autonomy over their own tax collection, such as the right to introduce or abolish taxes, set tax rates, define the tax base and grant allowances or relief to individuals and firms. Often the collection of particular taxes is not assigned to one specific level of the administration but it is shared between different levels of government. In such cases, sub-central authorities often collectively negotiate the tax sharing formulas with the central government (OECD/KIPF, 2016). As can be seen in Figure 2.3, in several countries sub-central authorities have considerable taxing powers.

According to the OECD/KIPF (2016), a higher sub-central tax share is desirable for several reasons related to efficiency and accountability: reliance on own tax revenue brings jurisdictions autonomy in determining public service levels in line with local preferences; it makes sub-central governments accountable to their citizens who will be able to influence spending decisions through local elections; it may enhance overall resource mobilisation in a country as local/regional authorities may tap additional local resources; and it creates a hard budget constraint on sub-central entities which is likely to discourage overspending.

At the same time, strong reliance on sub-central tax shares may raise equity concerns. Where sub-central authorities generate their own revenue, wealthier jurisdictions will be in a better position to provide adequate funding per student in their local systems than others. In the United States, for example, prior to the 1970s the vast majority of resources spent on compulsory schooling was raised at the local level, primarily through local property taxes. Because the local property tax base is generally higher in areas with higher home values, the heavy reliance on local financing contributed to the ability of wealthier to spend more per student (Kirabo Jackson et al., 2014).

Figure 2.3. **Proportion of taxes over which sub-central governments have power to set rates and/or the base, 2011**

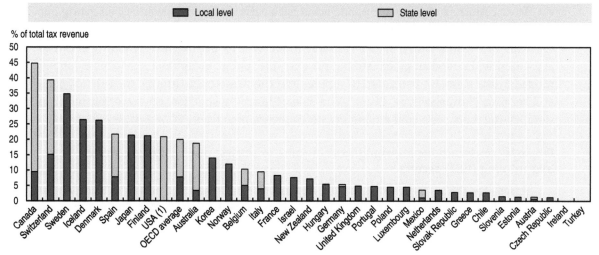

1. Tax autonomy of local governments in the United States varies across the states and is not assessed.
Source: OECD/KIPF (2016): *Fiscal Federalism 2016: Making Decentralisation Work*, http://dx.doi.org/10.1787/9789264254053-en.

In countries where school funding is heavily dependent on local tax bases, this may have adverse effects on matching resources to student needs, as areas with more disadvantaged students are likely to have fewer resources available to meet student needs. In such contexts, fiscal transfers or grants have an important role to play in equalising revenue levels across sub-central jurisdictions (more on this below).

Private funding plays an increasingly important role in the school sector

While the vast majority of school funding is provided from public sources, private sources of school funding have grown more quickly in recent years than public sources. Between 2008 and 2013, private sources increased by 16% on average across the OECD, while public sources increased by only 6%. Private sources typically play a more important role in secondary than in primary education. At the upper secondary level, there is a slightly stronger presence of private sources of funding in the vocational education and training (VET) sector than in the general sector (OECD, 2016a).

Schools may raise their own revenues through sales of services, rental of facilities and parental fees

While public schools are financed mainly through funding allocations coming from the different levels of the educational administration, individual schools may also have the ability to raise their own revenues from private (and/or public) sources. This typically involves the sale of services (particularly in the vocational sector), the rental of facilities and funds raised from parents and/or the community through obligatory fees or voluntary donations.

Among the OECD review countries, parental contributions are not uncommon in public pre-primary education with 9 of 17 systems charging tuition fees for pre-primary education that tended to be determined by either local or central authorities. While mandatory tuition fees are typically prohibited in public primary and secondary schools (Table 2.A1.2), the majority of education systems with available data permit public schools to benefit from voluntary monetary and non-monetary parental contributions as well as donations (Table 2.A1.3).

Most countries also permit public schools to raise additional revenue by renting out their materials and facilities (e.g. sports facilities), by providing extracurricular activities for a fee or – particularly in the vocational sector – by selling non-teaching services (e.g. catering, hairdressing). In Estonia, for example, public vocational schools are largely funded by the state but permitted to supplement their resources through the sale of goods and services (Santiago et al., 2016b). The sale of teaching services, on the other hand, is significantly more restricted among the OECD review countries (Table 2.A1.3).

Employer contributions are significant in some countries' vocational education and training (VET) sectors

Across the OECD, the average annual expenditure per upper secondary VET student in 2013 was 10% higher than that for students in general education (OECD, 2016a). There are often higher costs for the specialised equipment required to teach many technical and practical subjects. Unlike general education programmes, the funding of the VET sector in many countries involves contributions from employers. Given the larger set of actors engaged in the funding of VET, it is frequently based on agreements between public and private stakeholders determining their respective contributions to VET funding as well as their role in the provision of services like work-based learning and school-based learning. Employers tend to contribute to VET in the form of financial transfers (directly to VET providers or indirectly via training levies)[1] as well as through the provision of equipment, staff and training places. Given the direct benefits that students' acquisition of occupation-specific skills brings to the industry, employers sometimes bear the cost of work-based learning and contribute to covering costs for materials, trainers or the remuneration of trainees (for more information on the costs and benefits of apprenticeships see Kuczera, 2017). The school-based component of VET is more commonly publicly funded (Papalia, forthcoming).[2]

However, cost-sharing arrangements with significant private contributions are relatively rare in upper secondary VET programmes (see Figure 2.4). Private sector contributions tend to be significant in countries with a large apprenticeship system in which employers cover most of the costs of work placements (e.g. apprentice pay, instruction costs, tools and equipment). Among the 19 OECD and partner countries with available data for 2012, funding from private sources other than households typically accounted for less than 10% of total expenditure, with the notable exceptions of Germany and the Netherlands. The German VET system, as described in Box 2.1, provides an example of cost sharing arrangements involving contributions from all of the system's major stakeholders. In several countries, however, students have very few opportunities to engage in work-based learning or apprenticeships and there is no legal requirement for firms or industries to make financial contributions to the state-run vocational system (Santiago et al., 2016b).

Ensuring adequate involvement of companies in both the provision and funding of initial VET is a challenge shared by several OECD review countries. Evidence from across OECD countries indicates that labour market outcomes of vocational graduates improve if their programmes include substantial work-based learning, such as apprenticeships offered by companies (OECD, 2014a). In countries where practical training is primarily provided by schools, a number of efficiency challenges may arise. For schools, continuously updating their practical training offer to ensure its relevance to the requirements of the labour market involves significant investments into training, equipment and physical

Figure 2.4. **Private expenditure on upper secondary VET, 2012**

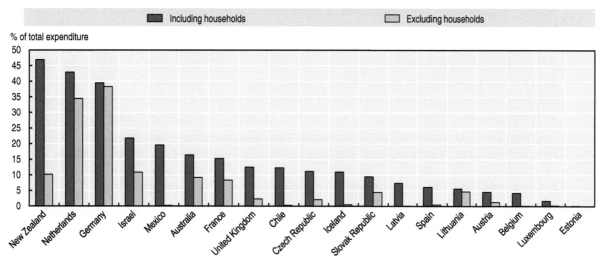

Note: Expenditure that is not directly related to education (e.g. for culture, sports, youth activities, etc.) is not included unless it is for the provision of ancillary services. Private expenditure includes contributions from households (students and their families) and other private entities such as firms.

Source: OECD (2016a), *Education at a Glance 2016: OECD Indicators*, *http://dx.doi.org/10.1787/eag-2016-en*.

Box 2.1. **Cost sharing arrangements in the German VET system**

The German dual VET system is characterised by high levels of per student expenditure, a strong enrolment in apprenticeship schemes and a high level of involvement among employers, with more than 60% of firms taking part in the provision of initial vocational education and training. The funding of VET involves all stakeholders. Public resources are provided by federal ministries (Ministry of Education and Research, Ministry of Economic Affairs and Energy, and the Ministry of Labour and Social Affairs), central agencies, such as the federal employment agency, as well as the federal states (*Länder*). Private sector resources are contributed by companies, unions, chambers as well as students and their families.

The school-based learning component is provided by vocational schools and funded primarily out of the federal states' budgets. The states are responsible for funding teaching staff and cover, on average, 80% of the vocational schools' expenses. Municipalities are the second main contributor, covering the largest share of material costs and investments out of their own revenue. The work-based learning provided through the apprenticeship system is largely self-financing and public authorities only indirectly contribute to its funding by providing students and employers with financial incentives to engage in training activities. German employers are required to contribute to the funding of work-based learning for their apprentices on the basis of collective agreements. The resources made available by employers include the apprentices' wages as well as the material and human resources necessary to provide adequate training conditions. With the exception of the construction sector, employers do not contribute to training levies.

Source: Papalia, A. (forthcoming), "The Funding of Vocational Education and Training: A Literature Review", *OECD Education Working Papers*, OECD Publishing, Paris.

---

infrastructure, which may discourage innovation and experimentation. The failure to provide opportunities for work-based skills development can thereby reduce the efficiency of VET provision and diminish its labour market relevance (Shewbridge et al., 2016b).

Countries such as Switzerland, Germany and Denmark operate so called dual systems whose VET pathways combine periods of school-based learning with alternating periods of work-based training which companies support through the contribution of financial and human resources. Regardless of whether employers are directly involved in the provision of VET, training levies are the most common mechanism to collect earmarked VET resources from the private sector. While some levies primarily serve to raise revenue for the provision of VET, for example through a tax paid by every employer, other levy schemes provide employers with incentives to actively engage in work-based training. These types of training levies are typically linked to a disbursement or exemption mechanism that redistributes the funds raised by the levy to employers that engage in the training of apprentices (Dar et al., 2003).

International funding may complement national sources of school funding

Funding from international sources including the European Commission and international agencies like the World Bank or the Inter-American Development Bank represents a significant share of investment to schooling in some countries. Several OECD review countries have significantly benefited from international funding to support educational initiatives and infrastructural investments (Box 2.2). The European Union's two structural funds – the European Regional Development Fund (ERDF) and the European Social Fund (ESF) – are designed to promote economic and social development and address specific needs of disadvantaged regions across the European Union. EU funds are allocated subject to the European Commission's approval of the recipient states' operational programme, in which they outline the funding's strategic objectives and propose an auditing framework. The managing authorities at the national level are then responsible for administering the funds and allocating them to projects and sub-central beneficiaries. Member states are also required to co-finance their operational programmes to varying extent.

Box 2.2. **International funding to support school education: Examples from OECD review countries**

In several OECD review countries, European Structural Funds have played an important role in the implementation of reforms and developments of the educational infrastructure. These included significant capital investments to upgrade existing facilities, widen access to high-quality early education and care and support the rationalisation of the school network. The Lithuanian Ministry of Education, for example, allocated EU funding to expand school transportation services and assist the creation of multi-function centres that combine day care, pre-primary and primary education as well as a community facility under a single management structure in rural areas (Shewbridge et al., 2016a). EU structural funds were also used to improve the provision of vocational education and training and fund the creation of vocational training centres in countries like Lithuania and the Slovak Republic. In Estonia, funding from the ESF was used to support the developments of the VET curriculum, while the ERDF funded corresponding infrastructural improvements (Santiago et al., 2016a). Another area supported by EU investments is teacher professional development, for example through Estonia's ESF-co-financed science teacher training programme and the initiative "Raising the qualification of teachers in general education from 2008 to 2014" (Santiago et al., 2016a). Other EU-funded projects have also focused on quality assurance and supporting schools' use of self-assessment tools as well as promoting equity through the integration of Roma communities in the Czech Republic and the Slovak Republic.

Box 2.2. International funding to support school education: Examples from OECD review countries (cont.)

Funding from international agencies such as the Inter-American Development Bank (IDB) or the World Bank has also been used to finance educational projects, often focused on capital expenditure and the improvement of infrastructures to support the expansion of educational services. In Uruguay, for example, loans from the World Bank were used to finance the Support Programme for Public Primary Education (*Programa de Apoyo a la Enseñanza Primaria Pública*, PAEPU), which provides investments into the infrastructure and equipment of full-time schools. The project is implemented in co-ordination with the Pre-school and Primary Education Council (*Consejo de Educación Inicial Primaria*, CEIP) and the Central Directive Council on Education (*Consejo Directivo Central*, CODICEN) of the National Administration for Public Education (*Administración Nacional de Educación Pública*, ANEP). Uruguay also co-operates with the IDB, whose loans have funded the country's Support Programme for Secondary Education and Training in Education (*Programa de Apoyo a la Educación Media y Formación en Educación*, PAEMFE), which funds strategic investments into the infrastructure and equipment of secondary education and teacher training institutions (Santiago et al., 2016b; INEEd, 2015).

Source: Shewbridge, C. et al. (2016a), *OECD Reviews of School Resources: Lithuania 2016, http://dx.doi.org/10.1787/ 9789264252547-en*; Santiago, P. et al. (2016a), *OECD Reviews of School Resources: Estonia 2016, http://dx.doi.org/ 10.1787/9789264251731-en*; Santiago, P. et al. (2016b), *OECD Reviews of School Resources: Uruguay 2016, http:// dx.doi.org/10.1787/9789264265530-en*; INEEd (2015), *OECD Review of Policies to Improve the Effectiveness of Resource Use in Schools: Country Background Report for Uruguay, www.oecd.org/education/schoolresourcesreview.htm*.

Making the most effective use of international funding requires effective procedures to evaluate the investments' impact, ensure their long-term sustainability and align them with strategic educational objectives (see also Chapters 4 and 5). In addition, a common challenge for countries benefiting from international funding is the need to develop adequate capacity to absorb and successfully use such funding for the implementation of agreed programmes at the local level. Particularly where individual schools need to apply for receiving project resources from international donors or the EU, limited management and implementation capacity and/or lack of experience in writing grant applications may prevent them from seizing the opportunities that such international funds provide. In some OECD review countries, such as the Czech Republic and the Slovak Republic, this has resulted in low absorption rates and underutilisation of internationally funded operational programmes (Shewbridge, 2016b; Santiago, 2016c). Variation across different schools' capability to attract funds can also exacerbate existing patterns of inequality, since large or urban schools may be better placed to make a successful bid for grants.

Responsibilities for school spending

This section looks at the different actors involved in making decisions on school spending. It discusses how common governance trends including fiscal decentralisation, school autonomy over budgetary matters and public funding of private schools have led to the emergence of a broad range of actors involved in the allocation, management and use of school funding in a number of countries. The section looks at each of these phenomena in turn. First, it analyses the degree of decentralised decision making on school funding across countries and explores opportunities and challenges related to the involvement of sub-central governments in making school funding decisions. Second, it describes the level of schools' budgetary autonomy across countries and the necessary conditions for more autonomous schools to be able to contribute to effective and equitable use of school funding. Third, it takes stock of countries' approaches to publicly funding private providers and reviews the potential benefits and risks of such approaches within overall school funding strategies.

Sub-central governments are the most important spenders in school education

Over the past two decades, sub-central jurisdictions have acquired increasing powers in the distribution of funding to education across OECD countries, with almost 60% of final funds allocated to schools by sub-central governments. This share is even higher in countries such as the United States (100%), Japan (98%), Canada (97%) and Germany (94%) where the funds are almost entirely coming from the sub-central levels (OECD, 2016a). However, while sub-central authorities are the most important spenders on schooling in many countries, there are wide variations across countries in the degree to which they actually have decision-making power over the distribution of funding between the individual schools in their jurisdiction (for a detailed analysis, see Chapter 3). In analysing the decision-making powers of sub-central authorities, it is important to note that the involvement of sub-central governments varies depending on the type of investment (e.g. capital versus current expenditure) and the levels and sectors of schooling (e.g. primary versus secondary schooling) that are being considered (for more detail see Chapter 3).

Sub-central spending responsibilities have grown faster than revenue raising capacities

As explained in the previous section, sub-central jurisdictions have acquired increasing powers for the collection of their own revenue. But at the same time, sub-central spending responsibilities have also grown, and they have done so much faster than tax collection responsibilities. Figure 2.5 illustrates the relative shares of sub-central revenue and spending in total government revenue and spending. The gaps between the revenue and the expenditure of sub-central jurisdictions are referred to as "vertical fiscal imbalances". Such imbalances are typically addressed through vertical fiscal transfers – or grants – from the central level to sub-central levels. They may also be addressed through horizontal transfers between sub-central entities. Fiscal transfers aim to offset gaps between revenue and expenditure, equalise fiscal disparities across regions and ensure similar ability to provide public services across all sub-central governments. Fiscal transfers represent an important share of overall central government spending and they have grown in recent years, from 6% to 7% of GDP between 2000 and 2010 (OECD/KIPF, 2016).

Fiscal transfers can also serve central governments in steering sub-central levels of the administration towards spending on certain purposes. Where central government grants are earmarked for a particular purpose, they allow the central level to exert considerable control over sub-central educational policy and spending (see Chapter 3 for more information on the design aspects of earmarked grants). OECD/KIPF (2016) report that across different public sectors, a slight trend from earmarked grants towards more non-earmarked grants could be observed in recent years. At the same time, they noted a parallel increase in regulatory frameworks and output control, which is another way for central governments to steer the use of resources at the sub-central level towards particular standards and expected performance levels (see Chapter 5 on the evaluation of school funding at sub-central levels).

Figure 2.5. **Sub-national revenue and spending across OECD countries**

Decentralisation ratios, 2014 or latest available year

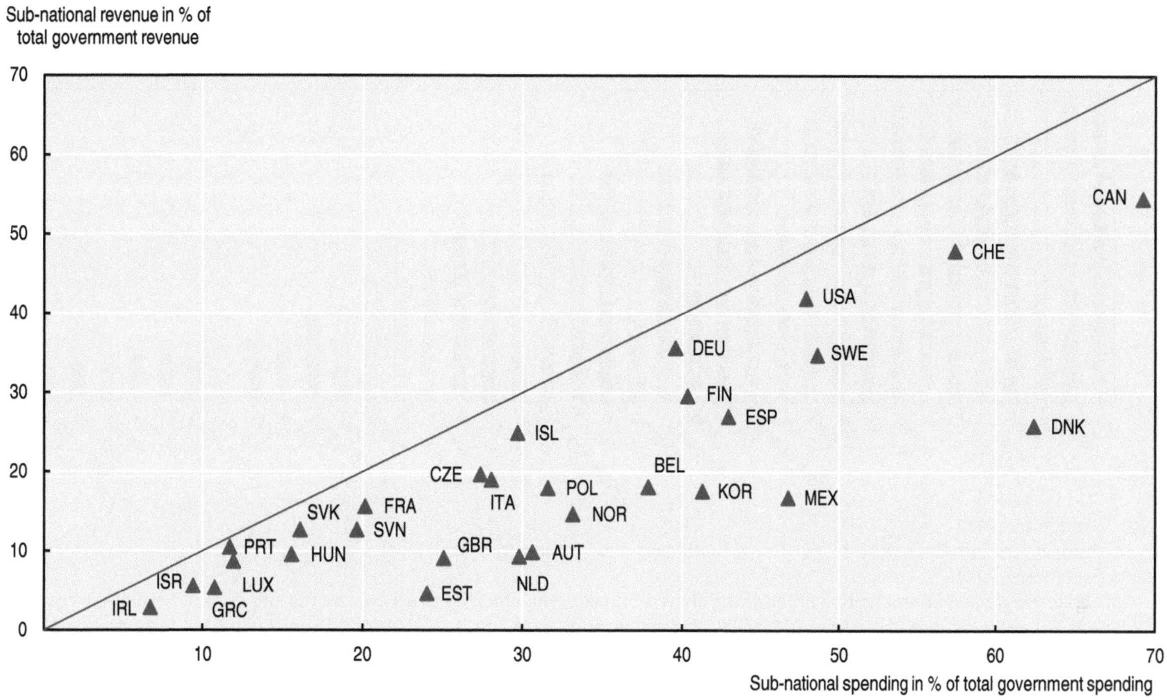

Note: Sub-national expenditures include intergovernmental grants, while sub-national revenues do not. Latest available data for Korea are from 2012 and for Mexico from 2013.

Source: OECD/KIPF (2016): *Fiscal Federalism 2016: Making Decentralisation Work, http://dx.doi.org/10.1787/9789264254053-en.*

Fiscal transfers can equalise sub-central revenue levels but have a number of drawbacks

The extent of transfers of public funds from central to sub-central levels of government varies widely between countries. The length of the bars in Figure 2.6 indicates the share of sub-central (regional and local level) funding allocated to schools in each country. The different shadings indicate how this sub-central funding is composed of initial funds originating at the sub-central level (dark shading) and transfers from the central government (light shading). The difference of funding power before and after transfers from central to sub-central levels of government represents more than 30 percentage points in Austria, Chile, Estonia, Finland and Hungary, and more than 40 percentage points in Korea, Latvia, Mexico and the Slovak Republic (OECD, 2016a).

The operation of fiscal transfer systems can help provide sub-central governments with revenues to support similar levels of educational service provision at similar tax rates. Less advantaged sub-central authorities in terms of private income and with a challenging socio-economic composition of the population typically receive higher grants from the central government. Box 2.3 provides examples from different countries that introduced equalisation schemes alongside decentralisation reforms which shifted responsibilities for school funding to the local level.

While fiscal transfers play an important role in providing sub-central revenue for service provision and equalising sub-central revenue levels, OECD/KIPF (2016) outline a number of disadvantages of strong reliance on inter-jurisdictional grants and equalisation transfers. First, while one might expect that grants help to stabilise sub-central revenue,

Figure 2.6. **Share and composition of final public funds allocated to schools by sub-central government in primary, secondary and post-secondary non-tertiary education, 2013**

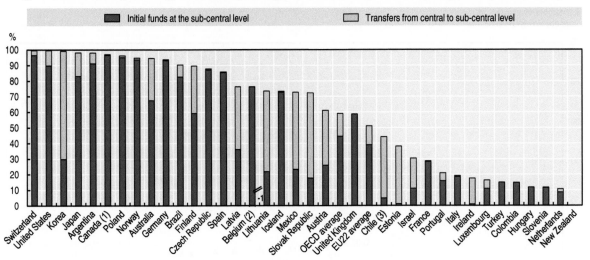

1. Year of reference: 2012
2. In Belgium, 76% of initial funds and 75% of final funds originate at the sub-central level
3. Year of reference: 2014

Note: Countries are ranked in descending order of the share of final funds allocated to schools by the sub-central level of government.
Source: OECD (2016a), *Education at a Glance 2016: OECD Indicators, http://dx.doi.org/10.1787/eag-2016-en,* Table B4.3. See Annex 3 for notes (*www.oecd.org/education/education-at-a-glance-19991487.htm*).

Box 2.3. **Introduction of equalisation funds in Brazil, Iceland and Poland**

When **Brazil** devolved authority from a highly centralised system to states and municipalities in the mid-1990s, it created a Fund for the Maintenance and Development of Basic Schools and the Valorisation of the Teaching Profession (*Fundo para Manutenção e Desenvolvimento do Ensino Fundamental e Valorização do Magistério,* FUNDEF) to reduce the large national inequalities in per-student spending. State and municipal governments were required to transfer a proportion of their tax revenue to FUNDEF, which redistributed it to state and municipal governments that could not meet specified minimum levels of per-student expenditure. FUNDEF has not prevented wealthier regions from increasing their overall spending more rapidly than poorer regions, but it has played a highly redistributive role and increased both the absolute level of spending and the predictability of transfers. There is evidence that FUNDEF has been instrumental in reducing class size, improving the supply and quality of teachers, and expanding enrolment. At the municipal level, data show that the 20% of municipalities receiving the most funds from FUNDEF were able to double per-student expenditure between 1996 and 2002 in real terms.

When **Iceland** moved responsibility for compulsory education to the municipalities in 1995, the cost of compulsory schooling was determined to be 2.84% of the total income tax received by the state. That percentage was decided by using the capital city, Reykjavík, as a zero point – calculating by how many percentage points the local income tax would have to go up for the city to cover the cost of operating the compulsory schools, which came to 2.07% of the states total income tax. In 1995, 2.07% of the national annual income tax was therefore permanently transferred to the local income tax which is collected centrally and transferred to the municipalities in order to even out salary costs in the compulsory schools and to cover other costs related to the transfer of responsibilities for schooling from the central to the local level. Following the calculations for the City of Reykjavík, the total cost of operating all the compulsory schools in the country was then determined, which came to a total of 2.84%

> ### Box 2.3. **Introduction of equalisation funds in Brazil, Iceland and Poland**
> *(cont.)*
>
> of the national income tax. The difference between the 2.84% and 2.07% – or 0.77% – was then allocated by the central government to The Local Governments' Equalizations Fund. The role of the fund is to even out the difference in expenditure and income of those local communities with a specific or a greater need, through allocations from the fund, based on the relevant legislation, regulation and internal procedures established for the operation of the fund. A part of the 0.77% is earmarked to cover proportionally the operational cost of the fund itself but the main part is reallocated to the local communities. 71% of this amount goes towards general support but the rest is earmarked for specific purposes.
>
> In **Poland**, education decentralisation was part of the overall decentralisation process of the country initiated in 1990. The main transfer from the central to local budgets is called "general subvention" and is composed of a few separately calculated components. Two main ones are the education component and the equalisation component. The education component is calculated on the basis of student numbers (with numerous coefficients reflecting different costs of providing education to different groups of students), and thus reflects different costs of service provision. The equalisation component is based on a formula and equalises poorer jurisdictions up to 90% of average per capita revenues of similar local governments. It thus reflects revenue equalisation.
>
> *Source:* OECD/The World Bank (2015), *OECD Reviews of School Resources: Kazakhstan 2015, http://dx.doi.org/ 10.1787/9789264245891-en;* Icelandic Ministry of Education, Science and Culture (2014), *OECD Review of Policies to Improve the Effectiveness of Resource Use in Schools: Country Background Report for Iceland, www.oecd.org/education/ schoolresourcesreview.htm.*

empirical evidence indicates that the opposite is often the case. Indeed, central government grants may exacerbate fluctuations in the revenue of sub-central government tiers because such transfers are often pro-cyclical, i.e. in times of strong growth, they are likely to increase whereas the amount of central transfers often decreases in times of crisis. This can reinforce pre-existing resource challenges at sub-central levels of administration and make it difficult for them to engage in medium-term planning (Chapter 4).

Second, grants may reduce the sub-central tax effort. For example, if grants are adjusted on the basis of local revenue, sub-central authorities might be discouraged from raising their own tax revenue because otherwise they might see their central grants reduced. In Estonia, for example, local governments have very limited revenue raising powers. The OECD review of Estonia found that this appears to encourage both local officials and their citizens to see any local financial difficulties as the result of insufficient national government support. The resulting "fiscal illusion" may reduce the willingness of both local officials and citizens to use local taxes to improve local services (Santiago et al., 2016a). Disagreement about the adequacy of central resources to fulfil decentralised responsibilities sometimes decreases the level of effective accountability of sub-central governments (Sevilla, 2006; see also Chapter 5). This is related to the difficulties that school systems face in objectively assessing the adequacy of funding (see Chapter 3).

Third, research and experience from different countries indicates that a high reliance on central grants may encourage overspending and thereby increase deficits and debt. There is evidence that a central government's commitment to a certain grant level is not always credible and that sub-central authorities may overspend in the hope that this overspending will then be compensated via additional grants (OECD/KIPF, 2016). Busemeyer (2008) finds that giving sub-central levels of government the power to spend without forcing them to raise their own revenues (by granting them autonomy in setting tax rates) sets strong incentives for overspending. A large misalignment between financing and spending responsibilities may lead to mistrust, lack of transparency and inefficiencies, as one actor – the central government – is responsible for most of the financing, whereas other actors – sub-central governments – are in charge of expenditures. This often creates worries at the central level about the misuse and waste of resources while sub-central authorities may see overspending as evidence that the grant level is insufficient or the transfer system unfair.

In Austria, for example, the vast majority of tax revenue is generated at the federal level (87% in 2014) rather than by the provinces and municipalities who are responsible for funding provincial schools. Through the Fiscal Adjustment Act, central funds are then partially redistributed among the provinces and municipalities based on quotas which are renegotiated among the different tiers of government every four years. This system creates a split of financing and spending responsibilities, typical for Austrian federalism (which is sometimes described as "distributional federalism"). While the federal government and the provinces agree on annual staff plans, the provinces are free to hire more teachers than foreseen in these staff plans and the additional expenditures are partly covered by the federal level. This system tends to encourage overspending on teaching staff by the provinces compared to agreed staff plan. Between 2006 and 2010, the number of teaching positions at general compulsory schools that were not included in the initial budget almost doubled from 1 039 to 2 063, leading to considerable additional costs (Nusche et al., 2016a).

Finally, the determination of grant levels and calculation methods themselves may also be problematic. In Kazakhstan, for example, the OECD review team found that one of the main concerns related to school funding was the importance of negotiations for the calculation of central transfers and the definition of education budgets at the sub-central level. The budget negotiations were found to lead to suboptimal allocations as objective indicators on potential revenues and expenditure needs were given little importance (OECD/ The World Bank, 2015). Given the potential disincentives and risks inherent in central grants, it is very important that such grants are skilfully designed so as to facilitate adequate spending across all jurisdictions while reducing the risk of fiscal slippage across levels of government.

Variations in sub-central funding approaches may mitigate equalisation effects

Even if well-designed fiscal equalisation mechanisms are in place, decentralised systems may still be characterised by considerable differences in educational spending across jurisdictions. This might indicate a potential for efficiency savings in some jurisdictions and/or potential inequities in the educational services provided to students in different jurisdictions. Little internationally comparable information is available on variations in school spending between sub-central entities. However, in an online supplement to the OECD *Education at a Glance 2016* sub-central data on annual expenditure per student is presented for three countries: Belgium, Canada and Germany.[3] This data shows that while spending per student does not differ much between jurisdictions in Belgium (between USD 11 221 and USD 11 856), it ranges between USD 7 900 and USD 11 400 across jurisdictions in Germany and between USD 8 732 and USD 19 730 across jurisdictions in Canada.

In several of the OECD review countries, there is evidence of discrepancies in the level of school funding across countries' different jurisdictions. In Israel, according to national data, more affluent local governments can provide up to 20 times higher funding per student for schools than less affluent local governments (OECD, 2016b). In Denmark, expenditure per student also varies strongly across municipalities despite existing equalisation mechanisms (Nusche et al., 2016b). Such differences might result from different levels of priority attributed by local authorities to education or different approaches to design local funding strategies. Where jurisdictions are autonomous in designing their own funding approaches, there may be only weak mechanisms to share and spread the related expertise and experience systematically across sub-central authorities so as to optimise funding mechanisms (for more information on the development of funding formulas at different levels of school systems, see Chapter 3).

In Denmark, more than half of the variation among municipalities can be explained by socio-economic conditions, with municipalities having more students from disadvantaged backgrounds spending higher amounts per student than other municipalities (Houlberg et al., 2016). However, there is still a large part of spending differences between municipalities that cannot be explained by socio-economic factors. This could indicate a situation where some municipalities prioritise spending on education more than others, but also a potential for efficiency savings in some municipalities. The spending differences across municipalities are also likely to result from differences in the approaches to school funding across jurisdictions. Each of the 98 municipalities designs its own formula to fund local schools. These formulas typically include parental background characteristics in addition to the number of students and the number of classes at the different year levels. However, the ways in which socio-economic differences are taken into account in the funding formulas vary greatly across municipalities. This suggests that the models vary not only as a result of deliberate decisions or different priorities (Nusche et al., 2016b).

In Kazakhstan, there is also evidence that regional and local differences in spending per students are not just related to objective cost factors. Expenditure per student varies greatly across regions – from 39% below the national average in the capital city to 50% above the national average in North Kazakhstan and marked differences in per student spending are also observed across school districts. The Ministry of Education and Science commissioned a report to UNICEF (United Nations Children's Fund) on the financing of 175 schools across Kazakhstan. The final report revealed important differences in spending per student between districts of the same region and between schools of the same type and size within the same district (UNICEF, 2012). Some sub-central governments spend significantly more of their resources on education than others and the existing differences are not always associated with the variation in the costs of provision (OECD/The World Bank, 2015).

Fiscal decentralisation may raise capacity challenges, especially in small jurisdictions

While their knowledge of local conditions and needs may allow sub-central authorities to allocate resources more effectively in line with school contexts, smaller authorities are very likely to face capacity challenges. Decentralised governance arrangements place significant demands on local authorities for budget planning and financial management. For example, they may be required to develop a funding formula, administer financial transfers, make decisions about investments in school infrastructure and maintenance and/or apply for a pool of targeted funding. But not all local authorities have sufficient capacity to implement sound budget planning and to manage their resources well. Administering a funding scheme requires considerable technical skills and administrative capacity and many school systems find it challenging to ensure these are available at the level of each educational provider.

Capacity constraints at the local level can also exacerbate inequities between individual authorities, in particular in countries that have many municipalities with a small number of inhabitants, such as the Czech Republic, France, the Slovak Republic, Hungary, Switzerland and Austria (Figure 2.7). In some countries, school providers (sub-central authorities or other school owners) are very small and responsible for only one or a few schools, which does not allow them to achieve the same extent of economies of scale, management capacity and support that can be offered by larger providers. Small providers typically have a very limited number of staff managing school services, and these do not necessarily have expertise regarding the design of effective resource management strategies. Some of the OECD review countries, such as Austria, the Czech Republic and the Slovak Republic, literally have thousands of municipalities involved in managing and funding their own schools, many of them with weak administrative capacity, which makes it difficult for them to maintain efficient school services.

Figure 2.7. **Municipal fragmentation in international comparison, 2014/15**

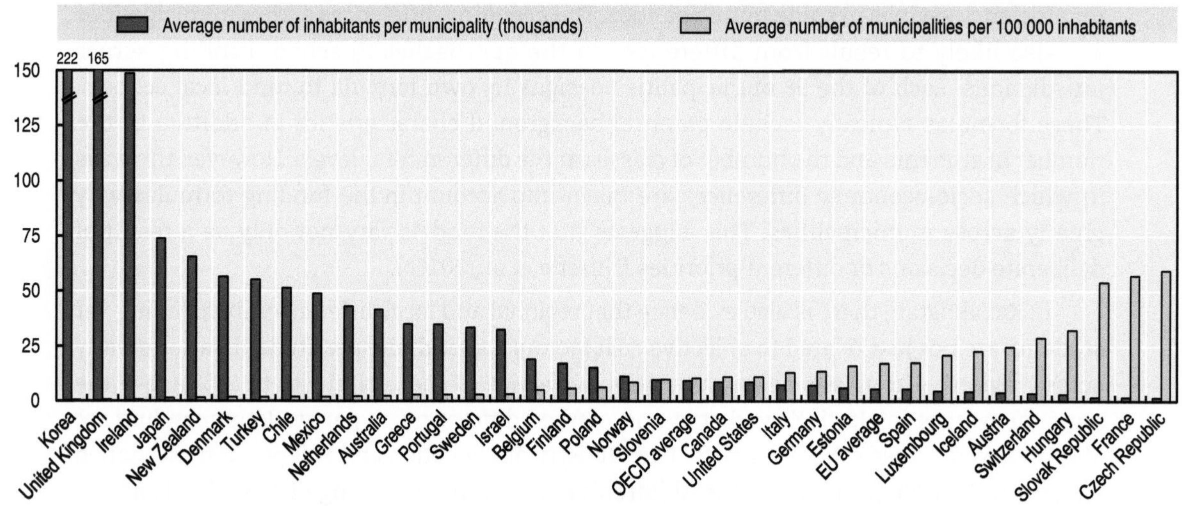

Source: OECD (2015a), "Sub-National Governments in OECD Countries: Key Data" (brochure), OECD, Paris.

While school leaders are typically accountable to their providers, not all providers have the professional capacity to provide effective feedback and support to their leaders. It can, therefore, be difficult for local authorities to fulfil their responsibility for managing financial resources and to collaborate with their school leaders to make resource use decisions that improve learning. In contexts where responsibilities for resource management and the pedagogical organisation of schools are shared between local authorities and schools, education leaders and administrators must be able to establish good relationships and to align resource management decisions with pedagogical aspects and needs. One way for building the capacity of local authorities lies in the creation of networks and collaborative practices (Box 2.4 provides an example from Norway), but these are still underdeveloped in many contexts.

One of the specific challenges of educational decentralisation is that while key decisions (e.g. distribution of financial resources, quality assurance) are typically transferred to regional or local authorities, most of the information and knowledge management capacities are retained by the institutions of the national administration. Therefore, many of them might require active support from the relevant national institutions to take and implement decisions.

Box 2.4. **Addressing the challenges of small size and limited capacity at the sub-central level**

Municipal networks for efficiency and improvement in Norway

In Norway, policy making is characterised by a high level of respect for local ownership. In such a decentralised system, it is essential that different actors co-operate to share and spread good practice and thereby facilitate system learning and improvement. Networking is a common form of organisation among municipalities in Norway and there are a range of good examples where networks and partnerships have been established between different actors as a means to take collective responsibility for quality evaluation and improvement. In Norway, there are many examples of localised collaboration initiatives launched and developed by small clusters of municipalities. As an example, in 2002, in Norway, the Association of Local and Regional Authorities (*Kommunesektorens interesse- og arbeidsgiverorganisasjon*, KS), the Ministry of Labour and Government Administration, and the Ministry of Local Government and Regional Development set up "municipal networks for efficiency and improvement" that offer quality monitoring tools for municipal use and provide a platform for municipalities to share experience, compare data and evaluate different ways of service delivery in different sectors. For the education sector, an agreement was established between KS and the Directorate for Education and Training to allow the networks to use results from the user surveys that are part of the national quality assessment system.

Local government reform in Denmark

Denmark re-organised its public sector through a Local Government Reform in 2007. This reform reduced the number of municipalities from 271 to 98 and abolished the 14 counties replacing them with five regions. Except for some smaller islands, most of the 98 municipalities have a minimum size of 20 000 inhabitants. The reform also redistributed responsibilities from former counties to municipalities, leaving the municipalities responsible for most welfare tasks, and reduced the number of levels of taxation from three to two as regions were not granted the authority to levy taxes. Regional revenues consist of block grants and activity-based funding from the central government and the municipalities. In addition, to ensure that the local government reform would not result in a redistribution of the cost burden between municipalities, the grant and equalisation system was reformed to take into account the new distribution of tasks. The reform sought to primarily improve the quality of municipal services, but also to address efficiency concerns (e.g. by creating economies of scale). Many of the 271 municipalities that existed prior to 2007 were considered too small to provide effective local services, in particular in the health sector.

The creation of Local Education Services in Chile

In Chile, a 2015 reform proposal intends to remove management of public schools from the 347 municipalities and create a new system of public education. The draft law proposes the creation of a National Directorate for Public Education (within the Ministry) which will co-ordinate 67 new Local Education Services, each of which will oversee a group of schools with powers transferred from the 345 municipalities). Prior to this reform, a number of different options for reforming the municipal school system were envisaged and a central concern was to ensure adequate accountability mechanisms to monitor the effective, efficient and equitable use of resources at sub-central levels (Santiago et al., forthcoming).

Source: Nusche, D. et al. (2011), OECD Reviews of Evaluation and Assessment in Education: Norway 2011, http://dx.doi.org/10.1787/9789264117006-en; Nusche, D. et al. (2016b), OECD Reviews of School Resources: Denmark 2016, http://dx.doi.org/10.1787/9789264262430-en; Santiago, P. et al. (forthcoming), OECD Reviews of School Resources: Chile, OECD Publishing, Paris.

Some countries have responded to size and capacity challenges at sub-central government level by merging several small education providers and thereby consolidating capacity for effective resource management (Box 2.4 provides an example from Denmark). Others are considering to move responsibilities to higher levels of the administration or to create new bodies to administer a larger number of schools (Box 2.4 provides an example from Chile).

Complexities in the governance of school funding risk leading to inefficiencies

Co-ordination is a very important and challenging aspect of governance in every system where sub-sectors of schooling operate under different political and administrative jurisdictions. The decentralisation processes developed in some countries have led to the emergence of increasingly autonomous and powerful local actors (e.g. regions, municipalities, schools) and raise the question of how to assure co-ordination in this new context of multi-level and multi-actor governance. The complexity of education governance might create inefficiencies in the use of resources due to duplication of roles, overlapping responsibilities, competition between different tiers of government and a lack of transparency obfuscating the flow of resources in the system (Chapter 5).

Efficiency challenges in using school resources may be linked with the potential isolation of sub-systems managed by different levels of administration and the rather rigid boundaries between them. The relative isolation of sub-systems might also be accompanied by a low intensity of communication between the administrative authorities responsible for these sub-systems. In Estonia, for example, while different levels of the administration offer competing services at most levels of education, the municipalities are the main provider of general secondary education while the state is the main provider of vocational secondary education. As a result, the general and the vocational sub-systems are relatively isolated from each other. This makes it difficult for sub-systems to share resources (for example teachers, special educational services or facilities) and to allow students to move easily between school types in line with their interests, talents and needs (Box 2.5). Challenges of isolated or competing sub-sectors are also faced by the Austrian school system where there is a parallel offer of federal and provincial schools at the lower secondary level, and in the Flemish Community of Belgium, where the school offer is organised within three different educational "networks" which each have their own legal and administrative structures (Box 2.5).

Challenges may also arise when several sub-central tiers of government are involved in distributing central funding thus establishing a hierarchy between the different levels. In the Czech Republic, for example, regions act as intermediaries in the funding between the central level and municipalities, which complicates the flow of resources from the central level to the end users (schools) (Box 2.5). Intermediary actors and additional layers of decision making can cause frictions and complicate monitoring and evaluation of resource use to the detriment of equity and efficiency. Such complex arrangements can also make it difficult to manage information on the use of school funding and how it translates into outcomes (Chapter 5). In decentralised school systems, the development of effective school funding mechanisms requires governance models that establish a clear division of responsibilities across different levels of the administration, build capacity at each of these levels and develop clear lines of accountability, using data and evidence effectively for policy making and reform (Chapter 5).

Finally, it is important to keep in mind that complexities may also arise in centralised governance settings if multiple actors or agencies are involved in school funding. In Uruguay, while the governance of education is highly centralised, it is also highly fragmented. The

Box 2.5. **Challenges related to the distribution of responsibilities for school funding**

In **Estonia**, the municipal and the state owned schools offer competing services in general education, in special needs education and – to a lesser extent – in vocational education and training. This results in reduced clarity of the responsibilities for setting the funding rules. At the time of the OECD review visit in 2015, the government was aiming to transfer responsibilities among tiers of government so as to provide greater clarity of funding and management responsibilities for each sector. The central government had a medium-term intention of establishing a more streamlined division of labour within public education, whereby municipalities should provide funding for pre-primary, primary and lower secondary education while the state should take responsibility for the entire upper secondary sector (both general and vocational schools) and special education schools. This was expected to reduce unnecessary duplication; provide the potential for better co-ordination within education levels (or school types); establish closer linkages between funding, school management and accountability; facilitate the alignment between education strategic objectives and school level management; reduce ambiguities in defining who is responsible for what; and assist with school network planning. For example, having the state take responsibility for both vocational and general upper secondary education is likely to facilitate bridges between the two sectors and allow upper secondary education to be managed as a unified sub-system.

In **Austria**, at the time of the OECD review visit in 2016, lower secondary education was offered both by the federal level (academic secondary schools) and the provincial level (New Secondary Schools, which are jointly funded by the federal government [responsible for teacher salaries] and the municipalities [responsible for all other funding]). The two types of lower secondary education share a common curriculum and similar educational goals but the systematic management and coherent funding of lower secondary education remain challenging due to the fragmented distribution of responsibilities between the federal, provincial and municipal level. At the time of the OECD review visit in 2016, the government was seeking ways to streamline the governance and funding of its school system. Reform proposals included the creation of a more unitary governance structure, which should overcome the formal division between federal and provincial schools. Given the history of political struggles between the federal and the provincial governments, the whole-sale delegation of funding for teachers, operational costs and infrastructure to either the federal or the provincial government appeared politically difficult. The OECD review team recognised that any future arrangement would most likely have to be a political compromise in the sense that both levels would continue to be involved.

In the **Flemish Community of Belgium**, school education can be classified in three "networks" providing school education. Two of these networks can be classified as providers of public education (Flemish Community schools and municipal and provincial schools). Within each network, schools provide education at the different levels of schooling from pre-primary through to upper secondary, as well as adult education. The different educational networks have different central organisations (the Flemish Community Education – GO! and the so-called "umbrella organisations" with a legal personality) employing administrative staff and operating their own pedagogical advisory services and student guidance centres funded by the Flemish government. Collaboration between schools pertaining to the different networks remains relatively rare. The division of public education in two educational networks involves considerable overhead and administration costs and leaves considerable potential for efficiency savings. At the time of the OECD review visit in 2014, several of the groups consulted argued that there would be benefits creating a single network that would

---

Box 2.5. **Challenges related to the distribution of responsibilities for school funding** *(cont.)*

cover all public schools, both the Flemish Community schools and the schools managed the municipalities and provinces. The review team considered that the potential merger of the two public networks deserved review and serious consideration as it would help reduce overhead and administration costs across the two smaller networks. In the context of reforms to optimise the structure of school administration, the review team also recommended reviewing the size of school boards within the different networks, with a special focus on determining the potential for merging school boards.

In the **Czech Republic**, the regional level has two separate roles in the education financing system. The first is receiving an education grant from the central budget to finance the schools under its managerial control (secondary schools), and allocating these funds to individual schools. In this respect, the Czech regions are just like any local governments among the post-communist countries. The second role is receiving an education grant from the central budget for schools managed by the municipalities (basic schools), and then redistributing these funds among the municipalities according to an allocation formula set by each region. In this regard, the Czech regions act like extensions of the national government and have much power over the municipal budgeting process. This double role of regions in the financing of the Czech education system is quite unusual among the post-communist countries. It creates a dependency of municipalities on regions, thus making the first tier of local government (municipalities) partially subordinate to the second tier (regions). The OECD review team in the Czech Republic suggested that direct transfers between the ministry and the municipalities that manage the schools could help promote policy dialogue and enable the central level to improve the central understanding of the challenges of the Czech school system and to better plan its development. The main difficulty confronting this approach is the extremely small size of the Czech municipalities and the fact that most of them have one school, if any at all. The review team suggested that a solution could be to entrust funding only to municipalities with extended powers, as is already the case with a number of locally delivered public services in the Czech Republic. In this way not all municipalities would be recipients of the grant. The review team recognised that transfers to municipalities with extended powers, completely bypassing the regions, would have to use more complex and flexible formulas. Nevertheless, the team had no doubts that these formulas could be designed to be far more simple and comprehensible than the current formulas for basic education used by the regions.

Source: Nusche, D. et al. (2016a), *OECD Reviews of School Resources: Austria 2016*, http://dx.doi.org/10.1787/9789264256729-en; Shewbridge, C. et al. (2016b), *OECD Reviews of School Resources: Czech Republic 2016*, http://dx.doi.org/10.1787/9789264262379-en; Santiago, P. et al. (2016a), *OECD Reviews of School Resources: Estonia 2016*, http://dx.doi.org/10.1787/9789264251731-en; Nusche, D. et al. (2015), *OECD Reviews of School Resources: Flemish Community of Belgium 2015*, http://dx.doi.org/10.1787/9789264247598-en.

system operates with four education councils for distinct sub-systems (pre-primary and primary education; general secondary education; technical-professional secondary programmes; teacher training) that operate in a rather independent manner. As a result, school education is not governed as a system, but as a number of rather isolated sub-systems. Each area of policy (e.g. human resources, curriculum, budget, infrastructure, planning) is independently addressed within each education council – each council has independent units covering these policy areas while a central governing council replicates the same units but with no oversight upon the corresponding units of the councils. This institutional design does not ensure enough co-ordination across educational levels and types.

Schools hold considerable responsibility for managing and allocating their funds

Over the past three decades, many education systems, including those in Australia, Canada, Finland, Hong Kong (China), Israel, Singapore, Spain, Sweden and the United Kingdom, have granted their schools greater autonomy in both curricula and resource allocation decisions (Cheng et al., 2016; Fuchs and Wößmann, 2007; OECD, 2016b; Wang, 2013). A higher degree of school autonomy typically involves greater decision-making power and accountability for school principals, and in some cases also for groups of teachers or middle managers such as heads of departments in schools. However, the school systems in OECD and partner countries have different points of departure and differ in the degree of autonomy granted to schools and in the domains over which autonomy is awarded to schools.

Figure 2.8 presents comparative data on the autonomy of schools from the OECD 2012 Programme for International Student Assessment (PISA), which also surveyed school principals about their degree of autonomy regarding decisions about the local school environment. The figure presents an index based on principals' responses regarding their autonomy in selecting teachers for hire, dismissing teachers, establishing teachers' starting salaries, determining the teachers' salary increases, formulating the school budget and deciding on budget allocations within the school (OECD, 2013a). As the figure shows, school autonomy in resource allocation was lowest in countries such as Greece, Italy, Germany, Austria, France and Portugal. On the opposite end of the spectrum, schools in countries such as the Netherlands, the Czech Republic, the United Kingdom, the Slovak Republic and Sweden had high degrees of autonomy in resource allocation.

Figure 2.8. **Index of school autonomy in resource allocation in OECD countries, 2012**

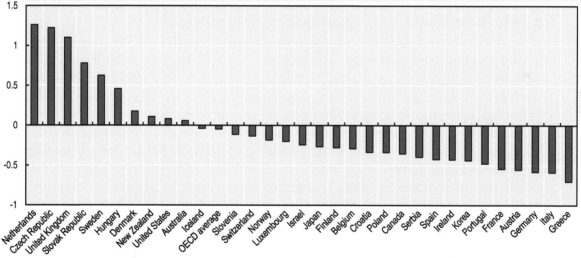

Source: OECD (2013a), PISA 2012 Results: What Makes Schools Successful (Volume IV)? Resources, Policies and Practices, http://dx.doi.org/10.1787/9789264201156-en, p. 131.

In countries with a strong focus on school autonomy in resource allocation, most funding going to schools is typically not earmarked, which gives schools flexibility to use resources to fit their specific needs. As a result, these schools are responsible for resource policy issues such as setting up budgeting and accounting systems, communicating with relevant stakeholders about resource use, recruiting and dismissing school staff, making decisions about the use of teacher hours, maintaining the school infrastructure, buying materials and establishing relationships with contractors and vendors. Autonomy in resource management decisions provides the conditions for schools to use resources in line with local needs and priorities.

By contrast, in countries where funding arrangements are established in a context of little resource allocation autonomy, schools typically need to follow strict rules to execute their budgets or they manage a very limited budget. They might also not be allowed to select their own staff or organise teacher hours the way they see fit. In addition, they might not be able to save up and transfer funds from one year to the next, take out loans, or generate own revenues. Also, in contexts of limited school autonomy, schools tend not to have their own accounts and, therefore, may depend entirely on education authorities for support in maintenance and operating costs. In highly decentralised systems, such as Chile and Iceland, the level of autonomy of schools may vary from jurisdiction to jurisdiction, with schools in some municipalities having greater autonomy than in others (Icelandic Ministry of Education, Science and Culture, 2014; Santiago et al., forthcoming).

In Chile, for example, the operation of schools that receive public funding is the responsibility of school providers (municipalities or private providers) but school providers may delegate responsibilities to schools. The precise distribution of tasks and responsibilities between school providers and schools, and therefore the degree of school autonomy for the use and management of resources, depends on individual school providers. This arrangement allows school providers to take over administrative and managerial tasks and thus free school leaders to concentrate on their pedagogical role. But for schools that have fewer opportunities to influence their providers' management decision, this makes it difficult to align resource management decisions with particular school needs (Santiago et al., forthcoming).

In many countries, schools have inequitable access to resources

While sub-central discretion over the distribution of funding allows sub-central actors to develop resource strategies in line with identified needs, in some countries it also raises concerns regarding the equity of resource distribution between their schools. In Chile, for example, it was noted that local autonomy regarding the allocation of basic grants to schools creates the opportunity for sharp differences in per student spending within municipalities, as well as a lack of transparency that may benefit schools with well-connected principals (Santiago et al., forthcoming). Also, in the Flemish Community of Belgium, where funding for operational costs is attributed to school boards and then further distributed among the schools, there is evidence that school boards responsible for several schools use their own weightings and strategies to allocate financial means to schools. As a result, there is no guarantee that central funding (which is weighted for socio-economic disadvantage of each school's student body) will indeed benefit the schools with the most challenging socio-economic characteristics (Nusche et al., 2015).

Another source of inequity may arise from differences in schools' ability to generate and use their own revenues. While the generation of own income can help complement school-level resources, it raises a number of equity concerns. First, in some countries not all types of schools have the same revenue generating powers. In Austria, for example, schools that are run and funded directly by the federal level have a certain degree of budgetary autonomy as they are able to rent out their school facilities and have control over their own accounts, even if the extent of revenues generated through such activities appears to be minor. By contrast, schools that are run and funded by the provinces and municipalities do not have such autonomy in financial matters, thus presenting an inequity in the system. They cannot generate additional income and depend entirely on their municipality for support in maintenance and operating costs (Nusche et al., 2016a).

Second, the capacity of schools to generate additional revenue is generally influenced by the socio-economic composition of community that they serve. To highlight socio-economic gaps in the ability of schools to raise funds, it is helpful to look at patterns in school systems which routinely collect the relevant income data, as is done in some school systems. In Western Australia, for example, it was shown that among schools of similar size, parental contributions rise in line with socio-economic status (SES) and are 16 times higher among the largest and highest SES schools than they are among the smallest and lowest SES schools. It is often small schools and those located in socio-economically disadvantaged areas that experience the greatest pressure of need, due to the concentration of multiple disadvantages in them. But these schools typically also have the least opportunity to generate additional revenue and thus the least flexibility in budget terms (Teese, 2011).

Third, in many countries the relevant school income data is not collected, thus leading to a lack of transparency regarding the real resource levels of individual schools. In the Slovak Republic, for example, financial contributions from parents in state schools are not sufficiently transparent with respect to the items they fund and how they are recorded. According to a study published in 2007 and cited in Santiago et al. (2016c), between 70% and 90% of parents pay for various services, such as school events, extracurricular activities or teaching materials. There is also some anecdotal evidence that suggests that some schools place pressure on parents to pay such contributions, which is inequitable. Households in the Slovak Republic contribute 15% of pre-primary education expenditure and 10% of primary and secondary expenditure. While private contributions to public services can have benefits, they require increased attention to integrity and equity considerations (Santiago et al., 2016c).

Limited resource autonomy may constrain strategic development at the school level

The relationship between school autonomy in managing own resources and performance outcomes is not clear cut. Evidence from PISA indicates that while student performance is higher where school leaders hold more responsibility for managing resources, this is only significant in countries where the level of educational leadership is above the OECD average (OECD, 2016c). The effect of delegating more autonomy for resource management to schools depends on schools' ability to make use of this autonomy in a constructive way and thus requires a strengthening of school leadership and management structures (more on this below). Furthermore, autonomous schools need to be embedded in a comprehensive regulatory and institutional framework in order to prevent adverse effects of autonomy on equity across schools. The results from PISA suggest that when autonomy and accountability are intelligently combined, they tend to be associated with better student performance (OECD, 2016c).

Findings from the OECD country reviews indicate that an absence of resource autonomy at the school level risks constraining schools' room for manoeuvre in developing and shaping their own profiles and may create inefficiencies in resource management. In Uruguay, for example, schools have very limited autonomy over the management or allocation of their budget. Not only do central authorities manage school budgets, the recruitment of teachers and the allocation of infrastructure and equipment but they also retain decision-making power over less fundamental aspects of school operation such as the acquisition of instructional materials, ad hoc repairs at schools and the approval of schools' special activities. Little local and school autonomy hinders effectiveness in the use of resources as local authorities and schools are unable to match resources to their specific needs, and in consideration of their conditions and context. Also, responses from central educational authorities to an emerging school need can prove very slow. In addition, limited autonomy disempowers school and local actors and makes it more difficult to hold local players accountable, in particular school leaders, as they do not have the responsibility to take most of the decisions (Santiago et al., 2016b).

Devolution of resource management to schools requires adequate leadership capacity

As part of a general move towards greater school autonomy, many countries have attributed greater resource responsibilities to their school leadership teams. While offering potential for effective strategic management at the school level, such budgetary devolution creates new challenges for resource management in schools. School leaders in such contexts are increasingly asked to fulfil responsibilities that call for expertise they may not have through formal training. Where resource management responsibilities are sharply increasing without additional support for leadership teams, it will be difficult for schools to establish robust management processes where resources are directed to improvement priorities and support learning-centred leadership (Plecki et al., 2006; Pont et al., 2008).

Where schools have autonomy over their own budgets, they must be able to link the school's education priorities with its spending decisions, for example by making connections between school development planning and budget planning (Chapter 4). In particular where targeted funding is available to provide disadvantaged schools with additional funding (Chapter 3), this is often tied to the requirement to develop a school improvement plan deciding how funds are used for the benefit of disadvantaged students and with accountability requirements (Chapter 5). Administrating and allocating such additional funding effectively requires time, administrative capacity and strategic leadership within schools. Evaluations of targeted programmes show mixed results and indicate that the success of these programmes depends on whether conditions for effective allocation and use of funding are in place at the school level (Scheerens, 2000).

If targeted funding is distributed to schools without further guidance and support, school staff may not know how to fit these special initiatives into their school development plans or they may use the additional money for measures that have not demonstrated to be effective (Kirby et al., 2003; Karsten, 2006; Nusche, 2009). In Chile, for example, school leaders often make limited use of school improvement planning which is required in return for additional funding through the preferential school subsidy (*Subvención Escolar Preferencial*, SEP). Resources from this subsidy can be used to contract external pedagogical-technical support, but schools and school providers do not always have the capacity to make an informed choice to select a service of high quality that meets actual needs and to monitor the implementation and the effects of the intervention (Santiago et al., forthcoming).

A further challenge concerns the potential tension between pedagogical and administrative/managerial leadership. On the one hand, school autonomy in resource management can be part of strategic learning-centred leadership as it allows aligning spending choices with the pedagogical necessities of schools. But on the other hand, school autonomy places an administrative, managerial and accounting burden on school leaders which may reduce their time available for pedagogical leadership (e.g. coaching of their teaching staff). This tension is also relevant for the training and evaluation of school leaders, which need to prepare school leaders for their financial and administrative responsibilities, but within a framework of pedagogical leadership (Pont et al., 2008; OECD, 2013b).

The public funding of private providers has strengthened private actors in schooling

Over the past 25 years, more than two-thirds of OECD countries have introduced measures to increase school choice (Musset, 2012), often by publicly funding private providers and letting students and families decide which schools to attend. Financial support for private providers is usually embedded in parental choice systems in which public funding may "follow the students" to whichever eligible school they choose to attend, or be used to compensate parents for their expenses on private school tuition fees through vouchers or tax credits. These measures have resulted in some countries developing a substantial publicly funded private sector (see Figure 2.9). For the year 2009, 9 out of 22 OECD countries with available data reported to have a voucher system in place for primary schools, five of which were targeted towards students from lower socio-economic backgrounds. At the lower and upper secondary level, vouchers were even more frequent, with 11 out of 24 countries operating such programmes. Of these, seven at the lower secondary level and five at the upper secondary level were targeted as disadvantaged students (OECD, 2011b).

Figure 2.9. **Percentage of students at age 15 by type of institution, 2015**
Results based on school principals' reports about the organisation managing the school and the sources of funding

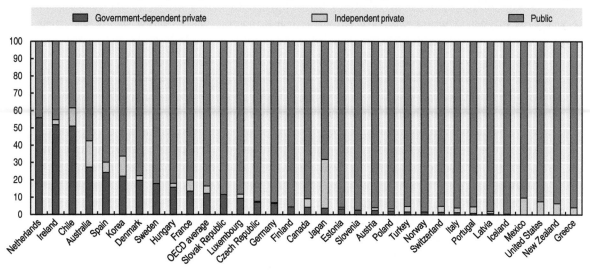

Note: Countries are ranked in descending order of the percentage of students enrolled in government-dependent private education.
Source: Adapted from OECD (n.d.), PISA 2015 Database, *www.oecd.org/pisa/data/2015database/*, Table II.4.7.

The public funding of private schools may be motivated by a range of different arguments whose relative importance varies across national contexts (for a review, see Boeskens, 2016). In some countries the policy focus is primarily on guaranteeing the rights of families to send their children to the school of their preference (e.g. in terms of quality, pedagogical approaches, religious denomination or geographical location), free of legal restrictions or financial barriers. While socio-economically advantaged families can often choose between different schools by virtue of their residential mobility and ability to pay tuition fees, these options may not be available to students with fewer means. Subsidising private provision has therefore been suggested as a means to promote equity by giving all students access to private providers (Boeskens, 2016). In other countries, there is greater focus on macro-level arguments supporting that such subsidies can provide incentives for schools to improve quality, stimulate greater diversity in the educational offer or encourage innovative pedagogical and governance arrangements that will increase efficiency and improve learning outcomes in the long run (OECD, 2010).

However, experience in several OECD review countries points to the risks of increased social segregation and a deprived public system if high-ability students and socio-economically advantaged students disproportionately leave the public system for private providers. These threats to equity are explored further below. On average across OECD countries, students enrolled in public schools scored lower in science than students in private schools in the OECD 2015 Programme for International Student Assessment (PISA). However, after accounting for socio-economic status, the opposite is true with students in public schools scoring higher than students in private schools on average across the OECD and in the majority of school systems. This remarkable difference in results before and after accounting for socio-economic status reflects the larger proportions of disadvantaged students enrolled in public schools than in private schools (OECD, 2016c).

Regulatory frameworks for the public funding of private schools vary considerably across systems

Experience from different countries indicates that the impact on equity and educational quality of publicly funding private providers is influenced by the institutional arrangements in which they are embedded. Among the OECD review countries, these regulations vary considerably. In some countries, publicly funded private schools do not only enjoy greater pedagogical freedom than their publicly managed counterparts but also greater autonomy in their admission and tuition policies. Other systems impose strict eligibility criteria on private schools seeking to qualify for public funding, binding them to follow national curricula and assessment procedures, excluding for-profit providers, and restricting their ability to charge add-on fees or engage in selective admission (Boeskens, 2016). In the Flemish Community of Belgium, for example, subsidised private schools are not permitted to select students on the basis of their academic achievement as a means to guarantee parents the right to exercise free school choice (see Box 2.6). Other systems use targeted funding schemes designed to exclusively benefit or provide additional support for private school students from disadvantaged backgrounds (Musset, 2012).

While it is relatively common for oversubscribed public schools to take into account non-academic factors such as a student's geographic proximity or the presence of their siblings, in some countries publicly funded private schools are permitted to select students on the basis of academic achievement, aptitude tests and parental interviews. These differential selection practices can restrict the exercise of school choice and risk increasing student segregation across providers. To address this challenge, Chile introduced a reform of its private school system in 2016 (presented in Box 2.7). Although its full effect remains to be seen, the 2016 reform of Chile's private school system (presented in Box 2.7) serves as a good example to illustrate the implementation of a regulatory framework that seeks to harmonise the admission and tuition policies of public providers and subsidised private schools.

Since the early 1990s, Sweden has operated an extensive school choice system whereby funding follows the student and private providers are entitled to receive subsidies equivalent to the local municipality's average spending per public school student. Publicly funded private schools have increased their share of the enrolment among 15-year-old students by almost 10 percentage points between 2003 and 2012 (OECD, 2013a). To receive the same funding as public schools, private providers need to be approved by the Schools Inspectorate and teach the same curriculum as municipal schools, although they can follow a special

Box 2.6. **Parental choice in the Flemish Community of Belgium**

The Flemish Community of Belgium has a long tradition of parental choice and is home to a large number of publicly funded private schools. One of the related umbrella organisations (*Vrij gesubsidieerd onderwijs*, VGO) enrolled the majority of the student population in 2012/13 (62.4% of primary school students and 74.8% of mainstream secondary school students). The majority of these "grant-aided private schools" are run by private foundations of Catholic denomination, while the non-denominational private providers typically follow a particular educational method or philosophy.

To facilitate school choice, the Flemish Community provides full funding to both public and grant-aided private schools. In turn, publicly funded schools are not allowed to charge tuition fees. Although parents can be asked to pay some fees for specific educational materials or supplemental activities, scholarships are available for some students at the secondary level to assist with these expenses. In addition, Flemish primary and pre-primary school students from low-income families are eligible for means-tested study grants. Additional provisions to ensure that families have equal access to the school of their choice include the prohibition of selective admission, although factors such as the access to information or school transportation arrangements remain potential sources of inequity and segregation since they may constrain the choices of disadvantaged families.

As a means to ensure equal access to educational opportunities and address the issue of socio-economic segregation, the 2002 Decree of Equal Educational Opportunities (*Gelijke Onderwijskansen*, GOK) provided for the establishment of local consultation platforms (*Locale Overlegplatformen*, LOP) which play an important role in co-ordinating the co-operation between schools and stakeholders and managing the enrolment process. LOPs are responsible for ensuring students' right to enrolment, analysing the socio-economic characteristics of the student population in the local area, acting as an intermediary in case of conflicts and implementing a local policy to co-ordinate schools' enrolment procedures within the framework of the decree (Lambrechts and Geurts, 2008). Particularly in urban areas with pressing demographic developments, LOPs play an important role in facilitating the distribution of students across local schools and networks and guaranteeing their right to enrolment.

Source: Nusche, D. et al. (2015), *OECD Reviews of School Resources: Flemish Community of Belgium 2015, http://dx.doi.org/10.1787/9789264247598-en.*

Box 2.7. **Regulating publicly funded private schools in Chile: The 2016 Inclusion Law**

The Chilean school system is characterised by a large network of publicly-funded private schools, enrolling 53% of its students in mainstream basic education (Year 1 to Year 8) and 51% at the upper secondary level in 2014. Historically, Chile allowed publicly funded private schools to charge tuition fees, operate for profit and select students based on academic achievement, aptitude tests or parental interviews. This practice has contributed to the country's high level of socio-economic segregation as middle-class students increasingly left the public school system to enter subsidised private schools with admission requirements that excluded large parts of the population. In order to address these concerns and facilitate the exercise of free school choice, a new law (*Ley de Inclusión*, Inclusion Law) was adopted in 2016, which imposes new eligibility criteria for public funding in order to restrict selective admission, for-profit ownership and top-up fees among subsidised private schools.

Box 2.7. Regulating publicly funded private schools in Chile:
The 2016 Inclusion Law *(cont.)*

The new regulations will be enforced by the Education Superintendence and gradually implemented over the coming years. In order to remain eligible for public subsidies, private schools will need to phase out their tuition fees and other obligatory parental contributions (e.g. for school materials) over the coming years and stop selecting students based on parental interviews or prior academic achievement. In order to facilitate this transition and compensate schools for the loss of revenues from parental "co-payment", the law provides a number of additional subsidies (*Aporte de Gratuidad*). Notably, the law provides for a 20% increase of the Preferential School Subsidy (*Subvención Escolar Preferencial*, SEP) which assigns additional resources to schools serving the most vulnerable 40% of students. In addition, schools that abolish co-payments will be eligible to receive a grant amounting to 50% of the SEP for students from the third and fourth quintile of the income distribution. The estimated fiscal cost of these transition arrangements are subject to debate, ranging from the official estimate of USD 914 million per year to about USD 1 170 million (Santiago et al., forthcoming).

Source: Santiago, P. et al. (forthcoming), *OECD Reviews of School Resources: Chile*, OECD Publishing, Paris.

---

orientation or profile like Montessori and Waldorf Schools. While subsidised private schools in Sweden have been prohibited from charging mandatory fees since 1997 and cannot select students in compulsory education based on their ability, they are allowed to operate for profit (Swedish Ministry of Education and Research, 2016). Similarly, in Estonia, publicly funded private schools can also make profits (Santiago et al., 2016a). While there is little robust and consistent evidence concerning the performance of for-profit schools in advanced economies, subsidising commercial providers without ensuring that profits are reinvested to improve the delivery of educational services raises concerns over the efficient use of public funding for education.

Inadequate private school regulations and school choice designs can generate inequities

One of the most commonly raised concerns with respect to school choice programmes is that they are disproportionately used by families with higher socio-economic status. Even in the absence of explicit admission criteria, students from disadvantaged backgrounds are less likely to make use of school choice and less frequently use academic quality as a criterion when deciding which school to attend. To address the socio-economic inequities that arise from differential participation rates, it has been recommended to raise awareness of school choice options, improve disadvantaged families' access to school information and to support them in making better-informed choices (Nusche, 2009; OECD, 2012). Progressive voucher schemes or weighted funding formulas have also been proposed as policy options to address the challenges of segregation along socio-economic and demographic lines (Musset, 2012). By channelling additional money to disadvantaged students, countries such as Chile and the Netherlands have used variants of these funding schemes to provide schools with the resources they need to adequately address their students' needs and diminish incentives that could exacerbate segregation.

The conditions which private schools must fulfil in order to qualify for public funding are central to the successful governance of school choice systems. Among these eligibility criteria, private schools' ability to select students and charge add-on tuition fees are particularly salient concerns for several OECD review countries. Allowing subsidised schools to select their students based on prior performance, aptitude tests or socio-economic background raises a number of concerns pertaining to both equity and educational quality. Selective admission permits private schools to "cream skim" high-ability students from the public sector, particularly where their public counterparts are required to operate on the basis of open enrolment or confine themselves to using non-academic criteria such as residential proximity to select students. Since parents often mistakenly evaluate a school's quality based on its student composition, engaging in selective admission can allow schools to attain a competitive advantage without actually improving their educational provision. Selectivity threatens to exacerbate student segregation between the public and private sectors and can widen existing achievement gaps. This process threatens to deprive the public school system of high-ability students, which is likely to harm those who are left behind and deplete public schools of vital resources since disadvantaged students may have greater resource needs (Boeskens, 2016).

School choice systems that permit private schools to demand significant parental contributions above and beyond the amount covered by the public subsidy risk exacerbating socio-economic segregation across schools. Most countries that subsidise private providers place restrictions on their ability to charge "add-on" tuition fees. In Sweden, for example, tuition fees among subsidised private are entirely prohibited, whereas countries such as Denmark provide fee-charging private schools with a proportionately lower amount of public funding (Houlberg et al., 2016). Regulations of add-on tuition fees usually aim to reduce financial barriers for low-income families seeking to make use of school choice and serve to ensure that private schools do not gain an unfair competitive advantage over free public schools. However, among the education systems participating in the review's qualitative survey, 9 of 17 reported not to have national regulations in place to restrict tuition fees among publicly funded private schools in general compulsory education (Table 2.A1.4). Evidence from Chile suggests that tuition fees among private schools were one of the reasons for the country's high level of student segregation (Elacqua, 2012) and empirical studies have also called into doubt whether private schools' revenue from parental contributions was effectively translated into higher educational quality. In the Chilean case, Mizala and Torche (2012) found no association between parental add-on fees and private schools' scores in national standardised tests (*Sistema de Medición de la Calidad de la Educación*, SIMCE) controlling for their student composition, which suggests that tuition fees may have primarily served as a means to cream-skim students from the public sector without raising their educational quality.

Monitoring the implementation of regulatory frameworks is important. In Chile, for example, publicly-funded private providers are subject to evaluations by the central education authorities through the Education Superintendence, which audits the use of public resources and monitors compliance with legislation, standards and regulations. It also enforces compliance with the recently introduced Inclusion Law, which prohibits publicly-funded private providers from making a profit, selecting students, and charging add-on student fees (Santiago et al., forthcoming). In addition, private school providers typically have to provide information on their use of the public financial resources they receive. In the Czech Republic, for example, private schools are required to report on the settlement of their public operating grants by a set deadline, provide analysis of the way the grant was used, and submit an annual report on the operation of the school. If the school has a school council in place, it must also provide information about the discussions that took place at their meetings (MŠMT, 2016).

There are concerns in some countries about inadequate monitoring of regulations for publicly funded private schools. In Germany, the basic law establishes central principles for the public funding of private schools that prohibit the selection of students to prevent social segregation in the education system. The introduction of precise regulations for the implementation of these principles and the monitoring and controlling of compliance with these regulations is the responsibility of the individual states. States should thus control aspects, such as the admission procedures and the social composition of private schools compared to public schools; however, according to Wrase and Helbig (2016), this is only rarely the case (Wrase and Helbig, 2016).

Policy options

This report does not aim to provide generic recommendations on effective governance arrangements that could be applied to all countries as such strategies need to be developed with an understanding of national (and sub-national) contexts, traditions and circumstances. However, there are a number of trends in the governance of school funding that can be observed across many countries, albeit in different combinations and to different degrees. These trends have been grouped in this chapter under the headings of fiscal decentralisation, school resource autonomy and involvement of publicly funded private actors. Depending on their different starting points, traditions and school system structures, countries have reacted to these trends in different ways and have developed unique responses to adapt their school funding systems to their own governance contexts. Their various responses to a set of similar challenges provide opportunities for peer learning across countries, keeping in mind that there is no one governance approach that would fit all systems. This section provides a set of options and examples of how the governance challenges most commonly observed in school funding systems might be addressed.

Align roles and responsibilities in decentralised funding systems

In the context of multi-level governance, school systems are increasingly involving sub-central governments in raising resources for schooling and making decisions on the allocation and management of school funds. However, for such decentralised funding approaches to work well, they need to be designed in ways that ensure sub-central jurisdictions have both adequate revenues to meet the needs of their students and relevant capacity to fulfil their funding responsibilities. In addition, it is key to ensure effective alignment between the roles and responsibilities of different levels of the educational administration. Creating such alignment involves reflection about both governance structures (e.g. the most efficient number of governance levels involved in school funding) and governance processes (e.g. stakeholder involvement, open dialogue and use of evidence and research).

Align sub-central revenue raising and spending powers

The distribution of responsibilities for spending on school education should be adequately aligned to the distribution of responsibilities for raising funds. In countries where sub-central authorities have large spending powers, consideration could be given to increasing, at the margin, their own revenue raising powers. As discussed above, reliance on own tax revenue brings jurisdictions autonomy in determining public service levels in line with local preferences; it makes sub-central governments accountable to their citizens who will be able to influence spending decisions through local elections; it may enhance overall resource mobilisation in a country as local/regional authorities may tap additional local resources; and it creates a hard budget constraint on sub-central entities which is likely to discourage overspending (OECD/KIPF, 2016).

In systems where sub-central decision making is a key principle of schooling, a case can be made for expanding the available choices for sub-central governments by increasing their fiscal autonomy. For example, the Nordic countries typically give local governments substantial control over personal income tax rates. Some Central and East European countries have also started to do this by giving local governments the right to impose a local surcharge – within limits set by law – on the national government's rate, while others are considering it. It should also be considered to accompany such an extension of revenue generating powers of local governments by a degree of jurisdictional consolidation to decrease the incentive such taxation might create for people to move from one jurisdiction to another – particularly from urban to suburban ones (Santiago et al., 2016a). However, it is important to recognise that such fiscal reforms require adjustments that go beyond the education system and need to be embedded in broader reflections on fiscal relationships across tiers of government.

Develop adequate equalisation mechanisms

Despite the advantages of raising the proportion of own revenue in sub-central education budgets, such an emphasis on using local tax bases for schooling also entails risks to create inequities in the availability of funding for schools across different localities. Typically, wealthier jurisdictions will be in a better position to raise their own revenues and to be able to provide adequate funding per student than others. In such contexts, the operation of fiscal transfer systems can help ensure that all jurisdictions have the necessary revenue to provide equal opportunities for their students. Such mechanisms aim to ensure that sub-central authorities are able to provide similar services at similar tax levels.

While the design of inter-jurisdictional relationships goes beyond the school sector (see above), getting the system right is particularly important for schooling as it often accounts for the largest share of the local budgets. Chapter 3 discusses key design principles to be considered when establishing effective fiscal transfer systems. In terms of governance, it is important to strike a balance between the need to reflect stakeholder views in the design of the transfer system and the risks of rent-seeking approaches and political distortions. A number of OECD countries have developed measures to limit the influence of special interests, for example through the establishment of independent agencies and bodies. Also, a two-stage budget procedure by setting the overall budget for equalisation and then negotiating the distribution formula may help reduce rent-seeking pressures (OECD, 2014b).

But even where well-designed equalisation schemes are in place, there may be marked differences among sub-central authorities in the level of funding they provide to schools and in the methods used for allocating these funds. To ensure a basic level of funding for all schools, one option is to introduce a funding approach whereby a part of central funding is earmarked for schools based on assessed needs while another part can be used at the discretion of sub-central authorities. In systems where each educational jurisdiction creates its own funding approach, the sharing of experiences among sub-central authorities should be encouraged and facilitated to create synergies and avoid duplication of efforts in designing optimal funding formulas (Chapter 3).

Build capacity for resource management at the sub-central level

In countries where sub-central authorities play a key role for providing education, the capacity building of sub-central actors should be a priority. Such capacity building should include a focus on resource management if this is a local responsibility. Competency frameworks for local leaders and administrators should reflect the related skills and be used to guide recruitment processes as well as training and professional development.

Part of the strategy involves professional development programmes to be made available to the staff employed by sub-central authorities and other school providers. These could emphasise, managing local school networks, engagement with community members, communication and consultation processes, school development, financial planning, human resources management and quality assurance in education (Chapter 5). But it is important to keep in mind that the professionalisation of local management does not depend only on the personal preparedness of local actors. In a wider professionalisation framework, the institutional settings within which local actors operate (e.g. co-ordination and co-operation among local authorities), the professional support provided, and the access of local actors to key information are important aspects to consider in improving capacity at the local level. For example, relevant training offers could be complemented by the establishment of a network of advisors to support the education work of local authorities. The central level and/or an association of local authorities could play a key role in this process.

Capacity for local education management can also be strengthened by encouraging local authorities to collaborate and share their administrative and managerial resources, e.g. jointly employing specialised staff for budgeting, financial control and the use of performance data, and working together to identify and disseminate effective practice. Associations of local authorities can take on a leading role in encouraging such collaborative practices and networks and in spreading good practices. Initiatives to develop and disseminate knowledge and tools for different levels of the school administration can support the implementation of effective processes for financial resource management. This could include support in areas such as planning resource use, budgeting and accounting, reporting on the use of financial resources, purchasing education materials and establishing contracts.

Finally, in countries where the high number and small size of providers limits their capacity for effective resource use, school funding could be rationalised by merging several small educational providers and thereby consolidating capacity for effective resource management. This would help ensure a more efficient and equitable administration of resources for a larger number of schools. Providers with adequate size and capacity will be better able to provide professional support for budgeting, accounting and other tasks to school leaders as well as offering regular leadership appraisal and feedback, thereby strengthening the strategic and pedagogical leadership at the school level.

Another option that has been considered by countries facing size and capacity challenges at sub-central levels is to re-centralise provision and funding of one or several sectors of schooling, either by moving responsibilities to higher levels of the administration or by creating new bodies to administer a larger number of schools. Re-centralisation of education services entails risks of weakening the links between education and local development planning. As a result, an important aspect to such re-centralisation processes is the establishment of mechanisms to ensure that local development objectives remain a relevant dimension in defining approaches to school funding. In countries where a decision for recentralisation has been made, it is important that schools remain responsive to local needs and that decision making involves consultation with the relevant local stakeholders. Systems that are re-centralising should also consider introducing flexible approaches to implementing such administration reform, which would recognise differences in capacity and performance between local providers. This could involve the possibility for willing municipalities or other providers to seek certification and continue to operate their local school system within a strengthened accountability framework.

Address the challenges of complexity in decentralised school funding approaches

Fragmented, overlapping and/or unclear governance and funding arrangements risk obfuscating resource flows, creating inefficiencies and reducing overall trust in the management of school systems. While governance arrangements have often been considered as a fixed feature of school systems, many countries are no longer willing or able to afford an inefficient distribution of responsibilities which may lead to costly duplication, overly complex funding formulas or waste of resources. Conclusions from the OECD country reviews clearly indicate that well-functioning governance arrangements are a key condition to allow for an effective and equitable distribution of resources across school systems.

One of the key ingredients of effective governance identified by OECD analysis on *Governing Complex Education Systems* is the need to align roles and responsibilities across the system as a way to address potential conflicts and overlap (Burns et al., 2016). In the context of school funding, this would require a clear division of labour between different levels of the school administration involved in the distribution of funding in order to increase the transparency and effectiveness of decentralised school funding. Where several tiers of government are funding schools at the same level of education and competing with each other for students, this may create conflicts of interests, barriers to collaboration and/or ineffective services for students who may not be able to transfer easily between sub-sectors run by different authorities. One option to address these challenges is to focus on developing a clear distribution of tasks, which assigns funding responsibilities for particular sub-sectors and/or particular types of resources to each tier of school administration.

Another option to address complexity challenges is to reduce the number of sub-tiers involved in channelling resources across a system. In countries where funding is channelled through several intermediary tiers of government before arriving at the school level, this might increase bureaucracy, reduce possibilities for central steering and dilute accountability for effective school funding. In such contexts, central governments could consider reducing the complexity of resource flows by introducing direct transfers for schooling to those levels of the administration which are directly responsible for managing and financing each education level. However, the precondition for such an approach is that the administrative units responsible for managing schools at have sufficient capacity to manage and distribute school funding.

While a whole-system approach that aligns roles and balances tensions is important for effective governance of school funding, Burns et al. (2016) caution against an excessive focus on governance structures rather than processes. For example, as systems seek to identify the most efficient number of governance levels, the focus on identifying an ideal structure may take a lot of time and energy without necessarily yielding lasting strategies to improve the effectiveness of the system. While an effective organisation of the different levels of the school administration is a crucial element of successful governance, thinking of structures in isolation without connecting them to supporting processes will not provide systemic and sustainable solutions to solve complexity challenges. Among the relevant processes that need to be considered alongside structural changes are: flexibility, adaptability, capacity building, open dialogue, stakeholder involvement and transparency (for more information, see Chapter 5). Changing governance structures without addressing the underlying processes may hinder effective implementation of the reforms (Burns et al., 2016).

Provide the necessary conditions for effective resource management at the school level

Some countries have taken steps to improve the conditions for schools to make decisions regarding the allocation of their operational budgets, for example by allowing them to have their own bank accounts and permitting a degree of carry-over of funds to the next financial year (for more information, see Chapter 4). Others are aiming to replace earmarked funding for schools by more general grants in order to allow school-level decision-making power in allocating such funding. To avoid that increased autonomy results in widening inequities across schools, it is important to develop framework conditions that ensure adequate levels of capacity, support and accountability for school leaders. If the right conditions are in place, being able to make budget decisions and recruit personnel can allow schools to more effectively shape their profiles and respond to local challenges.

First, increased school autonomy requires investment in school leadership and management capacity. The effects of school autonomy largely depend on the ability of schools to make use of this autonomy to manage their resources effectively. If schools hold considerable autonomy for resource management, education policies need to focus particularly on developing school leadership capacity and strengthening school management. This should be part of broader strategies to develop the school leadership profession such as the establishment of school leadership frameworks, the recruitment of qualified candidates, their preparation, induction, professional development, performance evaluation and career development over time (OECD, 2013b).

Second, depending on the tasks delegated to the school level, schools also require adequate administrative support staff, such as secretaries, accountants and/or financial managers who are based at the school or shared between several schools. Depending on the context, this does not necessarily mean an overall increase in staff numbers, but could involve a reflection on how human resources can be shifted to better meet schools' needs. It could also involve testing out innovative and cost-effective ways of organising schools and administrative support (e.g. through collaboration of schools or local authorities). In a number of countries, the responsibility for the maintenance of schools, including the provision of administrative staff, lies at the local level, which means that the availability of administrative support staff may depend on the willingness and resources of the responsible local authority. In such contexts, central authorities could consider the introduction of central guidelines regarding a minimum number of administrative staff for schools of a certain size, coupled with instruments to address resource inequities between local authorities (e.g. through an equalisation mechanism, see above). Adequate support structures with administrative staff and distributed leadership arrangements are important to reconcile administrative and managerial tasks with pedagogical leadership (Pont et al., 2008).

Third, schools may benefit from external support with budget management tasks. For example, local education providers can provide their school leaders with various degrees of help with the more technical aspects of school budgeting such as accounting and bookkeeping, allowing school leaders to focus more on strategic and pedagogical organisation of the school. They can also play an important role in the delivery of services

2. GOVERNING SCHOOL FUNDING

and can help their schools achieve scale economies, for example by buying materials and services for several schools at the same time. In addition, several countries have created consulting and advisory services that work with schools and provide support if needed, for example in the development of strategies to use targeted funds to improve learning for disadvantaged students.

Fourth, increased responsibility of schools over their own budget further needs to be accompanied by effective school self-evaluation and accountability mechanisms (Chapter 5). Requiring schools to develop school improvement plans connected to medium-term resource strategies can help inform resource allocation, as discussed in Chapter 4. Performance agreements with principals can also help holding school leadership to account (OECD, 2013b). Information generated through school evaluation needs to be systematically connected with future resource decisions. Additional support should be provided to schools identified as struggling with increased autonomy. School boards representing parents and the local community can provide horizontal accountability by reviewing school budgets.

Finally, a critical school size is also necessary in order for schools to be able to effectively use their autonomy. If schools are too small, delegating more responsibility to the school level may overwhelm leaders with additional workload. Considerations about school autonomy in managing their resources should therefore go together with discussions about desired school size. Supporting schools to group together and share financial resources in a rational way can help achieve economies of scale and a more efficient use of resources.

Develop adequate regulatory frameworks for the public funding of private providers

The conditions under which private schools are eligible for public subsidies influence the ways in which school choice programmes will impact on accessibility, quality and equity of the school system. To mitigate risks to equity, it is important that all publicly funded providers are required to adhere to the same regulations regarding tuition and admission policies, and that compliance with these regulations is effectively monitored.

Tuition fees for publicly funded private schools that are not covered by vouchers constitute a barrier to the exercise of school choice and can contribute to the socio-economic segregation of students between the public and private sectors. In the absence of appropriate eligibility criteria, private schools may invest public contributions to improve their educational quality without reducing their tuition fees, which places them at a relative advantage and risks draining the public sector of socio-economically advantaged students and resources. In order to ensure that vouchers and other forms of public funding increase the accessibility of private schooling options, regulations should therefore prevent subsidised private schools from charging fees that could constitute a barrier to entry. In countries where parental contributions are charged to make up for discrepancies between the funding of public and private providers countries should carefully monitor their effect and, if necessary, make adjustments to the public subsidy.

In order to support that school choice can improve access to high-quality education rather than leading to selectivity and "cream-skimming", governments should also regulate admission procedures and ensure that private providers adhere to the same standards of selection as public schools. If subsidised private schools are allowed to apply selective admission criteria based on factors such as academic achievement or parental interviews, they have a strong incentive to compete on the basis of selectivity, rather than their educational services. Favouring access of high-ability or socio-economically advantaged students that require fewer resources to teach and raise the school's average achievement threatens to exacerbate socio-economic segregation. Admission practices for oversubscribed schools should therefore be transparent and homogenous across school sectors. The use of lottery systems to assign places in oversubscribed schools or formula aimed to maintain a diverse student composition could be considered (Musset, 2012). Governments should also seek to reduce indirect forms of student selection through complicated application procedures or different expulsion practices across school sectors (Bellei, 2008). Finally, adequate accountability and transparency requirements are also important to ensure that subsidised private schools serve the public interest in providing high-quality education and to provide parents with the information they need to evaluate different schools' processes and outcomes (Chapter 5).

Notes

1. A training levy is a tax to be paid by companies to fund the government's training schemes.

2. Funding mechanisms sometimes allocate additional resources to school-based VET provision to compensate for the cost of specialised equipment and teaching, given the high degree of specialisation in some programmes as well as their higher share of students from disadvantaged backgrounds vis-à-vis general education pathways (see Chapter 3).

3. Data available at https://nces.ed.gov/surveys/annualreports/oecd/index.asp.

References

Ares Abalde, M. (2014), "School Size Policies: A Literature Review", *OECD Education Working Papers*, No. 106, OECD Publishing, Paris, http://dx.doi.org/10.1787/5jxt472ddkjl-en.

Bellei, C. (2008), "The public-private school controversy in Chile", in R. Chakrabarti and P.E. Peterson (eds.), *School Choice International – Exploring Public-Private Partnerships*, MIT Press, Cambridge, MA.

Boeskens, L. (2016), "Regulating Publicly Funded Private Schools: A Literature Review on Equity and Effectiveness", *OECD Education Working Papers*, No. 147, OECD Publishing, Paris, http://dx.doi.org/10.1787/5jln6jcg80r4-en.

Burns, T., F. Köster and M. Fuster (2016), *Education Governance in Action: Lessons from Case Studies*, OECD Publishing, Paris, http://dx.doi.org/10.1787/9789264262829-en.

Busemeyer, M. (2008), "The impact of fiscal decentralisation on education and other types of spending", *Swiss Political Science Review*, Vol. 14/ 3, Wiley-Blackwell.

Cheng, Y.C., J. Ko and T.T.H. Lee (2016), "School autonomy, leadership and learning: A reconceptualization", *International Journal of Educational Management*, Vol. 30/2, pp. 177-196, http://dx.doi.org/10.1108/IJEM-08-2015-0108.

Dar, A., S. Canagarajah and P. Murphy (2003), *Training Levies: Rationale and Evidence from Evaluations*, The World Bank, Washington, DC.

Elacqua, G. (2012), "The impact of school choice and public policy on segregation: Evidence from Chile", *International Journal of Educational Development*, 32, Elsevier, pp. 444-453.

Fuchs, T. and L. Wößmann (2007), "What accounts for international differences in student performance? A re-examination using PISA data", *Empirical Economics*, Vol. 32/2-3, pp. 433-464, http://econpapers.repec.org/RePEc:lmu:muenar:20303.

Hill, P., L.C. Pierce and J.W. Guthrie (1997), *Reinventing Public Education: How Contracting Can Transform America's Schools*, University of Chicago Press, Chicago.

Houlberg, K. et al. (2016), *OECD Review of Policies to Improve the Effectiveness of Resource Use in Schools: Country Background Report for Denmark*, Det Nationale Institut for Kommuners og Regioners Analyse og Forskning (KORA) [Danish Institute for Local and Regional Government Research], Copenhagen, www.oecd.org/education/schoolresourcesreview.htm.

Hoxby, C.M. (2000), "Does competition among public schools benefit students and taxpayers", *American Economic Review*, Vol. 90/ 5, pp. 1209-1238.

Icelandic Ministry of Education, Science and Culture (2014), *OECD Review of Policies to Improve the Effectiveness of Resource Use in Schools: Country Background Report for Iceland*, Iceland Ministry of Education, Science and Culture, *www.oecd.org/education/schoolresourcesreview.htm*.

INEEd (2015), *OECD Review of Policies to Improve the Effectiveness of Resource Use in Schools: Country Background Report for Uruguay*, National Institute for Educational Evaluation (Instituto Nacional de Evaluación Educativa), Montevideo, *www.oecd.org/education/schoolresourcesreview.htm*.

Karsten, S. (2006), "Policies for disadvantaged children under scrutiny: The Dutch policy compared with policies in France, England, Flanders and the USA", *Comparative Education*, Vol. 42/2, Taylor and Francis, pp. 261-282.

Kirabo Jackson, C., R. Johnson and C. Persico (2014), "The effect of school finance reforms on the distribution of spending, academic achievement and adult outcomes", *NBER Working Paper Series*, Working Paper 20118, National Bureau of Economic Research, Cambridge MA, *www.nber.org/papers/w20118*.

Kirby, S.N. et al. (2003), *A Snapshot of Title I Schools, 2000-01*, Department of Education, Washington, DC.

Kuczera, M. (2017), "Striking the right balance: Costs and benefits of apprenticeship", *OECD Education Working Papers*, No. 153, OECD Publishing, Paris, *http://dx.doi.org/10.1787/995fff01-en*.

Lambrechts, B. and E. Geurts (2008), *Educational Policies that Address Social Inequality, Country Report: Belgium/Flanders*, EPASI, Brussels.

Mizala, A. and F. Torche (2012), "Bringing the schools back in: The stratification of educational achievement in the Chilean voucher system", *International Journal of Educational Development*, Vol. 32/ 1, Elsevier, pp. 132-144.

Musset, P. (2012), "School Choice and Equity: Current Policies in OECD Countries and a Literature Review", *OECD Education Working Papers*, No. 66, OECD Publishing, Paris, *http://dx.doi.org/10.1787/5k9fq23507vc-en*.

Nusche, D. (2009), "What Works in Migrant Education?: A Review of Evidence and Policy Options", *OECD Education Working Papers*, No. 22, OECD Publishing, Paris, *http://dx.doi.org/10.1787/227131784531*.

Nusche, D. et al. (2016a), *OECD Reviews of School Resources: Austria 2016*, OECD Publishing, Paris, *http://dx.doi.org/10.1787/9789264256729-en*.

Nusche, D. et al. (2016b), *OECD Reviews of School Resources: Denmark 2016*, OECD Publishing, Paris, *http://dx.doi.org/10.1787/9789264262430-en*.

Nusche, D. et al. (2015), *OECD Reviews of School Resources: Flemish Community of Belgium 2015*, OECD Publishing, Paris, *http://dx.doi.org/10.1787/9789264247598-en*.

Nusche, D. et al. (2011), *OECD Reviews of Evaluation and Assessment in Education: Norway 2011*, OECD Publishing, Paris, *http://dx.doi.org/10.1787/9789264117006-en*.

OECD (2016a), *Education at a Glance 2016: OECD Indicators*, OECD Publishing, Paris, *http://dx.doi.org/10.1787/eag-2016-en*.

OECD (2016b), *Education Policy Outlook: Israel*, OECD, Paris, *www.oecd.org/education/policyoutlook.htm*.

OECD (2016c), *PISA 2015 Results (Volume II): Policies and Practices for Successful Schools*, OECD Publishing, Paris, *http://dx.doi.org/10.1787/9789264267510-9-en*.

OECD (2015a), "Sub-National Governments in OECD Countries: Key Data" (brochure), OECD, Paris.

OECD (2015b), "Steering education systems", *Education Policy Outlook 2015: Making Reforms Happen*, OECD Publishing, Paris, *http://dx.doi.org/10.1787/9789264225442-en*.

OECD (2014a), *Education at a Glance 2014: OECD Indicators*, OECD Publishing, Paris, *http://dx.doi.org/10.1787/eag-2014-en*.

OECD (2014b), *Fiscal Federalism 2014: Making Decentralisation Work*, OECD Publishing, Paris, *http://dx.doi.org/10.1787/9789264204577-en*.

OECD (2013a), *PISA 2012 Results: What Makes Schools Successful (Volume IV)? Resources, Policies and Practices*, OECD Publishing, Paris, *http://dx.doi.org/10.1787/9789264201156-en*.

OECD (2013b), *Synergies for Better Learning: An International Perspective on Evaluation and Assessment*, OECD Publishing, Paris, *http://dx.doi.org/10.1787/9789264190658-en*.

OECD (2012), *Equity and Quality in Education: Supporting Disadvantaged Students and Schools*, OECD Publishing, Paris, http://dx.doi.org/10.1787/9789264130852-en.

OECD (2011a), "Public governance", *Policy Framework for Investment User's Toolkit*, OECD Publishing, Paris, www.oecd.org/investment/pfitoolkit.

OECD (2011b), *Education at a Glance 2011: OECD Indicators*, OECD Publishing, Paris, http://dx.doi.org/10.1787/eag-2011-en.

OECD (2010), *Education at a Glance 2010: OECD Indicators*, OECD Publishing, Paris, http://dx.doi.org/10.1787/eag-2010-en.

OECD/KIPF (2016), *Fiscal Federalism 2016: Making Decentralisation Work*, OECD Publishing, Paris, http://dx.doi.org/10.1787/9789264254053-en.

OECD/The World Bank (2015), *OECD Reviews of School Resources: Kazakhstan 2015*, OECD Publishing, Paris, http://dx.doi.org/10.1787/9789264245891-en.

Papalia, A. (forthcoming), "The Funding of Vocational Education and Training: A Literature Review", *OECD Education Working Papers*, OECD Publishing, Paris.

Plecki, M.L. et al. (2006), *Allocating Resources and Creating Incentives to Improve Teaching and Learning*, Center for the Study of Teaching and Policy, The Wallace Foundation.

Pont, B., D. Nusche and H. Moorman (2008), *Improving School Leadership, Volume 1: Policy and Practice*, OECD Publishing, Paris, http://dx.doi.org/10.1787/9789264044715-en.

Santiago, P. et al. (forthcoming), *OECD Reviews of School Resources: Chile*, OECD Publishing, Paris.

Santiago, P. et al. (2016a), *OECD Reviews of School Resources: Estonia 2016*, OECD Publishing, Paris, http://dx.doi.org/10.1787/9789264251731-en.

Santiago, P. et al. (2016b), *OECD Reviews of School Resources: Uruguay 2016*, OECD Publishing, Paris, http://dx.doi.org/10.1787/9789264265530-en.

Santiago, P. et al. (2016c), *OECD Reviews of School Resources: Slovak Republic 2015*, OECD Publishing, Paris, http://dx.doi.org/10.1787/9789264247567-en.

Scheerens, J. (2000), "Improving school effectiveness", *Fundamentals of Educational Planning Series*, No. 68, UNESCO, Paris.

Sevilla, J. (2006), "Accountability and Control of Public Spending in a Decentralised and Delegated Environment", *OECD Journal on Budgeting*, Vol. 5/2, http://dx.doi.org/10.1787/budget-v5-art8-en.

Shewbridge, C. et al. (2016a), *OECD Reviews of School Resources: Lithuania 2016*, OECD Publishing, Paris, http://dx.doi.org/10.1787/9789264252547-en.

Shewbridge, C. et al. (2016b), *OECD Reviews of School Resources: Czech Republic 2016*, OECD Publishing, Paris, http://dx.doi.org/10.1787/9789264262379-en.

Swedish Ministry of Education and Research (2016), *OECD Review of Policies to Improve the Effectiveness of Resource Use in Schools: Country Background Report for Sweden*, Swedish Ministry of Education and Research, Stockholm, www.oecd.org/education/schoolresourcesreview.htm.

Teese, R. (2011), "The review of school funding in Western Australia: Background, key research findings and implications", *WA Corporate Executive Briefing*, Perth.

UNICEF (2012), *Developing the Methodology for a Per capita Financing Scheme in General Secondary Education in Kazakhstan and Piloting the Proposed Model*, UNICEF, Astana.

Wang, Y. (ed.) (2013), *Education Policy Reform Trends in G20 Members*, Springer, Dordrecht.

ANNEX 2.A1

National approaches to governing school funding

Table 2.A1.1. **Sources of public funding for education (ISCED 0-3), 2016**

Country	Administrative levels raising public financial resources	Level of education
Austria	Central authority Local authorities	ISCED 0-3 ISCED 0, ISCED 1-3 (state schools)
Belgium (Fl. and Fr.)	Central authority State authorities Regional authorities Local authorities	ISCED 0-3
Chile	Central authority Local authorities	ISCED 0-3
Czech Republic	Central authority Regional authorities Local authorities	ISCED 0-3 ISCED 3 ISCED 0-2
Denmark	Central authority Local authorities	ISCED 0-3 ISCED 0-2
Estonia	Central authority Local authorities	ISCED 0-3
Iceland	Central authority Local authorities	ISCED 3 ISCED 0-2
Israel	Central authority Local authorities	ISCED 0-3
Kazakhstan	Central authority Regional authorities Local authorities	ISCED 0-3
Lithuania	Central authority Local authorities	ISCED 0-3
Portugal	Central authority Regional authorities Local authorities	ISCED 0-3 ISCED 0-2
Slovak Republic	Central authority Local authorities Regional authorities	ISCED 02-3 ISCED 02, ISCED 1-2 ISCED 3
Slovenia	Central authority Local authorities	ISCED 1-3 ISCED 0-2
Spain	Central authority Regional authorities Local authorities	ISCED 0-3
Sweden	Central authority Local authorities	ISCED 0-3
Uruguay	Central authority	ISCED 0-3

Notes: The review team made every effort to ensure, in collaboration with countries, that the information collected through the qualitative survey on school funding is valid and reliable and reflects specific country contexts while being comparable across countries. However, given the qualitative nature of the survey, information should be interpreted with care.

For terms and definitions of levels of education and levels of administration, see Annex B. For country-specific notes to this table, see the end of this annex.

Table 2.A1.2. **Right for public institutions to charge tuition fees (ISCED 0-3), 2016**

Country	Institutions have the right to charge tuition fees	Level of education concerned	Responsibility for determining the level of tuition fees
Austria	Yes	ISCED 0	State authority Local authority
Belgium (Fl.)	No	x	x
Belgium (Fr.)	No	x	x
Chile	No	x	x
Czech Republic	Yes	ISCED 02	Central authority Individual school
Denmark	Yes	ISCED 0	Local authority
Estonia	Yes	ISCED 0	Central authority Local authority
	Yes (vocational)	ISCED 2-3	Other
Iceland	No	x	x
Israel	Yes	ISCED 0-3	Central authority
Kazakhstan	No	ISCED 0-3	x
	Yes (pre-vocational and vocational)	ISCED 3	Individual school
Lithuania	Yes	ISCED 0	Local authority
Portugal	No		x
Slovak Republic	Yes	ISCED 02	Local authority Individual school
Slovenia	Yes	ISCED 0	Local authority
Spain	Yes	ISCED 01	Regional authority Local authority
Sweden	Yes	ISCED 0	Local authority
Uruguay	No	x	x

x: not applicable

Notes: The review team made every effort to ensure, in collaboration with countries, that the information collected through the qualitative survey on school funding is valid and reliable and reflects specific country contexts while being comparable across countries. However, given the qualitative nature of the survey, information should be interpreted with care.

For terms and definitions of levels of education and levels of administration, see Annex B. For country-specific notes to this table, see the end of this annex.

Table 2.A1.3. **Right for public institutions to collect other private contributions (ISCED 0-3), 2016**

Country	Parental voluntary monetary contributions	Parental voluntary non-monetary contributions	Sale of teaching services	Sale of non-teaching services	Rental of materials or facilities	Philanthropy/ Donations	In-kind donations	Other
Austria	✓	✓		✓	✓	✓	✓	✓
Belgium (Fl.)	✓	✓		✓	✓	✓	✓	
Belgium (Fr.)	✓	✓		✓	✓	✓	✓	
Chile	✓	✓		✓	✓	✓	✓	✓
Czech Republic	✓	✓	✓	✓	✓	✓	✓	
Denmark	✓	✓			✓	✓	✓	
Estonia	✓	✓	✓	✓	✓	✓	✓	
Iceland								✓
Israel								✓
Kazakhstan	✓	✓	✓	✓	✓	✓	✓	
Lithuania	✓	✓	✓	✓	✓	✓	✓	
Portugal	✓	✓		✓	✓	✓	✓	
Slovak Republic	✓	✓		✓	✓	✓	✓	
Slovenia	✓	✓		✓	✓	✓	✓	
Spain					✓			
Sweden	✓	✓				✓		

Notes: Private contributions to public pre-schools and schools presented in this table do not include contributions to schools by employers.

Teaching services by individual schools refer to activities outside the scope of formal education such as training for workers in given industries or adult learning more generally.

Non-teaching services by individual schools refer to activities such as catering, hairdressing, car repair or plumbing typically associated with the education offer of a given school.

Philanthropy/Donations refer to donations by firms and non-governmental organisations to individual schools that are measured in monetary terms.

In-kind donations refer to donations by firms and non-governmental organisations to individual schools that are not measured in monetary terms, e.g. goods or services such as school equipment or time given to a school by a firm's staff member.

The review team made every effort to ensure, in collaboration with countries, that the information collected through the qualitative survey on school funding is valid and reliable and reflects specific country contexts while being comparable across countries. However, given the qualitative nature of the survey, information should be interpreted with care.

For terms and definitions of levels of education and levels of administration, see Annex B. For country-specific notes to this table, see the end of this annex.

Table 2.A1.4. **Right for publicly-funded private institutions to charge tuition fees (ISCED 0-3), 2016**

Country	Level of education	Tuition fees	Restrictions
Austria	ISCED 0-3	Yes	None
Belgium (Fl. and Fr.)	ISCED 0-3	No	x
Chile	ISCED 0-3	No	x
Czech Republic	ISCED 0-3	Yes	None
Denmark	ISCED 0-3	Yes	None
Estonia	ISCED 0	Yes	Tuition fees cannot exceed 20% of the state minimum salary if there are not enough places in the pre-school owned by the municipality and the municipality offers a pre-school place through a private provider.
	ISCED 1-3 (general education)	Yes	By law, it is not allowed to increase tuition fees by more than 10% between school years; from 2017 onwards, the increase can be larger than 10%.
	ISCED 2-3 (vocational)	No	x
Iceland	ISCED 0-2	Yes	The local authorities can stipulate restrictions at their own discretion based on locally determined funding formulas.
	ISCED 3	Yes	None
Israel	ISCED 0-1, ISCED 3	Yes	The central education authority (Ministry of Education) specifies the maximum fees that school can collect from parents.
Kazakhstan	ISCED 0	Yes	Fees are set by the school and public grants are excluded from the calculation of the tuition fee.
	ISCED 1-3	Yes	There are 20 Nazarbayev Intellectual Schools that are financed from the central (republic) budget. There are tuition fees at specific years in these schools.
	ISCED 3 (pre-vocational and vocational)	Yes	Tuition fees are set autonomously by the school and should not be less than the fees of students with a public grant (such grants are allocated for students with high academic performance).
Lithuania	ISCED 0-3	Yes	None
Portugal	ISCED 0-3	No	x
Slovak Republic	ISCED 02-3	Yes	None
Slovenia	ISCED 0-3	Yes	Teaching staff salaries must be defined in the same way as in public schools. Tuition fees cannot be used for higher salaries. Otherwise, there are no central or local regulations regarding tuition fees.
Spain	ISCED 0, ISCED 3	Yes	None
Sweden	ISCED 0-3	No	x
Uruguay	ISCED 0-3	No	x

x: not applicable

Notes: Tuition fees refer to the amount of money that students (and their families) have to pay to enrol in educational institutions.
The review team made every effort to ensure, in collaboration with countries, that the information collected through the qualitative survey on school funding is valid and reliable and reflects specific country contexts while being comparable across countries. However, given the qualitative nature of the survey, information should be interpreted with care.
For definition of levels of education, see Annex B. For country-specific notes to this table, see the end of this annex.

Table notes

Table 2.A1.1. Sources of public funding for education

Austria:

Almost all public financial means are raised at the central level and are subsequently allocated by a transfer funding mechanism, the Fiscal Adjustment Act (*Finanzausgleich*), to state (provinces) and local (municipalities) levels. State and local authorities spend these resources according to their respective competences, including in the area of early childhood education and care and school education.

Local authorities contribute through their tax-raising to the financing of early childhood education and care and school education (for state schools only) in their role as school maintainers (*Schulerhalter*) which bear the costs for establishing and maintaining schools and their infrastructure.

Belgium (Fl. and Fr.):

Federal taxes are distributed to all federal entities, including to the Communities, according to a funding formula based, among others, on demographic criteria. Taxes are also levied at sub-central levels and constitute part of the education budget.

The state authorities refer to the three Community authorities in Belgium. This is the level which is politically and administratively responsible for the funding of education in Belgium. Funding goes directly from the Communities to the school providers (school boards).

Regional authorities (i.e. provinces) and local authorities (i.e. cities and municipalities) can contribute resources for school infrastructure or other (non-directly teaching-related) provisions. These provisions do not represent institutional flows between levels, but are rather internal transfers between regional and local authorities, in their role as school providers, and schools.

Chile:

Local authorities (municipalities) are the school providers (*sostenedores*) of public schools and have revenues which may be allocated to the administration of public schools for which they are responsible. In 2012, municipalities raised 11% of the annual budget per student in public school-based education.

Czech Republic:

Table 2.A1.1 provides information for the most common sources of funding. All administrative levels raise funds for all levels of education, depending on the school provider (school founder). Legislation generally does not prohibit the central government, regional or local authorities from founding a school at any level of the education system. However, municipalities are the most common founders of basic education schools (ISCED 0: 98%, ISCED 1: 92%, ISCED 2: 80%), while regions are the most common founders of upper secondary schools (ISCED 3: 94%).

Estonia:

Local authorities also raise revenues for funding vocational education and training if the vocational school is owned by the local authority. This is only the case for schools offering upper secondary education.

Israel:

The central authority (Ministry of Education) pays the teacher salaries at ISCED levels 0-2 directly and transfers funds for teacher salaries to the local authorities (municipalities) for ISCED level 3 and to publicly-funded private providers. For all ISCED levels, the ministry provides funding for special programmes and other services like school renovation and transfers the related funds to the local authorities. It also provides the local authorities with funding for parts of the current expenditures on education (e.g. truant officer, services like concierges, school psychologists, etc.). Local authorities are responsible for the daily maintenance of schools. They cover any additional expenditure from their own revenues and can contribute with their own resources.

Kazakhstan:

Authorities at each administrative level are responsible for the schools and pre-schools under their jurisdiction. Legislative norms play an important role in budget approval negotiations as they determine the education funding levels claimed by regional and local authorities. Funding from higher administrative authorities can be directed to the lower administrative authorities (i.e. from central to regional and from regional to local levels) as part of transfers of a general character (budgetary subventions and budgetary extractions intended to equalise the level of fiscal capacity of regions) and targeted transfers (for instance, as in accordance with the implementation of the State Program of Education and Science Development in the Republic of Kazakhstan for 2016-19).

Portugal:

The autonomous regions of Madeira and the Azores have their own government. It is the competence of each regional parliament to legislate on matters related to the education system of each of these two autonomous regions.

Slovenia:

Table 2.A1.1 illustrates the most common sources of funding. The central level is the predominant provider in the areas of basic schooling (ISCED 1-2: 82%) and upper secondary education (ISCED 3: 99%). The municipalities mainly finance pre-school education (ISCED 0: 92%). For basic and upper secondary schools (ISCED 1-3), the local authorities are free to provide additional funds to ensure higher standards of education and provide additional services.

Table 2.A1.2. Tuition fees in public pre-schools and schools

Austria:

For early childhood education and care (ISCED 0), funding is typically mixed. Funding consists of federal funds, local co-funding as well as parental contributions. The precise funding mechanisms differ strongly between the states (provinces). The fees charged for the attendance of kindergarten before the age of five vary considerably among the states and local authorities. In some states, no tuition fees have to be paid (e.g. in Vienna), in other states fees have to be paid only for full-day care or the amount depends on parental income. The last year of kindergarten before primary education (the children are usually between five and six years old) is free of charge in all states. It is funded by the federal level based on an agreement according to the Federal Constitution Act (article 15a).

Denmark:

There are limits to the tuition fees which early childhood education and care institutions (ISCED 0) can charge. Parents' payments cannot exceed 25% of gross operating expenditure per child.

Estonia:

In early childhood education and care (ISCED 0), the central government decides the upper limit for the tuition fees which can be charged. The local authority as the owner of the pre-school has the right to decide to charge less than the upper limit.

In vocational secondary education (ISCED 2-3), schools are only permitted to charge tuition fees from students as a reimbursement for the cost of study who are not studying at state commissioned study places. The maximum rate for the reimbursement of the costs of education shall be the cost of the student place formed on the basis of state-commissioned education in the relevant curriculum group or relevant curriculum in the same calendar year. In practice, very few students pay tuition fees in public vocational schools.

Israel:

The central education authority determines the possible level of tuition fees in public schools at ISCED levels 0-3 with the approval of the Education Commission in the parliament.

Lithuania:

Tuition fees in early childhood education and care (ISCED 0) can only be charged for catering and educational purposes.

Slovak Republic:

While public institutions at ISCED 02 are allowed to charge tuition fees, no fees can be charged for children aged five, for socially disadvantaged children, and for children placed by court's decision. There are also no tuition fees in schools in hospitals and there is a ceiling for fees in schools run by the central government (mainly special schools). The level of tuition is determined by the local authority. Individual institutions under the authority of the central government can determine the level of tuition fees at ISCED 02 within a ceiling determined by the central authority. This is mostly the case for special schools.

Spain:

Early childhood education and care institutions at ISCED 01 are able to charge tuition fees. The decision to charge tuition fees rests with the regional or local authority. The level of tuition fees is determined by the same authorities using social and economic indicators concerning the schools of which each authority is the provider. From the last year of lower secondary education (ISCED 2) until the end of upper secondary education (ISCED 3), schools charge minimum insurance fees.

Table 2.A1.3. Other private contributions for public pre-school and school education

Austria:

The possibility to receive some of the types of private contributions specified in Table 2.A1.3 requires legal capacity and can thus be given only to federal schools. Schools can also raise private contributions through other means, such as advertisement for non-schooling purposes, for example.

Belgium (Fl.):

In the case of early childhood education and care and primary education (ISCED 0 and 1), parental contributions for extra (non-study) costs are capped at a maximum level and secondary schools (ISCED 2-3) have to comply with an obligation to keep their charges reasonable. Other voluntary donations are only allowed for covering expenses that are not directly related to core education tasks.

Chile:

Philanthropy and donations are regulated by Law No. 19.247. In early childhood education and care (ISCED 01), private providers which operate with funds transferred (*via transferencia de fondos*, VTF) from a specialised pre-school education institution (*Junta Nacional de Jardines Infantiles, JUNJI*) under the supervision of the Ministry of Education, may provide other monetary contributions.

Czech Republic:

The approval of the school provider (municipality or region for public schools) is required for the rental of facilities, materials and other resources that are the property of the school provider.

Denmark:

Public schools are free and schools should provide students with books and other materials necessary for learning without any charges. For example, if the school's teaching requires the use of a computer, the computers should be available to the students for free. There are no regulations on other forms of school-level private contributions to public schools, but this is estimated to only occur to a limited extent. Public schools are, however, not permitted to sell teaching or non-teaching services. At upper secondary level (ISCED 3), vocational schools can provide training for adults for a fee as regulated in legislation, such as the Act on Adult Vocational Education.

Iceland:

Early childhood education and care institutions and schools at ISCED levels 0-2 are permitted to charge fees for learning materials other than textbooks. Schools at ISCED level 3 are permitted to charge registration fees.

Israel:

It is at the discretion of the local authority to make decisions about the possibility of private contributions for public pre-school and school education. For example, local authorities decide about the parents' payments for the child's participation in other educational programmes, tours, etc.

Kazakhstan:

Revenues from paid services are deposited in the cash account of the Treasury and can be distributed according to school interests after consulting the school board or the parents committee. In-kind donations should be reflected in the account balance of school. According to Chapter 9 Article 63 of the Law on Education of the Republic of Kazakhstan (with amendments and additions as of 09.04.2016) governmental educational organisations have a right to offer the following paid services beyond the governmental requirements for education by signing the agreements for provision of paid services: i) realisation of additional educational programmes (child and youth creative development, supporting interests in sport and art, career enhancement training of professionals); ii) organisation of extracurricular activities with dedicated trainees by subjects (disciplines and discipline cycles) during the time outside of classes; iii) organisation of enhanced studies of elements of science with trainees (disciplines and discipline cycles); iv) organisation and implementation of various events – sport competitions, seminars, meetings, conferences for students, teachers and adults, as well as conferences of development and implementation of academic literature; v) offering trainings to use musical instruments and additional network services; vi) organisation of summer breaks, provision of food to students and participants of various events in educational organisations; vii) delivery of heat from power supply plants and boiler-rooms; viii) organisation of vocational training (retraining and further training of qualified human resources and middle rank specialists); ix) organisation and realisation of production of workshops, instructional farms and educational-experimental plots. The sale of non-teaching services, such as health-related services, is only possible in early childhood education and care (ISCED 0).

Slovak Republic:

The sale of non-teaching services by individual schools corresponds to revenues from business activities such as the sale of products. This is mainly relevant for vocational schools.

Sweden:

The Education Act regulates that education is free of cost. Donations and parental voluntary contributions (monetary and non-monetary) are permitted if not attached to specific terms.

Table 2.A1.4. Tuition fees in private early childhood education and care institutions and schools receiving public funding for current expenditure

Austria:

For private pre-school (ISCED 0), there are no general national rules and regulations on tuition fees of private institutions. Also for private schools (ISCED 1-3), the level of tuition fees charged is not regulated.

Chile:

Chile has introduced legislation in 2015 (Law No. 20.845) which progressively introduces school education free of charge in schools that receive public funding. Since the school year 2016, all public schools have been free of charge. Also, all early childhood education and care with public funding is to be free of charge.

Denmark:

The amount of the tuition fees is decided by the schools themselves.

Estonia:

In vocational secondary education (ISCED 2-3), it is not permitted to private schools receiving public funding to charge tuition fees.

Israel:

There are few independent private schools. Private schools referred to in this table are government-dependent private schools.

Kazakhstan:

Fees for early childhood education and care (ISCED 0) which operates within the framework of a public-private partnership are set by the public authority.

In pre-vocational and vocational upper secondary education (ISCED 3), fees for the education of a student with a public grant are defined by the central government or by a decree of the local authority.

Portugal:

Schools operating with "Association Contracts" (*Contratos de Associação*) receive public funds for their current expenditure. However, private schools cannot charge tuition fees to students covered by this type of contracts.

Chapter 3

Distributing school funding

This chapter presents an overview of different mechanisms used to allocate funding, whether this is between different levels of education administration or to individual schools. It presents a set of guiding questions that policy makers can follow in designing a funding allocation model that is aligned to the school system's governance structures. The chapter describes different approaches that countries take in distributing funding for current expenditures and capital expenditures. For current expenditures, the analysis focuses on the design of funding formulas that can be adjusted to support policy objectives aiming for greater efficiency, equity and quality. The chapter presents a range of policy options with key principles that can support the design and implementation of more effective funding mechanisms.

This chapter presents an overview of how different countries distribute funding. The focus is on the design of different mechanisms used to allocate funding, whether this is between different levels of education administration or to individual schools. The chapter is organised in three main sections. First, it presents the basic questions to be considered in designing a funding allocation model that is aligned to the school system's governance structures. Second, it presents approaches taken by OECD review countries in the allocation of funding for current expenditures and looks in particular at the design of funding formulas and considerations for related information needs. Third, it presents approaches taken by OECD review countries in the allocation of funding for capital expenditure. Finally, based on this overview of research and OECD review analysis of country practices, it presents a set of policy options for designing more effective allocation mechanisms. A profile of funding transfers between different administrative levels and to schools is provided for countries participating in the OECD review in Annex A.

Basic questions in designing a funding allocation model

The European Commission/Eurydice (2000) identified two factors in deciding on a procedure for determining the volume of resources to be allocated to schools: the responsibilities of those involved in the allocation, and the methods used to calculate the amount of resources allocated. However, there is in general a dearth of available research on the strengths and weaknesses of different funding models (Atkinson et al., 2005). This section presents a series of guiding questions that can be followed in designing a funding allocation model that best fits the established governance structure. It also shows some examples of how countries have reformed funding mechanisms to align to and support major changes in the governance structure of the school system (see Box 3.1).

Box 3.1. **Governance changes and the introduction of new funding allocation mechanisms**

In **New Zealand**, there was a significant change to educational governance structure in 1989 when the regional education boards were abolished and boards of trustees (composed primarily of parents) were made responsible for administering and managing individual schools. The former system of central regulation and funding supporting regional education boards that governed primary schools was broadly criticised as overly bureaucratic and not responding to student and local community needs (Ministry of Education, New Zealand, 2010). This change in school governance structure led to a change in how funding was allocated. State schools receive funding via four main allocation mechanisms (New Zealand Ministry of Education, 2015). First, each school is provided staffing entitlement in the form of a number of full-time teacher equivalents. The Crown directly meets the salary cost of teachers employed using staffing entitlement. The staffing entitlement received by a school is calculated using standard formula relating to school type, number of students and year level. The boards of trustees employ school principals and

---

Box 3.1. **Governance changes and the introduction of new funding allocation mechanisms** (*cont.*)

teachers. Pay and working conditions are centrally negotiated between unions and the Ministry of Education. Second, schools receive operational funding from the Ministry of Education in cash. This is based on a number of factors including: school type student number; Year level of students; socio-economic status of the community (a decile rated system 1 to 10); and schools location (adjustments for isolated schools). Third, the Ministry of Education may also directly provide schools with services and programmes (e.g. subsidised computers for teaching staff and in-service training). Fourth, the Ministry of Education centrally provides schools with property and building. Schools receive a five-yearly funding allocation to upgrade and modernise schools property. This must be spent according to a property plan prepared by the school and agreed by the ministry. Funding for additional property or major redevelopments is allocated on a needs basis and often the delivery of these projects is centrally managed by the ministry. The board of trustees controls the school's finances and is audited annually by the government's auditor (each school prepares an annual report on financial accounts for the Office of the Auditor-General). The professional standards for schools principals include the ability to effectively manage and administer finance, property and health and safety systems.

In the **Czech Republic**, a significant reform of public administration in 2002 saw the creation of 14 self-governing regions, including Prague the capital city (Shewbridge et al., 2016a). This move away from a centralised governance structure notably gave the 14 regions autonomy to govern their own education system. The Czech regions mainly operate schools providing upper secondary education. There are over 6 000 self-governing municipalities in the Czech Republic, of which only 453 are urban municipalities. Municipalities operate pre-school and basic schools (primary and lower secondary education), although not all Czech municipalities have a school. All current expenditures of schools are divided into two categories: the "direct costs" (central funding) and the "operational costs" (local funding). A central grant is allocated to regions using per student normative amounts to cover the direct costs which are regulated by the state. These include primarily salaries for teachers and other staff, textbooks, teaching aids, further professional development of teachers and other expenditures resulting from labour laws. Thus, for example, if the central government decides to increase teacher salaries or to strengthen curriculum, it has the mechanism to raise the national normative amounts to compensate local governments for the increased expenditures. The regions are responsible for allocating this funding to all schools on their territory (including municipal schools). The operational costs of schools are locally funded as expenditures depend on many diverse factors and on local prices of inputs. This component includes maintenance of schools, energy expenditures (heating, electricity, gas), communal services (provision of water, utilisation of garbage) and small repairs. A separate financial stream concerns investments in schools. This is the responsibility of school providers, that is, municipalities for basic schools and regions for secondary schools and private providers.

In **England (United Kingdom)**, a major reform to local government in 1972 saw the introduction of two tiers of local government, county and district councils, with the upper tier (counties) responsible for education. Since then, there have been a series of reforms and mergers of either counties and districts or various districts into "unitary authorities" to reduce the overall number of authorities and councillors. Counties remain responsible for education, including special educational needs, adult education and pre-school – in 2017 there were 27 county councils and 125 unitary authorities (which carry out all local government functions) (Sandford, 2016).

Box 3.1. **Governance changes and the introduction of new funding allocation mechanisms** (*cont.*)

In an overview of governance and funding distribution changes over the period 1988 to 2007, Levačić (2008) distinguishes three main periods in the governance of public schools: establishing local management of schools (1988-97), New Labour and consolidation (1997-2002) and centralising Labour (2002-07) (Labour being the major left-wing political party). From 1998 to 2002 schools were delegated greater financial responsibilities, while local authorities remained responsible for distributing central funding to public schools with a high degree of discretion (local authorities received a block grant from central authorities). However, local authorities were required to use a funding formula to allocate funding to public schools and this was to be mainly driven by student numbers and characteristics. In addition, the central government detailed a set of indicators that should be included in local funding formula. Over this period there were increasing tensions between central and local authorities surrounding the distribution mechanism and this culminated in the introduction of a centrally determined Dedicated Schools Grant in 2006/07, replacing the traditional block grant to local authorities.

In 2016, the Conservative government (right wing) has introduced some simplifications to the overall allocation mechanism to introduce greater flexibility at the local level: the block grants for schools are split into 3 notional blocks (schools block; early years block; high needs block) and most separate grants (targeted funding) have been incorporated into this major grant; and local authority funding formulas have been simplified, including 2 mandatory factors (minimum amounts per primary and secondary student; deprivation – using either an income deprivation index or free school meals data) and up to 12 other optional factors (e.g. sparsity/rural areas, prior attainment).

The introduction of academies (publicly-funded private schools outside the control of local authorities which receive funding directly from central authorities) constitutes a further key development in the governance and funding of school education in England. The academy school model was initiated under the Labour government in the early 2000s to address concerns about the quality of education in some local authorities, usually serving urban inner-city disadvantaged neighbourhoods, and was extended under successive Conservative governments. Like public schools run by local authorities, academies must follow legislation and guidance on admissions, exclusions and special educational needs and disabilities, but they benefit from greater autonomy (e.g. for setting pay and conditions for their staff or for changing the length of school terms). Publicly-funded private schools can operate as single academy trusts or under an umbrella of a multi-academy trusts.

Source: Levačić, R. (2008), "Financing schools: Evolving patterns of autonomy and control", *Educational Management Administration and Leadership*, http://dx.doi.org/10.1177/1741143207087774; New Zealand Ministry of Education (2015), *Education Report: Funding Review – Draft Stock-Takes and Next Steps*, https://education.govt.nz/ministry-of-education/consultations-and-reviews/education-funding-system-review; Shewbridge, C. et al. (2016a), *OECD Reviews of School Resources: Czech Republic 2016*, http://dx.doi.org/10.1787/9789264262379-en; Sandford, M. (2016), "Local government in England: Structures", *House of Commons Library Briefing Papers*, http://researchbriefings. files.parliament.uk/documents/SN07104/SN07104.pdf; OECD (2015), *Education Policy Outlook: United Kingdom*, www.oecd.org/education/policyoutlook.htm.

Who is responsible for the final allocation to schools?

As presented in Chapter 2, in many systems there is a complex distribution of responsibilities for funding transfers in the education sector. Funding may be initially transferred between different levels of authorities and may be specified for a particular educational purpose (earmarked funding), for compulsory education (block grant) or generally allocated for use in the public sector (lump sum funding) (see next section).

Depending on the type of conditions set in the initial transfer of funds, this will influence the degree of freedom that the authorities with final responsibility for allocating funds to school will have. Responsibilities may differ according to the resource category also. These distinctions are explored more in the sections on current expenditure and capital expenditure. Broadly, OECD (2016) data indicate three groupings of countries according to whether the major proportion of public funding to schools is allocated by local, regional, state or central authorities (Table 3.1).

Table 3.1. **Final stage in the transfer of public funds to schools, 2013**

Share of sources of public funds by level of government (after transfers between levels of government)

	Local	Regional	Central
Local authorities allocate the major proportion of resources			
United States	98	2	0
Norway	95	x	5
Poland	94	2	4
Finland	90	x	10
Canada	86	11	3
Latvia	76	x	24
Lithuania	74	x	26
Iceland	73	x	27
Slovak Republic	72	x	28
Korea	70	30	1
United Kingdom	59	x	41
State/regional authorities allocate the major proportion of resources			
Argentina	2	96	2
Australia	..	95	5
Japan	17	81	2
Spain	6	80	14
Mexico	0	73	27
Germany	22	72	6
Belgium	3	72	25
Czech Republic	26	62	12
Switzerland	39	60	0
Austria	12	49	39
Central authorities allocate the major proportion of resources			
New Zealand	0	x	100
Netherlands	11	0	89
Hungary	12	x	88
Slovenia	12	x	88
Turkey	..	15	85
Colombia	9	6	85
Luxembourg	16	x	84
Ireland	17	x	83
Italy	11	8	81
Portugal	15	6	79
France	12	17	71
Israel	30	x	70
Estonia	38	x	62
Chile	44	x	56
OECD average	**36**	**23**	**41**

.. : included in a different column of the table

x: not applicable

Note: "Regional" data refer to the first territorial unit below the national level. In federal countries this will be a state.

Source: OECD (2016), *Education at a Glance 2016: OECD Indicators*, http://dx.doi.org/10.1787/eag-2016-en.

The approach with allocation of funding mainly at the local level is typified by the United States where school districts have the major responsibility for funding allocation and there is a limited role for the states. Among the OECD review countries, Denmark, Lithuania, the Slovak Republic and Sweden also see local authorities allocating the major proportion of funding. In Denmark, Lithuania and Sweden this concerns the municipal authorities and in the Slovak Republic this concerns the school providers, whether municipal authorities, regional authorities or private schools.

The approach with allocation of funding mainly at the state level is typified by Australia where the states and territories have the major responsibility for funding allocation and there is a limited role for the Australian government, although the local level also plays an important role in funding allocation. A recent review of funding allocation in Australia noted the benefits that distribution via "systems" (government schools; Catholic schools; independent schools) brings as they can achieve efficiencies through economies of scale and use local knowledge of schools and communities to distribute funding to where it is most needed (Gonski et al., 2011). In particular, larger systems had the capacity to apply a greater range of measures of need in their funding formulas for distributing to individual schools and also had greater flexibility to provide additional support to schools where necessary, e.g. rural/remote schools, new schools, schools in financial difficulty. Among the OECD review countries, Austria (the provinces), Belgium (the Communities), the Czech Republic (the regions) and Spain (autonomous communities) have the major proportion of funding allocated at the regional or state level. However, in all cases authorities at different levels play a significant role in funding allocation also.

Finally, the approach with allocation of funding at the central level is typified by New Zealand where all funding is distributed by the New Zealand government directly to schools, as regional level authorities were abolished in 1989 (see Box 3.1). Among the OECD review countries, Uruguay provides an example of a system where funding is distributed directly from the central level to schools. There are four central education councils, each with responsibility to transfer resources in kind to schools in a particular sector. In Chile, Colombia, Israel, Luxembourg, Portugal and Slovenia, central authorities allocate the major proportion of funding to schools. However, in all cases local authorities also play a role in allocating funding to schools, most significantly in Chile and Israel.

As can be seen in Table 3.1, in many systems there is a complex mix of responsibilities for the final allocation of funding to schools. The balance of these responsibilities can be changed according to major governance changes (see for example the cases of New Zealand and the Czech Republic in Box 3.1) but also may be influenced by different conditions set on funding transfers between different administrative levels and/or central regulatory frameworks (see the example of England, the United Kingdom, in Box 3.1) and also by the use of targeted funding external to the main allocation mechanisms. These concepts will be further explored and illustrated below.

What conditions (if any) are set for funding allocation?

Different conditions can be set when a grant is allocated and these can have considerable influence on how the money is spent. A greater degree of decentralisation in funding allocation means that decision makers are better able to account for the particular needs of individual schools; but there is an increased likelihood of different treatment for schools across a country (see Chapter 2). The response to objectively similar circumstances will not always be the same (European Commission/Eurydice, 2000). A greater degree of centralisation can support greater transparency with all schools treated in a similar way; but it is difficult to take account of particular individual circumstances.

Conditions set by higher level authorities on initial funding transfers

Even if a local authority is responsible for funding allocation, central authorities may specify how (for what purpose) the money should be spent. The various restrictions with which local or regional authorities may need to comply provide a good indication of their room for manoeuvre (Atkinson et al., 2005).

Lump sum transfer. The greatest degree of administrative freedom is granted to local authorities when funding is transferred as a lump sum. The lump sum mechanism leaves discretion to sub-central authorities over the proportion allocated to school education. Among the OECD review countries, Belgium, Denmark and Sweden transfer lump sum grants to regional/state or local authorities (municipalities in Denmark and Sweden; the Flemish Community and the French Community of Belgium). Burns and Köster (2016) find that lump sum funding, along with stronger roles for stakeholders, horizontal accountability and the use of performance indicators to hold local authorities accountable, have helped move away from a hierarchical relationship between central, regional and local authorities to more mutual independence and self-regulation. However, establishing a fair allocation of resources may be more difficult for authorities with budgetary responsibilities for education and other sectors, as there is a need to be fair to schools and other public sectors (European Commission/Eurydice, 2000). Pressure on resources from other services may restrict funding to schools (Atkinson et al., 2005). It is also challenging to identify how much of the variation in expenditures across municipalities can be attributed to differences in municipal income (despite some equalisation via the central allocation), differences in socio-economic contexts and differences in how much public education is prioritised (Chapter 2).

Block grant. There may be funding allocated with the condition that it is spent on a certain type of expenditure, that is, current expenditure or capital expenditure. A block grant consists of funds that lower level authorities are required to use for current expenditure in pre-school or school education at their own discretion. This, therefore, leaves a high degree of discretion over the proportion of the grant that will be allocated to different categories of current expenditure, such as salaries, operational costs, and also over the amount allocated to each school (in the case that the local authority is responsible for more than one school).

Among the OECD review countries, Iceland transfers funding to municipalities in the form of a block grant for compulsory education; and for upper secondary education the bulk of the central transfer in the form of a block grant direct to schools (the central authorities are responsible for operating costs in upper secondary schools). In the Slovak Republic, the major funding transfer to school providers (regions, municipalities and private schools) comprises one block grant for salaries and operational costs. School providers are free to use this grant for any type of expenditure. However, there are limits imposed for the reallocation of funding among schools, with school providers permitted to reallocate a maximum of 10% of the grant calculated for salary costs and 20% of the grant calculated for operational costs. The OECD review in the Slovak Republic found that this gave flexibility to better meet local needs and to respond to difficulties some schools may experience in financing all their costs (Santiago et al., 2016a). However, funding for professional development is included in the block grant for salary costs (1.5% of the school's allocated amount for salaries) and the OECD review found that teachers reported difficulties in accessing professional development due to a lack of financial support from the school budget. In this context, it could be useful to earmark a certain percentage of the salary grant for professional development, or to set strong expectations that this proportion is spent on professional development or to give each teacher a personal allowance for professional development (Santiago et al., 2016a). In Chile, the major funding transfer to school providers (municipal authorities and private education providers) is a block grant for general education, but this is complemented by a series of earmarked funds and school-specific funds, e.g. to support students with special educational needs or to reward top performing schools respectively.

Earmarked grant. Central authorities may impose greater restriction by specifying a purpose for the grant. An earmarked grant consists of funds that lower level authorities are required to use for specific elements/items of current expenditure in pre-school or school education (e.g. teacher salaries).

In Estonia, the central authorities transfer a set of different earmarked funds to school providers (municipalities and private school operators) for specific educational purposes, the major funding transfer being for general education and covering teacher and school leader salaries and professional development, study materials and school lunches. The OECD review in Estonia found that the use of earmarked funding for teacher salaries offers the advantage that the costs of national policy decisions to raise minimum teacher salaries are not fully imposed on local authorities (Santiago et al., 2016b). It also makes it easy for the national government to ensure that funding has been spent for its specified purpose. In the Czech Republic, the central authorities transfer an earmarked grant to the higher tier of sub-central authorities (regions) to cover the "direct costs of education", including teacher and learning support staff salaries, textbooks and teaching aids and teacher further professional development. Similarly, the OECD review in the Czech Republic found that this allowed national authorities to align funding to policy changes on salaries and the curriculum (Shewbridge et al., 2016a) (see also Box 3.1). In Lithuania the central authorities transfer an earmarked grant for "teaching costs" to sub-central authorities (municipalities) calculated for each individual school, comprising teacher salaries, management, administration and professional support staff, textbooks for students and some school materials, teacher in-service training and pedagogical and psychological support services provided by local authorities. The use of earmarked funding for teaching costs enabled the national government to ensure a degree of control over the quality of education delivered in schools (Herczynski, 2011).

School-specific grant. Finally, the most restrictive type of transfer from central to lower level authorities implies reduced or no administrative discretion to reallocate funding among different schools (in the case that a local authority is responsible for more than one school). A school-specific grant consists of funds that lower level authorities are required to use for current expenditure in specific schools. In Chile, school-specific funds are allocated to reward top performing schools.

Conditions set on funding transfers to schools

Equally, different conditions can be set when allocating funds to individual schools. As noted, these funding allocations may come directly from central authorities or via other administrative levels. Depending on the type of conditions set, schools will have more or less freedom in administering the school budget. For an overview of different levels of school autonomy over the use of resources see Chapter 2.

Funds administered by the school

Schools enjoy most freedom over how to spend funding when they receive a block grant. The allocation of a block grant implies that the school may use this funding at its full discretion across all areas of spending. Authorities may impose some conditions on the particular area of spending that the funding should be used for, e.g. for non-teacher salary spending or operating costs, and transfer a restricted block grant. For example, in the Slovak Republic, the school provider must approve a school's request to use part of the salaries grant for operational costs, or vice versa.

Authorities may impose stricter conditions by transferring an earmarked grant. Fazekas (2012) cites the use of earmarked funding as a way for higher level authorities to constrain the school's room for manoeuvre. An earmarked grant is for a specific expenditure item or items, e.g. extra funds for special educational needs or teacher professional development, which the school is required to respect in its administration of the funds.

Resources received in kind or directly paid for/purchased by a body external to the school

Finally, schools may not receive funding directly and not administer the funds. Rather, the school receives resources in kind and/or costs are directly paid for by the relevant authority. In this case, a dedicated grant is issued for a specific use, e.g. teacher salaries or operating costs are paid directly by the relevant authority. Among the OECD review countries, dedicated grants are used for salary costs in Austria, the Flemish and French Communities of Belgium and Israel (all using a funding formula) and for both salary and operational costs in Chile and Uruguay (determined by administrative discretion/on a historical basis). In New Zealand, the Crown directly funds salary costs of teachers and principals employed using staffing entitlement (see Box 3.1). The salary costs of any additional staff (including teaching staff) are met by schools directly through their operational grant funding. An ongoing review of the funding mechanisms is careful to note that a block grant allocation to schools, inclusive of the salary cost of teachers, would not be introduced. This approach was experimented with in the 1980s and met with strong opposition from many stakeholders.

In Austria, there is a dual system for funding teachers at the federal and provincial levels, which sets some unintended incentives, including the possibility for provincial governments to overspend in general compulsory schools. Although the transfer is based on agreed staff plans, the federal government has no control over how provincial governments use these funds, including on policies to support small rural schools that lead to overspending. The OECD review in Austria recommended that the federal government fund all teachers directly, rather than the current complex transfer arrangement of teacher funding through the provincial administrations (Nusche et al., 2016b). Municipalities and provincial governments would continue to be responsible for funding maintenance costs and infrastructure investments.

What proportion of funding is distributed through the main allocation mechanism?

An important consideration in designing a funding allocation model is to determine how much of the public funding for schooling will be distributed via the main allocation mechanism and how much via other mechanisms (external to the main allocation mechanism), such as targeted funding offered via special programmes.

In the context of designing a funding formula as the main mechanism to distribute funding to schools, Levačić and Ross (1999) present several arguments for retaining a proportion of funding at the central level, including: the need to allow for short term or emergency expenditures with uneven incidence across schools (e.g. structural repairs, early staff retirement); where the central/local authorities hold statutory responsibilities for certain programmes; where central provision would allow significant economies of scale; situations where it is judged that schools would not make adequate provision (e.g. in-service training for staff); when the central level owns the school buildings; and earmarked grants for certain central projects.

Funding mechanisms external to the main allocation mechanism offer a certain degree of flexibility to the overall funding model and if well designed can offer important benefits. Burns and Köster (2016) identify the essential role of policy experimentation and risk-taking for innovation and the evolution of education systems. In this context, targeted funding can provide flexibility within the overall funding model to support pilots of innovative policies. For examples from Austria, the Czech Republic and Denmark, see Box 3.2.

Box 3.2. **Examples of targeted funds for specific programmes and priorities**

In **Austria**, federal funding is set aside for priority projects like the New Secondary School reform and the promotion of all-day schooling. However, the OECD review in Austria noted that the provision of targeted funding is not always sufficient incentive: the expansion of all-day schooling is slower than expected and provincial authorities had not requested all the available funds (Nusche et al., 2016b).

The **Czech Republic** uses a number of specific education grants to fund development programmes, that is, specific experimental or piloting programmes and new educational initiatives (Shewbridge et al., 2016a). These initiatives are often developed or proposed by some groups of teachers or by locally active and not well resourced non-governmental organisations, so require financial support from the state to be really tested. If these development programmes show positive outcomes, they may be expanded and eventually integrated into mainstream financing scheme, or they will be discontinued. The OECD review in the Czech Republic noted that, in this way, the use of targeted funding supports policy experimentation and by supporting localised, innovative projects can be a fruitful way to test out different approaches to address identified challenges in the education system.

In **Denmark**, there are very few specific or earmarked grants for compulsory public education (the *Folkeskole*) and these represent very low amounts compared to the overall spending in schools – compulsory education is almost exclusively financed by the lump sum from central government and local tax income (Nusche et al., 2016a). A recent example of earmarked funding is a grant for teacher competency development and a grant to facilitate implementation of the 2014 reform in compulsory public education. A key goal of the 2014 reform is to ensure that every teacher has the competencies and qualifications for the subjects they teach by 2020. The related central grant is earmarked to finance the necessary courses and written examinations for teachers to upgrade their skills (although schools must fund the release time for teachers to participate in these).

Source: Nusche, D. et al. (2016b), *OECD Reviews of School Resources: Austria 2016*, http://dx.doi.org/10.1787/9789264256729-en; Shewbridge, C. et al. (2016a), *OECD Reviews of School Resources: Czech Republic 2016*, http://dx.doi.org/10.1787/9789264262379-en; Nusche, D. et al. (2016a), *OECD Reviews of School Resources: Denmark 2016*, http://dx.doi.org/10.1787/9789264262430-en.

At the same time, there is an argument that efficiency is improved the greater the proportion of funding that is included in the main allocation mechanism. Levačić (2008) found that the efficiency of the allocation mechanisms from central authorities in England (United Kingdom) increased between 1998 and 2002 due to the fact that an increasing proportion of overall funding was delegated to schools, with only major capital expenditures and a few local services excluded from the main funding allocation. This was coupled by a requirement that the major proportion of local funding formula be driven by student numbers and characteristics.

Fazekas (2012) pinpoints the phenomenon of an increase in use of targeted funding programmes – external to the main allocation mechanism – as a direct result of high level authority frustration at not knowing how the allocated funding has been used at the school level. In the United Kingdom and the United States, for example, there was a growing concern that even if public authorities can determine and allocate the adequate amount of resources, it is unclear how schools spend the resources, particularly in settings where they are free to manage the allocated block grants. Levačić et al. (2000) warn that the accretion of numerous targeted funds can lead to a piece-meal re-centralisation of funding and undermine the advantages of formula funding. This also weakens administrative efficiency and a proliferation of "added on" grants can lead to obscurity of the funding mechanism. Chapter 5 discusses the administrative burden of monitoring and evaluating the use of targeted funding.

In Uruguay, there are over 130 programmes targeted at improving equity in education which involve the funding of specific groups of students or schools, including programmes for teachers, the provision of free meals in public primary schools, summer school programmes to extend the school year in selected schools and free transportation for all primary school students (Santiago et al., 2016c). The OECD review in Uruguay noted that the use of targeted funding conveys policy objectives and responds to emerging needs in the school system (e.g. a digital learning priority); it also promotes greater vertical equity (for definitions of equity, see Annex 1.A1). However, the multitude of programmes reduces transparency of funding to schools and makes the funding allocation complex and potentially inefficient due to the risk of duplication of efforts, a lack of co-ordination and greater administrative costs.

In Chile, a series of additional grants – external to the basic per capita grant – has been introduced to better address inequities, the major one being the preferential education grant that targets schools with at least 15% of their student population being socio-economically vulnerable, but also grants targeting rural or other specified areas, maintenance costs, special educational provision (Santiago et al., forthcoming). The OECD review in Chile found that the use of targeted funding has helped to address inequities and respond to new policy priorities, such as full-day schooling and an extended coverage of pre-school. However, the overall funding system has become overly complex over time with many different components. The growing share of grants earmarked for specific purposes has introduced high transaction costs, including those related to monitoring how the funding is used, and imposed restrictions on schools that often mean a less efficient allocation of resources at the school level.

How is the amount allocated to schools determined?

The OECD review has identified a range of different bases used to determine the amount of funding allocated to schools. Broadly speaking, there are four main approaches to funding allocation (OECD, 2012; Levačić, 2008; European Commission/Eurydice, 2000):

● Administrative discretion, which is based on an individual assessment of the amount of resources that each school needs. Although it can serve schools' needs more accurately, it requires extensive knowledge of each school and measures to prevent misuse of resources. While it might involve the use of indicators, the final allocation might not necessarily correspond to the calculations and these would not be universally applied to all schools.

- Incremental costs, which takes into consideration the historical expenditure to calculate the allocation for the following year with minor modifications to take into account specific changes (e.g. student numbers, school facilities, input prices). Administrative discretion and incremental costs are often combined, and usually these are used in centralised systems.

- Bidding and bargaining, which involves schools responding to open competitions for additional funding offered via participation in a particular programme or making a case for additional resources.

- Formula funding, which involves the use of objective criteria with a universally applied rule to establish the amount of resources that each school is entitled to. The relevant authority uses a formally defined procedure (a formula) to determine the level of public funds allocated based on a set of predetermined criteria, which in most cases are input-, output- or performance-oriented. These predetermined criteria are impartially applied to each recipient (e.g. sub-central authority or school). Formula funding relies on a mathematical formula which contains a number of variables, each of which has a coefficient attached to it to determine school budgets (Levačić, 2008). Formulas typically contain four main groups of variables (Levačić and Ross, 1999): i) basic: student number and grade level-based; ii) needs-based; iii) curriculum or educational programme-based; and iv) school characteristics-based.

The European Commission/Eurydice (2000) noted that methods based on the needs of a given school (i.e. administrative discretion and bidding and bargaining) are more direct than those based on a set of indicators of needs. In general, the greater the number of schools that authorities are responsible for, the harder it is to be aware of specific school needs and the more reliant they will be on indicators.

However, the distribution of funding on a discretionary or incremental basis is rarely efficient or equitable and tends to be associated with low levels of budget transparency (OECD/The World Bank, 2015). When funding is allocated on a historical basis, this funds existing staff year after year and typically involves the payment of invoices submitted by schools for supplementary costs (Levačić and Ross, 1999). Schools have no incentives to reduce their expenditures or increase their efficiency. Nor do they have incentives to improve the quality of their provision (European Commission/Eurydice, 2000). As noted in the OECD Review of School Resources in Kazakhstan, schools have incentives to run into deficits with the hope that others absorb them and to inflate their expenditures with the aim of obtaining larger allocations in subsequent years – a practice known as "deficit budgeting" (OECD/ The World Bank, 2015). Negotiation processes are driven by the relative priorities and strengths of local actors. Such perverse incentives lead to extensive regulation with a system of "norms" used to lower the expected allocation.

In Germany, 7 of the 16 states (*Länder*) determine supplementary funding to support the education of migrant children on the basis of the professional judgement of local school administrators (Table 3.2). While this offers the advantages to help address needs at the right time and control costs from year to year, it holds the disadvantages that some schools may receive less than their fair share of funding where school administrators underestimate funding needs and there have been heated parliamentary debates about the lack of transparency (Sugarman et al., 2016). Similarly, while the allocation of funding to schools based on the amount received in the previous year offers schools an accurate forecast of income, this may inhibit the expansion of schools with high educational demand, while supporting those whose development is lagging behind (European Commission/Eurydice, 2000).

The use of formula funding provides a high degree of transparency to the allocation system and when linked to the number of students provides good forecasting of public expenditure (European Commission/Eurydice, 2000). While administrative discretion plays an important role in funding allocation in many countries, the use of formula funding is well suited for the distribution of current expenditure and many countries have introduced this. The sections on current expenditure and capital expenditure below present an overview of different mechanisms used by countries. Broadly, among OECD review countries the major bases for determining funding allocation include: for current expenditure funding formula, administrative discretion, historical basis and negotiated process (Tables 3.A1.1 and 3.A1.2 and Annex A); and for capital expenditure the assessment of needs, administrative discretion and a competitive basis (Annex A).

How to ensure allocation mechanisms remain optimal?

The OECD review has highlighted the importance of conducting a periodic review of funding allocation mechanisms. The Ministry of Education, New Zealand (13 May 2015) provides some helpful insights into recent funding reviews conducted in Australia and in some of the Australian states and in England and Northern Ireland (United Kingdom). The funding reviews share some common procedural and design aspects. With the exception of England (United Kingdom), there is a substantive role for an independent body (whether an existing independent agency/office/commission or a panel of independent researchers) in providing recommendations for reform, with government officials providing administrative, data and analytical support. Indeed, two recent reviews in the Flemish Community of Belgium were conducted by the Belgian Court of Audit and a consortium of researchers commissioned by the Flemish Minister of Education (Nusche et al., 2015). In England (United Kingdom), the government led the review process, with an open and continued call for stakeholder input, but with an initial steering from the government to reach agreement on the broad aim of the review and intended direction of reform. Other common elements of the various funding reviews include:

- A *clear mandate for the review*: focus, scope and timeline; details of how the review sits within the broader policy context (e.g. ongoing reform plans).
- *Information on mechanisms for collecting evidence*: Consultation of stakeholders (in person, online surveys, online platform for submission of views/evidence); analysis of funding in a sample of schools (selection principles); research.

For example, the review commissioned by the Flemish government on school operating grants relied on a mix of qualitative interviews in 20 schools, a survey of school principals and a survey of municipalities (Nusche et al., 2015), whereas the Belgian Court of Audit's review of operating budgets relied on a direct analysis of school accounts.

How to ensure effective implementation of a new funding allocation mechanism?

A crucial aspect that should not be overlooked is that, no matter how well designed a new funding allocation mechanism is, there will always be winners and losers when implementing a new model unless additional resources are made available. Experiences in many countries highlight the importance of effectively managing the political economy of funding reform and also having a realistic estimate of the costs involved.

Political economy and stakeholder consultation

A World Bank (2011) study on the implementation of funding formula (per capita financing) in Armenia, Estonia, Georgia, Lithuania, Poland and the Russian Federation underlined the importance that policy makers pay sufficient attention to political economy pressures. The decline in school-age population in all countries studied put pressure on the efficiency gains expected with the introduction of per capita financing. The World Bank (2011) found that the incentives put in place by funding formula may be no match to the political economy pressures of keeping teachers on the payroll, transferring them to bigger schools, or finding alternative employment for them within the school system.

In Austria, there is a debate to introduce socio-economic criteria into the funding formula. The OECD review in Austria noted that while social partners support the introduction of an index-based formula, there may be political opposition from some provinces with a large share of rural schools, as such a formula would likely result in the redistribution of funding from rural to urban schools (since there are high concentrations of students from disadvantaged backgrounds in cities) (Nusche et al., 2016b).

In England (United Kingdom), Levačić (2008) argues that tensions between central and local authorities hindered the development of a rationally based and stable allocative mechanism over the period 1998-2007. Towards the end of this period, the government proposed to reform the allocation mechanism for the central grant for education (dedicated schools grant) to local authorities by introducing a needs-based formula but this met with tough political opposition. The proposed introduction of a needs-based formula aimed to achieve a more equitable and fairer distribution of funding to local authorities. However, in the face of political opposition, the government committed to ensuring each school received at least the national average and based this on historical funding levels (per student expenditure in 2005/06) – thus negating any of the expected benefits for equity and efficiency from the introduction of a national needs-based funding formula. The current government has held an initial consultation with stakeholders to introduce a national needs-based formula and this revealed broad support for the proposed reform (UK Department for Education, 2016). However, implementation has been delayed until 2018/19 as announced by the Education Secretary to underline "the importance of consulting widely and fully with the sector and getting implementation right" (Greening, 2016). Indeed, this is echoed in literature produced by the Ministry of Education in New Zealand in its ongoing review of the funding model, where "the need to bring stakeholders along on the journey" is emphasised.

Implementation costs

In the World Bank (2011) study, Armenia was the country that had seen most success in increasing the student-teacher ratio and there were two important factors to aid implementation: strong political commitment and additional funding provided for teacher redundancy packages. These two factors were also highlighted in the OECD review in Lithuania: the fact that the 2005 education law had made municipal authorities responsible for school network consolidation had supported the efficiency incentives set by the per capita funding formula; however, the OECD review underlined the need to secure funding to offer attractive redundancy packages to teachers (Shewbridge et al., 2016b).

Another example of the costs of implementation comes from the Flemish Community of Belgium, where recent changes to the system of distributing operating grants and staffing went in line with substantial increases in the overall budget (Nusche et al., 2015). In response to a major review of the funding model in Australia, the government explicitly made the promise that no school would lose funding (Australian Government, 2010). The aim of the review of the funding model was to better ensure adequate funding for students with greater educational needs and as such the government needed to commit significant additional resources to implement the funding reform.

Box 3.3. **Overview: Key questions in designing funding allocation mechanisms**

Who is responsible for the final allocation to schools?

- Central, regional or local authorities or school providers (i.e. division between authorities and private school operators); a mix of these (most typical) and if so, how clear are funding responsibilities?

- Which resource categories does this apply to? Current expenditures (Staff; operational costs); Capital expenditures (infrastructure; investment); or a mix of these? Is it clear which authority is responsible for allocating which resource category?

What conditions (if any) are set for funding allocation?

- Where there are initial transfers of funds between different level authorities, what conditions are set (lump sum transfer; block grant; earmarked grant)?

- What type of resource is allocated? Funding to the school budget (i.e. for schools to administer) or in kind or directly paid by a body external to the school (teaching equivalents)?

What conditions are set on funding transfers to schools?

- Do schools administer the funds? If so, what conditions are set? (block grant; restricted block grant; earmarked grant)?

- Does the school receive resources in kind? Or are resources paid for/purchased directly by a body external to the school?

What proportion of funding is distributed through the main allocation mechanism?

- What proportion of funding is allocated external to the main allocation mechanism (targeted funding)?

- What is the balance between the main allocation mechanism and additional grants?

How is the amount allocated to schools determined?

- Objective criteria with a universally applied rule or an individual estimate of what the school needs?

How to ensure allocation mechanisms remain optimal?

- How to design and conduct reviews of the funding model?

- How to determine adequacy of funding allocation?

How to ensure effective implementation of a new funding allocation mechanism?

- How to manage the political economy of funding reform?

- How to estimate the costs of implementation?

Distribution of current expenditure

OECD (2016) defines current expenditure as the "spending on goods and services consumed within the current year and requiring recurrent production in order to sustain educational services. Current expenditure by educational institutions other than on compensation of personnel includes expenditure on subcontracted services such as support services (e.g. maintenance of school buildings), ancillary services (e.g. preparation of meals for students), and rental of school buildings and other facilities. These services are obtained from outside providers, unlike the services provided by education authorities or by educational institutions using their own personnel". International data show that over 90% of annual expenditure by educational institutions (from public and private sources) is spent on school resources used each year to operate schools. In turn, the vast majority of current expenditure is used for the compensation of staff: 77% for both primary and secondary education in 2013 on average in the OECD (OECD, 2016, Table B6.2). While staff compensation primarily comprises salaries for teachers, compensation for other staff exceeds 20% of total current expenditure in Belgium, Estonia, France, Iceland and the United States (Figure 3.1). In contrast, compensation of other staff forms less than 10% of total current expenditure in Luxembourg and Mexico. The cross-country differences likely reflect the degree to which staff, such as school principals, guidance counsellors, bus drivers, school nurses, janitors and maintenance workers are classified as "non-teaching staff" (OECD, 2016).

Figure 3.1. **Compensation of staff as a share of total current expenditure in primary education, 2013**

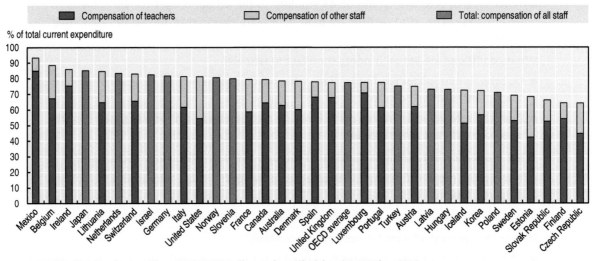

Source: OECD (2016), *Education at a Glance 2016: OECD Indicators*, http://dx.doi.org/10.1787/eag-2016-en.

However, there is sometimes significant variation within a country in terms of the proportion of current expenditure allocated to staff salaries. In Kazakhstan, payroll expenses account for 79% of urban school budgets and 93% of rural ones (UNICEF, 2012, in OECD/ The World Bank, 2015). Small class schools and primary schools in rural areas are particularly affected in this sense. On average, 99.6% of their budget is dedicated to salaries (Sange-SFK, 2012, in OECD/The World Bank, 2015).

Among the OECD review countries, the use of funding formulas to allocate funding for teacher salaries is prevalent and in only a few cases are these not used (Kazakhstan, Portugal and Uruguay) (Annex A). While local authorities have full discretion over the design of funding allocation mechanisms in Denmark and Sweden, the use of funding formulas is quite widespread among Danish and Swedish municipalities (Nusche et al., 2016a; Swedish Ministry of Education and Research, 2016). In Austria, where allocation at the upper secondary level is the responsibility of the central authorities, the predominant mechanism used is funding formulas, while administrative discretion mainly relates to addressing unplanned shortages such as the enrolment of refuges and asylum seekers during the school year (Annex A).

The remainder of this section explores three major aspects related to the distribution of current expenditure: designing funding formulas to meet different policy objectives; accounting for the fact that schools have different resource needs; and understanding the information and analytical needs for an effective allocation mechanism.

How can funding formulas be designed to meet different policy objectives?

Any funding distribution mechanism should be designed to fit the governance and policy context for the school system. There may be different goals that are more important than others depending on the overarching policy objectives.

There are three broad functions that funding formulas can aim to support (Levačić and Ross, 1999):

- Promoting equity (both horizontal equity, i.e. the like treatment of recipients whose needs are similar, and vertical equity, i.e. the application of different funding levels for recipients whose needs differ, see Chapter 1). This is one of the most important functions of a funding formula. To ensure horizontal equity it is crucial to ensure the same basic allocation per student differentiated by year level. Differential amounts can be added to the basic allocation according to the assessed degree of educational need to promote greater vertical equity.

- A directive function to promote certain behaviour in funding recipients. This can be a tool for central, state, regional or local authorities to set certain incentives and support particular policies. For example, an additional amount can be added to the basic allocation to support schools with lower student enrolments or to support the provision of teacher professional development in policy relevant areas.

- Or market regulation (supporting broader school choice policies). The more this function is emphasised, the greater the proportion of total funding to schools is allocated on a per student basis. The formula can establish the per student amount for each child and depending on the system this would be channelled directly to parents as a "voucher" to purchase school education or directly to the school.

A funding formula can be designed to support a balance of these different policy functions. For example, when Lithuania introduced a reform in funding distribution in 2001 (including a central funding formula to allocate funding for teacher and other pedagogical staff salaries), specific goals included an emphasis on eliminating rural-urban disparities (equity), enhancing parental school choice and the development of the private school sector (market regulation) and promoting the optimisation of local school networks and adjustment to the decreasing number of students (directive) (Herczynski, 2011). The specific policy objectives will dictate the different weightings given to each of the main components included in the funding formula. An overview of the funding mechanisms in Lithuania and an evaluation of how well they are meeting policy objectives in provided in Box 3.4.

Box 3.4. **Designing school funding formulas to meet policy objectives: Lithuania**

Policy context

Lithuania has seen steady emigration over the past 20 years. Between the official censuses in 2001 and 2011, the overall population declined by 12.6%. The population decline has dramatically impacted the school-age population in all school years from primary through upper secondary education and continues to exert pressures on schools. For example, in Years 6 and 7 (lower secondary education) there were almost half as many students in 2014/15, compared to in 2004/05. This demographic phenomenon has presented considerable challenges to the efficiency of the school network.

The vast majority of Lithuanian students are in public schools (just under 3% of students follow general education in the private sector). In Lithuania, the 60 municipalities are responsible for public schools providing general education; the state is directly responsible for vocational training institutions. The provision of public education is, therefore, highly decentralised (in 2014, 84% of students following regular compulsory education or upper secondary education attended a municipal school).

Policy functions emphasised in the funding formula

In 2001, Lithuania introduced an education finance formula which aimed to increase the efficiency of resource use in education and improve education quality. As well as creating a transparent and fair scheme for resource allocation, the reform aimed to promote the optimisation of local school networks and constant adjustment to the decreasing number of students.

Importantly, the funding allocation makes a clear distinction between "teaching costs" (state grant) and "school maintenance costs" (local funds). This design allows the state to directly influence the quality of education provided, as the central grant for "teaching costs" comprises salaries for teachers, school leadership, administration and professional support staff, textbooks for students and some school materials, teacher in-service training and pedagogical and psychological services. "School maintenance costs" cover salaries for maintenance staff, student transportation, communal and communication expenses (utilities), material expenditures and repair works to maintain school facilities. It is important to note that both parts of the school budget include some salary and some non-salary expenditures.

Choice of components within the funding formula and relative importance given to these

The major determinant of funding within the central grant is the number of students in the school. The grant is calculated as a fixed per-student amount ("student basket") multiplied by the number of "equivalent students" to give a weighted sum of students. This allows for cost differentials in teaching different students. The standard reference student (1.0) studies in a class of 25 students with a weekly number of lessons equal to the average in Years 1 to 10. In 2014, the funding formula contained 67 weighting coefficient values. The major student characteristics are school year, special educational needs and ethnic minority status. However, the funding reform also aimed to eliminate rural-urban disparities and as such the formula includes weights for the size, location and type of school. As a general rule, the final student weighting is the product of the weighting coefficients. For example, a student in a small, rural basic school would receive a weighted coefficient of 1.90, but a student with special educational needs in the same school would receive 2.60, that is 1.90 × 1.35 weighting for special educational needs. Schools exclusively providing specialised education receive an additional special weighting factor.

Box 3.4. **Designing school funding formulas
to meet policy objectives: Lithuania** (cont.)

Evaluation of how well the funding formula meets policy objectives

The allocation of a fixed per student amount has promoted greater efficiency. However, the per-student amount differs from a pure student voucher system in three ways:

● The grant is transferred to the municipality and not directly to the school. The municipality has the right to redistribute a certain proportion of funding across schools. In 2001, this was 15%, it was gradually reduced to 5%, but now stands at 7%. Municipal reallocation may weaken incentives for schools to compete for resources, as municipalities can choose to support "struggling schools".

● The grant takes into account school size. This aims to acknowledge that some smaller schools (with higher costs) have lower enrolment rates due to their rural location. However, school size also depends on municipal decisions to consolidate the network.

● The grant includes some specifications on minimal levels of required expenditure such as on textbooks and in-service teaching training.

The 2001 funding reform has helped to stop the declining efficiency of the school network. For example, the student teacher-ratio in primary education plummeted from 16.7 in 2000 to 11.0 in 2004, but was stabilised around 10 students per teacher from 2007 on. The annual adjustments over the exact weighting coefficients used in the funding formula are subject to fierce policy debate, notably around the area of the extent of support to small, rural schools. The use of the formula allows a high degree of transparency on decisions about funding priorities.

Source: Shewbridge, C. et al. (2016b), *OECD Reviews of School Resources: Lithuania 2016, http://dx.doi.org/10.1787/9789264252547-en.*

In addition, funding formula can incentivise greater efficiency at the school level. If the per student amount is allocated as a "fixed price contract" the school has incentive to use funding more efficiently and to spend savings in other areas (Levačić and Ross, 1999). In Estonia, the OECD review found that educational authorities with large numbers of schools (e.g. Tallinn) have developed clear and transparent formulas to allocate funds to schools for their operating costs (other than teacher and school leader salaries). These formulas have facilitated the operational autonomy of schools and have allowed school leaders to both save money and reallocate it across budget lines on an annual basis (Santiago et al., 2016b).

How can allocation mechanisms account for the fact that schools have different resource needs?

The overall level of investment in education is an important precondition to ensure the quality of educational provision, but beyond a certain level of investment what matters most is how funding is allocated to schools that are most in need of additional resources (Chapter 1). There are two broad approaches when designing mechanisms to allocate funding that recognises differing needs across schools: the inclusion of additional funding in the main allocation mechanism for particular schools, e.g. by including weighting to systematically allocate additional funding to certain categories; or the provision of targeted funding in one or a series of different grants external to the main allocation mechanism. In particular, the provision of targeted funding can be a useful mechanism for central authorities to address concerns over the equitable distribution of funding. Typically a mix of these funding mechanisms is found in many systems and different approaches are observed among the OECD review countries (Annex A). The OECD review has shed light on the different criteria included in funding formulas aiming to address differing resource needs, whether due to individual student needs, the provision of a specialised curriculum or specific school characteristics (Table 3.A1.1). For example:

- In the Flemish and French Communities of Belgium the main allocation mechanisms for operating grants and staff allocation to schools include weightings for student socio-economic characteristics and special educational needs and also for school location. Similarly, the provision of dedicated grants (the direct payment of educational staff salaries) takes into account student socio-economic characteristics and special educational needs. There is also additional targeted funding (allocated as a restricted block grant to school providers) for specific student groups, including students from disadvantaged backgrounds, newly arrived immigrants and refugees. In all cases, a funding formula is used either to allocate funding to school providers or to pay directly for staff salaries.

- In Chile, the main block grant for general education is allocated with a funding formula that incorporates different weightings for students from highly disadvantaged socio-economic backgrounds, for schools in rural or highly isolated areas and for special educational provision. Central authorities also allocate earmarked grants to school providers for students with special educational needs and from disadvantaged backgrounds and a salary complement for teachers working in "difficult schools" either due to their geographic location, marginalisation or extreme poverty. The calculation of these earmarked grants is also based on a funding formula.

- In Estonia, the main allocation mechanism (an earmarked grant for general education) is allocated with a funding formula that incorporates different weightings for student special educational needs and weightings for school location and different regions. Central authorities also provide targeted funding, for example, for teaching Estonian to students whose mother tongue is not Estonian or for newly arrived immigrants.

- In Israel, central authorities use a funding formula to determine the direct payment (dedicated grant) of teacher salaries. This incorporates weightings that account for student socio-economic characteristics and special educational needs and school location. There is no provision of targeted funding.

Table 3.A1.2 presents the OECD review countries that do not use funding formulas to allocate current expenditure. Although the same set of criteria is not used systematically to allocate funding, countries may take into account different criteria when making funding allocation decisions. In Uruguay, while the main annual grant does not use explicit criteria to determine the level of funding, the dedicated grant for the direct payment of teacher salaries does take into account different school types and educational programmes and there is targeted funding (also a dedicated grant) that may be allocated for teacher training in support of teaching students with special educational needs. The annual grant in Kazakhstan typically considers criteria such as the school type, location and size and the socio-economic composition of the school.

In most countries in Europe, central authorities provide additional resources targeting schools that are assessed to have additional funding needs (European Commission/EACEA/ Eurydice, 2016). Other educational authorities (regional or local) may also be responsible for allocating additional resources to support disadvantaged students. In Denmark and Norway, the initial transfer of a lump sum grant from the central government does account for certain demographic characteristics (the share of immigrant children in each municipality in Norway; an index of the socio-economic structure of the municipality in Denmark) – although municipalities have complete discretion in how they allocate funding to schools. In Sweden, municipalities are legally obliged to take into account the number of students enrolled and the "different preconditions and needs of different students" when designing their allocation mechanism (Annex A). In the United States, where a significant proportion of initial funding comes from the local level (50% of funding for primary and secondary education in 2013) (OECD, 2016) and where there are great variations among school districts in terms of income and wealth distribution, there is emerging evidence that revisions to funding mechanisms aiming to achieve a more equitable distribution of funding have had positive effects (Box 3.5). This is supplemented by the provision of targeted funding from the federal government.

Box 3.5. **Supporting disadvantaged schools with targeted funding and revised funding formulas: United States**

In the **United States**, the states are responsible for education (each implementing their own educational laws) and the federal government plays a limited role (in 2014, the federal government contributed 8.6% of public school system funding, varying from less than 5% in Connecticut, Massachusetts and New Jersey to over 13% in Arizona, Louisiana, Mississippi and South Dakota) (US Census Bureau, 2016). Federal funding is most commonly allocated to support a specific programme or need (Atkinson et al., 2005) and is "a means of filling gaps in State and local support for education when critical national needs arise" (US Department of Education, n.d.). Anti-poverty and civil rights laws in the 1960s saw the 1965 Elementary and Secondary Education Act launch a set of targeted programmes. The provision of targeted funding aiming to support schools with socio-economically disadvantaged student populations continues to be a major federal influence. For example, the United States Department of Education's Title 1 grants represented 2.2% of public school system funding in 2014 (US Census Bureau, 2016). In 2014/15, there were 18 260 school districts operating 98 373 schools, of which 69 531 schools were classified as "Title 1 eligible", that is, schools where the percentage of children from low-income families is at least 35% of children from low-income families served by the school district as a whole, and 54 623 as "school wide Title 1 eligible", that is, with at least 40% of children from low-income families in the school (NCES, 2016).

Since the 1970s, 28 states have introduced school funding reforms that have aimed to reduce inequality in school funding and to weaken the relationship between the level of expenditure and the school district's income and wealth. Recent research demonstrates positive estimated causal effects of school funding reforms with improved inputs and better school district-level outcomes (Lafortune et al., 2016) and high school completion and adult earnings and family income (Jackson et al., 2016). Both studies show, using different methodologies, that the school funding reforms were "productive" and cost effective. There are two main stages of school funding reforms: those undertaken from 1971 to the mid-1980s in response to legal challenges on equity grounds, i.e. local funding was found to violate the state's responsibility to provide a quality education to all children; and those undertaken from the late 1980s onwards on adequacy grounds, i.e. low per student spending levels in certain districts failed to meet the state's obligation to provide some adequate level of free education for children. Equity-based reforms tend to reduce the variance of expenditure with limited effect on overall expenditure levels – although there are some examples of a

---

Box 3.5. **Supporting disadvantaged schools with targeted funding and revised funding formulas: United States** (cont.)

"levelling down" of overall funding levels within a state. Adequacy-based reforms tend to increase overall expenditure (with higher funding allocations to all districts) with greater increases for low-income districts (high relative allocations in low-income districts).

Jackson et al. (2016) analyse funding reforms undertaken by 28 states in response to legal challenges on either equity or adequacy. In both cases, states changed the parameters in funding formulas and succeeded in reducing inequality in school funding, but employed different funding formula revisions to this end:

● "Foundation formulas" guarantee a base level of per student expenditure, estimate the district's required local contribution to fund this and provide the difference between the expected contribution and the foundation level. They are designed to increase per-student expenditure in the lowest-spending districts through redistribution of funding. These tended to be introduced in states that saw increased school expenditure overall.

● "Spending limits" prohibit per student expenditure levels above a predetermined amount. These tend to reduce expenditure in all districts in the long run with the most pronounced effect in the more affluent districts.

● "Reward for effort plans" incentivise local expenditure through provision of additional state funds to match locally raised funding and tend to lead to increased expenditure in all districts, particularly in low-income districts.

● Equalisation plans aim to equalise expenditure level by taxing all districts and redistributing funds to lower-income districts.

Lafortune et al. (2016) analyse funding reforms undertaken in 26 states in response to challenges to the adequacy of funding. Using data from 1990 onward from the National Assessment of Educational Progress, they demonstrate that the district-based funding reforms are quite effective at reducing between-district inequities. However, they do not closely target low-income students or minority students, as these students are not highly concentrated in school districts with low mean incomes. This points to the need for complementary policies aimed at reducing within-district resources and student achievement gaps.

Source: US Census Bureau (2016), "Public education finances: 2014", *Economic Reimbursable Surveys Division Reports, www.census.gov/content/dam/Census/library/publications/2016/econ/g14-aspef.pdf*; Atkinson, M. et al. (2005), *School Funding: A Review of Existing Models in European and OECD Countries*, National Foundation for Educational Research/Local Government Association, Slough; US Department of Education (2017), The Federal Role in Education, *www2.ed.gov/about/overview/fed/role.html*; NCES (2016), *Selected Statistics from the Public Elementary and Secondary Education Universe: School Year 2014–15, https://nces.ed.gov/pubs2016/2016076.pdf*; Jackson, C.K., R.C. Johnson and C. Persico (2016), "The effects of school spending on educational and economic outcomes: evidence from school finance reforms", *The Quarterly Journal of Economics, http://dx.doi.org/10.1093/qje/qjv036*; Lafortune, J., J. Rothstein and D. Whitmore Schazenbach (2016), "School finance reform and the distribution of student achievement", *NBER Woking Paper Series*, No. 22011, *www.nber.org/papers/w22011.pdf*.

Setting conditions on funding transfers

A recent overview of whether and how European countries allocate additional resources to schools with disadvantaged populations finds that the majority provide resources in kind, most typically additional staff (European Commission/EACEA/Eurydice, 2016). For example, in Ireland, EUR 55.48 million of the EUR 67.46 million allocated specifically to primary schools in 2015 funded additional teachers, head teachers or supporting teacher posts (Ireland Department of Education, 2017). Another form of in-kind allocation is the provision of professional development opportunities for staff (European Commission/EACEA/Eurydice,

2016). For example, the Danish government offers specific professional development for teachers working in schools with disadvantaged student populations. The French government, in its special professional development and support plan for teachers working in priority zones, guarantees teachers in the most difficult areas three days of training per year, plus mentoring for new teachers and special training for executive staff. Taking the example of mechanisms used to target funds to migrant background students, France and Germany mostly allocate resources in kind (in additional teaching hours or positions) and schools have little discretion over how these resources are used (Table 3.2). The main provision is via targeted funding external to the main funding mechanism (categorical funding), but four of the 16 states in Germany do apply weights within the main funding allocation formula. In France, general criteria on the school and neighbourhood demographic data are used. Where criteria are used in Germany, these are more specific and target migrant characteristics. However, in seven of the 16 states in Germany, no criteria are used to allocate funding.

Table 3.2. **Overview of different mechanisms to target funds to migrant students in Canada, France, Germany and the United States, 2015**

	France	Germany	Canada	United States
Initial funding	72% from the national government	75% from the 16 states (*Land*)	76% from the 13 provinces and territories	39% from the 50 states
Final distribution	71% national level	72% from the states	86% at the local level	98% at the local level
Degree of discretion over funding use	Mostly allocated as teaching hours; primary schools usually do not have discretion; secondary schools have some discretion in determining class sizes, subjects taught, etc.	Schools have little to no discretion; resource use is highly regulated. Typically involves the allocation of additional teaching positions, not discretionary funds.	In most cases, school districts have broad discretion over distribution to individual schools. Where a weighted formula is used, schools generally can decide how to use funds.	In most cases, school districts have broad discretion over distribution to individual schools. Where a weighted formula is used, schools generally can decide how to use funds.
Use of different funding distribution mechanisms	Categorical (all funding)	Categorical (9) Weighted formula (4) None (3)	Weighted formula (8) Categorical (1) None (4)	Weighted formula (34) Categorical (9) Reimbursement (3) None (4)
Basis to determine the level of the grant (e.g. criteria used, administrative discretion)	School and neighbourhood demographic data (including local unemployment rate)	Student migration background, citizenship (school data) Neighbourhood demographic data (including immigrant share of population) Expert judgement by local school administrators (7)	Student immigrant/ refugee status (school data, census data) Language proficiency tests	Language spoken at home (questionnaire) Language proficiency tests State share of Limited English Proficient students and recent immigrant students (census data)

Notes: Initial funding and final distribution data refer to funds for primary and secondary education in 2013. "Categorical" funding refers to targeted funding that is external to the main funding allocation mechanism and that is intended to be used for migrant-background students. The numbers in brackets denote how many states use the funding distribution mechanism.
Source: Compiled from information in Sugarman, J., S. Morris-Lange and M. McHugh (2016), *Improving Education for Migrant-Background Students: A Transatlantic Comparison of School Funding*, www.migrationpolicy.org/research/improving-education-migrant-background-students-transatlantic-comparison-school-funding and OECD (2016), *Education at a Glance 2016: OECD Indicators*, http://dx.doi.org/10.1787/eag-2016-en, Table B4.3.

In contrast, Canada and the United States give much more discretion to the local level in how to distribute funding and typically use weightings within the main funding allocation mechanism (Table 3.2 shows for example how targeted funding is allocated to support migrant background students). In general, this allows more discretion at the school level in how to use the funding. In a few European systems (Finland, the Flemish Community of Belgium, the Netherlands and England, Wales and Northern Ireland in the United Kingdom) schools receive additional funding and have discretion over how they use this funding

(European Commission/EACEA/Eurydice, 2016). A recent research study in the Flemish Community of Belgium found that 90% of the school principals surveyed were very positive about the additional funding they received to target socio-economic disadvantage (Groenez et al., 2015). The researchers found that the additional funding provided the necessary material conditions for teachers to do a good job and to cover specific expenditures to address the needs of disadvantaged students, such as specific teaching materials, in-service training or community school activities. It also concluded that it was logical for schools in more difficult financial situations to use these funds to address their most basic needs, such as urgent repair and heating costs. Recent evidence from England, however, indicates that the earmarking (or ring-fencing) of funding for a clearly defined target group (children receiving free school meals) was one of the factors associated with a more successful use of targeted funding (the Pupil Premium), as identified by the external school evaluation body in England (Ofsted, 2012). Less successful approaches included the indiscriminate spending of funds on teaching assistants, no clear audit trail for where the funding had been spent, and not including spending plans within the broader school development plan.

Accountability mechanisms play an important role in a context where schools have large discretion over the use of targeted funding (e.g. Ofsted, 2012; see also Chapter 5). Funding designs must manage the tension between flexibility, that is, allowing room for local judgement on how to most effectively use the funding, and accountability, that is, maintaining public confidence that funds are being used for their intended purpose and achieving the desired results (Sugarman et al., 2016). A recent review of funding allocation in Australia noted the benefits of funding distribution at the local level, but recommended greater transparency on methodologies used and analysis of the impact of funding (Gonski et al., 2011). The importance of striking this balance was raised in the OECD review in Denmark regarding the use of funding to support provision for students with special educational needs in regular schools (Box 3.6). Also, school accountability must manage the tension with unintended consequences for teaching and learning as schools comply with accountability requirements which may steer schools to focus on particular areas of the curriculum, for example (OECD, 2013).

Box 3.6. **Matching local flexibility over funding use with transparency on how funding is used: Denmark**

The OECD review in Denmark found that municipalities rely to a decreasing extent on earmarked funding to individual students with special educational needs and more on general funding. In the more general approach, resources for students with special educational needs are allocated across schools with respect to general criteria measuring the socio-economic background of students. This approach aims to give schools the flexibility to optimally use these resources, taking factors such as the characteristics of peers into account when allocating resources (Nusche et al., 2016a). Danish students have a legal right to receive teaching in accordance with their needs and school principals, in consultation with the school board, decide on the allocation of resources in their school, but must meet national regulations and ensure recruitment of the relevant teacher competency within the school's budget.

However, there are no national rules on how the additional needs of students recently included in regular schools (following a policy move to reduce the number of students in special education schools) should be translated into extra resources. This raises some concerns

---

> **Box 3.6. Matching local flexibility over funding use with transparency on how funding is used: Denmark** (*cont.*)
>
> over a lack of transparency on how resources follow students into regular schools and whether they receive adequate learning support (Nusche et al., 2016a). Regular schools typically employ pedagogues with a specific relevant education to work with students with special needs (pedagogues are not teachers, but focus on intellectual, social, emotional, neuromuscular, ethical, moral and aesthetic development). Municipalities may also apply to the central government for specific targeted funds for special needs education. The OECD review in Denmark recommended greater transparency to the school community about how the school uses resources to facilitate inclusion and the way this translates into learning outcomes for students with special educational needs.
>
> *Source:* Nusche, D. et al. (2016a), *OECD Reviews of School Resources: Denmark 2016*, *http://dx.doi.org/10.1787/9789264262430-en.*

Chapter 5 provides an overview of different approaches identified in OECD review countries to evaluate how schools use funding that is targeted for student groups with particular needs.

Determining the amount of additional funding allocated to schools

The use of a funding formula, if well designed, can promote greater equity and efficiency. However, a major challenge lies in estimating the different costs involved in providing different types of education. Within a funding formula, coefficients should adequately reflect different per student costs of providing education. This is a difficult task in systems where there is great variation in class size due to schools in rural or isolated locations. Different programmes and types of educational provision will also entail different costs (e.g. for specialised equipment, a specialised curriculum offer such as a recognised language minority). Judgments will also need to be made on the relative importance given to these different elements. Recent reviews of funding allocation mechanisms in Australia and the United Kingdom generally aim to distribute the major share of funding according to student rather than institutional requirements, with a preference for core funding per student supplemented by bands of funding to target particular needs (New Zealand Ministry of Education, 23 May 2015). Box 3.7 presents an overview of the major components that should be included in designing a needs-based funding formula. Table 3.A1.1 provides an overview of the extent to which OECD review countries using funding formulas include weightings for these different components.

> **Box 3.7. Which major components should a needs-based funding formula include?**
>
> **Which unit of funding?**
>
> What is being funded: the student, teaching group/class, school or school site? A formula may contain a number of different units.
>
> **Which major components?**
>
> There are four main components which are the building blocks of a formula. Each component relates to a main purpose for allocating funds to schools. Different weightings assigned to each of the major components below will be crucial in balancing the relative importance of the different policy functions for a funding formula (market regulation; promoting equity; directive function).

> ### Box 3.7. **Which major components should a needs-based funding formula include?** *(cont.)*
>
> **A basic allocation:** This could be an allocation per student or per class. If the unit is class, then the formula will include assumptions about the maximum permitted class size before an extra student demands the forming of two classes. There would be a year-level supplement differentiated according to the school year (grade level) or stage of schooling (e.g. primary, lower secondary, etc.). Setting a fixed amount per student in a particular year uses the assumption of the costs of educating a student with normal educational needs. This requires an analysis of expenditure requirements, e.g. activity-led costing. This – particularly with a per student unit – strongly supports the market regulation function.
>
> **An allocation for curriculum enhancement:** This component would adjust for the costs of providing a specific educational profile and would only apply to selected schools or students. For example, this could be the offer of a specialised curriculum such as a focus on the arts, sports or different vocational fields. It could also be the offer of an adjusted curriculum designed to meet specific educational needs of the school's student group. This allocation can support the directive function, helping to promote areas of the curriculum favoured by policy makers.
>
> **An allocation for students with supplementary educational needs:** This would aim to adjust for different student characteristics which would require additional resources to ensure the same level of access to the required curriculum. This allocation plays a major role in supporting the equity function.
>
> **An allocation for specific needs related to school site/location:** This would aim to adjust for structural differences in school site operation costs that are generally beyond the school management's control, e.g. schools located in rural or remote areas with significantly lower class sizes, schools with higher maintenance costs (linked to local economic factors and/or specialised equipment needs). School size is an important determinant of unit cost. Fixed costs (e.g. school leadership, premises, providing a selection of subjects) do not diminish with the number of students. Here it is key to define the "minimum efficient size" which represents the minimum size of a school at which average cost per student approaches its lowest feasible value. This involves a judgement about the extent to which small schools should be supported by additional allocations. This allocation can support the equity and directive functions.
>
> *Source:* Levačić, R. and K. Ross (1999), "Principles for designing needs-based school funding formulae?", in *Needs-Based Resource Allocation in Education: Via Formula Funding of Schools*, UNESCO International Institute for Educational Planning, Paris.

What are the information and analytical requirements for an effective allocation mechanism?

The OECD review has revealed the importance of paying adequate attention to data requirements and the choice of indicators for funding allocation and understanding the technical and analytical demands that the design and maintenance of effective allocation mechanisms requires.

Choosing indicators to distribute funding to schools

A range of different indicators is used in different countries and different regions of countries to determine the proportion of students with identified needs for additional resources. While each indicator has advantages and drawbacks, no perfect indicator exists that takes into account all needs students might have, ranging from disabilities to family problems. To construct such an indicator very detailed data on individual students would be required (West and Pennell, 2000).

Indicators vary in the share of the target population they actually reach. For all indicators, targeting areas, schools or students, there is a trade-off between the simplicity and transparency of the indicator and its accuracy (Levačić, 2006) and perceived sensitivity and fairness (Atkinson et al., 2005). Relatively simple indicators will always leave out some part of the target population. For more precise targeting to local contexts, more complicated indicators need to be established, although a higher degree of complexity makes these less transparent and understandable to a wider public (Fazekas, 2012). There are also examples where the use of simpler indicators did not make a large difference to schools' funding levels. For example, in Swidnik, Poland, a funding formula that included a large number of indicators was introduced initially in 1994. In 1996, this funding formula was replaced by a formula relying on the number of students only. This change did not lead to any major differences in individual schools' levels of funding (Levačić and Downes, 2004). The argument for targeting funding to certain areas is based primarily on the additional negative effects that socio-economic disadvantage has when concentrated in a particular area. It is also argued to be more efficient to target certain areas, as this will capture a greater proportion of the disadvantaged population than if funding were distributed more evenly. However, in the late 1990s the use of a "priority area" concept to target funding was challenged by several different studies coming out of European systems using this approach. In the United Kingdom, research on programmes targeting areas showed that these often left out a large proportion of the disadvantaged population and included many individuals who were not disadvantaged (Tunstall and Lupton, 2003; Smith, 1999). Similar results were found for programmes targeting specific areas in Ireland (Weir and Ryan, 2000). The area concept tended to presuppose that the formation of ghettos was inevitable and evidence from Belgium and France showed that the priority area label was stigmatising and encouraged flight of middle class families from these areas (European Commission/Eurydice, 2000; Moisan and Simon, 1997; Bénabou et al., 2004; Bénabou et al., 2007). As a result, there was a broad shift to using indicators that were more specific to the actual population in the school. For example, in the French Community of Belgium, the socio-economic index (*indice socio-économique*) is based on the student's residential area, using indicators such as income, qualification level and unemployment rate (Ministère de la Fédération Wallonie-Bruxelles, 2016). This is reviewed every five years. School leaders report this information in January of each year and this is centrally verified and each student is attributed a value on the socio-economic index. The average for each school is calculated and then schools are ranked according to their average socio-economic index value. In the primary school sector and the secondary school sector, the 25% of schools with the lowest values qualify for additional teaching periods or funding allocation.

In a comparison of different approaches to funding the education of migrant students, Sugarman et al. (2016) note that many German states use demographic characteristics such as country of origin as target indicators which acknowledges a wide range of needs and differences, compared to a narrower target indicator such as language proficiency as used in many school systems in Canada and the United States. The latter target indicator may not adequately account for other factors that undermine student success, whereas the former may provide resources to some students who no longer need such support. The precision of criteria used to allocate targeted funding is also being reviewed in Australia. There is an ongoing debate on how to further improve the targeting of need-based funding that was introduced as a result of a full funding review in 2010. Considerations include the actual index used to target additional funds to disadvantaged schools and identifying how additional funding has been used.

Paying attention to data collection and stakeholder consultation

The availability and quality of data is a key concern when compiling indicators. There are different challenges presented for data collection. In general, area-based measures may rely on data that is less up-to-date and sample-based, thus limiting the accuracy for targeting smaller areas. In recent years, OECD countries have implemented regular compliancy reporting systems for schools and many of these are now electronic reporting systems (OECD, 2013). This offers a wealth of data for indicators and can allow a more accurate targeting of resources. However, there are some concerns raised about the reliability of school reports when there is incentive to inflate or deflate numbers in order to benefit from additional resources.

A major issue of many indicators used to allocate additional resources to areas and schools is the lack of up-to-date data. This primarily concerns indicators that try to measure different aspects of specific areas. In many cases, census data, which is collected only very infrequently, is used. Harwell and LeBeau (2010), for example, criticise the free school lunch indicator in the United States that is used to allocate additional resources to schools with a large number of disadvantaged students for relying on the national poverty guidelines which have not been updated for a long time. Area-based indices used in Australia are also criticised for being out-of-date (Santiago et al., 2011). The additional educational needs index, used in the United Kingdom, relies on census data which is only collected every ten years and thus tends to be outdated (West, 2009).

A further problem is misclassification and missing data on part of schools, areas or students. For example, data on free school lunch status in the United States is missing for a significant number of students. Students without records or who do not complete the administrative procedure are often simply classified as not eligible for free school lunch (Harwell and LeBeau, 2010). In England, children are classified as eligible for free school meals in administrative data only if they are both eligible for and actually claiming free school meals (West and Pennell, 2000). Children eligible for free school meals but not claiming will not be captured.

The importance of regular review of the basis used to determine funding allocation is illustrated by a recent review in Ireland (Box 3.8). This highlights the possibilities that improved data availability offer to heighten the objectivity of the allocation mechanism. Also, it underlines the importance of ensuring adequate mechanisms for stakeholder consultation, which helps to increase the perceived fairness of the allocation system. Consulting stakeholders can ensure that funding mechanisms are able to reflect desired pedagogical innovations and respond to capacity-building challenges that are not anticipated in funding formulas (Sugarman et al., 2016).

Ensuring technical and analytical capacity

The OECD review has revealed that the design, implementation and maintenance of an effective allocation mechanism poses significant demands on technical and analytical capacity. This relates to the sophistication of information systems, analytical capacity to test out different allocation scenarios and to develop and adjust existing allocation

Box 3.8. **Data developments and opportunities to improve the basis for funding allocation: Ireland**

In **Ireland**, the government has undertaken a recent review (Ireland Department of Education, 2017) of the basis used to determine the allocation of additional funding to disadvantaged schools (the Delivering Equality of Opportunity in Schools [DEIS] action plan started in 2005 and is the main policy initiative to tackle educational disadvantage). The DEIS was established to bring together a range of existing policy interventions that aimed to tackle disadvantage and notably would use a standardised system for identifying levels of disadvantage in schools. The intention was to regularly review this system; however, the first major review was initiated in 2015. The plan included provision to conduct the identification process on a three-year cycle.

The 2005 standardised identification methodology

The initial identification process was managed by the Educational Research Centre (ERC) and approximately 20% of all schools were selected for inclusion. With the aim "to capture the socio-economic variables that collectively best predict the risk of educational disadvantage", two different approaches were used to identify schools eligible for additional funding:

● Primary schools (primary education): the ERC designed and administered a special survey to collect information from school principals on the percentage of students at the school: with an unemployed parent; in local authority accommodation; with a lone parent; whose family are travellers; from a large family (five or more children); who are eligible for free books. Primary schools were classified in three groups: rural; urban band 1 (the highest concentration of disadvantage); and urban band 2.

● Post-primary schools (secondary education): centrally held data were used, namely, student data on school-level retention rates and examination results (from the central database managed by the Department of Education), plus data examination fee waiver data which indicated that students held a medical card (data collected by the State Examinations Commission).

The ERC conducted analysis of the collected information and compiled a rank order of all schools according to their relative level of disadvantage compared to other schools. This ranking was verified by the Department of Education's Regional Office Network and the Inspectorate, based on local knowledge. As such, the identification procedure was extremely resource intensive. Some schools perceived that the procedure lacked objectivity (particularly the perceived subjectivity of information provided by school principals at the primary level) and also were critical of the fact that a school's social context was static as it was established at one point in time (2006) and did not capture demographic changes in school populations. This was compounded by the impact of the financial crisis which meant that no new schools were identified after September 2009. A review by the Economic and Social Research Institute (Smyth et al., 2015) highlighted the need to review whether the scale of funding is appropriate for those schools in urban band 1, given the complexity of their needs, and also the current "cut-off" point for schools to qualify for DEIS funding.

Data developments and opportunities to improve the identification basis

The technical review was conducted by a technical working group (comprising members of the ERC and Inspectorate) and the procedure comprised a review of the relevance of the 2005 identification basis, consideration of new options made possible by developments in data sources, consideration of stakeholder consultations and the input of additional technical expertise. Stakeholder consultation revealed a clear consensus on the need to

---

Box 3.8. Data developments and opportunities to improve the basis for funding allocation: Ireland (cont.)

establish a fairer basis for identification which is consistent for both primary and post-primary schools and more responsive to demographic change within individual schools. Further, the technical working group judged that the former approach to administer a survey to school principals was too resource intensive both for schools (administration burden) and for the central level (quality control). General developments in data collection in the public sector offer new possibilities and exploratory analysis by the technical working group identifies a strong indicator for a school's socio-economic profile that draws on two data sources:

- The Pobal Haase-Pratschke Deprivation Index (HP Index) based on census data collected every five years. The Central Statistics Office data from the Census of Population now provides socio-economic data at an individual level and for small areas of population. The HP Index uses this data to measure the relative affluence or disadvantage of a particular geographical area.

- The Department of Education's student data bases at the primary and post-primary levels (individual student data collected directly from schools on an annual basis). Individual student data at the primary level has only been available since 2016.

The combination of both these elements is necessary due to the fact that in Ireland students do not necessarily attend their local school. So the use of an area-based indicator in isolation would introduce a degree of inaccuracy. Research has shown that school choice is particularly prevalent among middle class families and in secondary education. School level data are geo-coded to the small area level, anonymised and then matched to the census small area level data.

The technical working group also recommends further exploratory analysis to complement this socio-economic profile information with other correlates of educational disadvantage. The review underlines the importance of ensuring adequate resources within the Department of Education to support the necessary data collection and analysis functions associated with the identification methodology. Such analytical capacity will also support broader policy work.

Source: Ireland Department of Education (2017), *Report on the Review of Deis, www.education.ie/en/Schools-Colleges/ Services/DEIS-Delivering-Equality-of-Opportunity-in-Schools-/DEIS-Review-Report.pdf*; Smyth, E., S. McCoy and G. Kingston (2015), "Learning from the evaluation of DEIS", *Research Series Number 39, www.esri.ie/pubs/RS39.pdf*.

---

mechanisms and building and sharing of capacity within systems. Chapter 2 explores more broadly questions of capacity at different governance levels and Chapter 5 examines different approaches to data and information management.

In the Slovak Republic, the Ministry of Education has capacity to operate a complex funding formula and has been investing in systems to support more efficient data collection at the school level, as part of the annual collection of a large and complex set of data underpinning the formula (Santiago et al., 2016a). Most schools maintain computer databases and export data electronically to the Ministry of Education. The proposed introduction of an information system collecting data on individual students and teachers would improve the reliability of data underpinning the allocation system. The dependency of school funding on student numbers creates an incentive for school leaders to inflate student numbers, but this is easier to do when reporting only aggregate numbers (Santiago et al., 2016a).

In Denmark, municipalities have detailed register data on their inhabitants, providing key information about the socio-economic background of individual students (Nusche et al., 2016a). Municipalities are free to decide on how to use this data in their calculations for school funding distribution. Each municipality develops its own formula based more or less on assumptions regarding school resource needs and some have commissioned research to identify student characteristics identified with learning difficulties. However, there is little system learning regarding effective school funding formulas, despite the fact that many municipalities invest significant effort in developing and maintaining funding formulas.

Herczynski (in Abu-Ghaida, 2011) presents arguments for using computer simulations for all schools in preference to experimental pilots in selected schools when preparing to introduce a per student funding reform. Simulations can be more appropriate and are certainly a more cost effective instrument to test different elements of an allocation formula and its coefficients. Different scenarios can be prepared and can be used to test compatibility with the overall levels of funding available or indeed to make the case for an increase in overall funding levels. In contrast, the use of experimental pilots in selected schools will necessarily be limited in scope and, as pilot schools typically receive higher funding allocations compared to non-pilot schools, it is difficult to draw lessons from the results.

The OECD review in the Czech Republic revealed that the technical complexities of the funding formulas used by two randomly selected Czech regions impaired the ability to adjust these to evolving strategic policy priorities (Shewbridge et al., 2016a). Both regions, in their allocations to pre-schools and basic schools (primary and lower secondary education) adjust two key parameters (the number of students per pedagogical and non-pedagogical staff) with the aim to account for different school sizes. Each uses a complex technical approach including logarithms and fractional powers in their funding formulas, making these incomprehensible to most education experts and meaning that these are either left unchanged from year to year or are only adjusted by external experts. Given the complexity of the funding formulas, the standard approach in each region is to provide a data file listing all the different possible values for key parameters in the formulas. This assumes a lack of analytical capacity by the regional administrators to calculate the parameters, to check whether the calculation is correct or to change the allocation formula and recalculate them. This means that the annual funding allocation follows a mechanistic and rigid approach, therefore, removing any discernment over how to adapt the allocation mechanism to evolving policy priorities. For lower and upper secondary general and vocational education, national law requires that parameters are set for each type of educational programme offered in the region. This may require the determination of between 200 and 400 different normative amounts each year and is a major bureaucratic task. It also obscures important aspects of education policy, such as which programmes or school types are allocated significantly higher amounts.

Distribution of capital expenditure

OECD (2016) defines capital expenditure as the "spending on assets that last longer than one year, including construction, renovation or major repair of buildings, and new or replacement equipment". Capital expenditure may be financed from current revenue or through borrowing. In 2013, on average in the OECD, the share of capital expenditure in annual expenditure by educational institutions (from public and private sources) was 8% in primary education, and 7% in both lower and upper secondary education (OECD, 2016, Table B6.1). This was 3% or less in Austria, Hungary, Italy, Mexico, Portugal, the Slovak Republic and the United Kingdom at both the primary and secondary education levels.

Following the OECD definition, expenditure on educational capital is expected to bring value beyond the allocation year. This is an important distinction and means that funding that is intended for maintenance and small repairs that are written off over the course of the school year (funding for "operational expenses") is included as a small proportion of current expenditure in many countries. In the OECD review countries, this is the case for Austria, Spain and Uruguay (Annex A). However, the actual type of maintenance activities included in current expenditure may be a grey area in many countries. An independent review of the funding mechanisms in Australia recommended a clear national definition of the maintenance and minor works responsibilities of schools and education authorities that should be addressed from funding for current expenditures (Gonski et al., 2011).

For capital expenditure, the resources used by schools constitute movable or immovable (fixed) assets, the value of which decreases annually in relation to their depreciation as they grow older and rises in accordance with any new investment in them (European Commission/Eurydice, 2000). This means that within a school system, schools differ in the state and value of their fixed assets. This has consequences for the type of allocation mechanism that is most suitable: an annual allocation calculated with a standard set of criteria would lead to inequalities, meaning that a general rule to allocate funding for capital expenditure would need to take the differing state of fixed assets across schools into account (European Commission/Eurydice, 2000). Among the OECD review countries, the majority do not provide an annual grant for capital expenditures. This is only the case in the Czech Republic, Denmark and (for upper secondary vocational programmes only) in Chile. In the French Community of Belgium an annual grant for instructional and non-instructional equipment as part of "operational expenditures" is provided to school providers. In all four systems, these are supplemented by other allocation mechanisms for capital expenditures. Another important aspect to consider in the allocation of funding for capital expenditures is that the management of capital resources is less frequently a school responsibility (Atkinson et al., 2005).

The main allocation mechanisms for capital expenditures among OECD review countries, therefore, include the ad hoc administration of grants, discretionary funding and infrastructure investment programmes (Annex A). More targeted funding may also be used to support projects in a broader policy context. For example, in Australia funding was earmarked for the building of new primary schools (also some secondary schools) in order to provide economic stimulus to every community in Australia in response to the global financial crisis. The Building the Education Revolution programme saw the delivery of 23 675 construction projects by 22 separate education authorities (government and non-government) (Commonwealth of Australia, 2011).

The major basis for allocation of funding for capital expenditures among OECD review countries is the assessment of needs. This often entails the targeting of funding to schools with the greatest needs of renovation or remodelling, including emergency repairs. Box 3.9 provides examples of different approaches in Australia and in England (United Kingdom).

Box 3.9. **Approaches to support more strategic use of capital funding: England (United Kingdom) and Australia**

Better targeting of funding for capital works and more efficient procurement

In **England (United Kingdom)**, there were three major allocations of public funding for capital expenditures (delivered as a capital grant) in 2013/15: basic need funding allocated to local authorities to provide additional school places where needed in their area (based on projections of need and enabling authorities to plan provision over the coming two years); maintenance capital (allocated to local authorities or direct to schools, depending on the management of the school); and devolved formula capital allocated direct to schools. Additional targeted funding (targeted basic need programme) was announced to provide additional support to local authorities with the greatest demographic pressures to expand the provision of school places.

A "Priority School Building Programme" was also established to target renovations/rebuilding of schools in the worst condition across the country (a total of 537 schools). The Education Funding Agency (which was merged with the Skills Funding Agency in April 2017 to form the Education and Skills Funding Agency) designed the programme to make more efficient use of public funding. First, schools are grouped into "batches" to improve efficiency in procurement time and costs. Second, the programme promotes a more standardised design to support construction efficiency and principles for future sustainability. It specifies standard design, works, services and performance requirements for each school. The facilities output specification comprises: a generic design brief with requirements for all schools; a school-specific design brief (e.g. reflecting special provision); schedules of accommodation comprising a list of rooms and spaces required in each school; and area data sheets which identify the requirements for each room and space listed in the schedule of accommodation (comprising services, environmental performance requirements, fittings, furniture and equipment and ICT provision). Key design principles relate to functionality, health and safety, a standardised approach, future-proofing (i.e. flexibility to adapt school facilities to changing enrolment patterns, curricular provision and teaching methods) and sustainability. These principles are illustrated in a set of "baseline designs for schools" which can be consulted at *www.education.gov.uk/schools/adminandfinance/schoolscapital/buildings anddesign/baseline*.

A funding stream to support better strategic planning of new school development

In **Australia**, a 2011 review of funding mechanisms found that funding for school capital and infrastructure was un-co-ordinated and lacked planning and that many schools, particularly in the government sector, were suffering from a lack of capital investment (Gonski et al., 2011). It supported the continued allocation of funding for maintenance as part of current expenditures, and the creation of two main capital expenditure funding streams for allocations from the Australian government: one to support new schools and school expansions; and the other to support investment in infrastructure in existing schools. The purpose of a central fund for new schools would be to encourage more efficient provision and planning across different sectors of the education system (government schools, non-government schools, Catholic schools, independent schools) and a balanced development of new schools in towns and new suburbs. A major recommendation was to establish School Planning Authorities in each state and territory that would be responsible for administering the central grant for establishing new schools (a school growth fund).

Source: Gonski, D. et al. (2011), *Review of Funding for Schooling – Final Report*, Australian Government, Canberra.

Policy options

Ensure a stable and publicly known system to allocate public funding to schools

A general principle for more effective funding distribution is to ensure that funds are allocated in a transparent and predictable way. Stability and predictability of financing allows all schools to plan their development in the coming years. This highlights the importance of ensuring continuity in the principles and technical details of the funding distribution system.

Funding formulas are used in many of the OECD review countries, and there are examples where the introduction or review of a formula has helped build general acceptance by stakeholders of formula funding as a fair method for funding allocation. The transparency of a formula can have a beneficial impact on policy debates at the national level. Fazekas (2012) cites the presentation of clear criteria that can be scrutinised and debated as a clear advantage of a funding formula for the allocation of public funding. A funding formula provides a clear framework for debates on the sufficiency and proper allocation of funding. Different parameters within the formula may be debated, which can help stakeholders to express their positions clearly and make agreements that are easy to monitor.

Follow guiding principles when designing funding formulas to distribute resources to individual schools

A well designed funding formula is, under certain conditions, the most efficient, equitable, stable and transparent method of distributing funding for current expenditures to schools. The distribution through a formula is more likely to lead to a more efficient and equitable allocation than other methods, including discretionary and incremental funding models. There is no single best practice funding formula. However, the OECD review has identified a set of guiding principles for designing funding formulas.

Align funding formulas with government policy and establish evaluation criteria accordingly

A number of criteria can be used to evaluate a funding formula, in particular efficiency, equity, integrity, administrative cost, accountability and transparency, and sensitivity to local conditions. The balance struck between the various criteria should reflect the government's policy preferences. With regard to meeting equity objectives, formula funding can be designed to combine both horizontal equity – schools of the same type (for example, primary schools) are funded at the same level – and vertical equity – schools of different types (for example, general programmes and technical-professional programmes) are financed according to their differing needs. However, inadequate formulas may exacerbate inequities and also inefficiencies.

Funding formulas should adequately reflect different per student costs of providing education

A major challenge in designing funding formulas is to adequately reflect that it does not cost the same to educate all students. There will be a need to fund schools differentially for legitimate differences in unit costs which are beyond the control of the school. This demands the introduction of different adjustment components in the formulas and could lead to a high degree of complexity. A balance needs to be struck between a simple formula, which might fail to capture school needs with full accuracy, and a sophisticated formula, which might be difficult to understand. As a guide for designing formulas to better meet differing needs, research has identified four main components:

- A basic allocation: This could be an allocation per student or per class and would be differentiated according to the school year (grade level) or stage of schooling (e.g. primary, lower secondary, etc.).

- An allocation for a specific educational provision: This component would adjust for a specific educational profile in a given school. For example, this could be the offer of a specialised curriculum such as a focus on the arts, sports or different vocational fields. It could also be the offer of an adjusted curriculum designed to meet specific educational needs of the school's student group.

- An allocation for students with supplementary needs: This would aim to adjust for different student characteristics which would require additional resources to ensure the same level of access to the required curriculum.

- An allocation for specific needs related to school site/location: This would aim to adjust for structural differences in school site operation costs, e.g. schools located in rural or remote areas with significantly lower class sizes, schools with higher maintenance costs (linked to local economic factors and/or specialised equipment needs).

Funding formulas should promote budgetary discipline

Funding formulas can be designed to set incentives for greater efficiency at the local and school levels. This entails not compensating overspending of schools unless justified by exceptional circumstances (i.e. emergency conditions, unexpected enrolment growth, small schools in remote locations). A per student funding allocation can impose greater fiscal discipline, which may be particularly necessary in a context of declining numbers in the student population that can lead to higher costs in terms of smaller school and class sizes. To acknowledge that not all costs are linear, a funding formula that essentially follows an allocation per student approach can incorporate compensation weights for smaller schools. The advantage of such an approach is that this can target more resources to particular schools (as set by a thorough analysis of national data), while keeping the incentive for the majority of schools in the system to reduce the number of classes by raising class size. This compensation allocation can be reviewed and adjusted to increase or alleviate financial pressure on local authorities with small schools and classes.

Ensure the periodical review of funding formulas to assess the need for adjustments

A periodical review of funding formulas is necessary to ensure they are fit for policy needs (which may change). There may be the need to improve the funding formulas as evaluated against the different criteria. This could include the need to increase or decrease the level of complexity in adjustments for student and school needs. The review of funding formulas should also take into account their position and weighting in the overall allocation of school education funding. For example, funding formulas could be better designed to adjust for differing student and school needs in favour of reducing the number of targeted funding programmes aimed at addressing differential funding needs.

Seek more efficient ways to address equity in funding mechanisms

Funding strategies play an important role in achieving equity objectives within school systems. A crucial aspect of policy is to decide on the best mechanisms to channel the extra resources to student groups with additional needs. This can typically be achieved through the regular allocation mechanism (e.g. a systematic weighted allocation to particular student groups within schools using a funding formula) or through funding directly targeted at specific students, schools or areas (e.g. extra funding to compensate for socio-economic disadvantage). The OECD review has highlighted the importance in striking a balance between targeted and regular funding to more efficiently support greater equity within a school system.

Targeted educational programmes may be used to allocate funding to priority areas. These can ensure responsiveness to emerging priorities and/or promote innovations within the school system. Funding will be earmarked for a specific purpose and can be used to promote specific educational policies. A range of examples are identified across countries, for example to help support mainstreaming of students with special educational needs or to support schools in rural locations. However, an excessive reliance on targeted programmes may generate overlap, difficulties in co-ordinating allocations, excessive bureaucracy, inefficiencies and lack of long term sustainability for schools. Targeted funding often comes along with greater transaction costs, including mechanisms to ensure it has been spent on the purposes it was intended for which may entail greater administrative and reporting burdens for schools (see also Chapter 5). There are, therefore, arguments to reduce transaction costs by including adjustments for vertical equity within the major part of funding allocation via a formula. This can simplify the funding system overall.

Pay adequate attention to the accuracy and reliability of data used as a basis for funding allocation

The OECD review has revealed that a wide range of different indicators are used across countries to distribute funding to schools. There is evidence of considerable refinement in indicators used over recent years and a policy consensus to use indices comprising multiple indicators in order to improve the targeting of socio-economic disadvantage. It is apparent that all indicators have shortcomings and that there is always a trade-off between the accuracy and the simplicity and transparency of an indicator. However, an additional consideration when choosing indicators is that data that cannot be manipulated by schools gives greater integrity to the funding allocation. One example is the use of census-based data as a proxy for data reported by schools on individual student characteristics (see below). While this would be less accurate in targeting individual students, authoritative national research can be used to choose the best proxy indicator or combination of indicators. This also holds the advantage of reducing reporting burden on schools. The accuracy and efficiency of the allocation system will rely upon the level of sophistication of information systems. Many school funding systems aim to strike a balance between using census-based and school-based indicators. All systems should also make sure to regularly review the indicators used to ensure that they reflect evolutions in data systems.

Needs-based allocation mechanisms are intuitive and can be perceived as fair, however, they may have some undesirable effects. For example, when funding is directly linked to the identification of individual students as having special educational needs, this may lead to excessive labelling of students which is stigmatising for individuals and can lead to considerable cost inflation. To avoid inflation of the numbers of students identified over time and inconsistent categorisations, the criteria used for assessing students as having physical or learning impairments should be transparent, unambiguous and applied impartially by educational psychologists. Several OECD countries use targeted funding for more severe special educational needs, complemented by a census-based funding approach for students with milder special educational needs or those linked to socio-economic disadvantage. Examples of such indicators are variables measuring social disadvantage (such as poverty, unemployment, poor housing, and low education level) in the immediate community of the school. Such indicators hold the advantage that schools cannot manipulate them.

Another way of reducing the incentive for excessive labelling of individuals as students with special educational is to allocate some of the funding for students with special educational needs to all schools, as a fixed percentage of their formula budget. Some systems may not use any earmarked funding and this may risk the perception that funding is not allocated to support the learning of students with special educational needs. In such a context, stronger accountability at the school level with scrutiny by school boards on the educational provision in the school for students with special educational needs and the impact it is having on their learning will play a key role.

Share experience about funding formulas developed at sub-national level for system learning

In countries where local authorities have responsibility for funding allocation, there is a great opportunity for system learning. While central authorities cannot directly influence funding allocation, more attention can be devoted to improving efficiency in different approaches used within the country. There will be many different funding formulas developed at the regional or local levels to distribute funding to schools. Many of these will share the aim of providing a more equitable funding allocation. There is, therefore, much potential for local authorities to learn from each other regarding the effective design of funding formulas. Some larger authorities with greater capacity may have developed funding formula with external expertise. Sharing knowledge across authorities can help to avoid duplication of efforts. At the central level there is room to identify and promote best practices in funding allocation.

Evaluate the costs of provision and the adequacy of funding regularly to review allocation efficiency

Improving financial distribution requires regular and detailed analysis of the adequacy of funding and its effects on the quality of teaching, the efficiency of schools and the equity of education. This requires compelling evidence from regular audit work and academic research (Chapter 5 examines these and other monitoring and evaluation mechanisms in depth). Funding mechanisms may be designed to assign additional funding to ensure vertical equity (i.e. providing education of similar quality to different students), but it is important to undertake regular evaluations of the actual costs. Reliable and detailed evidence should be gathered on the costs and adequacy of funding in general, and on specific elements that funding mechanisms aim to address, e.g. concerns for a more equitable distribution to support smaller schools in rural locations, the education of students with special educational needs and equity problems related to socio-economic disadvantages. This would entail an overview of the parameters used, for example, the assumptions for average class size and different school sizes for different educational levels. As funding mechanisms align to policy objectives, these are naturally framed by political preferences. However, comprehensive and compelling analysis and empirical evidence on the exact cost differences would strengthen the basis for policy decisions to review or adjust parameters included in funding mechanisms.

References

Abu-Ghaida, D. (2011), "Per capita financing of general education in Europe and Central Asia: Has it delivered on its promise? An overview of six country case studies", in J.D. Alonso and A. Sánchez (eds.), *Reforming Education Finance in Transition Countries: Six Case Studies in Per capita Financing Schemes*, World Bank, Washington, DC, *http://dx.doi.org/10.1596/978-0-8213-8783-2*.

Atkinson, M. et al. (2005), *School Funding: A Review of Existing Models in European and OECD Countries*, National Foundation for Educational Research/Local Government Association, Slough.

Australian Government (2010), "A future fair for all - School funding in Australia", Address to Sydney Institute, 15 April 2010, *https://ministers.employment.gov.au/gillard/future-fair-all-school-funding-australia-address-sydney-institute*.

Bénabou, R., F. Kramarz and C. Prost (2004), "Zones d'éducation prioritaire : quels moyens pour quels résultats ?", *Économie et Statistique*, Vol. 380, Insee, pp. 3-34.

Bénabou, R. et al. (2007), "The French Zones d'Éducation Prioritaire: Much ado about nothing ?", *Economics of Education Review*, Vol. 28/3, Elsevier, pp. 345-356.

Burns, T. and F. Köster (eds.) (2016), *Governing Education in a Complex World*, OECD Publishing, Paris, *http://dx.doi.org/10.1787/9789264255364-en*.

Commonwealth of Australia (2011), *Building the Education Revolution Implementation Taskforce. Final Report*, Commonwealth of Australia, Canberra.

European Commission/EACEA/Eurydice (2016), *Structural Indicators on Achievement in Basic Skills in Europe – 2016*, Eurydice Report, Publications Office of the European Union, Luxembourg, *https://webgate.ec.europa.eu/fpfis/mwikis/eurydice/images/1/1b/Achievement_in_Basic_Skills_.pdf*.

European Commission/Eurydice (2000), *Key Topics in Education in Europe Volume 2: Financing and Management of Resources in Compulsory Education - Trends in National Policies*, European Communities, Luxembourg.

Fazekas, M. (2012), "School Funding Formulas: Review of Main Characteristics and Impacts", *OECD Education Working Papers*, No. 74, OECD Publishing, Paris, *http://dx.doi.org/10.1787/5k993xw27cd3-en*.

Gonski, D. et al. (2011), *Review of Funding for Schooling - Final Report*, Australian Government, Canberra.

Greening, J. (2016), *Schools Funding*, Written statement to Parliament by The Right Honourable Justine Greening Member of Parliament, Department for Education and the Education Funding Agency, delivered on 21 July 2016, *www.gov.uk/government/speeches/schools-funding*.

Groenez, S. et al. (2015), *Analyse van het nieuwe financieringsmechanisme voor de werkingsmiddelen van scholen, Evaluatie van het Financieringsdecreet van 2008: Eindrapport [Analysis of the New Financing Mechanism for School Operating Grants, Evaluation of the 2008 Decree on School Funding: Final Report]*, KU Leuven.

Harwell, M. and B. LeBeau (2010), "Student Eligibility for a Free Lunch as an SES Measure in Education Research", *Educational Researcher*, Vol. 39/2, Sage, pp. 120-131.

Herczynski, J. (2011), "Student basket reform in Lithuania: Fine-tuning central and local financing of education", in J.D. Alonso and A. Sánchez (eds.), *Reforming Education Finance in Transition Countries: Six Case Studies in Per capita Financing Schemes*, World Bank, Washington, DC, *http://elibrary.worldbank.org/doi/abs/10.1596/978-0-8213-8783-2*.

Ireland Department of Education (2017), *Report on the Review of Deis*, Ireland Department of Education, Dublin, *www.education.ie/en/Schools-Colleges/Services/DEIS-Delivering-Equality-of-Opportunity-in-Schools-/DEIS-Review-Report.pdf*.

Jackson, C.K., R.C. Johnson and C. Persico (2016), "The effects of school spending on educational and economic outcomes: evidence from school finance reforms", *The Quarterly Journal of Economics*, Vol. 131/1, Oxford University Press, pp. 157-218, *http://dx.doi.org/10.1093/qje/qjv036*.

Lafortune, J., J. Rothstein and D. Whitmore Schazenbach (2016), "School finance reform and the distribution of student achievement", *NBER Woking Paper Series*, No. 22011, National Bureau of Economic Research, Cambridge, MA, *www.nber.org/papers/w22011.pdf*.

Levačić, R. (2008), "Financing schools: Evolving patterns of autonomy and control", *Educational Management Administration and Leadership*, Vol. 36/2, Sage, pp. 221–234, *http://dx.doi.org/10.1177/1741143207087774*.

Levačić, R. (2006), *Funding Schools by Formula*, paper prepared for International Conference on Educational Systems and the Challenge of Improving Results, 15-16 September 2006 University of Lausanne, Switzerland.

Levačić, R. and P. Downes (2004), *Formula Funding of Schools, Decentralization and Corruption: A Comparative Analysis*, International Institute for Educational Planning, UNESCO, Paris.

Levačić, R. and K. Ross (1999), "Principles for designing needs-based school funding formulae?", in *Needs-Based Resource Allocation in Education: Via Formula Funding of Schools*, UNESCO International Institute for Educational Planning, Paris.

Levačić, R. et al. (2000), "Funding schools by formula : Comparing practice in five countries", *Journal of Education Finance*, Vol. 25/4, University of Illinois Press, pp. 489–515.

Ministère de la Fédération Wallonie-Bruxelles (2016), *Examen de l'OCDE des Politiques pour un Usage Plus Efficace des Ressources Scolaires Rapport Pays*, Ministère de la Fédération Wallonie-Bruxelles, Bruxelles, *www.oecd.org/education/schoolresourcesreview.htm*.

Moisan, C. and J. Simon (1997), *Évaluation des ZEP*, Circulaire no. 97–233, Institut de Recherche sur l'Éducation, Paris.

NCES (2016), *Selected Statistics from the Public Elementary and Secondary Education Universe: School Year 2014-15*, Institute of Education Sciences, National Center for Education Statistics, Washington, DC, *https://nces.ed.gov/pubs2016/2016076.pdf*.

New Zealand Ministry of Education (2015), *Education Report: Funding Review – Draft Stock-Takes and Next Steps*, Summary Report for the Minister of Education, *https://education.govt.nz/ministry-of-education/consultations-and-reviews/education-funding-system-review*.

New Zealand Ministry of Education (2010), *OECD Review on Evaluation and Assessment Frameworks for Improving School Outcomes: New Zealand Country Background Report 2010*, New Zealand Ministry of Education, *www.oecd.org/education/school/47797042.pdf*.

Nusche, D. et al. (2016a), *OECD Reviews of School Resources: Denmark 2016*, OECD Publishing, Paris, *http://dx.doi.org/10.1787/9789264262430-en*.

Nusche, D. et al. (2016b), *OECD Reviews of School Resources: Austria 2016*, OECD Publishing, Paris, *http://dx.doi.org/10.1787/9789264256729-en*.

Nusche, D. et al. (2015), *OECD Reviews of School Resources: Flemish Community of Belgium 2015*, OECD Publishing, Paris, *http://dx.doi.org/10.1787/9789264247598-en*.

OECD (2016), *Education at a Glance 2016: OECD Indicators*, OECD Publishing, Paris, *http://dx.doi.org/10.1787/eag-2016-en*.

OECD (2015), *Education Policy Outlook: United Kingdom*, OECD Publishing, Paris, *www.oecd.org/education/policyoutlook.htm*.

OECD (2013), *Synergies for Better Learning: An International Perspective on Evaluation and Assessment*, OECD Publishing, Paris, *http://dx.doi.org/10.1787/9789264190658-en*.

OECD (2012), *Equity and Quality in Education: Supporting Disadvantaged Students and Schools*, OECD Publishing, Paris, *http://dx.doi.org/10.1787/9789264130852-en*.

OECD/The World Bank (2015), *OECD Reviews of School Resources: Kazakhstan 2015*, OECD Publishing, Paris, *http://dx.doi.org/10.1787/9789264245891-en*.

Ofsted (2012), *The Pupil Premium*, Ofsted Publications Centre, Manchester.

Sandford, M. (2016), "Local government in England: Structures", *House of Commons Library Briefing Papers*, No. 07104, House of Commons Library, London, *http://researchbriefings.files.parliament.uk/documents/SN07104/SN07104.pdf*.

Sange-SFK (2012), *Подушевое финансирование: за и против, аналитический отчет* [Per capita Funding: Pro and Contra], Soros Fund Kazakhstan, Almaty.

Santiago, P. et al. (forthcoming), *OECD Reviews of School Resources: Chile 2017*, OECD Reviews of School Resources, OECD Publishing, Paris.

Santiago, P. et al. (2016a), *OECD Reviews of School Resources: Slovak Republic 2015*, OECD Publishing, Paris, *http://dx.doi.org/10.1787/9789264247567-en*.

Santiago, P. et al. (2016b), *OECD Reviews of School Resources: Estonia 2016*, OECD Publishing, Paris, *http://dx.doi.org/10.1787/9789264251731-en*.

Santiago, P. et al. (2016c), *OECD Reviews of School Resources: Uruguay 2016*, OECD Publishing, Paris, *http://dx.doi.org/10.1787/9789264265530-en*.

Santiago, P. et al. (2011), *OECD Reviews of Evaluation and Assessment in Education: Australia 2011*, OECD Publishing, Paris, *http://dx.doi.org/10.1787/9789264116672-en*.

Shewbridge, C. et al. (2016a), *OECD Reviews of School Resources: Czech Republic 2016*, OECD Publishing, Paris, *http://dx.doi.org/10.1787/9789264262379-en*.

Shewbridge, C. et al. (2016b), *OECD Reviews of School Resources: Lithuania 2016*, OECD Publishing, Paris, *http://dx.doi.org/10.1787/9789264252547-en*.

Smith, G.R. (1999), "Area-based initiatives: The rationale and options for area targeting", *CASE Paper*, Centre for Analysis of Social Exclusion, London.

Smyth, E., S. McCoy and G. Kingston (2015), "Learning from the evaluation of DEIS", *Research Series Number 39*, The Economic and Social Research Institute, Dublin, *www.esri.ie/pubs/RS39.pdf*.

Sugarman, J., S. Morris-Lange and M. McHugh (2016), *Improving Education for Migrant-Background Students: A Transatlantic Comparison of School Funding*, Migration Policy Institute, Washington, DC, *www.migrationpolicy.org/research/improving-education-migrant-background-students-transatlantic-comparison-school-funding*.

Swedish Ministry of Education and Research (2016), *OECD Review of Policies to Improve the Effectiveness of Resource Use in Schools: Country Background Report for Sweden*, Swedish Ministry of Education and Research Stockholm, *www.oecd.org/education/schoolresourcesreview.htm*.

Tunstall, R. and R. Lupton (2003), "Is targeting deprived areas an effective means to reach poor people? An assessment of one rationale for area-based funding programmes", *CASE Paper 70*, Centre for Analysis of Social Exclusion, London.

UK Department for Education (2016), *Schools and High Needs Funding Reform: The Case for Change and Consultation Summary*, Department for Education, London, *https://consult.education.gov.uk/funding-policy-unit/high-needs-funding-reform/supporting_documents/Summary%20and%20case%20for%20change.pdf*.

UNICEF (2012), *Разработка методики подушевого финансирования организаций общего среднего образования и пилотная апробация предложенной модели* [Developing and Piloting the Methodology for a Per capita Financing Scheme in General Secondary Education in Kazakhstan and Piloting the Proposed Model], UNICEF, Astana.

US Census Bureau (2016), "Public education finances: 2014", *Economic Reimbursable Surveys Division Reports*, Educational Finance Branch, US Census Bureau, Washington, DC, *www.census.gov/content/dam/Census/library/publications/2016/econ/g14-aspef.pdf*.

US Department of Education (2017), The Federal Role in Education, US Department of Education, *www2.ed.gov/about/overview/fed/role.html*.

Weir, S. and C. Ryan (2000), *Interim Report on the Evaluation of the Breaking the Cycle Scheme in Rural Schools*, Educational Research Centre, Dublin.

West, A. (2009), "Redistribution and financing schools in England under Labour: are resources going where needs are greatest?", *Education Management, Administration and Leadership*, Vol. 37/2, Sage, pp. 158-179.

West, A. and H. Pennell (2000), "New labour and school-based education in England: Changing the system of funding?", *British Educational Research Journal*, Vol. 26/4, Wiley-Blackwell, pp. 523-536.

World Bank (2011), *Reforming Education Finance in Transition Countries: Six Case Studies in Per capita Financing Systems*, The World Bank, Washington, DC, *http://dx.doi.org/10.1596/978-0-8213-8783-2*.

ANNEX 3.A1

National approaches to distributing school funding

Table 3.A1.1. **Funding formulas: different criteria used for allocation of current expenditure among OECD review countries (ISCED 1-3), 2016**

Allocation mechanism		Purpose	Funding allocation		Level of education (ISCED)		Basic unit	School characteristics				Curriculum					Student characteristics			
Country			From	To				L	S	SES	Other	Lvl	SY	EdT	Pg	WbP	SES	SEN	Min/Imm	Other
Austria	DG	Teacher salaries	CA	St	2	3	S/C													
	EG	Teaching students with SEN	CA	Sc	1	3	T/S				✓							✓		
Belgium (Fl. and Fr.)	BG	Operational budget (inc. maintenance staff)	SA	SP	1	3	S	✓	✓			✓	✓	✓	✓	✓	✓	✓		
	RBG	Disadvantaged students; immigrants; refugees	SA	SP	1	3	S	✓	✓			✓	✓	✓	✓		✓	✓		
	DG	Staff salaries (teachers, management, admin)	SA	St	1	3	T/S	✓	✓			✓	✓		✓	✓	✓	✓		
Chile	BG	General and pro-retention subsidies	CA	SP	1	3	At/S	✓	✓			✓		✓			✓			
	EG	Complement for teacher salaries	CA	SP	1	3	T		✓	✓										
	EG	Students with SEN; disadvantaged students	CA	SP	1	3	T		✓	✓		✓								
	EG	Staff salary incentives in top performing schools	CA	SP	1	3	At/S				✓									
Czech Republic	EG	Direct costs of school education	CA	RA	1	3	S	✓	✓			✓		✓						
	RBG	Direct costs (inc. salaries)	RA	Sc	1	3	S				✓	✓		✓	✓					
Denmark	BG	For current expenditure	CA	Sc		3	S	✓	✓			✓								
Estonia	EG	General education (inc. salaries)	CA	SP	1	3	S	✓	✓					✓						
	EG	Policy priorities (specialised provision)	CA	SP	1	3											✓		✓	
	RBG	Schools owned by CA	CA	Sc	1	3	S	✓	✓					✓						
	EG	State commissioned VET study place	CA	LA	2	3	Study place						✓		✓			✓		
	EG	Study allowances (VET) to 3 municipalities	CA	LA	2	3	Study place						✓		✓			✓		
Iceland	BG	Any type of expenditure	CA	Sc		3	S	✓	✓			✓						✓		
	BG/EG	Equalise differences in LA income/expenditure needs	CA	LA	1	2	S				✓			✓	✓				✓	
Israel	EG	Non-teacher salaries and operational costs	CA	LA	1	3	S	✓				✓					✓			
	EG	Teacher salaries	CA	LA		3											✓	✓		
	DG	Teacher salaries	CA	St	1	2	S	✓				✓						✓		

Table 3.A1.1. **Funding formulas: different criteria used for allocation of current expenditure among OECD review countries (ISCED 1-3), 2016** (cont.)

Country	Allocation mechanism	Purpose	From	To	ISCED	Basic unit	School: L	School: S	School: SES	School: Other	Curr: Lvl	Curr: SY	Curr: EdT	Curr: Pg	Curr: WbP	Stud: SES	Stud: SEN	Stud: Min/Imm	Stud: Other
Lithuania	EG	Teaching and operational costs	CA	LA/Sc	1 2 3	S	✓				✓							✓	
Slovak Republic	BG	Salaries (forms one BG with operational costs)	CA	SP	1 2	S		✓			✓		✓	✓			✓		
	BG	Salaries (forms one BG with operational costs)	CA	SP	3	S				✓			✓	✓					
	BG	Operational costs (forms one BG with salaries)	CA	SP	1 2	S		✓		✓			✓	✓	✓				
	BG	Operational costs (forms one BG with salaries)	CA	SP	3	S				✓			✓	✓					
	EG	Socially disadvantaged students	CA	LA	1 2	S										✓			
	EG	Student competitions/international projects	CA	SP	1 2 3	S				✓									
Slovenia	BG	Any type of expenditure (except SEN/school meals)	CA	Sc	3	S							✓			✓	✓		
	EG	Students with SEN; School meals	CA	Sc	3	S										✓	✓	✓	
	EG	Operating costs of the educational programme	CA	Sc	1 2	S/T	✓										✓		
Spain	DG	Staff salaries; Teacher professional development	RA	St	1 2 3	S/T/C													✓
	EG	Supporting students with SEN	RA	Sc	1 2 3	S/T								✓			✓		
	EG	Operating costs/maintenance	RA	Sc	2 3	C	✓	✓			✓						✓	✓	
Denmark[1]	Dis	For current expenditure	LA	Sc	1 2	S/C	✓	✓	✓							✓			
Iceland[1]	BG/EG	Salaries/operating costs; support for specific students	LA	Sc	1 2	S	✓	✓		✓				✓			✓		
Sweden[1]	Dis	Typically for any type of expenditure	LA	Sc	1 2 3	S												✓	✓

1. While local authorities have discretion to design allocation mechanisms, many use funding formulas. The most typical criteria are presented in this table.

Notes: Allocation mechanism: DG = dedicated grant; EG = earmarked grant; BG = block grant; RBG = restricted block grant; Dis = discretionary funding

Funding allocation: CA = central authorities; SA = state authorities; RA = regional authorities; LA = local authorities; SP = school providers; Sc = schools; St = staff

Basic unit: S = student; C = class; T = teacher; At = attendance

School characteristics: L = location; S = size; SES = socio-economic status

Curriculum: Lvl = level of education; SY = school year; EdT = type of education; Pg = programme; WbP = work-based placement

Student characteristics: SES = socio-economic status; SEN = special educational needs; Imm = immigrant background; Min = minority

Full descriptive criteria are provided in the individual country profiles presented in Annex A.

The review team made every effort to ensure, in collaboration with countries, that the information collected through the qualitative survey on school funding is valid and reliable and reflects specific country contexts while being comparable across countries. However, given the qualitative nature of the survey, information should be interpreted with care.
For terms and definitions of allocation mechanisms, levels of governance and levels of education, see Annex B. For country-specific notes to this table, see the end of this annex.

Table 3.A1.2. **Predominant basis to determine allocation of current expenditure does not include funding formulas, OECD review countries (ISCED 1-3), 2016**

		Allocation mechanism	Funding allocation		Level of education (ISCED)			Basis to determine funding allocation	Typical criteria
			From	To					
Kazakhstan	AnG	For any type of current expenditure	CA/RA/LA	Sc	1	2	3	Administrative discretion Negotiated process Historical basis	SchT, L, S, SEC, Lvl, SEN
	EG	For equalising differences in regional/local revenues, and implementing specific government programmes and initiatives	CA/RA	Ad/Sc	1	2	3	Administrative discretion Negotiated process Historical basis	
Portugal	EG	Teacher salaries	CA	SP/Sc	1	2	3	Historical basis Administrative discretion	
	EG	Non-teaching staff salaries	CA	SP/Sc			3	Historical basis Administrative discretion	
	RBG	Operating costs	CA	SP/Sc		2	3	Historical basis Administrative discretion	
	DG	Salaries of non-teaching staff	LA	St	1	2		Historical basis Administrative discretion	
	Dis	Any type of current expenditure, except teacher salaries	LA	SP/Sc	1	2	3	Historical basis Administrative discretion	
Uruguay	AnG	For any type of current expenditure	CA	Ad	1	2	3	Negotiated process Historical basis	
	DG	Teacher salaries and professional development	CA/Ad	Sc	1	2	3	Administrative discretion	SchT, Pg, ER
	RBG	Operating costs	CA	Sc	1	2	3	Administrative discretion	SchT, Pg
	DG	Instructional material and telephone expenses	CA	Sc	1	2	3	Administrative discretion Historical basis	SchT, Pg
	DG	Teacher training in support of students with SEN	CA	Sc	1	2	3	Administrative discretion	SchT, Pg, SEN
	EG	School meals	CA	Sc		2	3	Administrative discretion	SchT, Pg

Notes: Allocation mechanism: AnG = annual grant; DG = dedicated grant; EG = earmarked grant; RBG = restricted block grant
Funding allocation: CA = central authorities; RA = regional authorities; LA = local authorities; Ad = administration; SP = school providers; Sc = schools; St = staff
Typical criteria: SchT = school type; L = school location; S = school size; SEC = socio-economic composition of school; Lvl = level of education; SEN = students with special educational needs; Pg = education programme: ER = enrolment rate
Full descriptive criteria are provided in the individual country profiles presented in Annex A.

The review team made every effort to ensure, in collaboration with countries, that the information collected through the qualitative survey on school funding is valid and reliable and reflects specific country contexts while being comparable across countries. However, given the qualitative nature of the survey, information should be interpreted with care.

For terms and definitions of allocation mechanisms, levels of governance and levels of education, see Annex B. For country-specific notes to this table, see the end of this annex.

Table notes

Table 3.A1.1. Funding formulas: different criteria used for allocation of current expenditure among OECD review countries

Austria:

The earmarked grant for teaching of students with special educational needs from the central education authority takes the school type as criterion into account.

Chile:

Earmarked grants for students with special educational needs and for disadvantaged students take historic school performance as an allocation criterion into account. The earmarked grant allocated to school providers as a salary incentive for education professionals is allocated based on performance within a comparable group in each region as determined by the National Performance Evaluation System of Subsidised Schools (*Sistema Nacional de Evaluación del Desempeño*, SNED). According to the Law 19.410 (Articles 15-17), the subsidy goes to school providers. Every trimester, the school provider distributes 90% of the subsidy among the school`s teachers, and the remaining 10% are used for salary incentives for remarkable teachers as defined by the teachers themselves, not the school provider.

Czech Republic:

The restricted block grant from regional authorities to schools for direct education-related costs typically also includes the school's specific infrastructure.

Iceland:

The block grant from local authorities to compulsory schools (ISCED 1-2) typically takes the proportion of low achievers into account.

Israel:

The earmarked grant from the central authority to local authorities for teachers' salaries in upper secondary education (ISCED 3) takes the characteristics of school network into account.

Slovak Republic:

The block grants from the central authority to school providers takes students with special educational needs integrated in mainstream education into account. The earmarked grant from the central authority to school providers for student competitions or participation in international projects takes the number of students placed in the first three positions in the competition and the number of international projects the school participates in into account.

Spain:

The funding formula for the dedicated grant for staff salaries and teacher professional development from the regional authorities includes identified needs of students as one criterion.

Sweden:

The criteria for allocating funds to schools are at the discretion of the municipality or district. The Education Act stipulates that the municipal funding mechanism should account for the number of students enrolled and also the "different precondition and needs of different students".

Table 3.A1.2. Predominant basis to determine allocation of current expenditure does not include funding formulas, OECD review countries

Kazakhstan:

The allocation of the annual grant from central, regional and local authorities to schools is based on schools' annual budget calls, the administrative levels' annual financial plans, and historical expenditures.

Chapter 4

Planning the use of school funding

This chapter describes practices and procedures involved in planning the effective use of school funding among OECD review countries and analyses the challenges involved in the process. First, the chapter reviews how budget planning procedures can be linked to educational targets and priorities as well as research and evaluation results to strategically guide the planning process and employ resources as effectively and equitably as possible. Following an overview of budget planning practices from the central to the school level, the chapter then discusses different techniques employed to render the process more flexible, responsive and efficient. Based on this overview and drawing on the OECD analysis of country practices, the chapter then explores how multi-annual perspectives and the effective use of targets or evaluation results can support the development of more efficient and effective planning procedures.

The statistical data for Israel are supplied by and under the responsibility of the relevant Israeli authorities. The use of such data by the OECD is without prejudice to the status of the Golan Heights, East Jerusalem and Israeli settlements in the West Bank under the terms of international law.

The process leading up to the formulation and implementation of funding plans is a key stage of the budgeting cycle. It provides an opportunity to reflect upon previous expenditure and future resource needs in order to develop financially sustainable budgets that support the provision of high quality education and effectively address policy priorities. Following this brief introduction, the chapter describes the practices and procedures underpinning the planning of school funding in different OECD and partner countries. First, it reviews different approaches to linking planning procedures to educational targets and strategic priorities as well as research and evaluation results. Second, it provides an overview of specific budget planning practices at the central, the intermediate and the school level. Third, the chapter discusses different techniques used to render the planning process more flexible, responsive and efficient. Based on the OECD review of country practices, the chapter then concludes with a set of policy options aimed at developing more effective planning procedures. Relevant data from the OECD review's qualitative survey is presented in the chapter annex.

Linking budget planning to policy objectives

As policy objectives evolve, countries face the challenge of aligning their funding strategies to best support these goals. Although countries emphasise them to different degrees at different times, typical education objectives include educational quality (e.g. improving overall achievement, improving the competencies of the teaching workforce), equity and inclusiveness (e.g. additional support for students from a low socio-economic background; integration of special needs students in mainstream schools), expansion (e.g. widening access to pre-primary education, diversity of offerings in secondary education) and excellence (e.g. targeting high performers). As a means to align their funding strategies with these objectives, countries have – to varying extent – integrated strategic considerations into their budgeting procedures. This may involve the use of strategic documents to guide the budget planning process or the development of expenditure frameworks that connect spending decisions to education priorities. To facilitate the integration of education strategies into the budgeting process, some countries have placed particular emphasis on developing clear targets, corresponding indicator frameworks and mechanisms to report on the system's use of resources to achieve these goals. This chapter focusses on the formulation of educational objectives and their connection to spending decisions, while Chapter 5 elaborates on the corresponding monitoring and evaluation procedures.

Formulating priorities and objectives

Effectively using education objectives to inform spending decisions depends on a shared understanding of educational quality and priorities to guide the budgeting process as well as the development of targets and reference standards against which its effectiveness can be assessed. Particularly in school systems with decentralised resource management responsibilities, the definition of well-defined and prioritised goals that can be translated into concrete targets at the local and school level has been central to guiding educational reforms (Nusche et al., 2016a). Box 4.1 provides an example from Denmark, showcasing the formulation of education priorities as a means to support the reform process in a decentralised budgeting system.

Box 4.1. **National targets guiding reform in Denmark**

As a school system characterised by a high degree of decentralisation in spending decisions, Denmark has developed an approach to educational steering that relies on the definition of clear education goals that translate into measurable targets at the local and school level. For the 2014 *Folkeskole* reform, it defined three core objectives pertaining to student achievement, equity and wellbeing along with a range of corresponding measurable indicators. The progress on all of these indicators was monitored for every school and reported to the municipalities. Similarly, the 2012 inclusion reform was guided by a clear target of an overall inclusion rate of 96% which provided a common objective for actors at all levels and appears to have been well-understood and taken on board by municipalities and schools to inform their local education planning.

Another noteworthy example of clearly formulated national targets is the Danish government's policy for teacher competency development and specialisation, which is part of the 2014 *Folkeskole* reform. The government established the target that 95% of teachers should be certified in all the subjects that they teach by 2020, including the short-term objectives of reaching 85% by 2016 and 90% by 2018. To facilitate the achievement of these objectives, the Ministry for Children, Education and Gender Equality has provided additional funding for teacher competency development along with evidence-based recommendations on how this funding could be spent. In order to apply for these funds, municipalities are required to develop a plan for their use, report back on their progress and repay any unspent money to the ministry by 2020.

Source: Nusche, D. et al. (2016a), OECD *Reviews of School Resources: Denmark 2016*, http://dx.doi.org/10.1787/9789264262430-en.

Many countries face challenges in establishing a shared understanding of educational quality that is suited to inform the planning of efficient resource use. In some countries, the use of idiosyncratic criteria, conflicting definitions or a failure to raise awareness of existing standards among all actors of the education system has created a lack of agreement over standards for educational quality. In Lithuania, for example, school and local level planning and evaluation are largely guided by idiosyncratic criteria, although the central level provides a framework for external school evaluation that sets out a detailed list of quality standards and 67 corresponding indicators (Shewbridge et al., 2016a). Likewise, not all countries set target dates for the completion of their educational objectives as part of planning process, which results in the absence of clear timeframes that could be used to subsequently evaluate spending decisions (Santiago et al., forthcoming).

Connecting spending decisions to targets and priorities

Education targets and priorities can be used to inform different stages of the budgeting process across administrative levels to ensure that the use of resources is aligned with educational objectives. An increasing number of OECD countries are making use of strategic documents to inform budget planning procedures and connect spending decisions to policy priorities. Developing these linkages between budget and strategy frameworks can provide governments with a clearer picture of where public finances are spent, facilitate the allocation of resources according to policy priorities and make it easier to track spending against the achievement of policy outcomes, particularly where targets and priorities are formulated in concrete terms (IIEP-UNESCO, 2010).

Although countries increasingly integrate annual budgets into strategically oriented medium-term expenditure frameworks (MTEFs), not all MTEFs are guided by concrete targets and priorities. For example, the five-year education budgets used in Uruguay were weakly linked to medium- and long-term strategic goals until annual targets and corresponding indicators were introduced with the most recent 2015-19 Budget Plan (Santiago et al., 2016b). Austria is another country that has taken significant steps to strengthen the link between spending decisions, performance and policy priorities by moving towards a performance-oriented budgeting approach at the national level. Building on a comprehensive reform launched in 2009, Austria introduced new budgeting principles in 2013 which led to the inclusion of performance targets in the federal budget alongside concrete actions envisaged to achieve these targets and criteria used to measure their success. The two education-related goals included in the 2015 budget are to improve gender equality in education and raise the level of education. Each goal is accompanied by three indicators whose progress is evaluated as part of the country's monitoring framework for educational quality (Nusche et al., 2016b). The broad goals are then linked and referred back to by specific budget programmes such as the one for "compulsory schooling – primary and secondary level" (Bruneforth et al., forthcoming).

However, even where performance- or outcome-oriented budgeting norms are followed at the national level, they are not always adopted at sub-central levels of administration. Some countries therefore mandate all levels of the education system from the central to the school level to develop their budgets and justify their spending decisions in light of a shared set of priorities. This may involve drafting their own medium- and short-term strategic plans and budgets in line with the central level expenditure framework or at least actively contributing to the preparation of local expenditure frameworks prepared at the central level. Estonia provides an example where co-ordination within and between ministries and different levels of administration are used to promote widespread awareness and understanding of the country's education goals and their effective integration into the budgeting process (see Box 4.2). However, in many countries, insufficient technical capacity at both the central and local levels constitutes a challenge when involving sub-central authorities in the implementation of strategic budgeting plans (IIEP-UNESCO, 2010).

Kazakhstan provides an example for strategically informed budgeting in a highly centralised planning system driven by an extensive system of norms which ensure that decisions issued at the central level filter down to local and school authorities. Strategic documents guiding the short-, medium- and long-term strategy contain specific indicators and targets which are translated into local implementation plans by intermediate authorities and regularly monitored for progress (OECD/The World Bank, 2015). Centralised top-down approaches provide clear expectations and priorities, ensure policy continuity and facilitate the monitoring of progress towards policy goals. On the other hand, limited spending discretion at the local level and a lack of consultation with stakeholders in the budgeting process will constrain the ability of school and local authorities to employ the mix of inputs deemed most appropriate to meet their local needs and efficiently deliver quality education. The engagement of a broad set of stakeholders and opportunities for participation are key to facilitating meaningful exchange, designing long term reforms and ensuring that education strategies adequately reflect resource needs across geographic and administrative areas of the system.

> ### Box 4.2. **Strategic education budgeting in Estonia**
>
> Estonia has taken important steps to integrate its annual budgeting processes into longer-term strategic frameworks at all levels of governance. By law, the national government, local governments and schools must have Strategic Development Plans. In the case of local and national governments, these plans must be linked to four-year medium-term expenditure frameworks (MTEF). These frameworks establish the parameters based on which annual budgets are drafted, before they are themselves adjusted in light of those budgets.
>
> At the national level, the National Reform Programme "Estonia 2020" constitutes the most important strategic document, which was adopted in the context of the Europe 2020 strategy. It identifies 17 major challenges facing the country and divides them into 4 basic fields, one of which is education. These educational priorities are further defined by the Estonian Lifelong Learning Strategy 2020, which in turn serves as the platform for financial planning in the sector between 2014 and 2020. Strategic priorities and goals are expressed in concrete financial terms by the Ministry of Education and Research's four-year MTEF and currently implemented through thirteen programmes.
>
> This expenditure framework is subject to inter-ministerial discussion and debate before being integrated into the government's overarching MTEF. In March of every year, the Ministry of Finance uses economic forecasts and the government's MTEF to give all line ministries a budget ceiling for the following four years. By April, line ministries must fit their priorities into these ceilings in accordance with their stated objectives and adjust their MTEFs accordingly. Negotiations between high-level civil servants result in further modifications of each ministry's budget and in September, the government submits its general budget proposal for the next fiscal year to parliament for debate. Local governments are also required to align their annual budgets with both four-year expenditure plans and longer-term Strategic Development Plans.
>
> School directors are responsible for developing school budgets. At the national level, most local governments operate according to well defined budget calendars and provide school directors with budget ceilings for the next fiscal year each spring. These figures are then adjusted in autumn when enrolment becomes clearer. In municipal schools, school budgets are reviewed by democratically elected boards of trustees composed of parents, teachers and students before receiving final approval by the local government. In state-run schools, budgets are also reviewed by boards of trustees or advisory bodies (in VET schools). These boards contain not only teacher and parent representatives, but also external experts and – in the case of VET schools – industry representatives. The Ministry of Education and Research grants final approval for the budgets of state schools.
>
> Source: Santiago, P. et al. (2016a), *OECD Reviews of School Resources: Estonia 2016*, *http://dx.doi.org/10.1787/9789264251731-en*.

Developing local capacity and providing support for strategic budgeting

Decentralising resource management responsibility and involving schools or local authorities in the implementation of strategic budgeting frameworks requires capacity at both the central and local level. While school and sub-system authorities require technical skills to prepare and monitor plans, the central level requires the capacity to oversee and provide effective guidance for the decentralised planning process (IIEP-UNESCO, 2010). Particularly smaller communities often lack the training or resources to engage in strategic budget planning. Making budgetary autonomy work may therefore require an investment in local administrative personnel as well as effective self-evaluation and accountability mechanisms (see Chapters 2 and 5). In some of the OECD review countries where schools bear significant responsibilities for the management of financial resources, like the Czech Republic, Estonia and the Slovak Republic, schools or school owners employ specialised administrative staff such as accountants and budget officers (Santiago et al., 2016a; Santiago et al., 2016b; Shewbridge et al., 2016b). Strengthening the capacity for effective budgeting at the sub-central level may also require training on financial resource management and goal-oriented budgeting to be integrated into professional development strategies for local and school-level leaders.

At the same time, even in systems with extensive local budgeting autonomy, the national or regional level can play an important role, not only in planning, triggering and steering education reform with a longer term systemic vision, but also in assisting local actors in the planning of their budget. Central education authorities can develop guidelines to assist with school finance and management procedures, provide feedback on the progress towards education goals, and co-ordinate the co-operation of actors across education levels for a whole-of-system approach to budgeting (Burns and Cerna, 2016). Several countries have also developed central consulting and advisory services that act as knowledge brokers, offering their services to schools and supporting them in making strategic spending choices. Box 4.3 describes how such forms of vertical and horizontal co-operation support local actors in Denmark in assuming their responsibility for strategic budgeting. The centralised provision of electronic budgeting platforms and the supply of relevant data through central information management systems can be another way for the central government to support schools and local authorities in their budget planning activities, as illustrated in Box 4.3 (OECD, 2013c).

Box 4.3. **Supporting budget planning activities at the sub-central level**

Supporting budgeting and resource management in Danish schools and municipalities

Danish school leaders enjoy extensive responsibility for the development of school budget plans and a high level of autonomy in their spending decisions since the largest part of school funding is not earmarked. To support school leaders in their resource management decisions, the Danish education system provides a number of support and accountability mechanisms.

Municipal education offices in Denmark help school leaders with technical aspects of school budgeting such as accounting and bookkeeping, which allows principals to concentrate more on the strategic and pedagogical organisation of the school. In addition municipalities co-operate with schools in the delivery of services and can help them achieve scale economies, for example by buying materials and services for several schools at the same time.

School boards play a formal role in approving school budgets, adding a degree of horizontal accountability to the budgeting process. The 2014 *Folkeskole* reform has therefore provided the national parents' association with financial support to further develop the competences and professionalism of school boards so they can exercise this role effectively.

If the biannual quality reports prepared by the municipalities provide evidence of consistent underperformance in some schools, the central level can provide additional support and recommend municipalities and schools to work with central learning consultants to improve processes and outcomes. In addition, the Ministry of Children, Education and Gender Equality has created a "resource centre for the *Folkeskole*" which mobilises knowledge to complement local expertise with research evidence (Nusche et al., 2016a).

Box 4.3. **Supporting budget planning activities at the sub-central level** *(cont.)*

Supporting school-level budgeting practices through central information systems

All schools in **Iceland** have access to IT systems supporting their budgeting and accounting procedures. The systems are provided by the central government and the respective municipalities but do not comprise tools that are specifically geared towards the planning of financial resources (Icelandic Ministry of Education, Science and Culture, 2014).

In **Estonia**, larger municipalities have developed remote electronic accounting systems for their schools. These systems relieve schools of the costs of keeping their own accounts while also giving them the ability to monitor their budgets on a day to day basis (Santiago et al., 2016a).

Lithuanian schools are supported in their budgeting and accounting through the ministry's education management information system (EMIS) which gives them ready access to indicators such as the average school area per single student or heating costs (Fakharzadeh, 2016).

Source: Nusche, D. et al. (2016a), *OECD Reviews of School Resources: Denmark 2016*, *http://dx.doi.org/10.1787/9789264262430-en*; Icelandic Ministry of Education, Science and Culture (2014), *OECD Review of Policies to Improve the Effectiveness of Resource Use in Schools: Country Background Report for Iceland*, *www.oecd.org/education/schoolresourcesreview.htm*; Santiago, P. et al. (2016a), *OECD Reviews of School Resources: Estonia 2016*, *http://dx.doi.org/10.1787/9789264251731-en*; Fakharzadeh, T. (2016), "Budgeting and Accounting in OECD Education Systems: A Literature Review", *OECD Education Working Papers*, *http://dx.doi.org/10.1787/5jm3xgsz03kh-en*.

Using data and evaluation results in the budgeting process

The effective planning of education funding strategies and reform initiatives requires not only the identification of future resource needs, but also the systematic mobilisation of knowledge generated through research, programme evaluations, monitoring and audit activities (Fazekas and Burns, 2012). Chapter 5 provides a detailed description of different approaches to collecting and reporting data on resource use, monitoring activities and managing relevant information. This section is concerned with the way information on previous budget executions, evaluation results and research evidence are employed to support ministries at the budget preparation stage, increase the efficiency of spending decisions and inform future reform initiatives during both the design and the implementation phase.

Strategic employment of evaluation results, value-for-money analyses and spending reviews

Evaluation results can be used to inform decisions throughout the budgeting cycle and serve as a basis for professional discussions among stakeholders concerning future reform initiatives. According to an OECD survey, approximately half of OECD countries reported the use of policy, programme or project evaluation results during budget negotiations between line ministries and the ministry of finance in 2005 (Curristine, 2005). Even more often than for the budget formulation itself, evaluation activities are commissioned and used internally by line ministries or national audit offices to inform their strategies and targets (Curristine, 2005). Not all evaluation activities explicitly assess the impact of programmes or policies relative to a set of previously established objectives. This can diminish their potential to help ministries in making spending decisions, prioritising among programmes and influencing their design or operation (Santiago et al., forthcoming).

Two evaluation techniques that explicitly aim to support effective spending decisions in the planning of educational resources are cost-benefit analysis and cost-efficiency analysis.

Both constitute value-for-money analyses that weigh the expected or observed benefits of education programmes, policies or investments against the costs of their implementation in order to ensure the efficient and effective use of resources and increase the transparency of budgeting decisions. Cost-benefit analysis and cost-efficiency analysis can take a variety of forms and be employed *ex ante* to compare the anticipated consequences of alternative spending proposals or *ex post*, as a means to evaluate the impact of programmes and policies after their implementation (Fakharzadeh, 2016). Both cost-benefit analysis and cost-efficiency analysis procedures can, under certain circumstances, provide spending authorities with valuable information to inform budget planning procedures, help them choose between projects and policy options, determine the scale and timing of investments and decide on the expansion or continuation of existing projects.

While cost-efficiency analysis takes a particular outcome or target as its starting point and compares the relative cost of different ways to achieve it, cost-benefit analysis aims to provide a holistic comparison of policy options, taking into account all of their associated costs and outcomes by expressing both inputs and benefits in explicit monetary terms. In most OECD countries, these types of analyses are used primarily to evaluate system-level investments in capital projects, with 17 of 32 countries reporting to use some type of value-for-money analysis in the evaluation of all capital investments, another 11 countries using it for capital projects that exceed a certain cost and 9 employing it on an ad hoc basis (OECD, 2014). Cost-benefit and cost-efficiency analyses are less consistently used to inform the budgeting process for other types of education expenditure. Given the difficulties involved in translating the benefits of education programmes (from social mobility and reduced dropout rates to better employment prospects) into monetary values (see Chapter 1), cost-benefit analyses in particular are less frequently used in the education sector than they are in other policy areas (Münich and Psacharopoulos, 2014).

In light of the uncertainty and complexities involved in value-for-money analyses, most decision makers use them to complement, rather than substitute for other sources of information during the budgeting procedure, acknowledging their limitations and underlying assumptions (Münich and Psacharopoulos, 2014). Although the scope to perform rigorous cost-benefit analysis and cost-efficiency analysis in the education sector may be restricted by data limitations and other constraints, elaborating frameworks for value-for-money evaluations alone can help stakeholders develop a clearer idea of the costs and benefits associated with specific proposals, which stakeholders they might accrue to over time and whether any side effects or unintended consequences should be taken into consideration (Münich and Psacharopoulos, 2014).

Since the financial crisis in 2008 and the increased fiscal consolidation pressures that followed, spending reviews have gained importance as another tool to implement strategic savings through the budgeting process, offering a procedure for "developing and adopting savings measures, based on the systematic scrutiny of baseline expenditure" (Robinson, 2014). Rather than evaluating new policies and expenditure proposals, spending reviews are primarily designed to identify potential areas for savings in existing budget lines and recurrent expenditure, either through improved efficiency or reductions in services and transfer payments. Spending reviews may be conducted with a pre-defined savings target, as a means to set MTEFs or to define sectoral expenditure ceilings during the budget preparation. The nature of the reviews varies considerably across countries with regards to their scope, frequency, and the types of saving measures they propose. Yet in 2012, half of the surveyed OECD countries reported to be engaged in a review process and most of these opted for a comprehensive format, identifying saving measures across a wide range of governmental expenditures (Robinson, 2014).

Spending reviews in OECD countries are usually initiated and designed by the finance ministries and political leaders who decide on the review's scope, timeframe and saving targets. Depending on country-specific factors, such as the composition of review teams, education ministries often play a central role when it comes to developing the final set of savings options to be proposed for implementation (Fakharzadeh, 2016). In order to identify areas for efficiency improvements, review teams rely on high-quality information generated through their own evaluation activities or drawn from existing data on educational efficiency. Routinely carrying out evaluation activities can therefore make an important contribution to the quality of spending reviews if their results are relevant, reliable and effectively integrated into the process (Robinson, 2014).

While spending reviews have traditionally been used by countries on an ad hoc basis, they are increasingly integrated into budget preparation processes (Fakharzadeh, 2016). This implies co-ordinating the frequency and timing of spending reviews with that of the country's ministerial budget allocations. In some cases, reviews are also timed so as to ensure that concrete saving options can be presented to the political leadership alongside the cost of newly proposed policy initiatives, which allows them to make a direct contribution to the budget planning process (Robinson, 2014). The simultaneous consideration of spending and saving options makes it possible for governments to adopt new high-priority spending proposals without increasing aggregate expenditure by implementing corresponding saving measures identified in the review process to balance their budget. This process encourages governments to engage in a direct comparison between the merits of new spending proposals and their baseline expenditure (Robinson, 2014).

Use of performance information in the budgeting process

Although there has been a general trend towards a greater emphasis on output criteria and performance information in the budget preparation and planning process (see Chapter 1), there is no consensus on the optimal use of performance data and the way it is employed to inform spending decisions varies considerably across systems (OECD, 2014). Broadly conceived, performance budgeting implies using information on what spending agencies are expected to accomplish with the resources they are allocated. As described above, this approach can entail the specification of measurable objectives and performance indicators for government programmes, the inclusion of targets and expected outcomes alongside expenditure information in budget documents as well as measuring, reporting and evaluating the results of government expenditure and using this information for strategic planning and budgeting (de Jong et al., 2013). Even among countries that routinely integrate performance targets into their budget documents, the use of performance information as a basis to decide future spending allocations is less frequent and often limited.

The information used for performance budgeting purposes can originate from multiple sources and take a variety of forms including operation and performance reports generated through regular evaluation practices, findings from spending reviews as well as various indicators pertaining to resource inputs, outputs and efficiency (Fakharzadeh, 2016; OECD, 2014). The means by which performance data influences spending decisions varies, ranging from its merely presentational use to direct links between performance measures and resource allocation (Curristine, 2005). Most commonly, the link is indirect and performance data serves as one of multiple types of information which decision makers consult for planning and allocation purposes. In theory, performance-based planning and allocation procedures can be used at different levels of the education system and at various points during the budgeting process.

Use of performance information at the system/programme level

Many OECD countries employ central-level frameworks that specify guidelines for the use of performance data during their budgeting processes. In most cases, the link between performance data and central-level spending decisions is flexible, suggesting that countries use performance information to inform budget allocations alongside fiscal considerations and policy priorities, rather than directly to allocate resources. In 2011, line ministries in OECD countries reported to draw on performance data for a variety of purposes during their budget negotiations with the Central Budget Authority (CBA), including decisions to allocate funding to specific programmes, strategic planning and prioritisation, increasing or reducing spending and, more rarely, terminating existing programmes. Still, around a third of OECD countries reported that line ministries make no use of performance information during the budget negotiations at all (OECD, 2014).

Correspondingly, systems differ in their response if performance goals are not met. In a few cases, the failure to meet targets can have direct funding consequences, resulting in the decrease, increase or freezing of the programme's budget. In other cases, poor performance is made public or initiates the intensified monitoring of organisations or programmes. In some systems, missed performance targets entail consequences for a programme's leadership evaluation or prompt the allocation of additional staff and training to agencies, yet few countries have automatic response mechanisms in place (OECD, 2014; OECD, 2013b).

Multiple reasons account for the limited use of performance data in the central level budgeting process. Given the difficulty involved in formulating appropriate performance indicators for the education sector alone, producing performance data or evaluation outputs that allow for strategic comparisons across programmes and ministries is complicated. This can also involve trade-offs between the comparability of evaluation results across sectors and their relevance for the resource decisions faced within the respective ministries. Even in countries with a strong evaluation culture, the decentralised way in which performance evaluations are conducted with a view to informing budgeting practices within specific ministries and agencies can therefore limit their use for budgeting processes at higher levels of authority (Shaw, 2016). Furthermore, using performance data to inform the budget preparation can be difficult in systems whose budget documents and procedures are organised along the lines of inputs, rather than output or outcome measures (see the section on programme budgeting below).

Use of performance information at the school-level

Performance data can also inform allocation decisions at the regional, local or school levels. The use of performance data for budgeting purposes and its impact on educational quality and efficiency is subject to debate and highly dependent on the context and details of its implementation. While performance-based allocation mechanisms have the potential to bring improvements to institutions' efficiency, increase accountability and encourage educational improvement, tying the allocation of resources to performance measures can also have undesired and unintended consequences. Besides the risk of exacerbating existing imbalances in the distribution of resources, performance-based components in the funding of individual schools can set perverse incentives resulting in lower quality standards or risk-avoiding behaviour among teachers and school leaders (Santiago et al., 2016b).

For example, funding vocational education and training programmes based on output criteria like completion rates may encourage institutions to improve student retention and increase their efficiency. However, performance-based funding criteria need to be designed with great care to avoid undesired consequences such as encouraging an excessively narrow focus on easily attainable and measurable outputs, the provision of short and easy-to-pass qualifications, a lowering of examination standards or cream-skimming practices that remove services from the students who need them the most (Papalia, forthcoming). Introducing performance-based funding components at a small scale, such as 2%-5% of funding, may suffice to draw attention to output measures and provide institutions with the desired incentive to improve educational quality without encouraging an excessively narrow focus on specific performance measures (Santiago et al., 2016a). As described in Box 4.4, Finland has implemented a performance-based funding system for VET education building on this principle. Regardless of the funding instrument's specific characteristics, the implementation of performance-based funding should be preceded by a pilot phase in a limited number of schools to carefully monitor its effects.

Box 4.4. **Performance based funding for vocational secondary schools in Finland, 2006**

Finland introduced the performance-based funding of VET providers in 2002, granting education providers additional state subsidies based on their performance. The system became a part of the country's unit price determination system in 2006 and makes up approximately 2% (roughly EUR 20 million) of the entire vocational education funding. The performance-based allocation of resources is based on a composite index that is composed of the following indicators (their relative weight is shown in brackets):

- Effectiveness: job placement (40%) and further studies in higher education (15%).

- Processes: dropouts (15%) and ratio of qualification certification holders to entrants (13%).

- Staff: formal teaching qualifications (11%) and staff development (6%).

Source: Kyrö, M. (2006), "Vocational education and training in Finland: Short description", *Cedefop Panorama Series*, No. 130, Office for Official Publications of the European Communities, Luxembourg.

In Denmark, the government operates a so-called taximeter system to allocate education resources to vocational and upper secondary schools. As part of this system, grants are allocated, among other criteria, based on the number of students enrolled in and completing their education at the individual school or college and afford them a high degree of budgetary autonomy (Houlberg et al., 2016). The taximeter system constitutes an activity-based budgeting tool that provides incentives for schools to increase their performance and efficiency, in particular by improving their student retention and reducing dropout rates.

Developing capacity for the use of data and research evidence across the system

Many OECD countries lack effective mechanisms to strategically integrate data and educational research into the process of evidence-based resource planning (OECD, 2007; Santiago et al., 2016b). Cross-country research indicates that systematic weaknesses in the ability to use data and research evidence can appear at every level of governance (Burns and

Cerna, 2016). As many systems devolve planning and budgeting powers to sub-central authorities, some have taken active measures to synthesise research evidence and feed the results back into the system to support principals and local actors in assuming these new responsibilities effectively.

The effective integration of research evidence into the policy-making and budgeting processes can be facilitated by developing fora that bring together researchers and policy makers to share relevant research evidence and discuss its application, as well as institutions that assess the legitimacy and rigour of research evidence, build trust and increase the co-operation between the policy and research communities (OECD, 2007; Santiago et al., 2016b). This may involve strengthening the capacity and mandate of existing evaluation bodies to assume a more active role as knowledge brokers and tasking them with strategically consolidating evidence from across the system and disseminating it to support policy development and budgeting procedures (Santiago et al., 2016b).

Key procedures and tools for planning the use of school funding

This section provides an overview of the procedures involved in the development of education budgets. It looks at each stage of the budgeting process from the initial planning phase to the budget's adoption as well as the distribution of responsibilities across different governmental actors throughout this process. Furthermore, the section presents planning procedures that can support the budgeting process at the central, sub-central and school-levels as well as forecasting techniques and multi-annual approaches to budgeting.

Stages of the budgeting process

In the most general terms, the budgeting process can be described as a succession of five stages consisting of: i) the budget preparation; ii) its review and adoption; iii) the budget implementation and execution; iv) parliamentary control of the budget implementation and v) financial reporting and external audit (OECD, 2004). This chapter looks into the planning stages of the budget preparation, review and adoption while the monitoring and control of its implementation as well as reporting and external audits are discussed in Chapter 5. Although the budgeting process involves different administrative levels contributing to and sharing decision-making responsibilities at each of these stages, a central budgeting authority (CBA) is usually responsible for co-ordinating the budgeting process at the central level, providing its timeframe, procedural rules and guidelines. In most OECD countries, the CBA is also charged with overseeing the development and submission of the final budget and is located in the Ministry of Finance or Economy. Exceptions to this rule include Australia, Canada and Ireland, where authority over the budgeting process is shared between several government entities, the United States, where it is located in the President's office and Belgium, where the CBA is part of the Federal Public Service Budget and Management Control (OECD, 2014).

Budget preparation and negotiation

The annual preparation of central education budgets conventionally requires education ministries to submit a budget proposal that is subject to negotiations with the CBA before it can be approved and implemented. Prior to the budget's initial draft, finance ministries may impose expenditure ceilings online ministries using a top-down approach, limiting the level of resources which education ministries have at their disposal when preparing their budgets. By contrast, in countries following a strict bottom-up approach, ministries and agencies submit budget requests and new spending proposals first, which the ministry of finance then takes into account when determining the ministries' final budget allocations (Fakharzadeh, 2016).

Few OECD countries, including France, Hungary and the United States, report to provide no ceilings for the initial budget requests of their line ministries (OECD, 2014). Imposing top-down ministerial budget ceilings is typically seen as a proactive way for the finance ministry to ensure that aggregate spending targets are not exceeded due to bottom-up spending pressures from individual ministries. It may also involve a greater responsibility among line ministries to use their operational knowledge to determine the most efficient allocation of resources while the CBA takes responsibility for controlling the aggregate spending level and providing line ministries with advice and technical support, such as expenditure projections for specific programmes (OECD, 2014). When defining ministerial budget ceilings, finance ministries may take into account executive policy priorities and forecasts alongside information such as previous spending levels. The resulting spending ceilings vary in their flexibility, sometimes allowing for the reallocation of resources between ministries after their requests and policy proposals have been taken into account (Robinson, 2013).

Once ministries have drafted and submitted their budget proposals, negotiations with the ministry of finance begin, which may deal with issues such as aggregate ministerial spending levels, specific programme allocations, strategic priorities and the termination or introduction of new budget lines. This process may be governed by formal rules or established conventions and the relative power, responsibilities and procedural roles of education and finance ministries vary across budgeting systems. Budget negotiations in systems following a bottom-up procedure usually last longer than those relying more heavily on a top-down approach, since bottom-up approaches require the finance ministry to negotiate details of individual ministries' proposals in order to meet aggregate fiscal expenditure targets. Across OECD countries, these budget negotiations can last from a few weeks to multiple months. During these negotiations, various forms of information including macroeconomic and fiscal estimates and, to varying extent, performance measures may be brought in to inform allocation decisions (see below for details on this process). Although most disputes arising during the budget formulation process are resolved in lower-level negotiations, the ultimate authority to settle allocation disagreements typically rests with the Cabinet Office, the Ministry of Finance (e.g. in Denmark, Slovenia and Spain) or the Chief Executive (e.g. in Australia, Chile and France). Less frequently, the power to resolve disputes is shared between more than one of these actors or, in the case of Belgium, vested in a ministerial committee (OECD, 2014).

Budget review and adoption

Following the budget negotiations, the ministry of finance usually presents its draft budget to the legislature for discussion and proposed amendments. The parliamentary review process can involve a range of accountability and scrutiny mechanisms, including hearings, plenary debates and reviews by dedicated committees. OECD countries increasingly entrust budget or finance committees with co-ordinating the parliamentary review process, ensuring consistency in the legislative budget actions and drawing on the expertise of other sectoral committees (Schick, 2003). To allow enough time for public scrutiny, parliamentary review and debate, draft budgets are submitted to the legislature at least two months before the start of the fiscal year in the great majority of OECD countries, allowing as much as four months in countries like Denmark and eight months in the United States (OECD, 2014).

The legislature's influence over the budgeting process and its relative authority *vis-à-vis* the executive varies across countries. In most systems, the parliament needs to adopt budgets before they can be implemented, yet in countries such as Greece or Ireland, its role is confined to approving or rejecting the budget proposal. Most OECD legislatures enjoy some power to amend the budget and demand spending to be reallocated at least within the executive's overall expenditure ceiling, although the use of this power may be limited by convention and parliamentary restraint in practice (OECD, 2014). Chapter 5 provides a more detailed account of the budget's implementation and subsequent evaluation.

Budget planning at the central government level

In most OECD countries, the ministry of finance establishes the procedural framework for the budgeting process in a budget circular which it provides to line ministries. The budget circular outlines the rules and timeline for the different budgeting procedures. In addition, it may provide guidelines for the use of fiscal projections, contain expenditure ceilings or targets and inform education ministries of specific government priorities. Throughout the budgeting process, the actors involved may draw on a wide range of information, consultation procedures and planning tools to guarantee that education budgets meet future resource needs.

In countries where the ministry of finance sets budget ceilings before line ministries draft their budget proposals, it may take into account factors such as fiscal targets for the aggregate budget, economic forecasts, past expenditure levels and policy priorities. In countries using bottom-up budgeting procedures, ministerial budget proposals tend to be more expenditure-driven, placing less emphasis on overall economic forecasts or system-wide policy priorities. In either case, some finance ministries offer education ministries their horizontal support during the budget preparation, providing them with procedural guidance as well as relevant financial and accounting documents (Curristine, 2005). Most education ministries also have a dedicated unit that is tasked with budgetary and funding matters, such as the Office of Information and Financial Affairs situated in the Icelandic Department of Education or the Finance Department within the Lithuanian Ministry of Education and Science (Fakharzadeh, 2016). These organisational units can play an important role in setting up budgeting and accounting systems and often take a lead in negotiating education budgets with the finance ministry.

Countries draw on a wide range of information during the central-level preparation of the education budget. Among OECD review countries, all 15 education systems with such central-level planning procedures reported the use of administrative data (e.g. the number of students, teachers and schools). Ten of them also made use of demographic information, such as population projections. Macroeconomic and fiscal forecasts (e.g. the GDP growth rate or the education expenditure's share of the national budget) as well as data on student flows (e.g. dropout or transition rates across education levels) are less common and used to prepare central education budgets in 8 and 5 out of the 15 systems respectively. Eight countries reported to make use of historical allocation techniques by drawing on previous years' budget data and systems frequently consider qualitative information such as policy priorities included in strategic documents (12 of 15) and identified needs (9 of 15) when planning their education budgets. In addition, some countries consult the results of programme and policy impact evaluations (Chile, Estonia, Kazakhstan and Spain) or performance data, for example Estonia, where the success relative to national education targets is taken into account during the budget planning process (see Table 4.A1.1). Not all countries have a systematic approach to the way this information is brought to bear on the budget planning process and the relative emphasis placed on different types of data during the formulation of initial spending ceilings, budget proposals and the subsequent negotiations may vary considerably, not least in light of the often highly politicised context in which budget negotiations take place.

The main types of education expenditure pertain to staffing, operating and infrastructure costs. Given the distinct characteristics of capital investment projects and current expenditure, 20 of 33 surveyed OECD countries used separate system-level budgets for capital and operating expenditures in 2012 (up from 15 countries in 2007). Even though some systems use "integrated budgets" covering both current and investment spending, they might still be separately accounted for before they are merged for allocation purposes (OECD, 2014). The planning tools employed in the budgeting process may vary across different expenditure types accordingly.

Particularly the planning and execution of spending on multi-year capital projects involves distinct budgeting procedures in many OECD countries. More frequently than is the case for operating expenses, decisions on the funding of capital projects are accompanied by *ex ante* value-for-money assessments. Nearly half of OECD countries reported funding the entire cost for capital projects up-front, while another 12 countries provided spending agencies with their capital funding appropriations incrementally over the course of multiple years. The remaining countries, including Austria, the Slovak Republic and the United Kingdom, determined the appropriate funding procedure on a case by case basis (OECD, 2014). In many countries, investment expenditure is also subject to distinct regulations concerning the carry-over of unspent appropriations across budgetary years and the permissibility for ministries to borrow against future appropriations.

Budget planning at sub-central levels

Given the trend towards decentralisation in many OECD countries, the relationships between central governments, ministries, regional and local actors as well as their respective responsibilities in the education budgeting process have been subject to change with local authorities increasingly involved in resource planning. As discussed in Chapter 2, although local actors may enjoy greater allocation and budgeting responsibilities for funds raised at their level of administration, resource raising and budgeting power do not necessarily align and some countries provide regional and local authorities with considerable responsibility for administering central grants (see Chapter 2). Local and regional actors may thus be responsible for developing budget proposals that outline the use of financial resources or their further distribution among sub-central levels of administration and schools.

Not all decentralised systems issue prescriptions concerning the use of particular budgeting and accounting procedures at the sub-central level. In Denmark, for instance, each municipality is responsible for devising and implementing its own budget planning approach (Nusche et al., 2016a). Iceland provides another example, which is discussed in Box 4.5. In other cases, regulations and requirements for local budgeting procedures are inscribed in national legislation, Education Acts and other statues. Guidance and requirements may be communicated through different methods, such as budget circulars, budget laws, generally accepted accounting standards, charts of accounts, and budget classifications. Furthermore, ministries of education and their budget planning units or ministries of finance may provide intermediate authorities with guidelines concerning financial management in education as well as budgeting and accounting practices (Fakhazadeh, 2016).

Box 4.5. **Budget planning responsibilities at the sub-central level in Iceland**

In Iceland, local municipalities are responsible for developing budgets for pre-primary and compulsory schools in consultation with local school leaders. In the aftermath of the financial crisis, Icelandic municipalities administered significant real term cuts to their education budgets, impacting operational expenditure as well as funding for the maintenance and development of facilities. The municipalities' responsibility for deciding when and how to reduce school funding and which services to prioritise or protect in the short- and medium-term underlines the need to develop the capacity for complex planning and funding strategies where such decisions are taken at the local level.

Source: Icelandic Ministry of Education, Science and Culture (2014), OECD *Review of Policies to Improve the Effectiveness of Resource Use in Schools: Country Background Report for Iceland, www.oecd.org/education/ schoolresourcesreview.htm.*

Budget planning in schools

As discussed in Chapter 2, school-level authorities across countries enjoy varying degrees of autonomy in planning their budgets and allocating resources. While staff and operating expenditure are centrally controlled in countries such as Uruguay, others afford school directors extensive control over their budgets including the ability to hire and dismiss teachers or determine their salaries, as is the case in Estonia. Within countries, the discretion over resource allocation and budgeting responsibilities can also vary across school types, levels of education and types of resources.

In the case of Estonia, leaders of municipal schools submit their budget proposals to be approved by the municipal authorities, while the central education authority is responsible for approving state school budgets. School boards, which are typically composed of staff, parents, students and sometimes community representatives, play a more active role in the budget planning process of countries such as Lithuania, where they approve school budgets and often take part in budgeting decisions concerning the use of personal income tax revenues (Shewbridge et al., 2016a). By contrast, in highly centralised systems, actors at the school level may not have any direct involvement in budgeting procedures since budgets are drafted and managed directly from the central level. Similarly, the budgets of most public primary and secondary schools in Chile are managed by local level administrators and indirectly defined through funding allocations transferred from the central level.

In the Flemish Community of Belgium, school boards, which are responsible for the governance of one or multiple schools, enjoy a high degree of autonomy concerning their use of resources and are responsible for setting up their own budgeting and accounting systems in compliance with the rules and procedures of their educational network. In general, the school boards of public providers need to follow the same budgetary rules as any public service while private school boards enjoy more flexibility and in some cases only have to follow the budgeting rules that apply to private enterprises or foundations. However, given that private schools receive public funding, recent changes to EU legislation which also apply to other EU member countries have mandated private school boards to align some of their budgetary procedures with those of public services (Flemish Ministry of Education and Training, 2015).

In many countries where school leaders or school boards are responsible for planning their own budgets, the type of information they use in the process is at their discretion. It often involves a combination of identified resource needs, student flow and enrolment data. To facilitate strategic budget planning at the school level, some countries require school authorities to provide strategic development plans linking the school's education objectives to proposed expenditures. Particularly if they are integrated into a wider multi-annual budget framework adopted at different levels of the system, school development plans can play an important role in facilitating a system-wide approach to educational resource planning.

Different horizontal and vertical support mechanisms can assist schools in their budget preparation. In Denmark, for example, school boards play a formal role in the approval of school budgets (Nusche et al., 2016a). In Estonia, school boards exercise an advisory function in the preparation of school budgets and some municipalities have developed remote electronic accounting systems which relieve schools of the cost of keeping their own accounts (Santiago et al., 2016b). Giving school leaders greater responsibility during the budget development and planning process can promote their ownership of the budget and enhance their ability to use their operational knowledge of the local context to efficiently and effectively respond to local challenges and needs. Enabling them to adequately perform this task requires a commitment to developing capacity at the school and local levels, which will be further discussed below.

Multi-annual budgeting frameworks

Over the past decades, a growing number of OECD countries have adopted medium-term expenditure frameworks (MTEFs) to carry out the budgeting process with a multi-year perspective. Budgeting based on MTEFs typically involves setting expenditure ceilings for a period of three to five years, rather than issuing them on an exclusive year-by-year basis. The ceilings prescribe limits of varying detail pertaining to aggregate and ministerial spending or, less frequently, expenditure levels for specific policy areas and line items. An expenditure framework can be updated on a rolling basis (as in Austria, Germany and Sweden) by adding a new ceiling to the end of the framework period each year. Alternatively, MTEFs can be updated periodically (as in France, the United Kingdom and Uruguay), which involves drawing up a new multi-annual sequence of ceilings once a certain number of years has passed or a new cabinet period started. The individual ceilings of a multi-year framework may be fixed or subject to regular adjustments and MTEFs with budget ceilings of any kind may be complemented by "descriptive forward estimates" of government expenditure and revenue levels under different economic or policy scenarios (OECD, 2014).

By 2012, 29 of 33 surveyed OECD countries reported the use medium-term expenditure frameworks which, in most cases, need to be approved either by the cabinet office or parliament before coming into force. Countries exhibit significant variation in the legal basis and authority of MTEFs, the compliance mechanisms used to enforce their budget ceilings, the entities charged with monitoring their execution and whether the respective decision-making powers rest with the legislature or the executive (OECD, 2014). In addition, countries have taken different approaches to balancing predictability and flexibility in their multi-annual budget frameworks. Most countries, such as the Czech Republic, treat budget ceilings beyond the first year of the multi-annual framework as indicative and allow for regular revisions of the ceilings to account for unforeseen events or unexpected fiscal developments such as significant deviations from inflation targets, although a variety of restrictions and procedural hurdles may apply. Other countries, such as the United Kingdom, provide fixed ceilings for each year of the multi-annual budget, which requires forward estimates of particularly high quality to ensure the ceilings' medium-term credibility (Robinson, 2013).

MTEFs also afford varying degrees of flexibility for ministries to reallocate funding between years or organisational units and while some MTEFs only provide aggregate expenditure ceilings at the central level, other countries formulate them for ministries, agencies and individual programmes (OECD, 2014). Box 4.6 provides an example of system-level multi-annual budgeting practices in Uruguay.

Box 4.6. **Multi-annual budget planning in Uruguay**

Uruguay uses a multi-annual budget planning process based on a five-year time horizon and prepared in negotiations between the institutions responsible for executing the budget and those that grant and monitor it (the final approval is made by the parliament). At the start of the budget negotiations, the Central Governing Council (*Consejo Directivo Central*, CODICEN) of the National Public Education Administration (*Administración Nacional de Educación Pública*, ANEP) prepares a five-year draft budget that covers the expenditures of the ANEP, which executes the majority of public spending on school education. The draft budget is then submitted to and negotiated with the Ministry of Economy and Finance (MEF). During the negotiations, the four education councils responsible for different school sectors are invited to submit their specific spending proposals based on guidelines established by the CODICEN. The CODICEN negotiates with the MEF until a five-year budget is agreed for ANEP's activities. Typically, only part of the budget requested by ANEP is granted by the MEF and once the five-year budget is established, the CODICEN reviews expenditure plans for all education councils and assesses the availability of resources to finance the proposed expenditures.

After the budget's adoption, the MEF transfers the allocated resources to the ANEP based on three types of expenditure (staff compensation, operating expenses and capital expenditure). The ANEP has some leeway in reallocating these funds from one type of expenditure to another, for example by transferring the designated funds for staff compensation and up to 10% of the funds for capital expenditure to cover operating expenses. Following discussions with the education councils, the CODICEN executes part of the budget itself (10.4% in 2013, mainly involving capital expenditure) and allocates the remaining budget, primarily for staff and operating expenditure among the four education councils of the ANEP (INEEd, 2015).

The multiannual nature of the budget induces stability in the allocation of funds and allows for spending authorities to plan expenditures over a longer time period. Although the allocations received by the councils have a degree of historical inertia, the budgeting process also allows for some flexibility to annual education budgets in response to unforeseen circumstances or the reassessment of priorities. For example, a recent drop in student enrolment has prompted surpluses in the CEIP's budget to be transferred to the budget of CETP (Santiago et al., 2016b).

Although the multi-annual budgeting process provides a good basis for medium-term planning, the five-year budgets in Uruguay have not been strongly linked to medium- and long-term strategies and educational priorities. In addition, the budget planning procedures in each of the four education councils are carried out relatively disconnected from each other, which limits the potential to align their budgets with a clear strategic vision encompassing the entire education system. Seeking to address these shortcomings, the ANEP has accompanied its 2015-19 Budget Plan with a set of annual targets covering 61 indicators for the period 2016-20.

Source: Santiago, P. et al. (2016b), *OECD Reviews of School Resources: Uruguay 2016*, *http://dx.doi.org/10.1787/9789264265530-en*.

Many countries face challenges in establishing a shared understanding of educational quality that is suited to inform the planning of efficient resource use. In some countries, the use of idiosyncratic criteria, conflicting definitions or a failure to raise awareness of existing standards among all actors of the education system has created a lack of agreement over standards for educational quality. In Lithuania, for example, school and local level planning and evaluation are largely guided by idiosyncratic criteria, although the central level provides a framework for external school evaluation that sets out a detailed list of quality standards and 67 corresponding indicators (Shewbridge et al., 2016a). Likewise, not all countries set target dates for the completion of their educational objectives as part of planning process, which results in the absence of clear timeframes that could be used to subsequently evaluate spending decisions (Santiago et al., forthcoming).

Multi-annual medium-term expenditure frameworks can guide budget planning procedures at different levels of the education system. Among the OECD review countries, 5 out of 17 reported to use multiannual education budgets at the central level, namely Austria and Slovenia, which operate a 2-year budget, Iceland and Kazakhstan, which use 3-year budgets and Uruguay, which uses a 5-year budget. In Estonia, while the central budget is annual, it is linked to four-year MTEFs. Some countries require spending authorities at the state, regional or local levels to formulate their budget proposals in line with the time-frame adopted at the central level (e.g. in Estonia, Iceland and Slovenia). This serves to increase the local capacity for strategic budgeting, co-ordinate budgeting procedures and ensure that all levels of the system actively contribute to central targets and priorities.

In some systems, as mentioned above, even schools are encouraged to prepare multi-annual budgets or development plans in accordance with the multi-annual perspective adopted at higher levels of administration. This can help local actors in making strategic spending decisions and provide an additional source of accountability, complementing the schools' annual financial reports with tangible objectives against which their progress can be assessed. While some countries apply a multi-annual budgeting approach across all levels of the education system, Estonia uses multi-annual budgets at the local level and annual budgeting procedures at the central levels, linking both to four-year medium-term expenditure frameworks. By contrast, countries including the Slovak Republic and Lithuania rely on single-year budgets at all levels of the education system, and Sweden gives municipalities discretion over the time period covered by their school budgets (see Table 4.A1.2).

MTEFs are widely acknowledged as an effective tool to assist strategic budget planning. They help ministries of finance and education ministries alike to maintain fiscal discipline by ensuring that policy proposals and programmes are backed by a medium-term budget and that varying costs at different stages of their implementation are adequately accounted for. In addition, MTEFs can give spending agencies the necessary resource security to strategically plan their operations and assist stakeholders in identifying the trade-offs and spending choices they need to make in order to adapt to future levels of funding. Adopting a multi-annual budgeting perspective can be particularly helpful when developing implementation plans for large capital projects whose operating costs are expected to change over time or reform projects whose fiscal impact is not immediately apparent due to their late implementation in the budget year (OECD, 2014).

Fiscal rules and control mechanisms

Rules and control mechanisms pertaining to expenditure and revenue, deficits or debt accumulation play a role in the budgeting process of nearly all OECD countries. Designed to ensure long-term fiscal sustainability, they impose constraints on the spending decisions of executives, ministries, legislatures or local authorities and specify potential sanctions in the case of their violation. Fiscal rules can derive their authority from different sources, including national legislation, executive commitments, constitutionally guaranteed instruments or international treaties. Practices regarding fiscal rules vary widely across national contexts and the policy goals they serve to support. Their effectiveness depends not only on a clear and transparent design, but also their integration with other budgeting practices and procedures including MTEFs, fiscal projections, effective monitoring and enforcement mechanisms (Schick, 2003).

An important development contributing to the increased use of fiscal rules among OECD countries has been the European Stability and Growth Pact, which limits the budget deficit European Union member states are allowed to run at 3% of GDP and their gross national debt at 60% of GDP. In addition, the Pact mandates the development of convergence or stability programmes that outline the countries' strategy to meet medium-term budgetary objectives. Since the Treaty on Stability, Co-ordination and Governance in the EU (the Fiscal Compact) came into force in 2013, members of the Eurozone have also had to adopt fiscal rules for a balanced budget into their national legislation (OECD, 2014).

An example of budgeting rules established in the aftermath of the financial crisis and in response to the European Stability and Growth Pact is the Budget Law passed in Denmark in 2012, which institutionalised a sanctioning mechanism that had been effective since 2010. Following negative GDP growth in 2009 and a significant budget overrun among Danish municipalities, the government introduced a sanctioning regime the following year which took effect in 2011. The Budget Law introduced binding multi-annual expenditure ceilings at the central, regional and municipal levels as well as an automatic sanction mechanism. In case municipalities fail to remain below the annually determined aggregate expenditure ceiling, significant sanctions are imposed and deduced partly from the grants of overspending municipalities (60%) and all other municipalities collectively (40%). Between 2011 and 2013, in the years following the Budget Law's introduction, municipalities reduced their expenditure and consistently underran their budgets (Houlberg et al., 2016; Nusche et al., 2016a).

Forecasting long-term and short-term resource needs

Strategic thinking and long-term planning are central to the successful governance of complex education systems (Burns, Köster and Fuster, 2016). Forecasts and projections of future resource needs can be used by different entities throughout the stages of the budgeting process to support this objective, to ensure the education system's long-term fiscal sustainability and develop clear implementation paths for educational reforms. In 2012, 24 of 33 OECD countries participating in the OECD Budget Practices and Procedures Survey, employed long-term fiscal projections covering more than ten years to inform the budgeting process at the central level. The simulation models used for these prognoses tend to be provided by the CBA, other core ministries or by government-independent institutions (OECD, 2014). Long-term fiscal projections need to be regularly revised, which tends to occur in regular annual or multi-annual intervals or following elections. Around half of OECD countries require their annual budgets or medium-term expenditure frameworks to be consistent with these projections (OECD, 2014).

Typically, the ministry of finance will use prognoses and forecasts to establish expenditure ceilings for line ministries, while the education ministry may use them to prepare and justify its expenditure requests during the budget negotiations. Some intermediate and school level authorities also use forecasting tools to estimate their future expenditure, prepare budgets and allocate resources. Forecasts and simulations can also be employed as a strategic planning tool to estimate revenues and expenditure under different scenarios. The Norwegian Ministry of Finance, for example, requires the education ministry to provide a baseline expenditure projection assuming no policy change along with its policy proposals. These scenarios then form the basis for political discussions on ministerial revenue and expenditure limits as well as the resources available for new policy initiatives (Anderson, Curristine and Merk, 2006). Forecasting resource needs in the education sector involves anticipating developments in the demand for services across different education levels and sectors as well as their implications for human, pedagogical, physical and financial resource needs. The precise methodologies used to estimate expenditure are not always publicly available and vary across countries as well as authorities within countries. At the central level, baseline data on demographic changes in the school-age population and information on previous budget allocations may be combined with additional parameters of varying complexity, for example projected enrolment rates and student flows, different modalities of resource utilisation and macroeconomic or budgetary indicators (Chang and Radi, 2001). Forecasting models can be purely extrapolative or take into account policy changes and normative targets (Fakharzadeh, 2016). At the school-level, the use of these tools tends to be at the discretion of school boards and school leaders.

The effective prediction of resource needs across education levels often requires both vertical and horizontal collaboration and the mobilisation of data from various sources within the education system. In Spain, for example, schools are requested to provide the respective education authorities with admission forecasts to inform the annual allocation of funding. This data is then used to guide subsequent resource planning and management activities. In addition, enrolment levels in pre-school services as well as data from municipal registers are used to inform demographic projections in co-ordination with local and regional authorities (INEE, 2016). In some cases, planning the budget for vocational education and training (VET) can also be supported by efforts to predict labour market trends and the demand for skills in different industries by employing systematic forecasts or consulting employers and unions. For example, Estonia's Qualification Authority has developed and implemented a system that seeks to provide the Ministry of Education and Research with ten-year labour market and skills forecasts on an annual basis to inform the planning of VET resources (Santiago et al., 2016a).

Budgeting techniques and structures

The structure of education budgets and the corresponding procedures for their planning, negotiation and execution differ considerably across countries. One way to distinguish between different budget structures is the extent to which they allocate expenditure to line items or programmes – a distinction that tends to correspond with a budget's orientation towards inputs or outputs respectively. Both techniques can in theory be adopted for budgeting procedures from the central to the school level and there are a variety of hybrid approaches that combine elements of line item and programme budgeting. Some countries use line item classifications alongside programme-based methods for different purposes during the budgeting process, sometimes distinguishing between the classifications used to allocate resources and the way budget information is presented to policy makers and stakeholders. In the United States, for example, funding is usually allocated to schools on the basis of line items while programme budgeting is used for planning purposes (NCES, 2003).

Line item budgeting

Line items constitute the lowest level of mandated spending in a given budget, detailing the use of allocated funds with varying degrees of specificity. Traditional line item budgets in education are organised along the lines of organisational units and objects of expenditure, allocating funding based on educational inputs such as personnel, infrastructure investments or maintenance. Countries' budgets vary considerably with respect to the number of line items they contain, the amount of detail with which allocations are specified and the levels of administration at which line item budgeting techniques are applied (OECD, 2014). The structure of line item budgets mirrors the organisation of authority and spending responsibilities within the administrative units that implement it. This – together with the separate listing of individual expenditure components – affords spending authorities a relatively high degree of oversight and input control. It also allows expenditure data to be easily summarised and monitored based on organisational units or item categories (NCES, 2003). Due to their intuitive structure and the relative ease of preparing them, line item budgeting remains the most widely used budgeting technique, particularly at the sub-central and school levels (NCES, 2003; Schaeffer and Yilmaz, 2008).

The way in which budgets are organised has implications for their planning, preparation, and subsequent evaluation (see Chapter 5). The fact that line item budgeting methods are focused on inputs – rather than the services or results that they are intended to deliver – makes it more difficult to link the cost of line items to specific services or outcomes. In contrast to programme-based budgets, the justification, prioritisation and expected impact of line item expenditures may therefore not be readily apparent based on the budget documentation alone. Some systems therefore supplement line item budgets with programme or performance information for presentational purposes and to allow decision makers to relate education spending to specific activities or purposes (NCES, 2003).

Programme budgeting

As part of a broader effort to reorient budgeting practices towards outcomes and results, some countries have moved from the use of line item budgets towards programme-oriented budgeting methods that assign funding to programmes of work and their associated outputs, rather than educational inputs. Conceived in the 1960s, programme budgeting "lays stress on estimating the total financial cost of accomplishing objectives" (Wildavsky, 1997) and promises to support the alignment of spending with policy objectives, for example by facilitating the integration of output targets and cost-effectiveness analyses into the budgeting process.

There is no consensus on the unit that should ideally constitute the basis of a programme budget in the education sector, which could be anything from the accomplishment of a specific educational objective to the implementation of an education reform or a certain type of activity. Identifying a set of appropriate programmes under which expenditures can be subsumed is key to designing effective programme budgets. Defining mutually exclusive and collectively exhaustive programmes is particularly difficult at any level of aggregation and involves dealing with the mutual dependencies between different government activities as well as those which contribute to multiple objectives at once (Wildavsky, 1997).

The use of programme over line item budgeting involves important trade-offs that policy makers need to take into account. Most importantly, while programme budgeting allows for more direct links between spending and outputs, line item budgeting gives spending authorities a higher degree of control over individual line item inputs. In addition, moving towards a programme budgeting approach places additional demands, particularly on sub-central authorities in terms of the capacity needed to implement the associated changes in accounting practices (Schaeffer and Yilmaz, 2008). As a consequence of their condensed format, programme-budget documents can also fail to provide comprehensive information on all aspects considered relevant by individual stakeholders, which means that they may have to be supplemented with additional financial documentation to ensure effective accountability (de Jong et al., 2013). Further challenges arise when administering budget programmes that span multiple organisational units responsible for different parts of the associated expenditures (NCES, 2003).

Nevertheless, under the right conditions, a programme-oriented approach to budgeting can facilitate the alignment of budgetary planning with performance targets and policy objectives. It can also facilitate the identification of opportunities for consolidation or co-ordination between activities and programmes that pursue similar goals. Line item budgets, on the other hand, are rarely organised in a way that allows policy makers to identify the cost of specific interventions and programmes or to disentangle the incremental cost of education reforms from that of regular school operations. Although carrying out cost-effectiveness analyses remains empirically and methodologically challenging (Belfield, 2015), programme budgeting can facilitate the process. Programme classifications can also be used to guide spending reviews in the identification of strategic savings options and to present performance information alongside expenditure data to facilitate subsequent evaluations (Robinson, 2014).

Regardless of whether countries adopt line item or programme-based budgeting methods, it is important to maintain coherence and clarity in the budget structure and establish clear spending responsibilities. A large number of separate programmes or budget lines can make the regular review of allocations and priorities challenging and may reduce flexibility in the use of allocated resources (for other factors conditioning budgetary flexibility, see below). Particularly when expenditure responsibilities for individual budgetary lines are unclear, a dispersed budget structure can give rise to inefficiencies due to the misalignment of spending and policy objectives or the failure to identify potential synergies (Santiago et al., forthcoming).

Budget flexibility and incentives for efficiency

Relaxing central input controls and increasing budget flexibility has been a common strategy to enable education authorities to pursue their objectives more efficiently and effectively. Measures to increase flexibility have been applied at the level of the executive, education ministries, local administrations and schools. More flexibility in the budget planning and execution process can serve to increase its responsiveness to unforeseen circumstances and changing priorities as well as providing incentives for the more efficient use of school funding at the planning stage.

Budget flexibility and reallocations

Within multi-annual budgeting frameworks, expenditure ceilings can be revised to account for unforeseen economic and fiscal developments or changing policy priorities. Even within a single year's budgetary cycle, some countries allow for budget allocations to be adjusted upwards or downwards after their adoption in response to circumstances that were not foreseen or unforeseeable during the planning stage. The rules and procedures governing this adjustment process vary across countries and different regulations may apply to spending cuts and increases, as well as to different types of expenditure, such as investment, operational and mandatory spending. The majority of OECD countries allow the executive to increase ministerial budgets after they were approved by the legislature, with the exception of some countries like Chile or France where such spending increases are prohibited. Most OECD countries also allow the executive to cut operational, investment and discretionary spending after the ministries' budgets have been approved, while cuts to mandatory spending tend to be more restricted with countries such as Austria, Belgium, Denmark and Estonia prohibiting the practice entirely, even though they permit reductions in other spending categories (OECD, 2014). With few exceptions, increases and cuts after the budget's adoption are limited by thresholds or contingent on their *ex ante* approval by the CBA or the legislature in case the reallocations exceed a certain threshold.

A whole-of-system approach to education planning needs to reconcile the importance of longer-term budgetary frameworks and the predictability they afford with a sufficient degree of flexibility to respond to unforeseen circumstances in the short term. In addition, the nature of the budget preparation schedule is often such that educational resource needs, particularly at the local level, are only imperfectly known by the time at which budgets need to be approved. Adjustment mechanisms can help to ensure, for example, that budget appropriations reflect the upcoming year's enrolment levels even if the initial adoption of the budget precedes the beginning of the new school year. In Estonia, for example, most local governments provide their school directors with budget ceilings for the upcoming fiscal year as soon as spring. Once enrolment levels become clearer towards autumn, budget allocations are adjusted accordingly, allowing schools to plan ahead without compromising their budget flexibility (Santiago et al., 2016a).

Carry-over of unused appropriations

Since budget appropriations are typically granted for a given fiscal year, carry-over rules regulate the extent to which actors at different levels of the education system can use unspent financial resources beyond this point. The right to carry savings forward from one year to the next can be subject to both quantitative and qualitative restrictions. These may include a ceiling for the amount that can be carried over in any given year or for the total accumulation of unspent resources. In other cases, requests to retain unspent funds may be subject to the evaluation and approval of the respective budgetary authority. At the ministerial level, the majority of OECD countries permit the carry-over of discretionary, operational and investment funding, usually subject to prior approval by the Central Budget Authority (CBA), the legislature or both (OECD, 2014). Belgium and Chile are among the countries that do not permit any ministerial carry-overs, while the Slovak Republic restricts the practice to discretionary and investment budgets (OECD, 2014).

There are arguments for and against the permission of budgetary carry-over practices (OECD, 2014). Carry-over rights have been argued to provide spending authorities with additional flexibility to compensate for rigidities in the budget execution. Allowing educational providers to use their savings beyond the budgetary cycle to fund other priorities also sets organisational incentives to improve the use of resources and reap the benefits of efficiency-producing innovation (OECD, 2015). By contrast, prohibiting providers from retaining savings between budget years may lead to inefficient spending patterns towards the end of the fiscal year and rigid restrictions on carry-over practices can compound other sources of inefficiency such as shortcomings in national planning procedures. For example, it is estimated that 20% of infrastructure investments in Chile are lost to the education sector due to delays in the execution of national programmes and the failure to spend appropriated funds within the approved period (Santiago et al., forthcoming). At the same time, unrestricted carry-over rights may lead schools to accumulate excessive surpluses and reduce the executive's control over the timing of expenditures. Carry-over can thereby cause spending fluctuations and the allocation of resources to student cohorts for whom they were not originally intended unless they are accompanied by appropriate fiscal rules.

The rules regulating carry-over at the school level vary between countries and may not apply universally across different school types or regions within a system. In Iceland, for example, each municipality decides whether their pre-primary and compulsory schools are permitted to carry surpluses and losses forward to the next financial year while upper secondary schools governed by the state are authorised to retain unused funds without restrictions and subtract debts from the following year's allocations (Icelandic Ministry of Education, Science and Culture, 2014). In Lithuania, by contrast, annual school budgets are based on their expenditure during the previous year and any surpluses must be refunded to the state at the end of the cycle, providing no incentives for educational institutions to reduce their cost or save funds for future expenditures. Likewise, targeted state grants transferred to municipalities can only be used for education purposes during the year in which they were allocated (National Agency for School Evaluation [NASE], 2015).

Among the OECD review countries, four reported not to allow public schools to carry-over any budget surpluses at the primary level, while another four systems imposed no restrictions on the practice. In Denmark, Estonia, Iceland and Portugal, budgetary carry-over is subject to the approval of central or local educational authorities, while the Czech Republic, Israel and the Slovak Republic allow for the carry-over of funds either up to a certain limit or restricted to a specific type funding. In most countries, the budgetary regulations concerning carry-over practices are similar at the lower secondary level. At the upper secondary level, schools are more frequently permitted to retain unspent allocations, with 6 of 17 systems reporting no restrictions on the practice. By contrast, three systems reported not to permit any carry-over at the upper secondary level and seven systems impose some restrictions or mandate the approval of educational authorities. In Uruguay, for example, surplus income generated by product sales at the school level goes into a central budget and is redistributed to the school in the next school year. The Slovak Republic mandates retained funds to be spent until March of the following year. In Austria, carry-over rights for federal lower and upper secondary schools are subject to the discretion of the central education authority and in Estonia, subject to the approval of central or local authorities, depending on the school owner (see Table 4.A1.3).

Even where the retention of funds across budget years is permitted in principle, the failure of many schools to do so (as seen, for example, among municipal schools in Estonia) highlights that carry-over procedures need to be transparent and easy to navigate for schools with limited administrative capacity (Santiago et al., 2016a). Otherwise, problems in the carry-over process can lead school authorities to engage in inefficient expenditures at the end of the budgetary year and discourage them from saving for larger investments or mobilising additional revenues through donations, asset income and the sale of goods and services.

Policy options

Adopt a multi-annual approach to budget planning

Adopting a multi-annual approach to planning education expenditure and making effective use of budgeting tools such as medium-term expenditure frameworks (MTEFs) is key to ensuring the efficiency and financial sustainability of high-performing education systems. MTEFs constitute a strong framework to combine medium-term economic and fiscal estimates with projected resource needs in order to assist spending authorities in making informed and sustainable budgeting choices. In order to achieve and maintain fiscal discipline, multi-annual expenditure plans should be adopted with a view to ensure that policy proposals and programmes are backed by a medium-term budget and that varying costs at different stages of their implementation are adequately accounted for.

Adopting a multi-annual budgeting process can provide spending agencies with a means to strategically plan their operations, take into account potential trade-offs between alternative spending options and their longer-term expenditure implications, thus giving them additional security when planning longer-term investments. The development of multi-annual budgets should be guided by high-quality forecasting mechanisms to ensure the reliability of indicative spending ceilings or create the conditions necessary to commit to longer-term allocations. In order to maximise their value for strategic planning, MTEFs should integrate budgeting processes at different levels of the education system by encouraging actors across administrative levels to align their spending proposals with central expenditure frameworks.

Strategically link spending decisions to policy priorities

Aligning funding strategies with policy objectives is crucial to ensure that financial resources are effectively employed to drive educational improvement and reforms. This requires both the formulation of clear goals and their connection to the budget planning process. Central-level educational goals should be well-defined and prioritised and – particularly in school systems with decentralised resource planning responsibilities – translatable into concrete objectives at the sub-central level. Fostering widespread awareness and a shared understanding of this strategic vision for education among different stakeholder groups and levels of authority can increase the coherence of budget planning activities across the education system. In addition, it would be beneficial for planning purposes if educational objectives were accompanied by a range of targets with a defined time horizon to promote accountability, increase their value for strategic resource planning and facilitate the subsequent evaluation of spending decisions.

Countries should ensure that these targets and policy priorities are taken into consideration when planning the use of school funding by integrating them into strategic documents and the procedural mechanisms that guide the budget preparation at different levels of the education system. Particularly when combined with multi-annual budgeting procedures, strategic frameworks containing short- and medium-term objectives should be used to inform negotiations and decisions on medium-term expenditure frameworks. Information on policy objectives and expected outcomes should also be presented alongside budget allocations in order to facilitate the distribution of resources according to policy priorities, provide authorities with a clear picture of the purposes that expenditures serve and facilitate the subsequent evaluation of spending decisions against the achievement of policy outcomes. Countries should seek to establish these links between strategic objectives and educational expenditure beyond the central level, for example by encouraging the alignment of spending decisions with school development plans. This may require a commitment to building technical and strategic capacity where local actors and school authorities play an active role in the budgeting process.

Strategically use evaluation and research evidence in the budgeting process

The effective planning of educational resource use relies on the systematic mobilisation of evidence generated through research, evaluations and monitoring activities. Evidence on the efficiency of spending decisions should be used to inform discussions among stakeholders and help the responsible authorities in making informed decisions throughout the budget preparation process. To effectively inform evidence-based budget planning, the data generated by evaluation activities should explicitly assess the impact of programmes and policy initiatives, ideally relating it to previously established objectives and expenditure information. If they are well co-ordinated with the budgeting process, spending reviews can prove another important source of information to support efficient spending choices. To this end, the timing and frequency of spending reviews should be aligned with the central-level budget planning procedures to ensure that concrete saving options are identified and presented to the political leadership at a time when they can be considered alongside the cost of newly proposed policy initiatives.

Education systems should also promote the creation of fora that foster co-operation between researchers and policy makers as well as institutions that can act as knowledge brokers and strategically consolidate, evaluate and disseminate evidence to facilitate its integration into the budgeting processes. Particularly in decentralised systems, school principals and local authorities should be encouraged and enabled to use data and research evidence for budgeting purposes through training as well as vertical and horizontal support. It is important to ensure that stakeholder groups can contribute to discussions regarding the design of evaluations, the evidence collected and the interpretation of evaluation outcomes.

Provide sufficient budget flexibility and incentives for efficiency

Introducing an appropriate degree of flexibility into the budgeting process can improve its responsiveness to unforeseen circumstances and promote more efficient spending decisions at the sub-central level. Particularly in the context of multi-annual budgeting procedures, countries should seek to reconcile the importance of long-term reliability and stability in funding allocations with their responsiveness to changing conditions in the short term. Allowing for the regular adjustment of multi-annual budget ceilings to take into account changing resource forecasts and permitting funding to be shifted across budget items in response to emergencies or reassessed priorities can significantly improve the allocation of educational resources if appropriately regulated. Schools and local authorities should also be provided with some room to carry unused appropriations forward from one budget year to the next. This can discourage inefficient expenditures towards the end of the budget cycle and provide schools and local authorities with incentives to mobilise additional revenue or improve the efficiency of their operations, although appropriate regulations should prevent the accumulation of excessive surpluses and spending fluctuations across years.

References

Anderson, B., T. Curristine and O. Merk (2006), "Budgeting in Norway", *OECD Journal on Budgeting*, Vol. 6/1, *http://dx.doi.org/10.1787/budget-v6-art2-en*.

Belfield, C. (2015), "Cost-benefit analysis and cost-effectiveness analysis", in H.F. Ladd and M.E. Goertz (eds.), *Handbook of Research in Education Finance and Policy*, Routledge, New York.

Bruneforth, M. et al. (forthcoming), *OECD Review of Policies to Improve the Effectiveness of Resource Use in Schools: Country Background Report for Austria*, Bundesministerium für Bildung und Frauen, Vienna.

Burns, T. and L. Cerna (2016), "Enhancing effective education governance", in *Governing Education in a Complex World*, OECD Publishing, Paris, *http://dx.doi.org/10.1787/9789264255364-13-en*.

Burns, T., F. Köster and M. Fuster (2016), *Education Governance in Action: Lessons from Case Studies*, OECD Publishing, Paris, *http://dx.doi.org/10.1787/9789264262829-en*.

Chang, G.-C. and M. Radi (2001), "Educational planning through computer simulation", *Education Policies and Strategies*, No. 3, United Nations Educational, Scientific and Cultural Organization (UNESCO), Paris, *http://unesdoc.unesco.org/images/0012/001242/124209e.pdf*.

Curristine, T. (2005), "Performance Information in the Budget Process: Results of the OECD 2005 Questionnaire", *OECD Journal on Budgeting*, Vol. 5/2, *http://dx.doi.org/10.1787/budget-v5-art13-en*.

de Jong, M., I. van Beek and R. Posthumus (2013), "Introducing accountable budgeting: Lessons from a decade of performance-based budgeting in the Netherlands", *OECD Journal on Budgeting*, Vol. 12/3, *http://dx.doi.org/10.1787/budget-12-5k455r12vs37*.

Fakharzadeh, T. (2016), "Budgeting and Accounting in OECD Education Systems: A Literature Review", *OECD Education Working Papers*, No. 128, OECD Publishing, Paris, *http://dx.doi.org/10.1787/5jm3xgsz03kh-en*.

Fazekas, M. and T. Burns (2012), "Exploring the Complex Interaction between Governance and Knowledge in Education", *OECD Education Working Papers*, No. 67, OECD Publishing, Paris, *http://dx.doi.org/10.1787/5k9flcx2l340-en*.

Flemish Ministry of Education and Training (2015), *OECD Review of Policies to Improve the Effectiveness of Resource Use in Schools: Country Background Report of the Flemish Community of Belgium*, Brussels, *www.oecd.org/education/schoolresourcesreview.htm*.

Houlberg, K. et al. (2016), *OECD Review of Policies to Improve the Effectiveness of Resource Use in Schools: Country Background Report for Denmark*, KORA, Copenhagen, *www.oecd.org/education/schoolresourcesreview.htm*.

Icelandic Ministry of Education, Science and Culture (2014), *OECD Review of Policies to Improve the Effectiveness of Resource Use in Schools: Country Background Report for Iceland*, Icelandic Ministry of Education, Science and Culture, Reykjavik, *www.oecd.org/education/schoolresourcesreview.htm*.

IIEP-UNESCO (2010), "Strategic planning: Techniques and methods", *Education Sector Planning Working Paper*, No. 3, International Institute for Education Planning – United Nations Educational, Scientific and Cultural Organization, Paris, *http://unesdoc.unesco.org/images/0018/001897/189759e.pdf*.

INEE (2016), *OECD Review of Policies to Improve the Effectiveness of Resource Use in Schools: Country Background Report for Spain*, Instituto Nacional de Evaluación Educativa (National Institute for Educational Evaluation), Madrid, *www.oecd.org/education/schoolresourcesreview.htm*.

INEEd (2015), *OECD Review of Policies to Improve the Effectiveness of Resource Use in Schools: Country Background Report for Uruguay*, Instituto Nacional de Evaluación Educativa (National Institute for Educational Evaluation), Montevideo, *www.oecd.org/education/schoolresourcesreview.htm*.

Kyrö, M. (2006), "Vocational education and training in Finland: Short description", *Cedefop Panorama Series*, No. 130, Office for Official Publications of the European Communities, Luxembourg.

Münich, D. and G. Psacharopoulos (2014), "Mechanisms and methods for cost-benefit/cost-effectiveness analysis of specific education programmes", *European Expert Network on Economics of Education (EENEE) Analytical Report*, No. 19, Prepared for the European Commission.

Musset, P. (2012), "School Choice and Equity: Current Policies in OECD Countries and a Literature Review", *OECD Education Working Papers*, No. 66, OECD Publishing, Paris, *http://dx.doi.org/10.1787/5k9fq23507vc-en*.

NASE (National Agency for School Evaluation) (2015), *OECD Review of Policies to Improve the Effectiveness of Resource Use in Schools: Country Background Report for Lithuania*, National Agency for School Evaluation, Vilnius, *www.oecd.org/education/schoolresourcesreview.htm*.

NCES (2003), *Financial Accounting for Local and State School Systems*, US Department of Education, National Center for Education Statistics, Washington, DC, *http://nces.ed.gov/pubs2004/2004318.pdf*.

Nusche, D. et al. (2016a), *OECD Reviews of School Resources: Denmark 2016*, OECD Publishing, Paris, *http://dx.doi.org/10.1787/9789264262430-en*.

Nusche, D. et al. (2016b), *OECD Reviews of School Resources: Austria 2016*, OECD Publishing, Paris, *http://dx.doi.org/10.1787/9789264256729-en*.

OECD (2016), *Education at a Glance 2016: OECD Indicators*, OECD Publishing, Paris, *http://dx.doi.org/10.1787/eag-2016-en*.

OECD (2015), *The Innovation Imperative in the Public Sector: Setting an Agenda for Action*, OECD Publishing, Paris, *http://dx.doi.org/10.1787/9789264236561-en*.

OECD (2014), *Budgeting Practices and Procedures in OECD Countries*, OECD Publishing, Paris, *http://dx.doi.org/10.1787/9789264059696-en*.

OECD (2013a), *PISA 2012 Results: What Makes Schools Successful (Volume IV): Resources, Policies and Practices*, OECD Publishing, Paris, *http://dx.doi.org/10.1787/9789264201156-en*.

OECD (2013b), *Government at a Glance 2013*, OECD Publishing, Paris, *http://dx.doi.org/10.1787/gov_glance-2013-en*.

OECD (2013c), *Synergies for Better Learning: An International Perspective on Evaluation and Assessment*, OECD Publishing, Paris, *http://dx.doi.org/10.1787/9789264190658-en*.

OECD (2007), *Evidence in Education: Linking Research and Policy*, OECD Publishing, Paris, *http://dx.doi.org/10.1787/9789264033672-en*.

OECD (2004), "The Legal Framework for Budget Systems an International Comparison", *OECD Journal on Budgeting*, Vol. 4/ 3, OECD Publishing, Paris, pp. 14-22, *www.oecd.org/unitedkingdom/35933542.pdf*.

OECD/The World Bank (2015), *OECD Reviews of School Resources: Kazakhstan 2015*, OECD Publishing, Paris, *http://dx.doi.org/10.1787/9789264245891-en*.

Papalia, A. (forthcoming), "The Funding of Vocational Education and Training: A Literature Review", *OECD Education Working Papers*, OECD Publishing, Paris.

Robinson, M. (2014), "Spending reviews", *OECD Journal on Budgeting*, Vol. 13/ 2, OECD Publishing, Paris, *http://dx.doi.org/10.1787/budget-13-5jz14bz8p2hd*.

Robinson, M. (2013), "Aggregate expenditure ceilings and allocative flexibility", *OECD Journal on Budgeting*, Vol. 12/3, *http://dx.doi.org/10.1787/budget-12-5k468nqj1f7g*.

Santiago, P. et al. (forthcoming), *OECD Reviews of School Resources: Chile*, OECD Publishing, Paris.

Santiago, P. et al. (2016a), *OECD Reviews of School Resources: Estonia 2016*, OECD Publishing, Paris, *http://dx.doi.org/10.1787/9789264251731-en*.

Santiago, P. et al. (2016b), *OECD Reviews of School Resources: Uruguay 2016*, OECD Publishing, Paris, *http://dx.doi.org/10.1787/9789264265530-en*.

Santiago, P. et al. (2016c), *OECD Reviews of School Resources: Slovak Republic 2015*, OECD Publishing, Paris, *http://dx.doi.org/10.1787/9789264247567-en*.

Schaeffer, M. and S. Yilmaz (2008), "Strengthening local government budgeting and accountability", *Policy Research Working Paper*, No. 4767, The World Bank, Washington, DC.

Schick, A. (2003), "The Role of Fiscal Rules in Budgeting", *OECD Journal on Budgeting*, Vol. 3/3, *http://dx.doi.org/10.1787/budget-v3-art14-en*.

Shaw, T. (2016), "Performance budgeting practices and procedures", *OECD Journal on Budgeting*, Vol. 15/3, *http://dx.doi.org/10.1787/budget-15-5jlz6rhqdvhh*.

Shewbridge, C. et al. (2016a), *OECD Reviews of School Resources: Lithuania 2016*, OECD Publishing, Paris, *http://dx.doi.org/10.1787/9789264252547-en*.

Shewbridge, C. et al. (2016b), *OECD Reviews of School Resources: Czech Republic 2016*, OECD Publishing, Paris, *http://dx.doi.org/10.1787/9789264262379-en*.

Wildavsky, A. (1997), "The political economy of efficiency: Cost-benefit analysis, systems analysis, and program budgeting", in R.T. Golembiewski and J. Rabin (eds.), *Public Budgeting and Finance*, Marcel Dekker, New York.

ANNEX 4.A1

National approaches to planning the use of school funding

Table 4.A1.1. **Information used in the preparation of the central education budget (ISCED 0-3), 2016**

Country	Administrative data	Results from impact evaluations	Demographic information	Policy priorities	Identified needs	Macroeconomic and budgetary indicators	Data on student flows	Data on pedagogical orientations	Information about previous budget	Performance information
Austria	✓		✓	✓	✓			✓		
Chile	✓	✓	✓	✓	✓	✓	✓		✓	✓
Czech Republic	✓		✓		✓		✓	✓		
Denmark	✓			✓		✓	✓		✓	
Estonia	✓	✓	✓	✓	✓	✓	✓	✓	✓	✓
Iceland	✓		✓							
Israel	✓		✓	✓	✓			✓		
Kazakhstan	✓	✓	✓	✓	✓	✓	✓	✓	✓	
Lithuania	✓									
Portugal	✓			✓					✓	
Slovak Republic	✓			✓	✓	✓				
Slovenia	✓		✓	✓	✓	✓			✓	✓
Spain	✓	✓	✓	✓	✓	✓			✓	✓
Sweden	✓		✓	✓						
Uruguay	✓			✓		✓		✓	✓	

Notes: General note on Belgium (Fl. and Fr.): There is no central education budget and budget planning, but an annual lump sum transfer originating from central (federal) taxes to the states (Communities). Communities can use funds from the lump sum transfer for all policy domains they are responsible for at their own discretion. Budget planning happens at the state (Community) level. Therefore, this table does not provide information for Belgium (Fl. and Fr.).

The review team made every effort to ensure, in collaboration with countries, that the information collected through the qualitative survey on school funding is valid and reliable and reflects specific country contexts while being comparable across countries. However, given the qualitative nature of the survey, information should be interpreted with care. For country-specific notes to this table, see the end of this annex.

Table 4.A1.2. **Budgeting of public expenditure at the central and sub-central level (ISCED 0-3), 2016**

Country	Level of education	Level of administration	Responsibilities for setting up the education budget	Budget duration
Austria	ISCED 0-3	Central	• Central financial authority and central education authority negotiate • Central government (Council of Ministers) proposes • Central legislative authority (National Council) approves	Multiannual (2 years)
	ISCED 0, ISCED 1-3 (state schools)	State	• State financial authority and state education authority negotiate • State legislative authority approves	Not specified by the regulatory framework
		Local	• Local financial authority and local education authority negotiate • Local legislative authority approves	Not specified by the regulatory framework
Belgium (Fl. and Fr.)	ISCED 0-3	Central	• Central financial authority (not exclusively for education)	Annual
		State	• State government and state education authority negotiate • State government proposes to state legislative authority • Other (social partners) advise • State legislative authority approves	Annual
Chile	ISCED 0-3	Central	• Central education authority proposes • Central financial authority negotiates, approves and proposes to central government • Central government proposes to central legislative authority • Central legislative authority approves	Annual
	ISCED 0	Local	• Central education authorities (*Junta Nacional de Jardines Infantiles* [JUNJI], Integra) • Local education authorities	Annual
	ISCED 02-3	Local	• Central education authority (*Ministerio de Educación*, MINEDUC) • Local education authorities	Not specified by the regulatory framework
Czech Republic	ISCED 0-3	Central	• Central education authority proposes • Central financial authority advises • Central government negotiates • Central legislative authority approves	Annual
	ISCED 3	Regional	• Central education authority advises (according to normatives set by the Ministry of Education, Youth and Sports) • Regional education authority proposes (through a system of regional normatives) • Regional government negotiates • Regional legislative authority approves	Annual
	ISCED 0-2	Local	• At the discretion of local authorities	Annual
Denmark	ISCED 0-3	Central	• Central government proposes • Central legislative authority approves	Annual
	ISCED 0-2	Local	• Local government	Annual
Estonia	ISCED 0-3	Central	• Central education authority proposes • Central financial authority negotiates • Central government approves • Central legislative authority approves	Annual
		Local	• Local government proposes • Local legislative authority approves	Multiannual (4 years)
Iceland	ISCED 3	Central	• Central education authority proposes and approves • Central financial authority negotiates • Central legislative authority approves • Central government approves	Multiannual (3 years)
	ISCED 0-2	Local	• At the discretion of local government authorities	Multiannual (4 years)
Israel	ISCED 0-3	Central	• Central education authority proposes and approves • Central financial authority negotiates and approves • Central government adopts • Central legislative authority finally approves	Annual
		Local	• At the discretion of local education authorities	Annual

Table 4.A1.2. **Budgeting of public expenditure at the central and sub-central level (ISCED 0-3), 2016** *(cont.)*

Country	Level of education	Level of administration	Responsibilities for setting up the education budget	Budget duration
Kazakhstan	ISCED 0-3	Central	● Central education authority proposes ● Central financial authority negotiates ● Central government approves ● Central legislative authority approves	Multiannual (3 years)
		Regional	● Regional education authority proposes ● Regional financial authority negotiates ● Regional government and regional legislative authority approve	Multiannual (3 years)
		Local	● Local education authority proposes ● Local financial authority negotiates ● Local government and local legislative authority approve	Multiannual (3 years)
Lithuania	ISCED 0-3	Central	● Central financial authority negotiates ● Central education authority proposes ● Central government approves	Annual
		Local	● Central education authority approves ● Local legislative authority approves	Annual
Portugal	ISCED 0-3	Central	● Central education authority (Ministry of Education) proposes ● Central education authority and central financial authority (Ministry of Finance) negotiate ● Central government approves ● Central legislative authority approves	Annual
	ISCED 0, ISCED 1 (first 4 years)	Local	● Central financial authority proposes general budget ● Local government approves budget for school education	Annual
Slovak Republic	ISCED 1-3	Central	● Central education authorities ● Central financial authorities and other (social partners, mainly the teachers' union) negotiate draft budget ● Central financial authorities propose draft budget to the central government ● Central government after discussion approves draft budget and proposes the budget to the central legislative authority ● Central legislative authority approves	Annual
	ISCED 3	Regional	● Regional education authority	Annual
	ISCED 02	Local	● At discretion of local education authority	Annual
	ISCED 1-2	Local	● Local education authority	Annual
Slovenia	ISCED 1-3	Central	● Central government proposes ● Central financial authority and central education authority negotiate ● Central legislative authority approves	Multiannual (2 years)
	ISCED 0-2	Local	● At the discretion of local authorities	Multiannual (2 years)
Spain	ISCED 0-3	Central	● Central financial authority proposes draft budget after negotiations with government (including the central education authority) ● Central legislative authority and others (groups from civil society) negotiate ● Central legislative authority approves	Annual
		Regional	● Regional financial authority proposes ● Regional financial authority and regional education authority negotiate ● Regional legislative authority approves	Annual
	ISCED 0-1	Local	● Local financial and education authorities negotiate and propose ● Local government approves	Annual

Table 4.A1.2. **Budgeting of public expenditure at the central and sub-central level (ISCED 0-3), 2016** (cont.)

Country	Level of education	Level of administration	Responsibilities for setting up the education budget	Budget duration
Sweden	ISCED 0-3	Central	• Central financial authority and central education authority negotiate • Central government proposes • Central legislative authority approves	Annual
		Local	• Local government • At the discretion of local authority	Annual
Uruguay	ISCED 0-3	Central	• Central education authorities propose • Central financial authority negotiates • Central legislative authority proposes and approves	Multiannual (5 years)
Slovak Republic	ISCED 1-3	Central	• Central education authorities • Central financial authorities and other (social partners, mainly the teachers' union) negotiate draft budget • Central financial authorities propose draft budget to the central government • Central government after discussion approves draft budget and proposes the budget to the central legislative authority • Central legislative authority approves	Annual
	ISCED 3	Regional	• Regional education authority	Annual
	ISCED 02	Local	• At discretion of local education authority	Annual
	ISCED 1-2	Local	• Local education authority	Annual
Slovenia	ISCED 1-3	Central	• Central government proposes • Central financial authority and central education authority negotiate • Central legislative authority approves	Multiannual (2 years)
	ISCED 0-2	Local	• At the discretion of local authorities	Multiannual (2 years)
Spain	ISCED 0-3	Central	• Central financial authority proposes draft budget after negotiations with government (including the central education authority) • Central legislative authority and others (groups from civil society) negotiate • Central legislative authority approves	Annual
		Regional	• Regional financial authority proposes • Regional financial authority and regional education authority negotiate • Regional legislative authority approves	Annual
	ISCED 0-1	Local	• Local financial and education authorities negotiate and propose • Local government approves	Annual
Sweden	ISCED 0-3	Central	• Central financial authority and central education authority negotiate • Central government proposes • Central legislative authority approves	Annual
		Local	• Local government • At the discretion of local authority	Annual
Uruguay	ISCED 0-3	Central	• Central education authorities propose • Central financial authority negotiates • Central legislative authority proposes and approves	Multiannual (5 years)

Notes: The level of administration describes the level of the system for which the budget is set. For example, the central level of administration refers to the "central budget".

The review team made every effort to ensure, in collaboration with countries, that the information collected through the qualitative survey on school funding is valid and reliable and reflects specific country contexts while being comparable across countries. However, given the qualitative nature of the survey, information should be interpreted with care.

For terms and definitions of levels of administration and governance and levels of education, see Annex B. For country-specific notes to this table, see the end of this annex.

Table 4.A1.3. **Regulations on budget carry-over for public schools**

Country	Level of education	Right for budget carry-over
Austria	ISCED 0, ISCED 1-3 (state schools)	x
	ISCED 2-3 (federal schools)	At the discretion of central education authority
Belgium (Fl. and Fr.)	ISCED 0-3	Yes, with no restrictions
Chile	ISCED 0 (operated directly or indirectly by the central education authority *Junta Nacional de Jardines Infantiles* [JUNJI])	No
	ISCED 0 (operated directly or indirectly by the central education authority Integra)	Yes, with some restrictions
	ISCED 02-3	Yes, with no restrictions
Czech Republic	ISCED 0-3	Yes, but only funding provided by local authority
Denmark	ISCED 0-2	At the discretion of local education authority
	ISCED 3	Yes, with no restrictions
Estonia	ISCED 0	At the discretion of individual school
	ISCED 1-3	At the discretion of school provider (central education authority, local education authority)
Iceland	ISCED 0, ISCED 1-2	At the discretion of local education authority
	ISCED 3	Yes, with no restrictions
Israel	ISCED 0-3	Yes, but only any surplus from petty cash and parental contributions
Kazakhstan	ISCED 0-3	No
Lithuania	ISCED 0-3	No
Portugal	ISCED 0-3	At the discretion of central education authority
Slovak Republic	ISCED 0-3 (school with the status of a legal entity)	Yes, but needs to be spent after a given period of time (until March the following year)
	ISCED 0-3 (school without the status of a legal entity)	Yes, but only the amount received in last two calendar months of a year (November and December) and only a specified maximum
Slovenia	ISCED 0-3	Yes, with no restrictions
Spain	ISCED 0-3	Yes, with no restrictions
Sweden	ISCED 0-3	No
Uruguay	ISCED 0-1	No
	ISCED 2-3	No, but the income of product sales can be retained in the event of surplus

x: not applicable.

Notes: Budget carry-over refers to the possibility for public schools to retain any budget surplus for the next budget year.

The review team made every effort to ensure, in collaboration with countries, that the information collected through the qualitative survey on school funding is valid and reliable and reflects specific country contexts while being comparable across countries. However, given the qualitative nature of the survey, information should be interpreted with care.

For definitions of levels of education, see Annex B. For country-specific notes to this table, see the end of this annex.

Table notes

Table 4.A1.1. Information used in the preparation of the central education budget

Chile:

Additional information includes recurring expenses form existing programmes.

Czech Republic:

Information about identified needs at different levels of the system is used to some degree for planning of infrastructure needs and investments on a central level.

Estonia:

Administrative data refers to the number of students in general education. Performance information refers to an assessment if previous national education targets have been achieved or not. Additional information used in the preparation of the central education budget includes forecasts of labour market demand in the case of vocational education and training.

Iceland:

The budget of upper secondary schools (ISCED 3) is determined through the central budget, based on the number of full-time equivalent students and the line of study. The education budget of pre-primary and compulsory schools (ISCED levels 0-2) is determined at the local level at the discretion of local authorities. In addition the Municipality Equalisation Fund distributes central funds to municipalities based on formulas and regulations.

Kazakhstan:

Additional information includes data on teacher professional qualifications.

Lithuania:

Administrative data refers to the number of students.

Portugal:

Administrative data refers to the number of students and the type of educational offer. Additional information includes the draft budget prepared by schools for operating costs.

Slovak Republic:

Administrative data refers to the number of students. Macroeconomic and budgetary indicators include, among others, economic growth projections in terms of GDP and fiscal forecasts. Identified needs at different levels of the system refers, for example, to the infrastructure investments, e.g. to expand supply of early childhood education and care and to meet growing demand in certain geographical areas. Policy priorities as described in education strategic documents refers, for example, to teacher salaries which are determined in collective bargaining and make up a substantial share of public expenditure on education.

Slovenia:

Administrative data refers to the number of students per educational programme and the number of teachers. Performance information is used in negotiations between the central financial and the central education authority.

Spain:

Administrative data refers to the number of students and the number of teachers. Results from impact evaluations of policies and programmes refers to international and national evaluation results. Macroeconomic and budgetary indicators refer to educational and economic indicators. Demographic information refers to population projections. Policy priorities as described in education strategic documents refer to specific current needs. Identified needs at different levels of the system refers, for example, to computer equipment, language learning, etc. Performance information describes whether previous national education targets have been achieved or not.

Sweden:

Administrative data refers to the number of students and the number of teachers. Demographic information refers to population projections.

Uruguay:

Administrative data refers to the number of students and the number of teachers. Macroeconomic and budgetary indicators are considered by the central legislative authority to propose a budget reduction. Data on pedagogical orientations are used by type of school and level of education.

Table 4.A1.2. Budgeting and planning of public expenditure at the central and sub-central level

Austria:

Budgeting procedures differ according to the type of costs, i.e. personnel costs versus costs for maintaining the school infrastructure and according to the type of school, i.e. federal schools versus state schools.

For state schools, the general principles for the transfer of funds from the federal to the state level for teaching resources are set out in the Fiscal Adjustment Act (*Finanzausgleichsgesetz*). For Years 1-8 (state schools), the federal government fully compensates the states for their expenditures on pedagogical staff within the limits of staff plans approved by the Minister of Education and the Minister of Finance. For federal schools, i.e. academic secondary schools and vocational schools and colleges, the resource allocation for federal schools is planned and implemented by the Federal Ministry of Education and the state school boards. Short-term planning for federal schools is an annual procedure that stretches over several months (from April to October every year) and involves the Federal Ministry of Education, the state school boards and the schools. Teaching resources (measured as "value units", *Werteinheiten*) are allocated by the Federal Ministry of Education to the state school boards, which redistribute these to individual schools.

As a general rule, the federal level is responsible for providing and maintaining the infrastructure for federal schools (about 550 schools, mainly general academic schools – lower and upper cycle as well as vocational schools and colleges), whereas municipalities are mostly responsible for state schools (about 4 500, mainly primary schools, schools at the lower secondary level, special needs schools and pre-vocational schools, some part-time vocational schools for apprentices). There are also schools owned and maintained by the states (about 300, mainly part-time vocational schools for apprentices and vocational schools at upper secondary level).

State and local budgets are determined by a multiannual transfer mechanism, the Fiscal Adjustment Act (*Finanzausgleich*) which usually covers four to six years.

Belgium (Fl. and Fr.):

There is no central education budget and budget planning for education. The central budget in this table describes the annual lump sum transfer originating from the federal level to the Communities. The lump sum transfer can be used for all policy domains that Communities are responsible for at their own discretion. The state level (Communities) is responsible for planning the education budget.

Chile:

The central education budget is determined by a law which establishes the budget for the whole public sector each year. The central budgeting process starts with a sectorial request. For instance, the Ministry of Education makes a proposal to the Ministry of Finance which co-ordinates the national budget as a whole that is then presented by the central government to parliament.

In early childhood education and care (ISCED 0), there are local budgets for pre-school providers that operate with funds transferred from the central education authority [*Junta Nacional de Jardines Infantiles via transferencia de fondos*, JUNJI VTF]) and from the central education authority (Integra) on the basis of agreements. Accordingly, the budget of public pre-school providers is mainly established through fund transfers by these central authorities. In addition, public providers also budget and plan expenses of funds that complement those transferred by the central education authority. Similarly, publicly-subsidised private providers budget and plan expenses of funds that complement those transferred by the central education authority.

At ISCED levels 02-3, the budget of public school providers (municipalities) is mainly established by the central education authority (*Ministerio de Educación*, MINEDUC). In addition to managing education funding transferred by the central education authority, public school providers also budget and plan expenses for funds collected at the local level. They can allocate additional resources to the administration of public education in their jurisdiction from their own revenues. The budgeting process is the same for publicly-subsidised private school providers which organise the use of complementary school funds they may receive (e.g. through donations).

Czech Republic:

The budget of some parts of EU structural funds for the regional level administered by the Ministry of Regional Development is planned largely independently by central authorities.

At the local level, the administration of the part of the budget coming directly from the municipality is undertaken independently by the municipality without any restrictions or rules other than the general fiscal rules that apply to local authorities.

Denmark:

On an annual basis, the central government and Local Government Denmark, the association of Danish municipalities, negotiate the overall tax and expenditure for the municipalities collectively. The result of the annual negotiations is then included in the budget proposal that the central government introduces every year in August. The proposal for the

Finance Act is then negotiated by parliament. The act is usually passed by parliament in December. The central government acts, negotiates and introduces the budget proposal as one actor. The Ministry of Finance is responsible for the budget proposal and the negotiations.

For budget planning at the local level, each municipality is led by a democratically elected council. Each council is elected for four years and elects a chairman among its members – the mayor. It is the mayor's duty to prepare, call and chair all meetings of the local council. Furthermore, the mayor is the chief executive of the local administration. Each municipal council must set up a finance committee which is chaired by the mayor. Committee structures vary greatly across municipalities. However, municipalities often have a social services committee, a technical and environmental committee, and a committee for education and culture.

Estonia:

By law, the central government, local governments and schools must have Strategic Development Plans. For central and local governments, these plans must be linked to four-year medium-term expenditure frameworks (MTEF). The MTEFs establish the parameters around which annual budgets are planned.

Iceland:

The budget of upper secondary schools (ISCED 3) is determined through the central budget, based on the number of full-time equivalent students and the line of study. The education budget of pre-primary and compulsory schools (ISCED levels 0-2) is determined at the local level at the discretion of local authorities. In addition, the Municipality Equalisation Fund distributes central funds to municipalities based on formulas and regulations.

Israel:

The central education authority (Ministry of Education) builds the education budget. The central financial authority (Ministry of Finance) negotiates and approves it. The central government approves the educational budget, but can change it. A special increase can be approved for individual projects. Conversely, a decrease can be approved too and the central education authority and the central financial authority negotiate to decide where the reduction will be applied. Finally, the central legislative authority (Finance Committee in the parliament) approves the budget.

Kazakhstan:

Despite the budget planning being multiannual at all levels of the system, a budget adjustment is held annually.

Lithuania:

The central education authority approves the local budget for learning needs. The local legislative authority approves the local budget for maintenance needs.

Portugal:

As established by the central general budget, central funds are transferred to a social municipal fund (Fundo Social Municipal), which are then distributed, according to legally established criteria across the different municipalities. Municipalities then decide how these are allocated to school education among other purposes.

Slovak Republic:

Formally, the regional and local authority as the school provider (founder) approves the budget of their schools (in the case of publicly-funded private schools, this is the responsibility of the private school provider). However, 95% of funding is decided at the central level by the Ministry of Education and comes from the central budget. Only a small proportion is decided at the regional and local levels and comes from authorities' own revenues.

Pre-school education (ISCED 02) is financed from local resources, i.e. local taxes and personal income tax centrally redistributed in the form of a lump sum. As a result, there is no central budget for pre-primary education. The local authority as school provider decides the total budget at its own discretion. For private ISCED 02 institutions, the local authority must allocate 88% of the resources allocated to its own public institutions. The central budget contributes to pre-primary education of 5-year-old children.

Salaries make up a substantial share of public expenditure on education. The social partners are therefore involved in the setting of the budget level in as far as the teachers' union negotiates teacher salaries in collective bargaining.

Spain:

The central government manages public funds for its sphere of management, the autonomous cities of Ceuta and Melilla and educational institutions abroad. Additionally, the budgets for the education system are defined at central level by the General Law for Central Government Budgets and at regional level by each of their corresponding Education Budget Laws. The General Budget in Education prepared at the central level includes a yearly foresight for the public expenditure that is managed by the central government. These funds, mainly allocated as a lump sum to regions are used at the regional level to cover costs with general administration of education, culture and sports (including teachers' professional development), teaching in all education levels (including costs with Spanish schools out of Spain), special needs programmes, ICT programmes, grants and fellowships for students, transport to school, canteens, textbooks, teaching and learning resources, among others. The procedure governing the elaborations of the general budget is established by a Ministerial Order of the Ministry of Finances and Public Administration, which establish the criteria that must adapt the income and expenses to fulfil the targets of budgetary stability and public debt approved by the parliament (Congress and Senate). In the process of preparation, the Ministry of Finance and Public Service and the Minister of Education closely co-operate with the other members of government to elaborate the General Budget and transfer it to the parliament. At the parliament, there is a period of debate and negotiation by means of amendments in which the proposals of civil society, other ministries and political groups with parliamentary representation are channelled. The approval in the parliament by means of voting turns the final text into the General Law of State Budgets.

Regional authorities (Autonomous Communities) manage public funds within their territories and decide on the amounts earmarked for education and their distribution among the different types of provision, programmes and services, which is annually established in their budgets based on demand and previous proposals of education authorities. Advice for budget implementation at the regional level is given by the government council, the regional education board, and civil society and the educational community in particular, through the regional school council.

Local education authorities (municipalities) have the ownership of pre-primary and primary education institutions and provide basic services of water, gas, light, electricity and cleaning. Also, they assume the responsibilities related to the maintenance and supervision of buildings used for pre-primary and primary education and special education, in co-operation with the relevant education authorities to obtain the sites necessary for the construction of new schools - for which regional authorities are responsible for. Advice for budget implementation at the local level is given by the education council, and civil society and the educational community in particular, through the municipal school council. Additionally, local authorities may establish specifics agreements with regional educational authorities to take into account in their budgets some special or important needs of schools in their own municipality from any ISCED level (not only ISCED 0-1). This includes, for instance, the arrival of immigrant children, rapid increase of adults in need of education, some accident or serious problem of infrastructure, among others.

Uruguay:

The central education authorities (Central Governing Council of the National Public Education Administration [CODICEN-ANEP]) and the individual education councils for the different sub-sectors of the system only allocate the budget by items (wages, investment, expenditure). The legislative authority cannot propose increases on the budget, but only reductions. At ISCED level 2-3 (pre-vocational and vocational), the respective education council has started a process of decentralisation with the creation of regional campuses. Also at ISCED level 2-3 (general), the respective education council has created regional offices of the inspectorate. The system, however, remains highly centralised and there is no regional level of governance.

Table 4.A1.3. Regulations on budget carry-over for public schools

Austria:

At ISCED 0, no general central rules apply as responsibility for this level of education lies with the states. For general compulsory schools at ISCED levels 1-3, there is essentially no budget planning at individual school level as most financial aspects are pre-determined by administrative regulations. State schools lack the legal capacity to contract, In practice, however, state schools are often given some discretion in making minor spending decisions from budgets co-administered with the local school authority. Nevertheless, this differs across municipalities.

Belgium (Fl. and Fr.):

The operational budget is determined by the state education authorities and distributed to school providers (school boards) according to a funding formula. School boards are responsible for planning the use of the operational grant.

Belgium (Fl.):

In the public Flemish Community Education (Onderwijs van de Vlaamse Gemeenschap, GO!) school network, the financial autonomy of individual schools varies across the school clusters (scholengroepen). In some cases, the latter acquire operational goods and services for a number of schools in order to benefit from buying on a larger scale. In other cases, the school cluster undertakes the acquisition of operational goods and services, but the school determines both the amount and the nature of the resources concerned. By way of very specific budgets coming from the Ministry for Education and Training of the Flemish Community, school clusters can sometimes directly cover some expenditure on immovables and repairs.

Chile:

Individual schools are responsible for the implementation of their school educational project (*Proyecto Educativo Intitucional*, PEI) to offer an education that complies with the overall normative framework. In addition, school providers may delegate further tasks and responsibilities to schools, while retaining the final overall responsibility for the operation of their schools. The precise distribution of tasks and responsibilities between school providers and schools, and therefore the degree of school autonomy for the use and management of resources, will always depend on individual school providers and their schools. Also, school providers and schools do not have complete discretion in the use of their financial resources. There are several subsidies with specific purposes and legal restrictions, such as the Preferential School Subsidy (*Subvención Escolar Preferencial*, SEP), the Support for Special Education Programme (*Programa de Integración Escolar*, PIE), the Pro-Retention Educational Subsidy (*Subvención Educacional Pro-Retención*), the Subsidy for Boarding Schools (*Subvención de Internado*), and a Subsidy for the Strengthening of Public Education (*Subvención de Reforzamiento Educativo*).

Czech Republic:

All schools have been independent legal entities since 2003. With this status, schools enter legal relations under their own name and bear full responsibility for these. The status of independent legal entities has given school principals greater autonomy for decisions about financial matters, for the management of the school property to the extent determined by the school provider (school founder), for the independent management of labour affairs, the possible development of additional school activities and the management of own profits and losses, as well as their own accounting. While all schools are independent legal entities, public schools can have three specific legal forms: subsidised organisations, school legal entities, or organisational units of the state. School principals at schools which have the legal status of a subsidised organisation or a school legal entity, i.e. most public schools, are the authorised body of these schools and as such hold full responsibility for the quality of education, the management and administration of the school, the school's budget and finances, human resource management, and community relations. For most schools, budgeting constitutes a bi-directional process. The school leadership proposes the budget and the school founder approves the budget. In addition, the school founder determines the share of the budget for non-teaching expenses that originates from its own resources.

Denmark:

At ISCED 1-2 (*Folkeskole*), the school budget is formulated at the school within the limits decided by the municipal council and the budgetary conditions decided by the council. The school leader is responsible for formulating a budget proposal for the school within principles set and discussed by the school board.

Israel:

School principals have little flexibility for the expense budget which is allocated to the school.

Kazakhstan:

Schools can have different levels of financial autonomy depending on their legislative organisational form. Thus, some schools can have a partial autonomy for budget use after paying the priority fields of expenditures (teacher salary, dues, housing and communal services). Such schools can carry-over surplus funds to the next year.

Portugal:

The central authority can decide to allow schools to retain a budget surplus from their own revenue.

Slovenia:

The school's budget surplus must be used for the development of education.

Uruguay:

In general, there is no budget surplus at any level of the education system. Any budget surplus from the income of schools' product sales at ISCED 2-3 can be retained, but these funds go to a universal fund from which they are redistributed to schools. These funds cannot exceed UYU 3 000.

Chapter 5

Evaluating the use of school funding

This chapter analyses the role of evaluation in school funding to hold decision makers accountable and to ensure available resources are used effectively and equitably. First, it discusses key aspects of evaluating the use of school funding in complex governance systems. Second, the chapter provides a description of the processes for evaluating the use of resources by agents at all levels of the system. This includes internal management and control, accounting, financial reporting, external audits and evaluations, and individual performance management. It discusses the key role of data and information management, indicator frameworks and benchmarking systems to facilitate an effective monitoring of the use of school funding. Third, the chapter offers an overview of processes to evaluate particular types of school funding, such as targeted funds for equity. The chapter concludes with a set of policy options for evaluating the use of school funding.

The statistical data for Israel are supplied by and under the responsibility of the relevant Israeli authorities. The use of such data by the OECD is without prejudice to the status of the Golan Heights, East Jerusalem and Israeli settlements in the West Bank under the terms of international law.

Evaluating the use of school funding is essential for both accountability and improvement purposes. Evaluation provides information on what a planned budget actually delivers beyond the intentions for the use of resources as expressed in the budget allocation. Evaluating the use of school funding thus gives a fuller picture of the educational experience that is provided to students with the available resources. Evaluation also helps to ensure that resources are managed effectively and used in line with stated purposes and the requirements and regulations attached to funding, while leaving some room for uncertainty in the execution and implementation of the budget (Johansen et al., 1997).

In practice, budgets are rarely implemented exactly as approved. This can be for legitimate reasons, such as adjustments in policies in response to emerging challenges. But the effective implementation and execution of a budget may also be hindered by a lack of capacity (e.g. to budget adequately for expenses or to comply with the planned budget), mismanagement, unauthorised expenditures, inefficiencies, and corruption and fraud (Vegas and Coffin, 2013; Ramkumar, 2008). Ensuring integrity has gained new and increasing relevance in a context in which levels of public trust in government have decreased in the wake of the financial and economic crisis in many countries (Burns and Cerna, 2016).

Continuously monitoring the execution and implementation of a budget helps to reallocate funds during the fiscal year, if needed, and to avoid both overspending as well as underspending. Among other things, this may help to avoid losing claims in subsequent fiscal years (Johansen et al., 1997). Also, in a context where resources are channelled across varies levels and actors in the education system (from one level of government to the next, and ultimately to schools and students),monitoring and evaluation help to reveal potential mismanagement and inefficiencies at different levels of the system, provide transparency of sub-central spending, and facilitate accountability of authorities and decision makers.

Monitoring and evaluation are also crucial for determining the efficiency and effectiveness of resource use by providing information on whether resources have been allocated productively. Monitoring and evaluation facilitate learning about the ways in which financial resources are used at different levels of the system, the extent to which the use of financial resources translates into outcomes for different groups of students, and how resources could be used more efficiently and effectively to achieve the goals of a system. Such information can then inform budget debates and processes for planning a future budget with robust evidence as analysed in Chapter 4. The relationship between decision making and the availability of information is a crucial one as both the range and quality of decisions are dependent on the knowledge that is available (Baines, 2000). The good use of information and analysis in allocation decisions can increase the amount of government resources dedicated to education and improve the efficiency of spending (Vegas and Coffin, 2013).

It is important to keep in mind that monitoring and evaluation arrangements fundamentally depend on the overall school funding architecture, in terms of governance, planning and budgeting, as well as distribution mechanisms. The degree of decentralisation and school autonomy determine the necessary level of accountability and transparency at the lower levels of a system. The organisation of monitoring, evaluation and reporting varies across OECD countries and tends to be adapted to the management needs of public spending (see Tables 5.A1.1 and 5.A1.2 for an overview of responsibilities for monitoring and evaluation in OECD review countries). Typically, however, internal and external control systems work at each level of government, with a national supreme audit institution overseeing the whole system and with international audit standards being generally applied both for internal and external audits (Sevilla, 2006).

This chapter uses the term evaluation in a broad sense, encompassing elements such as monitoring, reporting and auditing. When a distinction between monitoring and evaluation is made, monitoring refers largely to an ongoing assessment of the use of financial resources, that is an assessment of the implementation and execution of the budget, for example through accounting and the recording of transactions. Evaluation refers largely to an assessment of the use financial resources in retrospect, that is once the budget has been executed, for example in the form of internal management and controls, external audits, and staff performance management. Evaluation and monitoring may entail different reporting processes and requirements, such as in-year financial reports of the central budget or reports on the closing budget of individual schools.

Evaluating the use of school funding in complex governance systems

As analysed in Chapter 2, education systems today are increasingly characterised by multi-level governance with shared responsibilities between central and sub-central governments. In such systems, the question of which actors at which levels should be held accountable for which decisions and outcomes becomes central (Burns and Koester, 2016). Giving sub-central authorities the power to make funding decisions may enhance the quality of public services. At the same time, the expansion of sub-central spending, revenue collection and borrowing powers creates challenges for fiscal control and financial reporting (Schaeffer and Yilmaz, 2008). It is therefore important to ensure through monitoring, evaluation and reporting that funds transferred from the central to sub-central governments are used efficiently and in line with laws and regulations and as approved by the legislative (Sevilla, 2006).

Ensuring accountability in the use of school funding at different levels of governance

As Hooge's (2016) work on multiple school accountability in OECD countries highlights, when the national level is increasingly held accountable for the outcomes of the education system while goal-setting and decision making take place at the local level, making accountability work at lower levels of governance within the overall accountability framework becomes a critical topic. The central government remains responsible for ensuring high quality, efficient and equitable education at the national level despite decentralisation and the introduction of new governance mechanisms (Burns and Koester, 2016).

In this context, the central government may have an interest in taking on a strong role in monitoring and controlling sub-central spending and performance. Some central governments seek to control and monitor sub-national spending and performance through the use of input-related control mechanisms, such as the allocation of funds through earmarked grants (Lotz, 2006; see also Chapter 3). For example, in Denmark, the use of funding at a local level is generally not monitored or evaluated by central authorities, but there has been a deliberate emphasis on monitoring the use of specific grants provided to the municipalities (Nusche et al., 2016b). Similarly, in Sweden, the central government increasingly tries to steer municipalities by means of specially allocated subsidies (Swedish Agency for Public Management, 2016). Sub-central authorities and governments, on the other hand, may perceive central monitoring and controlling as interference in their areas of responsibility. This can lead to tensions between different governance levels (Schaeffer and Yilmaz, 2008). Accountability in multi-level governance systems thus needs to be carefully balanced with trust between actors at different levels of governance (Burns and Cerna, 2016).

Governance arrangements characterised by fiscal decentralisation or a network of publicly funded private schools (Chapter 2) require adequate accountability and controls of the quality of spending in terms of legality and efficiency (Sevilla, 2006). In a well-functioning sub-central government budget and managerial structure, sub-central governments face different types of accountability (Schaeffer and Yilmaz, 2008):

- As part of **bottom-up accountability**, citizens act through the electoral process or indirectly through civil society organisations or the media. Beyond the electoral process, citizens can also hold their local authorities accountable through accessing publicly available local government financial information, involvement in the budgetary process through participatory budgeting practices, and through independent budget analysis.

- **Horizontal accountability** covers the range of public entities responsible for checking local government abuses and inefficiencies, such as local government councils, court systems or auditing agencies.

- **Vertical accountability** entails rules set by higher-level governments often for the operation of local governments and requirements for financial reporting in return for the provision of financial resources through fiscal transfers.

As discussed in Chapter 2, private school providers may be subject to distinct or additional regulatory frameworks, particularly if they benefit from public subsidies. To qualify for the receipt of public funds, private providers typically have to fulfil certain requirements and comply with rules and regulations that need to be accompanied by adequate monitoring and compliance mechanisms.

In decentralised governance contexts, it is important that each level of government is accountable for its specific spending decisions. This requires a clear and transparent division of responsibilities and adequate financial capacity to fulfil these responsibilities, as discussed in Chapter 2. Effective accountability of sub-central authorities also requires reliable and co-operative control structures across levels of government. The line ministry or the ministry of finance should collaborate with sub-central internal controls. Central audit bodies should collaborate with sub-central audit bodies. Effective co-operation, and thus overall accountability, can be facilitated by clear rules regarding the scope of external audit institutions and their relationship with managers and other controllers at each level of government as well as valuable and reliable information (Sevilla, 2006). In the absence of adequate collaboration and the sharing of information, accountability and transparency across the system suffer. The OECD country review of the Czech Republic, for example, identified a lack of co-ordination across different information sources as a major challenge for transparency and accountability. It thus recommended deepening collaboration within the governance structures while at the same time strengthening accountability mechanisms, including the transparent reporting of key information (Shewbridge et al., 2016a).

Effective internal and external controls also require consistent data that are gathered through homogeneous statistics and accounting and reporting systems across levels of government. Consistent data help to produce more accurate findings and recommendations (Sevilla, 2006). However, countries with decentralised governance structures can face challenges in providing a robust data base with comparable information on sub-central expenditures. In Denmark, for example, different accounting practices and ways of organising the local school systems can make it difficult to compare municipal spending data and to effectively monitor the use of funding by municipalities and schools. Accounting data are available to the public, but the variation in the use of account plans by different municipalities makes these data difficult to analyse and to monitor the impact of funding. For example, some staff categories are counted as local employees in some municipalities and as school employees in others (Nusche et al., 2016b). Estonia provides another example. Here, the mixing of local and national government funds both by level of education (e.g. pre-primary and primary education) and by function (e.g. salaries for support staff are not covered by the central education grant) complicates the audit of local education spending (Santiago et al., 2016a).

Involving stakeholders in the evaluation of the use of school funding

While a growing number of increasingly vocal stakeholders also increases the complexity of education governance (Burns and Koester, 2016), bottom-up accountability through the direct engagement of citizens can play an important role in complementing vertical and horizontal accountability of public authorities, including of sub-central governments. Bottom-up accountability can help safeguard against a misuse of budgetary resources. Citizens, however, must have the ability and the opportunity to demand accountability (e.g. through access to budgetary information) and governments must have the means and incentives to respond to citizen demands for accountability and better delivery of services (Schaeffer and Yilmaz, 2008).

Budget transparency, as defined by the OECD, is the full disclosure of relevant fiscal information in a timely and systematic manner. Transparency is important throughout the whole budgeting process (from preparation and approval to execution and evaluation) for accountability and participation and is affected by several factors. This includes efforts to ensure the quality and integrity of information, the legal framework regulating the disclosure of information, the existence of a clear chain of responsibility within the budget process, and the degree of legislative participation in the budget process (OECD/IDB, 2014; OECD, 2002). In some OECD review countries, the dissemination of information on the education budgets of sub-central authorities could be improved. Four out of 16 OECD review countries reported that information about education budgets of sub-central authorities is only available upon request and/or at the discretion of the concerned authority. In one country (the Czech Republic), general information is published by the concerned education authority but detailed information is only available upon request by the central financial authorities. Another three countries reported that no information is publicly available at all (see Table 5.A1.3).

Also at the local and school level, there has been a trend to move towards more explicit multiple accountability designs that involve stakeholders in decision making and accountability. Burns et al. (2016) note that a diverse set of stakeholders in a local education system (such as unions, employer organisations, foundations, non-state education providers, and education practitioners) are important actors to include in monitoring and evaluation. They can also act to increase the sustainability of initiatives and help in their implementation. Accountability measures in schools that involve multiple stakeholders can usefully complement traditional measures of vertical accountability.

In some countries, school boards, which usually comprise representatives of parents, teachers, the local community and sometimes students, can play a key role in monitoring the use of funding at the school level and in providing horizontal accountability of school-based resource management (see Box 5.1). Multiple accountability, however, is still a fairly new concept and the amount of available research on how to make it work is modest. While it provides opportunities, such as new sources of information to learn, improve and steer, it also carries a risk of information overload, and it can be difficult to involve less powerful voices in multiple accountability processes (Hooge, 2016). The impact that school boards can have for financial oversight depends on the definition of their roles and responsibilities, their capacity, and their access to sufficient, relevant and comprehensible information. School boards, for example, should be aware of the funding that is available and how resources are allocated and used for teaching and learning (Vegas and Coffin, 2013).

Box 5.1. **The financial monitoring responsibilities of school boards in selected OECD review countries**

In **Denmark**, school boards play a role in evaluating school quality. It is part of the school boards' role to set principles and long term goals for the school and to follow up on school budgets, policies and results. In most schools, the school leader prepares the school budget with input from the teaching staff and presents it to the school board. By law, it is the role of the school board to hold the school leader accountable and make the final decision on the school budget (Nusche et al., 2016b).

In **Estonia**, boards of trustees play a strong role for horizontal accountability and for ensuring that decision makers use funds in compliance with the law. Boards of trustees also typically review budgets, revenues, and expenditures at the school level (Santiago et al., 2016a).

In **Iceland**, school boards have a crucial statutory responsibility regarding the operation of compulsory schools in each municipality. School boards are responsible for ensuring that laws and regulations are complied with and for making recommendations for improvements to the municipality. In addition, compulsory schools are required to establish a school council which should also discuss the school's annual operational plan. At the upper secondary level, school boards are, among other things, responsible for the annual operating and financial plan of the school (Icelandic Ministry of Education, Science and Culture, 2014).

In **Lithuania**, legislation promotes the importance of self-governance at the school level and the particular role of the school council as the highest self-governance body at school level. The OECD country review of Lithuania suggests a strong role of school councils for decisions about and oversight of the use of resources. (Shewbridge et al., 2016a).

In the **Slovak Republic**, the school board acts in an advisory capacity with respect to the school budget. The school director presents the school budget plan to the board for its consideration and is also required to submit an annual school economic report (Santiago et al., 2016b).

Source: Nusche, D. et al. (2016b), *OECD Reviews of School Resources: Denmark 2016*, *http://dx.doi.org/10.1787/ 9789264262430-en*; Santiago, P. et al. (2016a), *OECD Reviews of School Resources: Estonia 2016*, *http://dx.doi.org/ 10.1787/9789264251731-en*; Icelandic Ministry of Education, Science and Culture (2014), *Review of Policies to Improve the Effectiveness of Resource Use in Schools: Country Background Report for Iceland*, *www.oecd.org/education/ schoolresourcesreview.htm*; Shewbridge, C. et al. (2016a), *OECD Reviews of School Resources: Czech Republic 2016*, *http://dx.doi.org/10.1787/9789264262379-en*; Santiago, P. et al. (2016b), *OECD Reviews of School Resources: Slovak Republic 2015*, *http://dx.doi.org/10.1787/9789264247567-en*.

Central education authorities can provide individual school boards with guidance to fulfil their role. In England (United Kingdom), for example, the Governors' Handbook gives guidance to governors in schools maintained by local authorities, academies and free schools on financial requirements and the accountability of the bodies on financial matters (Fakharzadeh, 2016). Central education authorities can, furthermore, support parent associations in providing training and guidance to school boards. In Denmark, for example, the Ministry of Education provided the national parents' association with substantial funding to raise the competencies and professionalism of the school boards to strengthen democratic involvement of stakeholders and horizontal accountability at the school level (Nusche et al., 2016b).

However, in various countries there are concerns about the capacity of school boards to get involved in the monitoring of school funding. The OECD country review of Kazakhstan, for example, noted that the involvement of parents and other key stakeholders in holding the school accountable is still incipient and that boards of trustees, which were created in 2007, are only rarely involved in overseeing the financial performance of their school, even though this is among their functions (OECD/The World Bank, 2015).

Evaluating the use of school funding at different levels of the school system

A number of countries have introduced performance-oriented approaches to central budgeting, often as part of wider public sector reforms (see Chapters 1 and 4) (Sevilla, 2006). Among the OECD review countries, Austria, for example, introduced performance-based budgeting to increase the transparency of central budgets and to establish links between resource inputs and outcomes (Bruneforth et al., 2016; Nusche et al., 2016a). The Slovak Republic constitutes another example having initiated a reform for a more efficient, reliable and open public administration in 2012 that also aims to establish a new quality management system to monitor and assess performance efficiency (Santiago et al., 2016b). An approach to the evaluation of funding that sets inputs in relation to the performance of a system, such as the quality of teaching and learning and educational outcomes, has the potential to improve decision making and make the use of available resources more effective. However, in the field of education, the OECD country reviews found that the analysis of the impact of school funding on school system quality is still not very common. Monitoring and evaluation mostly concentrate on budgetary compliance and pay limited attention to linking inputs with outcomes.

Evaluating the use of school funding at the system level

Given the complex nature of education, countries face a number of challenges in monitoring and evaluating the use of school funding in relation to educational processes and quality and equity outcomes. Costing inputs, quantifying outputs and relating particular outcomes to particular inputs is difficult to realise in an educational context. Considering the role that factors outside of education play for outcomes and the time it may take for an intervention to have an effect, conclusions may be difficult to draw even where both costs and outcomes can be realistically assessed (Burns and Koester, 2016; Simkins, 2000).

The evaluation of school system performance requires the setting of goals and objectives, the identification of appropriate indicators and the collection of relevant data for these indicators (OECD, 2013). It can, however, be difficult to agree which objectives to use and preference may be given to outcomes that are measurable at the expense of other valuable, but more intangible outcomes (Levačić, 2000; Simkins, 2000). In some countries, comparable measures of student outcomes may not be available at all or only for particular stages of education and/or in discrete skills. This runs the risk of policy being driven primarily in areas where there are measures available (OECD, 2013). Setting goals and objectives also requires a weighting of different outcomes and, at times, certain outcomes may only be produced at the expense of other outcomes (Levačić, 2000). There are inevitable trade-offs between different goals in school systems and the focus on one goal may lead to a smaller focus on other goals. The orientation towards certain goals and objectives can lead to distortions in the education process, such as an excessive focus on teaching students the specific skills that are assessed as part of a policy or programme evaluation (OECD, 2013).

The analysis of efficiency and effectiveness requires sufficient analytical capacity and the ability to interpret the available data, for example by identifying the value added of a particular education policy or programme (OECD, 2013). Making sound judgements about the effectiveness with which resources are used requires professional experience and expertise, a willingness to draw on a broad range of indicators, and an awareness of the partial nature of evidence (Baines, 2000). The implementation of performance audits, for example, requires considerable expertise. To evaluate and report on the performance of a programme, the performance audit team must be familiar with the programme's technical and managerial aspects. As a result, performance audits are often also resource intensive and require large expenditures (OECD, 2016b).

Evaluating the use of school funding at sub-central levels

Evaluating how funding relates to the quality of teaching and learning is even more challenging in systems with a large extent of decentralisation. Given sub-central autonomy in using funds in many countries, central oversight of sub-central funding may be limited by legislation or regulations to monitor budgetary and regulatory compliance. In Estonia, for example, audits of local government expenditures funded by their general budgets carried out by the ministry of finance and the national audit office can only assess legal compliance. Broader questions of efficiency and effectiveness can only be assessed when audits concern expenditures from earmarked grants (Santiago et al., 2016a). In Chile, similarly, evaluations through the Education Superintendence assess the legality of expenses declared by school providers as part of their financial reporting but legislation, specifies that the Superintendence should not analyse or evaluate the effectiveness with which resources are used. However, at the time of writing this report, the Superintendence was in the process of focussing its audits and evaluations towards a model that seeks to not only determine the use of financial resources in line with legal requirements, but to contribute to educational quality and to improve school resources management (MINEDUC, AQE and ES, 2016).

Measuring the results of sub-central spending may be further complicated by the difficulty of agreeing on targets and objectives as well as the technical complexity of defining indicators and results. This can be complicated by political situations, such as different political parties governing in central government and sub-central governments which may impede the use of information on the performance of different policies and programmes.

In addition, reporting on inputs assigned to a certain policy or programme implies an accounting exercise and typically the use of a generally accepted accounting system. It also requires the timely submission of complete information and possibly the homogenisation of accounting systems. Reporting on outputs and outcomes requires basic co-operation between levels of government to develop a consensus about the definition and measurement of objectives and results (Sevilla, 2006).

It is also important to recognise the inherent tension between accountability and innovation. Tightly controlled accountability mechanisms seek to minimise risk and error, both of which are fundamental elements in the innovation process. As Burns and Koester (2016) argued, "strong accountability systems [should] thus keep a clear focus on achievement and excellence, while being nuanced enough to allow for innovation, creativity and a rounded learning experience".

Combining the evaluation of financial aspects of school operation with pedagogical considerations

Evaluating the impact of funding in schools involves a review of how resource use affects the achievement of teaching and learning goals (Glover, 2000). This requires professional judgement and appropriate management processes to combine knowledge about school effectiveness with considerations of resource use and costs (Levačić, 2000).

Within schools, school management and leadership require both budget as well as a general cost consciousness to achieve an efficient and effective use of their resources. While budget consciousness describes an awareness of the financial implications of an activity or decision in the school, a general cost consciousness entails an understanding that costs in education are not only borne by the school, but by a number of parties involved, such as parents' and students' in terms of their time. The management of school funding that is oriented towards performance in terms of the quality of teaching and learning involves the regular analysis of cost drivers and the monitoring of some key efficiency data, at least on an annual basis. This can facilitate the effective planning and management of resource provision and offer the opportunity to achieve higher levels of efficiency, for example by changing curriculum staffing patterns or by utilising economies of scale (Simkins, 2000).

A school's view of how the budget is running can be regularly informed by monitoring reports of income and expenditure. These can be automatically produced by the school's financial information software. In Slovenia, for example, the budget management of schools entails self-evaluations and the adoption and discussion of reports on the realisation of the annual work plan and the financial and human resources plans (Slovenian Ministry of Education, Science and Sport, 2016).

Considering the importance of teaching staff costs for the school budget, resource management and self-evaluation in schools may involve an assessment of how the school uses its staff (e.g. student-teacher ratio for the school as a whole or for particular age groups, the proportion of the school budget spent on teachers, teacher contact time) (McAleesee, 2000). Such analyses can help determine the costs of different patterns of staff deployment to the curriculum and help evaluate the cost implications of different use and deployment of learning support staff, different policies of class size, and the use and deployment of support services, such as psychologists (Simkins, 2000).

The financial and resource management of schools may also be evaluated as part of external school evaluations and audits. The processes which OECD review countries have in place are described further below. The evaluation of financial and budgetary aspects in schools should focus on the ways in which the use of school funding promotes school improvement and development. As a recent OECD study on evaluation and assessment highlighted, school evaluations must go beyond compliance with regulations, focus directly on the quality of teaching and learning, and provide meaningful feedback, to contribute towards school improvement. The same is true for the performance management of school leaders, which needs to include a strong focus on pedagogical leadership considering the role this type of leadership can have on the learning environment (Radinger, 2014; OECD, 2013). However, in practice, the evaluation of financial aspects of school operation may rather focus on schools' compliance with rules and regulations and shift the focus away from the evaluation of pedagogical aspects and the quality of teaching and learning.

The evaluation of financial aspects in relation to educational processes and outcomes may be complicated by various factors. It may stem from an overall lack of a shared focus on effectiveness and efficiency at all levels of a system, particularly at the level of sub-central authorities and schools. Governance arrangements and the distribution of responsibilities between different authorities can also be a factor. In the Czech Republic, for example, school providers typically fail to take educational aspects into account in the financial oversight over their schools and in the evaluation of individual school leaders and focus on budgetary and regulatory compliance only as they rely on the school inspectorate to evaluate pedagogical processes (Shewbridge et al., 2016a). Also, responsibilities for the management of financial resources and for organising pedagogical aspects of school operation may be distributed between school providers and schools. This can not only complicate the strategic management of financial resources in light of pedagogical considerations, but also the effective monitoring and evaluation of resource use in relation to teaching and learning.

The evaluation of financial and pedagogical aspects of school operation can be integrated in a single process or carried out separately (see Box 5.2). Both approaches entail potential benefits and drawbacks. On the one hand, the separation of responsibilities provides favourable conditions for the implementation of school evaluations that contribute to school improvement. On the other hand, such arrangements may make it more difficult to connect resource use decisions with pedagogical considerations, as this requires sufficient co-ordination and links between both processes, and entails the risk of overloading schools with external processes, pressures and expectation in complex environments of multiple accountabilities.

Box 5.2. **Different approaches to evaluating financial and pedagogical aspects of school operation**

In the **Netherlands**, until recently, financial and pedagogical-didactical inspections were conducted separately by two different units of the inspectorate. However, a number of cases of financial and organisational mismanagement of schools led to calls for stronger supervision of educational governance. As a result, the inspectorate has integrated the two lines of inspection, also in recognition of substantial linkages between the quality of financial and human resource management at the level of schools and school boards and the quality of education (Nusche et al., 2014).

In **Chile**, responsibilities for financial and pedagogical oversight are largely distributed between the Agency for Quality Education and the Education Superintendence. While the agency focuses on pedagogical processes and the quality of education in schools, the Superintendence focuses on the compliance of schools and school providers with legal requirements. The agency evaluates schools against a central evaluation framework, the Performance Standards for Schools and School Providers, which entail a "resource management" domain and six standards related to the management of financial resources. Evaluations of the Superintendence check that school providers and schools meet the minimum requirements for official recognition and other issues, such as building and

---

> ### Box 5.2. **Different approaches to evaluating financial and pedagogical aspects of school operation** (cont.)
>
> infrastructure standards, safety standards, labour standards, and compliance with the Inclusion Law which prohibits school providers and schools with public funding from making a profit, from selecting students, and from charging student fees. As school providers tend to be responsible for the management of resources, evaluations by the Superintendence focus on the evaluation of school providers. There are some links between the two processes. Evaluation reports by the agency should take into account the results from evaluations of the Superintendence as one element (Santiago et al., forthcoming).
>
> Source: Nusche, D. et al. (2014), *OECD Reviews of Evaluation and Assessment in Education: Netherlands 2014*, www.oecd.org/edu/evaluationpolicy; Santiago, P. et al. (forthcoming), *OECD Reviews of School Resources: Chile*, OECD Publishing, Paris.

Evaluating equity outcomes of the use of school funding

Countries typically invest considerable resources to improve the educational opportunities and outcomes of disadvantaged students. To ensure that resources are targeted effectively towards the needs of different student groups, monitoring and evaluation should pay adequate attention to equity issues and how resources translate into outcomes for disadvantaged students. As the OECD Review of Evaluation and Assessment in Education recommended, monitoring performance across specific groups of students should be a priority (OECD, 2013). While evaluating equity in terms of outcomes is important to ensure that the investment of resources has an impact on equity, it is also important to ensure that the funding arrangements overall meet the equity goals of a system and that any inequities in available resources between different schools and providers that may be linked to funding and governance arrangements are made transparent (see Chapters 2 and 3).

Countries typically set certain goals and objectives for improving the outcomes of particular student groups and have processes in place to monitor and evaluate the achievement of these goals (OECD, 2013). The OECD country reviews, however, suggest that some countries could pay more attention to the ways in which inputs translate into outcomes for different groups of disadvantaged students. The OECD country review of Lithuania, for instance, notes that there is a commitment to providing additional support to students growing up in families at risk of poverty. The focus, however, is on providing inputs rather than on monitoring the outcomes of disadvantaged groups of students to determine the extent to which the education system serves their needs (Shewbridge et al., 2016b). Similarly, in the Flemish Community of Belgium, although additional resources are targeted to students with particular characteristics of disadvantage, there is no national strategy for assessing the outcomes and progress of different groups of students (Nusche et al., 2015).

Monitoring the impact of school funding on priority groups is particularly important in complex governance systems where resources intended for disadvantaged groups are channelled through different authorities or providers. Depending on the governance context, sub-central governments can play an important role both in providing additional funding and in influencing the distribution and use of financial resources in schools (Chapter 2). Sub-central or school level autonomy to make such decisions can make it difficult to measure expenditure outputs for specific student groups. The expenditure output is the real cost of educating a student as opposed to the centrally planned funding per student. The difference between inputs and expenditure outputs lies in spending decisions made at the different levels of the school administration, and often even at the school level, which are not always transparent.

Local autonomy in school funding decisions may mean that steps to ensure an equitable resource allocation taken at the central level, for example through a central funding formula (also see Chapter 3), may be undermined at the local level. It is therefore important to ensure transparency about the distribution and use of funding and the actual resource outputs for specific student groups in each school. A lack of transparency will make it difficult to analyse the extent to which financial resources are distributed equitably among schools. Such concerns about the equitable distribution of school funding within and across school districts in the United States have led to new federal data collections on school-level expenditures (see Box 5.3).

Box 5.3. Developing and implementing systems to collect school expenditure data: A study about the experience of states and school districts in the United States

Concerns about the equitable distribution of school funding within and across school districts in the United States have led to new federal data collections on school-level expenditures. However, many school districts in the United States do not have experience in systematically tracking expenditures at the school level, and the quality of these large-scale data collections is uncertain. To better understand the feasibility of broadening the collection and reporting of detailed school-level expenditure data, and improving the quality of such data, a mixed-method study by the United States Department of Education examined five states and four school districts that have developed their own accounting systems for school-level expenditures. While findings are not generalisable, the study findings may be useful to inform efforts to implement school-level expenditure reporting systems, particularly in large urban areas that were the subject of this study.

The states and districts that participated in the study had been collecting and reporting school-level expenditure data for varying amounts of time and reported similar motivations for developing or expanding their school expenditure data systems. Reasons include a response to the introduction of state laws intended to promote equity and transparency in school spending and district efforts to give schools more authority over spending decisions. To implement a system for collecting school-level expenditure data, authorities typically had to invest in new hardware and software, make changes to charts of accounts, and train their staff. They incurred both personnel and non-personnel expenses, which included staff time spent to choose and/or design the data system, to plan system roll-out strategies and to develop training materials, as well as contracts with vendors or consultants and technology upgrades. Commonly identified challenges in developing a system to track school-level expenditure data included staff capacity and training.

As the study demonstrates, collecting and reporting high-quality school-level expenditure data is feasible and has perceived benefits for transparency, equity, and the efficient use of resources. A key challenge in the process of collecting and reporting school-level expenditure data lies in ensuring consistency in practices surrounding the attribution of funds to schools both within and across districts and states.

Source: US Department of Education, Office of Planning, Evaluation and Policy Development, Policy and Program Studies Service (2017), Exploring the Quality of School-Level Expenditure Data: Practices and Lessons Learned in Nine Sites, www2.ed.gov/about/offices/list/opepd/ppss/reports.html.

In systems where schools have considerable resource autonomy, school leaders also need to make equity judgements when allocating resources between different age groups, curriculum areas, courses, and students with different learning needs (Levačić, 2000). Monitoring and evaluation of the use of financial resource at the school level may, however, not pay sufficient attention to the ways in which resource use decisions in schools promote equal learning opportunities and outcomes for all students, including those from disadvantaged backgrounds. Differentiated analysis is necessary to understand whether certain interventions may have differential effects on students from different groups and to design adequate strategies to meet specific learning needs (OECD, 2013).

In Denmark, for example, municipalities recognise the additional needs of schools with a disadvantaged student intake, and invest heavily in schools enrolling students from such backgrounds, but there is generally little evaluation of how this additional funding is used and in how far it contributes to improving learning opportunities for these students. While there is increasing focus on analysing student assessment results to formulate improvement strategies, it does not seem to be common practice to analyse results separately for different groups at risk of underperformance (Nusche et al., 2016b). Similarly, in the Flemish Community of Belgium, the OECD country review noted that the impact and effectiveness of additional resources for equal opportunities in schools is not sufficiently monitored (Nusche et al., 2015).

Key procedures and tools for evaluating the use of school funding

Reporting

Transparency in the use of school funding is important in terms of public sector integrity and accountability for the use of public resources that are derived from citizen's expenditures and earnings (OECD/IDB, 2014). Transparency about financial resource flows reduces the risk for corruption and misuse of resources if it enables public stakeholders to hold authorities and schools accountable (Wodon, 2016). Reporting on the use of financial resources is an important element for creating transparency in school funding flows. It can provide information to different stakeholders about the flow and use of funding and the effectiveness and efficiency with which the available financial resources are used. This is a precondition to enable stakeholders (such as teachers, parents, students, professional organisations and labour unions) to participate in discussions and decisions about the use of school funding.

Reporting at the central level

In the central budget cycle (see Chapter 4), the monitoring and reporting of school funding begins at the budget execution stage. During the budget execution stage, expenditure transactions are recorded in accounting books and accounting and budgeting reports are produced. This also involves a continuous analysis and assessment of how funds are actually spent to implement the policies, programmes and projects outlined in the budget. Monitoring the implementation and execution of a budget typically involves an analysis of the differences between projected and actual revenues and expenditure in total and by account as well as the debt levels. It can focus on the responsibilities of individuals or organisations and take the form of *ex ante* or *ex post* control. While the former seeks to limit managerial discretion, the latter assesses the execution of a decision after operation.

Budget execution is monitored through accounting and reporting practices. During the course of the financial year, accounting officers or their delegated staff members record all of the outstanding revenue and expenditure transactions. Accounting follows certain accounting standards which are set by the ministry of finance or an independent professional advisory body and may be described in public budgeting documents. Accounting standards can help achieve integrity, control and accountability objectives and influence the quality of financial data and information. Accounting standards, therefore, also influence the quality of reporting of financial data (e.g. in terms of comparability) and the quality of decision making to plan the use of financial resources (for detailed information on accounting practices, see Fakharzadeh, 2016).

The recorded transactions form the basis for accounting and budgeting reports that help to inform the executive, the legislative and the public on the budget execution (OECD, 2014). Reporting requirements for central governments can be stipulated by law or policy that has been approved by the legislature (OECD/IDB, 2014). Information about the execution and implementation of budgets may also be available to citizens thanks to legislation on transparency and public access to information. In Chile, for example, a transparency law (Law No. 20.285) implemented in 2008 ensures the right of any person to request and receive information available in any body of the public administration. Based on this legislation, all government services report information such as the number of staff, administrative acts, purchases, and budget details through a dedicated platform. The same law also regulates requests to access public information (MINEDUC, AQE and ES, 2016).

Throughout the financial year, in-year and mid-year reports compare the actual expenditures with the approved budget to show whether the budget provisions are being adhered to during the execution phase. In-year reports help to identify budget implementation issues and to develop appropriate responses in a timely manner, but they generally do not monitor service delivery and performance. According to the OECD Budget Practices and Procedures Survey 2012-13, three out of four participating OECD countries issue a consolidated mid-year report (OECD, 2014).

Reporting at the sub-central level

Permanent and transparent reporting structures are necessary for fiscal discipline and for accountability and control in systems with decentralised public spending. This regards both reporting about grants that are transferred from the central to sub-central governments as well as reporting about the total spending and financing activity of sub-central authorities (Sevilla, 2006).

Countries may have certain requirements for accounting and financial reporting for sub-central authorities and other school providers in place. Among OECD review countries, legislation in Iceland, for example, requires municipalities to produce annual financial plans and reports for their services and institutions. It is up to municipalities to work within this legal requirement (Icelandic Ministry of Education, Science and Culture, 2014). In Kazakhstan, the Ministry of the National Economy establishes reporting requirements on operations of regional and local authorities. In education, specifically, monitoring and reporting on resource use takes place at multiple levels and is operated in a bottom-up cascade. Every unit and level regularly reports to the hierarchically superior level about itself and the levels below (OECD/The World Bank, 2015).

Reporting at the school level

Schools typically have to comply with requirements regarding accounting and reporting practices to describe the nature, sources, and amount of their revenues, the allocation of revenues within the school to various domains, and the actual expenditures in these domains. Accounting provides the basis to meet reporting requirements by education authorities and to inform the school community about the fiscal and educational activities of the school. Among OECD review countries, Slovenia provides one example. Here, all public schools must send a financial report each semester to their school provider, that is the municipality in the case of basic schools (primary and lower secondary education) and the Ministry of Education, Science and Sport in the case of upper secondary schools. These reports enable authorities to monitor the operations of the individual user of the budget and, in case of identifying an interim deficit of funds, take steps to ensure that the amount of funds set out in the financial plan will not be exceeded by the end of the year. Upper secondary schools record the spending of annual funds in their books of accounts and submit reports on the use of funds received and on the realisation of their financial plans to the ministry. All public schools must also submit reports on the use of funds (balance sheets) to the Agency for Public Legal Records and Related Services (AJPES) which publishes the financial data from the annual accounts of public institutions on its website (Slovenian Ministry of Education, Science and Sport, 2016).

New Zealand provides another example. The country's Education Act 1989 sets the requirements for school boards in relation to annual reports and provides general guidelines and standards applicable to the annual financial statements. Accordingly, annual reports should include annual financial statements and performance information that provides an analysis of any discrepancy between the school's performance and the relevant aims, objectives, directions, priorities, or targets set out in the school charter (Fakharzadeh, 2016). In addition, a school's view of how budget is running is reported to their board of trustees by the monthly monitoring reports of income and expenditure. The Ministry of Education can request these monthly reports if a school is at financial risk.

While requirements for reporting are in place in most systems, the OECD country reviews pointed to concerns about transparency in the reporting of school budgets. Financial reports may have room for improvement with regards to the type of information that is reported. In the Flemish Community of Belgium, for example, schools are required to follow the general regulations on the sound application of accountancy rules in relation to the legal structure of the school provider and have to give proof that funding has been used according to the objective of the allocation and that there is no diversion of resources (Flemish Ministry of Education and Training, 2015). The Court of Audit, however, found that school reports on their financial activities varied and that schools' accounts often lacked cost details. The OECD review of the Flemish Community indicated that the real cost of running programmes and services at the school level was not reported. In addition, information on income from non-public sources is not collected by the Department of Education and Training, even if it might be exhumed from audit reports for the Ministry of Finance where the emphasis is on accounting compliance rather than educational use and value (Nusche et al., 2015).

More generally, the OECD review suggests that the public disclosure of budgetary information at the school level could be improved in a number of countries. Among the 17 systems participating in the OECD review's qualitative survey, only 5 systems (Chile, Iceland, Israel [for central funding], the Slovak Republic and Slovenia) reported that information about budgets of individual schools is published. In six systems, information is available upon request from the school or a public authority (the Czech Republic, Estonia, Lithuania, Portugal, Sweden and Uruguay) while in three systems (Denmark, Israel [for local funding] and Kazakhstan) information is available at the discretion of schools and/or the relevant education authority. In four systems, no such information is available (Austria, the Flemish and French Communities of Belgium and Spain) (see Table 5.A1.4).

It should be noted that there is a tension between the benefits of transparency and reporting at the local and school level and the administrative burden this entails. In Chile, for example, school providers, the Ministry of Education and the Education Superintendence have to dedicate considerable resources to monitor and check daily attendance records. The monitoring of student attendance alone involves 640 million entries per month that need to be checked. This is related to the system of school funding which allocates resources to school providers based primarily on a block grant in return for effective provision as measured by student attendance. Reporting requirements for the multiple programmes serving schools are typically different which multiplies the time and effort involved (Santiago et al., forthcoming). Kazakhstan is another case in point where general extensive reporting requirements raise concerns about the administrative burden this involves for national and local authorities (OECD/The World Bank, 2015).

Auditing and evaluating the use of funding at different levels of the system

Auditing and evaluating the use of school funding at the central level

Budget evaluation is the last stage of the budget cycle that assesses whether financial resources have been used appropriately and effectively. This entails both internal and external audits and financial reporting. It can be an annual end-of-year activity or based on an ongoing process throughout the budget year. The production and publication of a year-end report concludes the financial year. It is the main accountability document of the government towards the legislature and the public and demonstrates compliance with the level of expenditures and revenue authorised by parliament. Internal audit, for example within ministries of education, constitutes a key part of the public financial management system. Internal auditors carry out the first review of the quality of budget, financial and accounting information concerning the extent to which organisations have achieved previously established objectives. Internal audit units are subordinate to the head of the entity within which they reside, but are organisationally and functionally independent. Internal audit findings and recommendations can facilitate informed and accountable decision making, which enhances effectiveness and produces greater value for money. Moreover, internal auditing allows decision makers and public managers to focus their attention on areas in need of improvement (OECD/IDB, 2014). Box 5.4 provides examples of internal audit procedures in OECD review countries.

Most countries have external audit processes in place (see Table 5.A1.1). National audit bodies such as the supreme audit institution, the national audit office, the auditor general, or the state comptroller, are in charge of overseeing public expenditures, of evaluating the effectiveness of internal audit operations, and of verifying expenditures in the year-end report for accuracy (Fakharzadeh, 2016; OECD/IDB, 2014; Ramkumar, 2008). Auditing follows certain standards that apply to the auditing process in general (e.g. in terms of qualifications and independence), for field work (e.g. in terms of planning and internal controls), and for reporting (e.g. distribution of audit reports) (Thai, 1997).

Auditing typically involves a survey phase, a review phase and a reporting phase. The end product of an auditing process is the auditing report which provides information about the operations and audit recommendations. The usefulness of the auditing process

> ## Box 5.4. **Internal audit of school funding in select review countries**
>
> In **Estonia**, the internal audit department of the Ministry of Education and Research analyses the efficiency and lawfulness of the preparation of the budget, financial reporting and organisation of accounting and evaluates the expediency, economy and lawfulness of the use of resources. The reports prepared as a result of the internal audits are internal documents and available only to internal parties (Ministry of Education and Research, 2015).
>
> In the **Slovak Republic**, the Ministry of Education carries out financial audits and controls the use of the state budget and of funds from the European Union through its Department of Control. The ministry co-ordinates its audits with the Ministry of Finance and the Supreme Audit Office. The department presents the annual plan of its activities to the minister of education. A Summary Financial Management Report and individual auditing reports are presented to the Ministry of Finance. There are also governmental audits which assess the setup and efficiency of management and control systems (Education Policy Institute, 2015).
>
> In **Uruguay**, the internal audit unit of the National Public Education Administration (ANEP) controls and monitors the execution of the expenditure and reports to the ANEP's central governing council (CODICEN). The internal audit has jurisdiction over all the education councils of the central governing council and programmes operating within ANEP. Its tasks include monitoring the use of resources within the school system, assessing compliance with laws and regulations, analysing information systems to assess their reliability, and providing advice to ANEP in the fulfilment of its objectives. It can "propose corrective measures deemed appropriate in order to achieve greater efficiency and effectiveness in the use of resources, both human and material". ANEP's internal audit has free access to all offices managed by ANEP, including individual schools. The internal audit comprises one internal general auditor, three central internal auditors, and delegated internal auditors (INEEd, 2015).
>
> *Source:* Ministry of Education and Research (2015), *OECD Review of Policies to Improve the Effectiveness of Resource Use in Schools: Country Background Report for Estonia, www.oecd.org/education/schoolresourcesreview.htm;* Educational Policy Institute (2015), *OECD Review of Policies to Improve the Effectiveness of Resource Use in Schools: Country Background Report for the Slovak Republic, www.oecd.org/education/schoolresourcesreview.htm;* INEEd (2015), *OECD Review of Policies to Improve the Effectiveness of Resource Use in Schools: Country Background Report for Uruguay, www.oecd.org/education/schoolresourcesreview.htm.*

depends on the effectiveness of the actions taken to follow up on audit recommendations (Thai, 1997). Public sector audits generally take one of the following three forms: Financial audits (which verify the accuracy and fairness of the presentation of financial statements); compliance audits (which assess if the expenditure has been authorised by a competent authority, if it has been authorised by the budget appropriation law and made in accordance with the terms of the law); and performance audits (which report on economy, efficiency and effectiveness). More recently, countries' supreme audit institutions have increasingly begun measuring budget impact through value-for-money audits, but there is wide variation among countries in terms of the frequency with which they undertake such audits (for more information, see Fakharzadeh, 2016; OECD, 2016b). Box 5.5 provides some examples of external auditing of central school funding in select OECD review countries.

Other public bodies and institutions may hold additional responsibilities for financial monitoring and oversight (see Table 5.A1.1). In Kazakhstan, for example, the Department for Combating Economic Crimes and Corruption and the General Prosecutor's Office implement inspections in the case of complaints or in the frames of the thematic planned controls (OECD/The World Bank, 2015). In Sweden, the Agency for Public Management

---

Box 5.5. **External audit of school funding in select OECD review countries**

In **Austria**, the Federal Court of Audit can carry out audits on all aspects and levels of the school administration, whether operated by federal or state (provincial) authorities, and typically publishes a number of reports on audits in the area of school administration every year (Bruneforth et al., 2016).

In **Belgium**, the Court of Audit provides budgetary advice and exercises financial control, which includes a control of the legality, compliance and good use of public funds. Its competencies extend to the Communities. The Court of Audit can perform audits on the public funding mechanisms applied by public authorities, including for education. In the area of education in the Flemish Community, the Court of Audit examined a number of issues over the last decade (Ministère de la Fédération Wallonie-Bruxelles, 2016; Flemish Ministry of Education and Training, 2015).

In **Lithuania**, the National Audit Office is responsible for supervising the legitimate management and use of public property and the execution of the public budget. It examines and evaluates the legitimacy of the use of funds allocated to education. The National Audit Office also provides occasional independent scrutiny of the activities of the Ministry of Education through its performance audits. The office, for example, audited non-formal education during the period 2011-13. After a reform of the education finance system in Lithuania, the audit office also prepared several reports evaluating the reform (Shewbridge et al., 2016b; NASE, 2015).

Source: Bruneforth, M. et al. (2016), *OECD Review of Policies to Improve the Effectiveness of Resource Use in Schools: Country Background Report for Austria*, *www.oecd.org/education/schoolresourcesreview.htm*; Ministère de la Fédération Wallonie-Bruxelles (2016), *Examen de l'OCDE des politiques pour un usage plus efficace des ressources scolaires : Rapport Pays*, *www.oecd.org/education/schoolresourcesreview.htm*; Shewbridge, C. et al. (2016b), *OECD Reviews of School Resources: Lithuania 2016*, *http://dx.doi.org/10.1787/9789264252547-en*; NASE (2015), *OECD Review of Policies to Improve the Effectiveness of Resource Use in Schools: Country Background Report for Lithuania*, *www.oecd.org/education/schoolresourcesreview.htm*.

(*Statskontoret*) is responsible for conducting studies in all areas of government for the central government and ministries with the aim of making the public sector more efficient (Swedish Ministry of Education and Research, 2016).

Auditing and evaluating the use of school funding at the sub-central level

Sub-central authorities may have to comply with legal requirements to implement internal auditing and controlling processes. This is, for example, the case in Estonia where municipal governments, like all government agencies, are legally required to have internal audit commissions in place. These commissions are required to make judgments if an institution has complied with the law and if it is spending financial resources efficiently and effectively (Santiago et al., 2016a).

Various OECD review countries have external audits and evaluations of sub-central authorities in place which may build on internal financial management processes and assess and validate financial statements and reports produced by sub-central authorities (see Table 5.A1.1). Central auditing bodies, such as national audit offices, may control sub-central financial activities, including expenditure on school education, although the model and scope of such audits differs between countries (Sevilla, 2006). This is, for example, the case in Chile, Estonia and Lithuania. In a range of OECD review countries, external monitoring and evaluations of the use of school funding by sub-central authorities may also involve central government authorities more broadly, such as the ministry of finance or the ministry of the interior.

Expenditures by sub-central authorities that receive grants from higher levels of government may, furthermore, be part of broader evaluations of performance in the provision of local services. In Denmark, for example, annual negotiations between the central government and Local Government Denmark (KL/LGDK), the interest group and member authority of the Danish municipalities, provide an important space for discussing municipal economic performance and the development of municipal services. They are thus an important mechanism to keep the balance between central regulations and local autonomy and provide space for discussing and evaluating progress towards established goals across the system. Since 2013, the implementation of a major reform of compulsory education (2014 *Folkeskole* reform) has been an important part of these negotiations (Nusche et al., 2016b).

The role of central education authorities (e.g. ministries of education or education inspectorates) in overseeing the finances of sub-central authorities and other school providers differs between OECD review countries (see Table 5.A1.1). In some countries, central education authorities may not get involved in monitoring and evaluating the use of school funding by sub-central authorities. In Denmark, for example, the Ministry for Education does not get involved in monitoring individual municipal budgets as long as national framework laws are respected. Individual municipalities are autonomous in their spending decisions and the central level only follows up if there is evidence that laws are not respected. The ministry may, however, monitor and supervise municipal quality reports and follow up in case of any concerns.

In some countries, central education authorities supervise the use of financial resources by individual sub-central authorities and other school providers. In the Slovak Republic, for example, the Ministry of Education controls local and regional authorities in the financing of basic and secondary schools with a focus on the transparency of financing, the correctness of the methods and procedures applied and the data provided, and the purpose of the use of the granted funds in accordance with the law. The Ministry of Education also performs governmental audits with the permission of the Ministry of Finance (Education Policy Institute, 2015). In Sweden, the central education inspection services in the form of the National School Inspectorate monitor that municipalities comply with education legislation and regulations (Swedish Ministry of Education and Research, 2016). Some countries have set up specialised institutions to carry out external audits and evaluations of public and publicly-subsidised private school providers (see Box 5.6).

At a sub-central level, audit institutions control local public spending and provide horizontal accountability in a number of countries (Sevilla, 2006) (see Table 5.A1.1). In Lithuania, for example, municipal control and audit services supervise the use and management of municipal assets and government property and conduct external financial and performance audits in municipal administrative entities (Shewbridge et al., 2016b; NASE, 2015). Requirements to commission external audits by independent providers constitute an alternative to such sub-central audit institutions (see Table 5.A1.1). In Iceland, for example, municipalities are required to commission an external audit by an independent accounting professional as specified in the legislation for local governments. It is up to municipalities to work within this legal requirement (Icelandic Ministry of Education, Science and Culture, 2014).

Box 5.6. **Evaluation of resource use by school providers through dedicated agencies: the cases of Chile and England**

In **Chile**, the Education Superintendence (*Superintendencia de Educación*) is responsible for evaluating the use of public financial resources by all school providers (and individual schools) that receive public funds from a compliance perspective and for communicating the results of its audits to the educational community. It was established in 2012 as part of the national System for Quality Assurance which was created through the enactment of the General Education Law (*Ley General de Educación*, LGE, 2009) and is represented at a central as well as a regional level. The Superintendence audits the annual financial statements of school providers for consistency with administrative data. The Education Superintendence also evaluates the compliance of school providers (and individual schools) with legislation, standards and regulations, investigates any claims or complaints against school providers (and schools) and applies any pertinent penalties. The audit programme is based on school samples and uses a risk management model that considers both the probability of transgressions and their potential negative effects on the quality of education. In 2015, the Superintendence undertook about 20 000 audit visits to over 9 000 schools.

In **England (United Kingdom),** the Department for Education has delegated its responsibility for oversight to the Education Funding Agency (which was merged with the Skills Funding Agency to form the Education and Skills Funding Agency from April 2017 onwards). The agency was responsible for overseeing financial management and governance in local authorities (which oversee public/maintained schools) and in publicly-funded school providers (academy trusts). Oversight of local authorities' management of schools' finances follows a light-touch approach. Local authorities must inform their regional schools commissioner when they plan to take certain actions, such as issuing a warning notice to a school. Beyond this, the agency does not routinely collect data on how local authorities exercise their responsibilities. The agency does, however, intervene with local authorities in case of concerns, such as persistent excessive surpluses and deficits. In contrast to schools operated by local authorities, the agency has more responsibilities for the oversight of academy trusts. It directly funds academy trusts and the agency's accounting officer must be satisfied and assure the Department of Education that academy trusts have appropriate arrangements for financial management and governance. The agency also has a process for assessing financial risk in academy trusts.

Source: Santiago, P. et al. (forthcoming), *OECD Reviews of School Resources: Chile*, OECD Publishing, Paris; Ministry of Education, Agency for Quality Education and Education Superintendence (2016), *OECD Review of Policies to Improve the Effectiveness of Resource Use in Schools: Country Background Report for Chile*, www.oecd.org/education/schoolresourcesreview.htm; National Audit Office (2016), *Financial Sustainability of Schools: Report by the Comptroller and Auditor General*, www.nao.org.uk/report/financial-sustainability-in-schools/.

Auditing and evaluating the use of funding at the school level

Depending on the level of school autonomy for the management of financial resources, the use of financial resources by schools may be evaluated or audited. Box 5.7 provides examples of evaluating resource use by school providers through dedicated agencies. There is often limited room for misuse of funds at the school level given the limited degree of their financial autonomy in some countries and the large share of funding going to teacher salaries. But there are a number of areas that need to be monitored for compliance. Potential forms of non-compliance include the inflation of data that form the basis for funding allocations, possible incentives for schools to categorise a greater number of students as

---

Box 5.7. **Evaluating financial risk and sustainability**

In England (United Kingdom), the Department for Education launched a Schools Financial Health and Efficiency programme to help schools manage their budgets effectively and to ensure their financial health while maintaining or improving student outcomes. This programme includes a financial health check service provided by accountancy and consultancy firms, other schools or local authorities. The Education Funding Agency, a public body responsible for financial oversight of publicly-funded private schools (academies) and local authorities, has processes in place to intervene in local authorities in case of deficits or surpluses and for assessing financial risk in academies (National Audit Office, 2016).

Northern Ireland (United Kingdom) implemented a viability audit in 2011 to ensure the viability and long-term sustainability of schools. The Department of Education commissioned all education and library boards to identify those schools which were evidencing stress in relation to sustainable enrolment levels, delivery of quality education and financial viability (Northern Ireland Audit Office, 2015).

In the **Netherlands**, financial sustainability has also been a concern to the country's school inspectorate. The inspectorate pays attention to schools' financial situation as part of its evaluations. The inspectorate sees risks in the financial sphere as an indication of quality problems and has the possibility to place school boards under special financial supervision (OECD, 2016a; Inspectorate of Education, 2015).

Source: National Audit Office (2016), *Financial Sustainability of Schools: Report by the Comptroller and Auditor General*, www.nao.org.uk/report/financial-sustainability-in-schools/; Northern Ireland Audit Office (2015), *Department of Education: Sustainability of Schools*, www.niauditoffice.gov.uk/publication/department-education-sustainability-schools; OECD (2016a), *Netherlands 2016: Foundations for the Future*, http://dx.doi.org/10.1787/9789264257658-en; Inspectorate of Education (2015), *The State of Education in the Netherlands in 2013/14*, https://english.onderwijsinspectie.nl/documents.

"disadvantaged" or "with special educational needs" to receive additional funding, and the misuse of earmarked funding.

This was evident in some review countries. In Lithuania, for example, the national audit office reported that there is scope to increase the reliability of the data provided by schools. Although considerable progress has been achieved in this respect since the introduction of the education finance reform, the data on enrolment and student characteristics used for calculating the funding are still not considered sufficiently reliable (Shewbridge et al., 2016b).

Financial risk and sustainability, possibly linked with the development of student enrolments, is another area that needs to be monitored to ensure stable teaching and learning environments for students. Education officials and others need to anticipate short- and long-term fiscal problems, also to take the necessary remedial steps. Assessing the financial condition of schools can, however, be challenging. The monitoring of financial condition requires a wide range of fiscal and economic information that should be accessible to non-financial experts, such as school board members, who may be interested in understanding and evaluating financial performance as well. It could, for example, involve the analysis of financial and related reports and an assessment of liquidity, debt burden and other indicators of financial condition and outlook (Ammar et al., 2005).

Some countries have implemented specific processes to assess the financial management or financial risks of their schools (see Box 5.7). Financial condition indicator systems can assist education officials, including those at sub-central levels, to evaluate schools' fiscal health and identify areas they are at risk in the short and long run by providing detailed and readily available financial information (Ammar et al., 2005).

Depending on the overall governance arrangements, different authorities may take responsibility for monitoring and evaluating the use of financial resources in schools (see Table 5.A1.1). In many countries, central or state education authorities, such as the ministry of education, the school inspectorate or an evaluation agency, have responsibility for reviewing financial statements, verifying data that determine funding allocations or carrying out financial audits. This is the case for example in Chile, the Czech Republic, the Flemish and French Communities of Belgium, Iceland, Lithuania, Portugal, the Slovak Republic, Slovenia, Spain, Sweden and Uruguay. The evaluation of the use of school funding may then be part of broader school evaluation processes, such as in the Czech Republic and Lithuania (see Box 5.8). Finally, central financial and auditing authorities contribute to evaluating and auditing the use of financial resources in schools in a number of countries, such as for example in Estonia, Iceland, Lithuania, Portugal, the Slovak Republic and Slovenia.

Box 5.8. **Evaluating the use of resources as part of school evaluation processes**

In the **Czech Republic**, the school inspectorate is responsible for evaluating the operation of all schools and school facilities that are in the school registry irrespective of the school provider (school founder). The inspectorate controls compliance with legal regulations related to the provision of education and school services and checks and audits public funding from the central budget (Shewbridge et al., 2016a).

In **Lithuania**, the National Agency for School Evaluation evaluates all schools on a seven-year cycle against a standard framework. As part of the five focus areas of this framework, evaluations consider a school's strategic management which includes a school's strategy (including implementation and impact of the school's strategic plan) and asset management (including fund management, asset management and space management) as two key themes of performance (Shewbridge et al., 2016b).

Source: Shewbridge, C. et al. (2016a), *OECD Reviews of School Resources: Czech Republic 2016*, *http://dx.doi.org/10.1787/9789264262379-en*; Shewbridge, C. et al. (2016b), *OECD Reviews of School Resources: Lithuania 2016*, *http://dx.doi.org/10.1787/9789264252547-en*.

In countries with a large degree of decentralisation, sub-central authorities may bear the key responsibility for monitoring and evaluating the use of funding by their schools. This is, for example, the case for primary and lower secondary education in Denmark where municipalities are responsible for ensuring and controlling the quality of their schools. Typically, municipalities monitor closely that schools operate within their allocated budget and follow up with school leaders in case of financial problems. In one of the municipalities visited as part of the country review undertaken by the OECD, all school leaders jointly followed the budgets for all schools in the municipality and municipal staff and school leaders communicated regularly about their spending. This allowed the municipality to shift resources between schools when necessary (Nusche et al., 2016b).

In some countries the evaluation of school leaders considers their responsibilities for the management of financial resources. In the Czech Republic, for example, regions and municipalities place a strong focus on budgetary compliance in their evaluation of individual school leaders (Shewbridge et al., 2016). In Slovenia, the performance of a school leader is assessed by the school council on an annual basis and the evaluation takes financial results of activities as one criterion into account. The performance evaluation has a certain impact on the possibility of promotion and also a financial impact in terms of pay, even if this was frozen at the time of writing this report as a consequence of austerity measures (Ministry of Education, Science and Sport, 2016). In other countries, personnel evaluations do not include financial management aspects. In Iceland, for example, financial resource management is not part of individual performance evaluations (Icelandic Ministry of Education, Science and Culture, 2014). Financial management aspects and the use of financial resources may rather be assessed for the school as a whole in these cases.

Data and information management systems

Information management systems are a key tool to ensure that the various facets of resource management are carried out effectively and efficiently (Baines, 2000). Countries have been investing in the creation of central databases and information systems and the computerisation of data collection processes. The Baltic review countries provide two noteworthy examples. Estonia has invested heavily in the public sector use of information technologies and has developed a network of databases to track taxation, public sector expenditure, the labour market, social welfare services, and the education system. Of particular importance is the Estonian Education Information System (*Eesti Hariduse InfoSüsteem*, EHIS) which entails comprehensive registers for teachers, students, educational institutions, curricula and licences, and educational research. Much of the data contained in the system are available to the general public (Santiago et al., 2016b). Also Lithuania has developed several tools and techniques to assess effectiveness and efficiency in education. The country's Education Management Information System (EMIS) collects key data on various areas of education including human and material resources. The system enables decision makers to analyse the current state of human and material resources at the national, municipal or school level and to adopt data driven decisions (Shewbridge et al., 2016b).

However, it can be challenging to manage knowledge and data across a system in order to facilitate the effective monitoring and evaluation of school funding. This may be linked to a large number of sources of funding and/or a split of the available data across different levels of governance and different institutions and authorities reflecting governance arrangements (e.g. distribution of responsibilities for different levels of the education system and sub-sectors or different areas of expenditure). In systems with a large degree of decentralisation, it can be challenging to bring decentralised knowledge and analysis together. Making sure that the data resulting from monitoring and evaluation are easily accessible for use at different levels of the system can be another challenge. While it is important to bear broader policies and data protection issues in mind, data may not be sufficiently disaggregated to allow for monitoring and analysis of different geographical areas or individual schools. In some cases, the lack of integration of data and evidence may also stem from a lack of political will to present and examine the available information.

Well-developed data and indicator systems can facilitate the monitoring and benchmarking of sub-central authorities by allowing comparisons of their performance with that of others to identify areas of improvement. In this sense, benchmarking is an efficiency tool that aims to improve value for money offered by public services, such as education (Fakharzadeh, 2016; Cowper and Samuels, 1997). Well-designed indicator systems are information tools that can enhance the quality of decision making by reducing information asymmetries, and promote the accountability of public services to national, sub-national, and citizens' priorities (Mizell, 2008).

Indicator and benchmarking systems may be developed and provided by central government authorities and cover all services for which sub-central authorities are responsible, including education. In Denmark, for example, the Ministry of Social Affairs and the Interior is responsible for monitoring the overall performance of the municipalities and manages *Nøgletal* (Key Figures), a system that makes available data on the social conditions, economic background, local finances, and outputs for municipalities and regions (Nusche et al., 2016b). In England and Wales in the United Kingdom, the Audit Commission, a non-departmental public body tasked with auditing local authority expenditure, has been monitoring local performance according to a set of key performance indicators since implementation of the Local Government Act 1992. The Audit Commission produces annual comparative indicators of local authority performance which include, for instance, the percentage of three- and four-year-olds with a school place within the local authority, expenditure per primary school student, expenditure per secondary school student, and the percentage of draft special educational needs statements prepared within six month periods (Fakharzadeh, 2016). Other systems for benchmarking sub-central authorities and evaluating the efficiency of sub-central spending include the Australian Review of Government Service Provision (*www.pc.gov.au/research/ongoing/report-on-government-services*) and Norway's KOSTRA (Municipality-State-Reporting) system (*www.ssb.no/en/offentlig-sektor/kostra*). Both these data and benchmarking systems monitor the extent to which services achieve equity, efficiency, and effectiveness goals, including in the area of education (Mizell, 2008).

Associations of sub-central authorities may develop and provide their members with their own tools and indicator systems to facilitate mutual benchmarking. In Denmark, for example, Local Government Denmark has been developing a common business management system for all Danish municipalities (*Fælleskommunal ledelsesinformationsystem*, FLIS [Joint Municipal Information System]). The development of this system was intended to enhance the transparency and accountability of municipal decision making in the new governance context following a structural reform of governance in 2007 (Nusche et al., 2016b). In Iceland, the Association of Local Authorities gathers data and statistics on pre-primary and compulsory schools, their operation and basic resource use on an annual basis. Municipalities and individual schools are encouraged to use the available information to compare their status to that of others with the aim of improving both operations and efficiency (Icelandic Ministry of Education, Science and Culture, 2014). Box 5.9 provides a detailed description of the characteristics of some of these systems for the case of Denmark and Iceland.

Countries may also have systems in place to use information and indicator systems for benchmarking individual schools on their use of funding. In England (United Kingdom), for example, the Department for Education has developed a framework for better value for money in the education sector that emphasises the use of benchmarking. It publishes performance tables annually that include information on schools' spending, classified by income and expenditure type. With this publicly available data, various interested parties can track schools' spending and the outcomes achieved. There is also a website allowing schools to benchmark their own spending and performance. Measures of attainment are also displayed as part of this framework, with data available on progress measures, absence levels and finance (Fakharzadeh, 2016).

Box 5.9. **Data and information systems in decentralised systems: The cases of Denmark and Iceland**

Denmark has placed growing emphasis on data collection, analysis and evaluation. Since 2013, the National Agency for IT and Learning of the Ministry for Education has developed a new data warehouse (*www.uddannelsesstatistik.dk*) to monitor key aspects of education. The data warehouse seeks to promote data-driven approaches at the level of schools, municipalities and the central ministry and to facilitate the analysis of data in relation to national goals. It aims to bring together data from different sources in a single location to allow policy makers and stakeholders at different levels of the system to access information easily for evaluation and planning purposes. Municipalities and schools are required to enter specific information into the data warehouse. It is mandatory for municipalities to draw on the data included in the data warehouse to prepare their biannual quality reports. The data warehouse system appears to be particularly useful for smaller municipalities which may have little capacity to organise their own data collection and analysis. The system includes a function for schools to generate a statistical and quality report based on data for their own school. The information in the data warehouse is also available to the public with the exception of confidential data on results from national assessments at the level of individual schools and municipalities.

At the time of writing this report, the data warehouse encompassed 35 indicators to monitor compulsory education, including examination and national test results from student wellbeing surveys, transition rates to upper secondary education, the number of students in special schools or classes, student absences, and annual expenditure per student. It includes information on teacher competencies based on information entered by teachers regarding their formal education. There were plans to further broaden the information on human resources in schools and to include information on the number of lessons received by students.

The Ministry of Social Affairs and the Interior manages a system for monitoring municipal performance (*Nøgletal* [Key Figures]). The system makes available data that describe social conditions, economic background, local financial data, and outputs for municipalities and regions. Information is kept at a relatively general level to avoid excessive bureaucratisation. In the area of education, it includes information on per student expenditure, the number of primary and lower secondary schools, the number of regular classes, average school and class size, expenditure on private schools and continuation schools, and the proportion of students in private schools relative to the number of students in the public *Folkeskole*. It allows comparing basic financial indicators such as expenditure per student across municipalities.

The municipalities have put in place a common business management system for all Danish municipalities (*Fælleskommunal ledelsesinformationsystem*, FLIS [Joint Municipal Information System]). The development of this system was intended to enhance the transparency and accountability of municipal decision making in the new governance context following a major structural reform that redistributed responsibilities between levels of governance. The system has been operational since 2013 and collects both financial and administrative information from the individual municipalities, thus providing the possibility to compare indicators across municipalities. It covers key service areas for which the municipalities are responsible (schools, eldercare and social services). Regarding the school sector, the system includes information on aspects such as: spending per student, school size, class size, teachers' age, teachers' salaries, inclusion, and student characteristics (such as age, gender and ethnic background). The data can be viewed for individual municipalities.

Box 5.9. Data and information systems in decentralised systems: The cases of Denmark and Iceland (*cont.*)

In **Iceland**, the Association of Local Authorities, in partnership with selected schools, piloted a data management system in 2007 to address concerns about the availability of robust data and the possibility to monitor the financial and professional operation of pre-school education and compulsory schooling. After the successful pilot, the system, *Skólavog* (*www.skolapulsinn.is*), was put in place on a permanent basis in 2011. The system collects different data, including the operational cost per student. It also collects operational information for compulsory schools, such as information on the educational background of the teachers, student performance results in the nationally standardised tests and the results of attitude surveys for students, parents and school staff. Participation by municipalities in the system is voluntary. Municipalities can access the data for their schools, along with information on how their schools compare to the other participating schools as a whole. It is up to each municipality to decide how the available information is shared.

In 2012, the central government established an additional information system, *Upplýsingaveita sveitarfélaga* (*http://upplysingaveita.samband.is*) that gathers financial information from the municipalities. This system allows for an easier and much more detailed analysis of the costs of education than before. The information is used for calculating the various cost elements that are then published in annual reports such as the school report (*Skólaskýrsla*) and on the website of the Association of Local Authorities.

Source: Nusche, D. et al. (2016b), *OECD Reviews of School Resources: Denmark 2016, http://dx.doi.org/10.1787/ 9789264262430-en*; Icelandic Ministry of Education, Science and Culture (2014), *Review of Policies to Improve the Effectiveness of Resource Use in Schools: Country Background Report for Iceland, www.oecd.org/education/ schoolresourcesreview.htm.*

Evaluating particular types of school funding

Evaluating the use of targeted funds for equity

The receipt of targeted funds may be conditional on the compliance with specific monitoring, evaluation and reporting requirements (see Box 5.10). Since targeted funds are typically linked with monitoring, evaluation and reporting requirements they may provide central authorities a possibility for steering how resources are used (see Chapter 3). Ensuring adequate monitoring and evaluation is key to ensure equity funds are used to the benefit of target groups.

At the same time, it should be noted that excessive administrative and evaluation requirements attached to targeted funds may set disincentives for school providers and schools to apply for such funds. In the state of Berlin in Germany, for example, state education authorities have been providing socio-economically disadvantaged schools with additional funds through a "bonus programme". To receive these additional funds, disadvantaged schools must develop a performance agreement with the school inspection on the targets and objectives that should be achieved with the additional funds. As an intermediate programme evaluation of the programme highlights, school leaders most often criticised the bureaucracy and administrative burden and the amount of time the administration of the programme takes in the school day in the implementation of the programme (Maaz et al., 2016).

In Sweden, a study on the central steering of municipalities also assessed school leaders' perspectives of and experience with the use of targeted funds. While they appreciated that

Box 5.10. **Approaches to the evaluation of targeted funds**

In the **Flemish Community of Belgium**, the provision of resources for secondary schools implementing additional educational support for disadvantaged students through the 2002 Decree on Equal Educational Opportunities is linked with evaluation and monitoring requirements. Secondary schools have considerable flexibility as to how to use the resources, but must follow a three-year cycle of policy and planning in Year 1, evaluation in Year 2, and inspection in Year 3 (Nusche et al., 2015). More generally, school evaluations carried out by the Flemish inspectorate evaluate the use of earmarked funding for specific purposes (Flemish Ministry of Education and Training, 2015).

In **Chile**, the education system has developed a financial scheme (preferential school subsidy, SEP) that provides additional resources for schools serving vulnerable children and youth. The design of SEP is progressive as subsidy amounts increase for schools that enroll students with specific disadvantages. Schools that receive funding through the preferential school subsidy (SEP) are required to develop a school improvement plan and school providers must sign an agreement of equal opportunities and excellence in education (*Convenio de Igualdad de Oportunidades y Excelencia Educativa*) in which they commit to use the additional resources to put the school improvement plan into practice while respecting certain regulations for how the funds can be used. The school improvement plan itself should describe support initiatives that target priority students and technical-pedagogical actions to improve the achievement of low-performing students. It should aim to improve school processes as a whole and set annual objectives, indicators, measurements for evaluation and monitoring, timelines, and sources of funding. School improvement planning typically involves a school self-evaluation to analyse the school's management and operation and to identify strengths and weaknesses.

At present, there are more than 8 000 schools that have committed themselves to engage in school improvement planning in return for SEP subsidies. As some studies suggest, the preferential school subsidy has led schools to focus on students with learning difficulties, to introduce new pedagogical methods and evaluation and assessment processes, to develop their own innovative projects, and to create multidisciplinary professional teams, something which is greatly appreciated by schools and school leaders. The additional resources have enabled schools to establish psycho-pedagogical assessments of students through educational psychologists and to provide additional support for students with special needs and students showing low performance. However, there is also some evidence that school improvement plans as part of the preferential school subsidy predominantly function as an accountability tool to justify additional resources. School improvement planning is often strongly geared towards the achievement of targets in national standardised student assessments. As a result, school improvement planning tends to turn into a bureaucratic process that is based on gathering information and documenting processes and achievements to meet external accountability demands rather than as a process that contributes to the improvement of school-internal processes (Santiago et al., forthcoming).

In **England (United Kingdom)**, The Department for Education has established an additional funding scheme provided to schools attending disadvantaged students (Pupil Premium). Pupil Premium funds are provided on a per-student basis and schools have autonomy on how these resources are spent. Schools are expected to spend these resources on strategies that better support learning for disadvantaged students and close the achievement gap between disadvantaged and advantaged students. Since 2012 schools are required to publish online information about how the Pupil Premium is used and the interventions they are implementing to address the needs of disadvantaged students as

> **Box 5.10. Approaches to the evaluation of targeted funds** (*cont.*)
>
> well as the impact they are having. Schools receiving the Pupil Premium are required to monitor and report achievement of all students and to report achievement specifically of disadvantaged students. Ofsted, the English inspection agency, monitors closely the attainment and progress of disadvantaged students and how schools are addressing the needs of disadvantaged students. If the inspection identifies issues regarding the provision for disadvantaged students, then a more thorough review (the pupil premium review) is conducted. The purpose of this review is to help schools to improve their pupil premium strategy so that they "spend funding on approaches shown to be effective in improving the achievement of disadvantaged pupils". The Department for Education uses information reported by schools to highlight and reward those schools reaching good results for disadvantaged students (Santiago et al., forthcoming).
>
> *Source: Nusche, D. et al. (2015), OECD Reviews of School Resources: Flemish Community of Belgium 2015, http:// dx.doi.org/10.1787/9789264247598-en; Flemish Ministry of Education and Training (2015), OECD Review of Policies to Improve the Effectiveness of Resource Use in Schools: Country Background Report of the Flemish Community of Belgium, www.oecd.org/education/schoolresourcesreview.htm; Santiago, P. et al. (forthcoming), OECD Reviews of School Resources: Chile, OECD Publishing, Paris.*

targeted subsidies would help ensure that funds benefit education and not just municipal budgets as a whole, they raised concerns about the efforts required to administer targeted funds, with amounts that are often considered too low in relation to the required bureaucracy (Swedish Agency for Public Management, 2016). There may also be inequities among school providers due to the fact that while some will offer support (including evaluating on how funds are used), others will not.

Evaluating the use of funding for particular education programmes

Programme evaluation plays an important role as part of broader strategies to evaluate the use of school funding. Programme evaluation comprises the internal or external assessment of particular initiatives and programmes funded by ministries and agencies against a set of objectives or criteria and using a variety of quantitative or qualitative methodologies before (*ex ante*), during, or after (*ex post*) implementation (OECD, forthcoming; Fakharzadeh, 2016; OECD, 2016b). Rigorous programme evaluation can facilitate decisions about the introduction and continuation of programmes, or about their phasing out if they are not effective. While many OECD review countries have processes in place to evaluate policies and programmes (see Table 5.A1.2), the OECD review suggests that the impact of education programmes is not always systematically and rigorously evaluated.

The implementation of a systematic and robust approach to evaluating education policies and programmes can be hampered by a lack of financial resources. Authorities may give priority to implementation rather than evaluation in their resource allocation decisions. A lack of political will can be a further obstacle to systematic evaluations. The results of a programme evaluation might become available during a time considered as inconvenient in the political cycle and carry political risks, e.g. if it is closely tied to the programme of a political party (Rutter, 2012). A lack of analytical capacity or sufficient information on student learning outcomes can be a further obstacle to the implementation of robust programme evaluations (OECD, 2013).

Research organisations and civil society can provide an important source of analytical capacity for providing knowledge about the efficient and effective use of funding. But the education research community may not benefit from the necessary structures and resources to engage in such research. In Denmark, for example, researchers interviewed for the respective country review reported that relatively little research evidence was available regarding the relationship between inputs and outputs and the causal links between interventions and outcomes in the school system (Nusche et al., 2016b).

The effective monitoring and evaluation of specific programmes may sometimes require a broader whole-of-government perspective to ensure effective collaboration and make best use of the available evidence, create synergies, and avoid duplications. For example, government authorities in different policy areas may develop and implement policies and programmes that seek to address social disadvantage, provide relevant data and statistics, and carry out evaluations of the social impact of government policies. Chile and Uruguay provide two examples among OECD review countries in this respect. In both countries, the respective Ministries of Social Development are responsible for broader social protection policies which influence education, provide indices of deprivation that are used for the allocation of targeted funds to disadvantaged students and evaluate the social impact of policies (Santiago et al., forthcoming; INEEd, 2015).

The existence of different programmes that target socio-economic disadvantage which may be funded and administered by different authorities, however, requires ongoing monitoring to avoid inefficiencies. Chile provides a case in point. There is a strong sense among budget officials both in the Ministry of Education and in the Ministry of Finance that multiple programmes are in place that serve similar goals and that efficiencies could be gained through consolidation or better co-ordination. There is, for instance, more than one programme focused on student retention. One of these programmes has been introduced by the National Board of School Assistance and Scholarships (*Junta Nacional de Auxilio Escolar y Becas*, JUNAEB) which provides cash and in-kind support to disadvantaged students. Another programme has been implemented by the Ministry of Education (Santiago et al., forthcoming).

Evaluating the use of funds from international sources of funding

As analysed in Chapter 2, funding from international sources including the European Commission and international agencies like the Inter-American Development Bank (IDB) or the World Bank represent a significant share of investment to schooling in some countries. Making the most effective use of international funding requires effective procedures and sufficient capacity to evaluate the impact of the investments. The receipt of these funds is thus typically linked to particular monitoring and evaluation processes. For the receipt of EU funds, for example, member states must propose an auditing framework in their operational programme together with the strategic objectives of the funding. Central education authorities then have structures and processes in place to monitor the effective use of this funding. In Estonia, for example, the internal audit department of the Ministry of Education and Research also analyses and evaluates the organisation and lawfulness of the use of foreign aid, including management and control systems of subjects related to granting and using allocations from the EU structural funds and carries out project audits according to need. It co-ordinates the audits of EU structural funds in the area of government of the ministry, including organising the preparation of the annual work plan of auditing EU structural funds (Ministry of Education and Research, 2015).

The OECD country reviews indicate that there is often a lack of capacity for monitoring and evaluating these funds at different levels which can present a challenge for the effective implementation of funding. In the Czech Republic, for example, one of the main challenges for the implementation of EU funding for 2007-13 included a lack of evaluation capacity which resulted in poorly defined objectives and the inefficient monitoring of individual projects (Shewbridge et al., 2016a). The country review of Estonia notes that improvements are required in the monitoring of the implementation and the design of impact evaluations (Santiago et al., 2016a). In the Slovak Republic, financial support from EU structural funds is managed by the Ministry of Education through individual operation programmes. The ministry is responsible for the implementation and the correct and efficient use of European resources and ensures compliance with rules set by the European and Slovak legislation (Education Policy Institute, 2015). A general weakness of policy impact assessment and weak operational and project management capacity, also at regional and local levels, however, present major challenges for the evaluation of the longer-term impact of EU-funded development interventions (Santiago et al., 2016b).

Policy options

Pay greater attention to evaluating how school funding translates into educational processes and outcomes

Countries should create the necessary conditions for financial monitoring systems at all levels to also focus on evaluating how the use of funding translates into educational processes and outcomes. An approach to evaluating the use of funding which involves analysis of both financial and educational data and the identification of effective policies and programmes has the potential to improve decision making and to make better use the available funding for teaching and learning.

Monitoring and evaluating the effectiveness with which financial resources are used requires comprehensive information about resource inputs, educational processes and outcomes. Effective monitoring, therefore, requires an ongoing and regular assessment of the state of education and the flow of resources. At the same time, the long-term outcomes of education, which are more difficult to measure, need to be kept in mind. The OECD Review of Evaluation and Assessment in Education (OECD, 2013) provides an in-depth discussion of the evaluation of the education system and policy pointers to improve system-level monitoring. Policy pointers include, among others, the adoption of a broad concept of education system evaluation; a recognition that policy making needs to be informed by high-quality data and evidence, but not driven by the availability of such information; the situation of education system evaluation in the broader context of performance measurement frameworks for the public sector; the development of an education indicator framework for the systematic mapping of available information against education system goals; the design of a national strategy to monitor student learning standards; and collection of qualitative information on the education system (OECD, 2013).

As a result of governance arrangements and split responsibilities, existing data on different aspects of a school system are often split across levels of governance and different institutions. This can obfuscate resource flows and prevent a full picture of the available data on inputs, processes and outcomes. To facilitate the monitoring of the effectiveness of school funding, countries should make efforts to integrate the different existing databases. This would help to link resource use decisions with results, facilitate better decision making, and create transparency of resource use. In decentralised school systems, integrated data systems should make disaggregated data available to meet the information needs of sub-central levels of governance. To ensure comparability of data, common reporting standards for budgeting and accounting should be developed, even though one needs to take into account the costs this implies. Effective evaluation of the use of school funding would, furthermore, benefit from the development of strong analytical capacity, systematic and robust processes of policy and programme evaluation, a culture of using evidence as well as the implementation of a strategic budget planning processes as suggested in Chapter 4.

Evaluate the impact of school funding on specific student groups

Many countries show considerable financial commitment to providing additional support for students at risk of underperformance. This focus on additional inputs needs to be matched with sufficient attention to monitoring the outcomes of different student groups such as socio-economically disadvantaged students, students with a migrant background, indigenous students, and students with special educational needs. This would help to determine the extent to which the school system meets their needs. Monitoring equity issues at a system level can inform resource use decisions to address inequities, help to target financial support more effectively, and increase the overall focus on equity in resource use decisions among different stakeholders across the system, including at the level of sub-central authorities and schools. Analysing the relationship between investments in equity strategies (e.g. through targeted programmes) and student outcomes can be a key step to understanding what works to improve equity in schooling.

Countries should set clear equity goals for the system and develop related indicators to monitor the achievement of these equity goals. This should entail the collection and analysis of data on the demographic characteristics of schools and students and the learning and other outcomes of disadvantaged students, for example through national assessments and labour force surveys. Learning outcomes should be analysed for specific groups of students and key performance data should be sufficiently broken down for different student groups to facilitate the analysis of the challenges particular groups of students face. Data that are sufficiently disaggregated can also help to facilitate peer-learning among schools with a similar student intake and similar challenges. Commissioning thematic studies on the use of resources for equity is another option for monitoring the equity of the school system.

Countries may have implemented different policies and programmes to address social disadvantage over time. This includes programmes introduced by different ministries or authorities, such as the ministry of social affairs. To avoid duplications and inefficiencies, countries should make sure the existence and effectiveness of multiple programmes are monitored over time.

It is also important to monitor how schools use their funding to provide high quality teaching and learning for all of their students. This is particularly relevant in the case of targeted programmes that provide additional resources to disadvantaged students, even though one needs to also consider the potential disincentives such monitoring requirements can entail. School boards can play an important role in discussing the use of funding for different student groups with the school leadership.

Consider the use of school funding as one element of school evaluation

In countries that have extended a great degree of autonomy for the management of resources to schools, other elements of a country's evaluation and assessment framework, such as external school evaluations, school self-evaluations and school leader evaluations, should also include an evaluation of the effective use of school funding. This could promote a more effective use of resources that takes into account pedagogical considerations and the impact of resource use on teaching and learning. And it ensures that schools are held accountable for the use of their resources. The same is true for the performance management of school leaders, which needs to evaluate resource management while maintaining a strong focus on pedagogical leadership.

Evaluating the effectiveness of the way in which funding is used at the school level should go beyond budgetary and financial compliance and financial stability. It should also assess how schools use their funding to promote the general goals of the school system, implement their school development plan and ultimately improve teaching and learning for all students based on a common vision of a good school. It should combine both pedagogical and financial aspects of school operation, and review how resource use affects the achievement of strategic goals and the quality of teaching and learning. In countries where different authorities hold responsibilities for different aspects of school operation, they should be encouraged to collaborate and to take the information resulting from different evaluation processes into account. This could ensure that both pedagogical and financial aspects and the links between them receive sufficient attention. The information from external and internal evaluations should result in helpful feedback to schools to inform their decision making on how to make better use of their resources and promote school development.

Strengthen local capacity for evaluating the use of financial resources

Oversight of the use of school funding at the local level can help ensure that decisions about the use of financial resources meet local needs and provide conditions for strong local accountability. However, sub-central authorities may have little capacity for monitoring and evaluating the use of funding, in particular how the use of funding relates to teaching and learning. Local agents may focus on budgetary and legal compliance only and rely on other actors of the system, such as central education authorities and central inspection services, to evaluate the pedagogical aspects of school operation.

Broader strategies to build local capacity that are discussed in Chapter 2 should also pay attention to the competencies of education administrators for implementing financial monitoring and evaluation processes. This should involve training in skills to make connections between resource use decisions and the quality of teaching and learning and the ability to use the resulting data for improvement. A review of existing approaches by different sub-central authorities can serve to identify and share examples of good practices. In decentralised systems with incipient monitoring and evaluation practices by sub-central education authorities, establishing reporting requirements may provide a stimulus to develop evaluation practices. However, it is important to bear in mind that such reporting requirements increase administrative burdens on local actors and may also encourage authorities, and thus schools, to focus on the goals that they are required to report on. Formulating competency profiles for local officials can also be one way to clarify expectations.

It is important to build the evaluation and monitoring capacity of school leaders and school boards. School leaders need to be able to collect and report data on school budgets and student outcomes to their responsible authorities as well as the school community in effective ways. Central authorities could provide exemplars of good practice in data analysis, reporting and communication to make sure some minimum requirements are met. The school community, including teachers, should have a prominent role in monitoring the use of funding at a local level as part of their overall role for school development and receive training in this area. This needs to involve the identification of key stakeholders, which includes less powerful or inactive voices. Providing them with the tools to interpret and analyse data and other evaluation processes is an important part of giving them the expertise they need to take part in multiple accountability systems.

Also schools need to be ready and open to stakeholder involvement. School leaders play a key role here in ensuring the openness of their school to parents and members of the local community. This could involve the introduction of requirements for stakeholder involvement in financial oversight. For example, it could be a requirement for schools to seek the school community's formal approval for the school's annual budget plan and it could be mandatory for school leaders to present quarterly finance reports for discussion by their community. However, this should be accompanied with steps so such requirements do not lead to excessive bureaucracy.

Promote budgetary transparency

Countries should promote the transparency of the central education budget and the way in which financial resources are used. Budgetary reporting can provide decision makers with clear information about resource use on which to base their decisions and facilitate the robust analysis of financial and non-financial data and thus enhance the quality of policy decisions. It can also strengthen public participation and oversight.

Reports about the central education budget should make available information about expenditure by levels of education and different sub-sectors, different expenditure categories, localities and possibly even individual schools, as well as information about the sources of funds for investment in the school system. Budgetary reporting should be linked to evidence about the quality and equity of the school system in relation to established policy objectives and targets. This could help to communicate the goals of the investments in the school system and build social consensus about fiscal efforts for schooling. To this end, countries could develop a national reporting framework that brings together financial indicators and performance indicators, including information on the learning outcomes for students at risk of low performance. In decentralised systems, sub-central authorities, such as regions or local authorities, should provide adequate information about their sub-central education budgets. This should include reporting on the use of central resources to increase transparency about the flow of resources. In contexts where sub-central authorities determine the amount of expenditure on different schools and/or contribute their own resources raised at a sub-central level to the central funding of schools, sub-central authorities should make information about the average amount of financial resources (e.g. average per-student expenditure) of their schools publicly available. This would facilitate the monitoring of equity of available resources across different sub-systems and geographical areas. To minimise the administrative burden, sub-central authorities could collaborate in their reporting, for example through their membership associations.

Make information about the use of financial resources in schools publicly available

Countries with a large degree of school autonomy for the use and management of financial resources should encourage the dissemination of information about school budgets together with information about the school development plan and other activities at the school. Countries could consider introducing a school-level reporting framework that is developed together with schools which enables schools to examine the impact and improve their decisions. School-level reporting can also ensure that the school community knows how schools operate and how funding is used. In particular, it would be important to disclose the public resources each school receives alongside the use of those resources and, possibly, the educational outcomes at the school. Of course, school-level information about school performance needs to be put into broader national contexts and policies, e.g. on school choice, and the particular context of a school, such as students' socio-economic background. In systems with school choice, however, such information could also improve the basis for parents to make informed decisions as analysed in Chapter 2.

In countries where public schools are allowed to raise their own financial resources in addition to public funding (e.g. through the provision of extracurricular activities, meal provision and rental of facilities), these resources should be accounted for in their school budgets. Public schools should make information about the amount of private income and how it has been spent publicly available. Publicly-funded private schools should be required to be transparent not only on the expenditure of public funding, but on their other sources of revenue, such as parental fees, and how these have been spent.

Reporting of school-level information needs to be weighed against the administrative burden involved. To cope with the administrative burden, schools should have sufficient administrative support, through staffing and their school provider, to comply with reporting requirements. The administrative burden could also be reduced by providing schools with easy access to national data sufficiently disaggregated for use at the school level. Depending on the nature of the school-level report, reports could also be prepared directly by higher-level authorities, to not impose any additional paperwork on schools.

References

Ammar, S. et al. (2005), "Avoiding fiscal stress: The use of expert systems to assess school district financial condition", in W.J. Fowler, Jr. (ed.), *Developments in School Finance, 2004: Fiscal Proceedings from the Annual State Data Conference of July 2004*, US Department of Education, National Center for Education Statistics, Government Printing Office, Washington, DC, *https://nces.ed.gov/pubs2005/2005865.pdf*.

Baines, E. (2000), "Managing information as a resource", in C. Coleman and L. Anderson (eds.), *Managing Finance and Resources in Education*, SAGE Publications, Thousand Oaks, CA, pp. 200-214.

Bruneforth, M. et al. (2016), *OECD Review of Policies to Improve the Effectiveness of Resource Use in Schools: Country Background Report for Austria*, Bundesministerium für Bildung und Frauen, Vienna, *www.oecd.org/education/schoolresourcesreview.htm*.

Burns, T. and L. Cerna (2016), "Enhancing effective education governance", in *Governing Education in a Complex World*, OECD Publishing, Paris, *http://dx.doi.org/10.1787/9789264255364-13-en*.

Burns, T. and F. Koester (2016), "Modern governance challenges in education", in *Governing Education in a Complex World*, OECD Publishing, Paris, *http://dx.doi.org/10.1787/9789264255364-3-en*.

Cowper, J. and M. Samuels (1997), "Performance benchmarking in the public sector: The United Kingdom experience", Paper prepared for an OECD Meeting on Public Sector Benchmarking, *www.oecd.org/unitedkingdom/1902895.pdf*.

Educational Policy Institute (2015), *OECD Review of Policies to Improve the Effectiveness of Resource Use in Schools: Country Background Report for the Slovak Republic*, Educational Policy Institute, Ministry of Education, Science, Research and Sports of the Slovak Republic, Bratislava, *www.oecd.org/education/schoolresourcesreview.htm*.

Fakharzadeh, T. (2016), "Budgeting and Accounting in OECD Education Systems: A Literature Review", *OECD Education Working Papers*, No. 128, OECD Publishing, Paris, *http://dx.doi.org/10.1787/5jm3xgsz03kh-en*.

Flemish Ministry of Education and Training (2015), *OECD Review of Policies to Improve the Effectiveness of Resource Use in Schools: Country Background Report of the Flemish Community of Belgium*, Brussels, *www.oecd.org/education/schoolresourcesreview.htm*.

Glover, D. (2000), "Financial management and strategic planning", in C. Coleman and L. Anderson (eds.), *Managing Finance and Resources in Education*, SAGE Publications, Thousand Oaks, CA, pp. 117-132.

Hooge, E. (2016), "Making multiple school accountability work", in *Governing Education in a Complex World*, OECD Publishing, Paris, *http://dx.doi.org/10.1787/9789264255364-7-en*.

Icelandic Ministry of Education, Science and Culture (2014), *Review of Policies to Improve the Effectiveness of Resource Use in Schools: Country Background Report for Iceland*, Ministry of Education, Science and Culture, Reykjavik, *www.oecd.org/education/schoolresourcesreview.htm*.

INEEd (2015), *OECD Review of Policies to Improve the Effectiveness of Resource Use in Schools: Country Background Report for Uruguay*, Instituto Nacional de Evaluación Educativa (National Institute for Educational Evaluation), Montevideo, *www.oecd.org/education/schoolresourcesreview.htm*.

Inspectorate of Education (2015), *The State of Education in the Netherlands in 2013/14*, Inspectorate of Education, Utrecht, *https://english.onderwijsinspectie.nl/documents*.

Johansen, C.K., L.R. Jones and F. Thompson (1997), "Management and control of budget execution", in R.T. Golembiewski and J. Rabin, *Public Budgeting and Finance*, 4th edition, Marcel Dekker, New York, pp. 575-585.

Levačić, R. (2000), "Linking resources to learning outcomes", in C. Coleman and L. Anderson (eds.), *Managing Finance and Resources in Education*, SAGE Publications, Thousand Oaks, CA, pp. 3-24.

Lotz, J. (2006), "Accountability and Control in the Financing of Local Government in Denmark", OECD Journal on Budgeting, Vol. 5/2, *http://dx.doi.org/10.1787/budget-v5-art11-en*.

Maaz, K., S. Böse and M. Neumann (2016), *BONUS-Studie: Wissenschaftliche Begleitung und Evaluation des Bonus-Programms zur Unterstützung von Schulen in schwieriger Lage in Berlin, Zwischenbericht über die erste Schulleiterbefragung aus dem Schuljahr 2013/2014* [BONUS study: Scientific monitoring and evaluation of the Bonus Program for schools in challenging circumstances in Berlin, intermediate report about the first school leader survey fort he school year 2013/2014], Deutsches Institut für Internationale Pädagogische Forschung [German Institute for International Educational Research], Deutsches Institut für Internationale Pädagogische Forschung, Berlin, *www.dipf.de/de/forschung/projekte/pdf/steubis/bonus-studie-zwischenbericht*.

McAleese, K. (2000), "Budgeting in schools", in C. Coleman and L. Anderson (eds.), *Managing Finance and Resources in Education*, SAGE Publications, Thousand Oaks, CA, pp. 3-24.

Ministère de la Fédération Wallonie-Bruxelles (2016), *Examen de l'OCDE des politiques pour un usage plus efficace des ressources scolaires : Rapport Pays*, Ministère de la Fédération Wallonie-Bruxelles, Bruxelles, *www.oecd.org/education/schoolresourcesreview.htm*.

Ministry of Education, Agency for Quality Education and Education Superintendence (2016), *OECD Review of Policies to Improve the Effectiveness of Resource Use in Schools: Country Background Report for Chile*, MINEDUC, AQE and ES, Santiago, *www.oecd.org/education/schoolresourcesreview.htm*.

Ministry of Education and Research (2015), *OECD Review of Policies to Improve the Effectiveness of Resource Use in Schools: Country Background Report for Estonia*, Tartu, *www.oecd.org/education/schoolresourcesreview.htm*.

Mizell, L. (2008), "Promoting Performance – Using Indicators to Enhance the Effectiveness of Sub-Central Spending", *OECD Working Papers on Fiscal Federalism*, No. 5, OECD Publishing, Paris, *http://dx.doi.org/10.1787/5k97b11g190r-en*.

MŠMT (2016), *OECD Review of Policies to Improve the Effectiveness of Resource Use in Schools: Country Background Report for the Czech Republic*, Czech Ministry of Education, Youth and Sports, Prague, *www.oecd.org/education/schoolresourcesreview.htm*.

NASE (2015), *OECD Review of Policies to Improve the Effectiveness of Resource Use in Schools: Country Background Report for Lithuania*, National Agency for School Evaluation, Vilnius, *www.oecd.org/education/schoolresourcesreview.htm*.

National Audit Office (2016), *Financial Sustainability of Schools: Report by the Comptroller and Auditor General*, National Audit Office, London, *www.nao.org.uk/report/financial-sustainability-in-schools/*.

Northern Ireland Audit Office (2015), *Department of Education: Sustainability of Schools*, Northern Ireland Audit Office, Belfast, *www.niauditoffice.gov.uk/publication/department-education-sustainability-schools*.

Nusche, D. et al. (2016a), *OECD Reviews of School Resources: Austria 2016*, OECD Publishing, Paris, *http://dx.doi.org/10.1787/9789264256729-en*.

Nusche, D. et al. (2016b), *OECD Reviews of School Resources: Denmark 2016*, OECD Publishing, Paris, *http://dx.doi.org/10.1787/9789264262430-en*.

Nusche, D. et al. (2015), *OECD Reviews of School Resources: Flemish Community of Belgium 2015*, OECD Publishing, Paris, *http://dx.doi.org/10.1787/9789264247598-en*.

Nusche, D. et al. (2014), *OECD Reviews of Evaluation and Assessment in Education: Netherlands 2014*, OECD Publishing, Paris, *www.oecd.org/edu/evaluationpolicy*.

OECD (forthcoming), *Building a Common Understanding of Education Evaluation Policy Analysis: A Framework for Analysis*, OECD Publishing, Paris.

OECD (2016a), *Netherlands 2016: Foundations for the Future*, OECD Publishing, Paris, *http://dx.doi.org/10.1787/9789264257658-en*.

OECD (2016b), *OECD (2016), Supreme Audit Institutions and Good Governance: Oversight, Insight and Foresight*, OECD Publishing, Paris, *http://dx.doi.org/10.1787/9789264263871-en*.

OECD (2014), *Budgeting Practices and Procedures in OECD Countries*, OECD Publishing, Paris, *http://dx.doi.org/10.1787/9789264059696-en*.

OECD (2013), *Synergies for Better Learning: An International Perspective on Evaluation and Assessment*, OECD Publishing, Paris, *http://dx.doi.org/10.1787/9789264190658-en*.

OECD (2002), "OECD Best Practices for Budget Transparency", *OECD Journal on Budgeting*, Vol. 1/3, *http://dx.doi.org/10.1787/budget-v1-art14-en*.

OECD/IDB (2014), *Government at a Glance: Latin America and the Caribbean 2014: Towards Innovative Public Financial Management*, OECD Publishing, Paris, *http://dx.doi.org/10.1787/9789264209480-en*.

OECD/The World Bank (2015), *OECD Reviews of School Resources: Kazakhstan 2015*, OECD Publishing, Paris, *http://dx.doi.org/10.1787/9789264245891-en*.

Radinger, T. (2014), "School leader appraisal — A tool to strengthen school leaders' pedagogical leadership and skills for teacher management?", *European Journal of Education*, Vol. 49/ 3, Wiley-Blackwell, pp. 378-394, *http://onlinelibrary.wiley.com/doi/10.1111/ejed.12085/abstract*.

Ramkumar, V. (2008), *Our Money, Our Responsibility: A Citizens' Guide to Monitoring Government Expenditures*, The International Budget Partnership, Washington, DC, *www.internationalbudget.org/publications/our-money-our-responsibility-a-citizens-guide-to-monitoring-government-expenditures/*.

Rutter, J. (2012), *Evidence and Evaluation in Policy Making: A Problem of Supply or Demand?*, Institute for Government, London, *www.instituteforgovernment.org.uk/sites/default/files/publications/evidence%20and%20evaluation%20in%20template_final_0.pdf*.

Santiago, P. et al. (forthcoming), *OECD Reviews of School Resources: Chile*, OECD Publishing, Paris.

Santiago, P. et al. (2016a), *OECD Reviews of School Resources: Estonia 2016*, OECD Publishing, Paris, *http://dx.doi.org/10.1787/9789264251731-en*.

Santiago, P. et al. (2016b), *OECD Reviews of School Resources: Slovak Republic 2015*, OECD Publishing, Paris, *http://dx.doi.org/10.1787/9789264247567-en*.

Santiago, P. et al. (2016c), *OECD Reviews of School Resources: Uruguay 2016*, OECD Publishing, Paris, *http://dx.doi.org/10.1787/9789264265530-en*.

Schaeffer, M. and S. Yilmaz (2008), "Strengthening local government budgeting and accountability", *Policy Research Working Paper 4767*, The World Bank, Washington, DC.

Sevilla, J. (2006), "Accountability and Control of Public Spending in a Decentralised and Delegated Environment", *OECD Journal on Budgeting*, Vol. 5/2, *http://dx.doi.org/10.1787/budget-v5-art8-en*.

Shewbridge, C. et al. (2016a), *OECD Reviews of School Resources: Czech Republic 2016*, OECD Publishing, Paris, *http://dx.doi.org/10.1787/9789264262379-en*.

Shewbridge, C. et al. (2016b), *OECD Reviews of School Resources: Lithuania 2016*, OECD Publishing, Paris, *http://dx.doi.org/10.1787/9789264252547-en*.

Shewbridge, C. et al. (2011), *OECD Reviews of Evaluation and Assessment in Education: Denmark 2011*, OECD Publishing, Paris, *http://dx.doi.org/10.1787/9789264116597-en*.

Simkins, T. (2000), "Cost analysis in education", in C. Coleman and L. Anderson (eds.), *Managing Finance and Resources in Education*, SAGE Publications, Thousand Oaks, CA, pp. 168-186.

Slovenian Ministry of Education, Science and Sport (2016), *OECD Review of Policies to Improve the Effectiveness of Resource Use in Schools: Country Background Report for Slovenia*, Ljubljana, *www.oecd.org/education/schoolresourcesreview.htm*.

Swedish Agency for Public Management (2016), *Central Government's Steering of Municipalities*, *www.statskontoret.se/In-English/publications/2016---summaries-of-publications/central-governments-steering-of-municipalities-201624/*.

Swedish Ministry of Education and Research (2016), *OECD Review of Policies to Improve the Effectiveness of Resource Use in Schools: Country Background Report for Sweden*, Swedish Ministry of Education and Research, Stockholm, *www.oecd.org/education/schoolresourcesreview.htm*.

US Department of Education, Office of Planning, Evaluation and Policy Development, Policy and Program Studies Service (2017), *Exploring the Quality of School-Level Expenditure Data: Practices and Lessons Learned in Nine Sites*, US Department of Education, Washington, DC, *www2.ed.gov/about/offices/list/opepd/ppss/reports.html*.

Vegas, E. and C. Coffin (2013), "What matters most for school finance: a framework paper", *Saber Working Paper Series*, World Bank, Washington, DC.

Wodon, Q. (2016), "What matters most for equity and inclusion in education systems: A framework paper", *Saber Working Paper Series*, World Bank, Washington, DC.

ANNEX 5.A1

National approaches to evaluating the use of school funding

Table 5.A1.1. Monitoring and evaluating how different levels of the system use public financial resources (ISCED 1-3, public schools only)

Country	Level of education				Level of governance	Responsibility for monitoring and evaluation
Austria		1	2	3	Central level	● Central audit services (Federal Court of Audit) ● Central education authorities (Federal Ministry of Education, state school boards)
		1	2	3	State level (state schools)	● Central education authority (Federal Ministry of Education) ● Central audit services (Federal Court of Audit) ● State audit services (State Courts of Audit) ● State legislative authorities
					Local level (state schools)	● State education authorities ● State financial authorities ● State audit services (State Courts of Audit) ● Local education authorities ● Local financial authorities ● Central audit services (Federal Court of Audit)
					School level (state schools)	● State education authorities ● State audit services (State Courts of Audit) ● Central audit services (Federal Court of Audit)
			2	3	School level (federal schools)	● Central education authorities (Federal Ministry of Education) ● Central education authorities (state school boards) ● Central audit services (Federal Court of Audit)
Belgium (Fl.)		1	2	3	Central level	● Central audit services (Belgian Court of Audit)
					State level	● Central audit services (Belgium Court of Audit) ● State education inspectorate (Flemish Education Inspectorate)
					School level	● State education authority (Flemish Agency of Educational Services) ● State education inspectorate (Flemish Education Inspectorate)
Belgium (Fr.)		1	2	3	Central level	● Central audit services (Belgian Court of Audit)
					State level	● State financial authorities (Inspection des Finances)
					School level	● State education authority (Administration générale de l'enseignement du Ministère de la Fédération Wallonie-Bruxelles)
Chile		1	2	3	Central level	● Central audit services (General Comptroller Office of the Republic, *Contraloría General de la República*)
					Local level	● Central education authority (Ministry of Education) Central financial inspectorate (Superintendence of Education) ● Central audit services (General Comptroller Office of the Republic) ● Central financial authority (Tax Administration Service)
					School level	● Central financial inspectorate (Superintendence of Education) ● Central education authority (Ministry of Education) ● Central audit services (General Comptroller Office of the Republic)
Czech Republic	0	1	2	3	Central level	● Central audit services (Supreme Audit Office) ● Central financial authority
					Regional level	● Regional audit services ● Other (Ministry of the Interior)
					Local level	● Local audit services ● Other (Ministry of the Interior)
					School level	● Central education inspectorate (Czech School Inspectorate) ● Local education authorities (as school founders) ● Regional education authorities (as school founders) ● Other (Ministry of the Interior)
Denmark		1	2	3	Central level	● Central education authorities ● Central audit services ● Central financial authority
		1	2		Local level	● Local audit services
					School level	● Local education authorities ● Local financial authorities ● Other (local legislative authorities) ● Local audit services ● Central financial authorities
				3	School level	● Central education authorities ● Central audit services ● Other (private auditors)

Table 5.A1.1. **Monitoring and evaluating how different levels of the system use public financial resources (ISCED 1-3, public schools only)** (cont.)

Country	Level of education			Level of governance	Responsibility for monitoring and evaluation
Estonia	1	2	3	Central level	● Central audit services (National Audit Office of Estonia) ● Central financial authority
				Local level	● Central audit services (National Audit Office of Estonia)
				School level	● Central audit services (National Audit Office of Estonia) ● Local audit services (in the case of municipal schools)
Iceland	1	2	3	Central level	● Central audit services (National Audit Office) ● Central financial authority (Ministry of Finance)
	1	2		Local level	● Other (monitoring board under the Ministry of the Interior) ● Other (requirement to commission an external audit)
				School level	● Local financial authorities
			3	School level	● Central education authorities (Ministry of Education, Science and Culture) ● Central audit services (National Audit Office)
Israel	1	2	3	Central level	● Central education authority (Ministry of Education) ● Central financial authority (Ministry of Finance) ● Central audit service (State Comptroller)
				Local level	● Central education authority (Ministry of Education) ● Central audit services (State Comptroller)
				School level	● Central education authority (Ministry of Education) ● Local education authorities ● School board (ISCED 1 only)
Kazakhstan	1	2	3	Central level	● Central audit services (Account Committee) ● Central financial authorities and inspectorate (Department for Combating Economic Crimes and Corruption, General Prosecutor's Office, Ministry of Finance's committees of financial control, audit committees) ● Central education authorities
				Regional level	● Regional audit services ● Regional education authority ● Central audit services (Account Committee) ● Central financial authorities and inspectorate (Department for Combating Economic Crimes and Corruption, General Prosecutor's Office, Ministry of Finance's committees of financial control, audit committees)
				Local level	● Regional audit services ● Local education authority ● Central audit services (Account Committee) ● Central financial authorities and inspectorate (Department for Combating Economic Crimes and Corruption, General Prosecutor's Office, Ministry of Finance's committees of financial control, audit committees)
				School level	● Central education authority (depending on school's jurisdiction) ● Local education authorities (depending on school's jurisdiction) ● Regional education authority (depending on school's jurisdiction) ● Central financial authority (Ministry of Finance) (all schools irrespective of jurisdiction)
Lithuania	1	2	3	Central level	● Central audit services (National audit office)
				Local level	● Central audit services (National audit office) ● Local audit services
				School level	● Central education authority ● Central education inspectorate ● Central audit services ● Local audit services
Portugal	1	2	3	Central level	● Central education inspectorate (*Inspecção Geral da Educação e Ciência*, IGEC) ● Central financial inspectorate (*Inspecção-Geral de Finanças*, IGF) ● Central audit services (*Tribunal de Contas*, Account Court)
	1			Local level	● Central education inspectorate (IGEC) ● Central financial inspectorate (IGF) ● Central audit services (Account Court)
	1	2	3	School level	● Central education inspectorate (IGEC) ● Central financial inspectorate (IGF) ● Central audit services (Account Court)

Table 5.A1.1. **Monitoring and evaluating how different levels of the system use public financial resources (ISCED 1-3, public schools only)** *(cont.)*

Country	Level of education			Level of governance	Responsibility for monitoring and evaluation
Slovak Republic	1	2	3	Central level	• Central education authority (Ministry of Education) • Central financial authority (Ministry of Finance) • Central audit services (Supreme Audit Office)
			3	Regional level	• Central education authority (Ministry of Education) • Regional government authority • Central financial authority (Ministry of Finance) • Central audit services (Supreme Audit Office)
	1	2		Local level	• Central education authority (Ministry of Education) • Regional government authority • Central financial authority (Ministry of Finance) • Central audit services (Supreme Audit Office)
				School level	• Central education authority (Ministry of Education) • Central financial authority (Ministry of Finance) • Central audit services (Supreme Audit Office) • Local education authority • School leadership
			3	School level	• Central education authority (Ministry of Education) • Central financial authority (Ministry of Finance) • Central audit services (Supreme Audit Office) • Regional education authority • School leadership
Slovenia	1	2	3	Central level	• Central audit services (Court of Audit)
	1	2		Local level	• Central audit services (Court of Audit)
	1	2	3	School level	• Central audit services • Central financial authorities • Central education authority • Other (Independent audit services contracted by individual schools)
Spain	1	2	3	Central level	• Central financial inspectorate (General Inspection of Services) • Central education inspectorate (Educational Central Inspection of Non-University Education) • Other (General Intervention of the State Administration)
				Regional level	• Regional financial inspectorate (Regional Inspection of Services) • Regional educational inspectorate (Educational Inspection of Non-University Education) • Other (General Intervention of the Regional Administration)
	1	2		Local level	• Regional financial inspectorate (Regional Inspection of Services) • Regional education inspectorate (Educational Inspection of non-university education) • Other (General Intervention of the Regional Administration)
				School level	• Central education inspectorate • Regional and local education authorities
Sweden	1	2	3	Central level	• Central audit services
				Local level	• Local audit services • Central education authority (National School Inspectorate)
				School level	• Local financial authorities • Local education authorities • Central education authorities (National Agency for Education; National School Inspectorate)

Table 5.A1.1. **Monitoring and evaluating how different levels of the system use public financial resources (ISCED 1-3, public schools only)** (cont.)

Country	Level of education			Level of governance	Responsibility for monitoring and evaluation
Uruguay	1	2	3	Central level	• Central audit services (Court of Audit) • Central education authority (internal audit of the National Public Education Administration [ANEP])
				School level	• Central education authorities (Treasury Division of Education Councils, Sectorial Infrastructure Directorate and Sectorial Programming and Budget Directorate of the CODICEN)

Notes: Information presented in this table refers to the evaluation and monitoring of the use of public financial resources in public schooling. Further information in the table notes at the end of the annex may provide information on responsibilities for monitoring of the use of public financial resources in publicly-funded private schooling for some countries. Countries may also have in place additional processes for monitoring and evaluation in public schooling which are not reported in this table. The level of governance describes the level of the education system at which school resources are used and managed.

The review team made every effort to ensure, in collaboration with countries, that the information collected through the qualitative survey on school funding is valid and reliable and reflects specific country contexts while being comparable across countries. However, given the qualitative nature of the survey, information should be interpreted with care.

For terms and definitions of levels of governance and levels of education, see Annex B. For country-specific notes to this table, see the end of this annex.

Table 5.A1.2. **Responsibility for evaluating central education programmes/policies**

Country	Responsible authorities
Austria	• Central education authorities (Federal Ministry of Education, Federal Institute for Education Research, Innovation and Development of the Austrian School System) • Central audit services (Court of Audit)
Belgium (Fl. and Fr.)	• Central audit services (Belgian Court of Audit)
Chile	• Central education authority (Ministry of Education) • Other (Ministry of Social Development)
Czech Republic	• Central education inspectorate (Czech School Inspectorate) • Central education authority (Ministry of Education)
Denmark	• Central education authorities • Central audit services • Central financial authority
Estonia	• Central education authority
Iceland	• Central education authority (Ministry of Education, Science and Culture)
Israel	• Central education authority (The National Authority for Assessment and Evaluation in Education [RAMA])
Kazakhstan	• Central education authorities
Lithuania	• Central education authority (Ministry of Education and Science)
Portugal	• Central education authority (Ministry of Education)
Slovak Republic	• Central education authority (Ministry of Education)
Slovenia	• Central education inspectorate
Spain	• Central education authority
Sweden	• Central education authorities (National Agency for Education, Ministry of Education and Research) • Other (Swedish Agency for Public Management)
Uruguay	• Central education authorities (CODICEN-ANEP) • Other (Ministry for Social Development MIDES)

Notes: This table describes responsibilities for the evaluation of central education policies and programmes. The type of policies and programmes that are evaluated depends on the distribution of responsibilities and the levels of education for which the central education authorities are responsible.

The review team made every effort to ensure, in collaboration with countries, that the information collected through the qualitative survey on school funding is valid and reliable and reflects specific country contexts while being comparable across countries. However, given the qualitative nature of the survey, information should be interpreted with care.

For country-specific notes to this table, see the end of this annex.

Table 5.A1.3. **Public availability of information on education budgets of sub-central authorities (ISCED 1-3)**

Country	Systematically published by relevant education authority	At the discretion of the relevant education authority	Available upon request	Not published
Austria	✓			
Belgium (Fl. and Fr.)	✓			
Chile			✓	
Czech Republic	✓		✓	
Denmark	✓			
Estonia	✓			
Iceland	✓			
Israel				✓
Kazakhstan		✓	✓	
Lithuania				✓
Portugal			✓	
Slovak Republic		✓	✓	
Slovenia				✓
Spain	✓			
Sweden	✓			

Notes: This table describes the public availability of information on education budgets of sub-central education authorities. The levels of sub-central governance and the level of education for which they are responsible depend on the particular context. For example, for Austria, the information presented in this table refers to the level of states and local authorities (ISCED 1-3 state schools). For the Czech Republic, the information presented refers to the level of regional (ISCED 3) and local authorities (ISCED 1-2).

General note on Uruguay: The school system is highly centralised and there are no sub-central levels of administration as such, even though there have been some steps towards some decentralisation at ISCED levels 2-3.

The review team made every effort to ensure, in collaboration with countries, that the information collected through the qualitative survey on school funding is valid and reliable and reflects specific country contexts while being comparable across countries. However, given the qualitative nature of the survey, information should be interpreted with care.

For country-specific notes to this table, see the end of this annex.

Table 5.A1.4. **Public availability of budgetary information for individual public schools (ISCED 1-3)**

Country	Systematically published	Available upon request	At discretion of school or relevant authority	Not published
Austria				✓
Belgium (Fl.)				✓
Belgium (Fr.)				✓
Chile	✓			
Czech Republic		✓		
Denmark			✓	
Estonia		✓		
Iceland	✓			
Israel	✓		✓	
Kazakhstan			✓	
Lithuania		✓		
Portugal		✓		
Slovak Republic	✓			
Slovenia	✓			
Spain				✓
Sweden		✓		
Uruguay		✓		

Notes: Budgetary information may be systematically published by or be available upon request from the school, the relevant education authority, the central financial authority, etc.

The review team made every effort to ensure, in collaboration with countries, that the information collected through the qualitative survey on school funding is valid and reliable and reflects specific country contexts while being comparable across countries. However, given the qualitative nature of the survey, information should be interpreted with care.
For country-specific notes to this table, see the end of this annex.

Table notes

Table 5.A1.1. Monitoring and evaluating how different levels of the system use public financial resources (ISCED 1-3, public schools only)

Austria:

All levels of administration, the federal (Ministry of Education, Ministry of Finance), the state (governments of the provinces [*Länder*]), and the local (municipalities) levels are involved in the monitoring of resource use. The monitoring of resource use for infrastructure and other investments for state schools is the responsibility of the municipalities and the state governments (financial and education authorities). Monitoring systems also exist at the level of the provinces, but differ considerably. There are no uniform principles for controlling and budgeting in place across the provinces and municipalities. For federal schools, controlling for all expenditures (current and extraordinary investments) rests within the sphere of the state school boards. The Federal Ministry of Education monitors expenditures for infrastructure and teaching staff for federal schools based on information provided by the state school boards and by the schools themselves.

The State Courts of Audit can audit aspects of state school administration and also individual schools. The Federal Court of Audit publishes a number of reports on audits in the area of school administration every year which cover both the schools administered by federal authorities and those administered by the provinces. The Federal Court of Audit can also carry out audits on all aspects and levels of the school administration including schools administered by the provinces, but in general it does not audit individual schools.

At the local level, the states provide rules to the local authorities on their financial management. At the level of schools, there are no specific instruments in place for efficiency assessment as general compulsory schools generally have no (state schools) or rather little responsibility (federal schools) for budget and teaching resources. The Federal Ministry of Education monitors expenditures for infrastructure and teaching staff for federal schools based on information provided by the state school boards and by the schools themselves. Budget autonomy of federal schools is subject to supervision and audit by the state school boards, which check compliance with budget and procurement legislation as well as the general principles of economy, efficiency and expediency of public administration. A particular focus is on the coherence of investments with curricula and on their pedagogical necessity. Also the Federal Ministry of Education has the right to exercise control over individual schools in this context. Similar systems of controlling exist at state level for state schools.

Belgium (Fl. and Fr.):

Since there is no specific education budget at the central level, the Belgian Court of Audit does not perform audit tasks specifically on education.

In both the Flemish and the French Communities, the financial management, oversight and controlling of accounts of different school providers and schools differ depending on the educational network a school/school provider belongs to.

Belgium (Fl.):

The state education authority (Flemish Agency of Educational Services) is responsible for verifying whether the budget allocated to the school matches with the enrolments, student and school characteristics and other administrative data on the basis of which the operation grant and teaching and staff hours were calculated. The state education inspectorate (Flemish Education Inspectorate) is responsible for quality evaluations and for controlling the allocation of earmarked budgets for "equal educational opportunities" in secondary education.

Belgium (Fr.):

The state financial authorities (Inspection de Finances) issue a preliminary opinion on the expenses defined in the budget of the French Community of Belgium (state level) and presents an opinion on spending opportunities.

The state education authorities control the use of subventions and allocations in schools and are responsible for verifying the count of the number of students in a school.

Chile:

The central audit services (General Comptroller Office of the Republic, *Contraloría General de la República*) ensure that the acts of the central administration are legal. They can also implements financial audits of individual school providers and schools, but of public school providers and schools only.

The central financial inspectorate (*Superintendencia de Educación*) carries out financial audits of both public and publicly-subsidised private school providers and individual public and publicly-subsidised private schools. However, in practice, financial audits focus predominantly on the school provider. The inspectorate has the mission to ensure that schools and their communities follow the educational regulations; to inspect the legal use of resources by all publicly funded schools through an accountability system; for the use of resources to penalise schools failing to follow the educational laws; and to address complaints and information requirements from members of the schools communities and citizens in general regarding the violation of educational rights. The central education authority (*Ministerio de Educación*, MINEDUC) reviews the expenditure of some components of the per student funding voucher The Tax Administration Service is responsible for monitoring and collecting all internal taxes of Chile. It ensures that each taxpayer complies fully with its tax obligations, implementing and overseeing the internal taxes effectively and efficiently. It might carry out financial audits of school providers in case of inconsistencies in their tax declaration.

Czech Republic:

Local and regional authorities (in their role as school providers) inspect the economic management of the financial means of schools and school facilities. This mostly entails carrying out a general inspection of economic management – correctness, transparency, completeness and clarity of bookkeeping, observation of budget discipline, effective and economical use of the means provided, observation of generally binding legal regulations, etc.

Denmark:

At ISCED levels 1-2 (*Folkeskole*), the local administrations are responsible for monitoring and evaluating the use of public financial resources in schools. The finance committees of the municipalities are responsible for the accounting and the yearly account is approved by the municipal councils and sent to the auditor and the central financial authorities. Local Government Denmark (LGDK, KL), the association of Danish municipalities, provides advice to the municipalities on their budget implementation. At ISCED level 3, schools' accounting is audited by private auditors and approved by the school board. The central education authorities and central audit services monitor the use of resources.

Estonia:

Central financial authorities are responsible for monitoring and evaluating the use of resources from international funding at the central level.

Israel:

At the central level, an internal auditor within the Ministry of Education and the general accountant of the Ministry of Finance are in charge of financial control and payment depending on performance. The State Comptroller oversees and inspects the executive branch of the governing administration. It audits the economy, the property, the finances, the obligations and the administration of the central state and of government ministries. It inspects the legality, integrity, managerial norms, efficiency and economy of the audited bodies, as well as any other matter which it deems necessary.

At the local level, the Ministry of Finance and the Ministry of the Interior provide advice on budget implementation and approve the closing budget of municipalities. Municipalities report on the actual performance of activities and services on which they receive funding. The Ministry of Education transfers the funds according to these execution reports.

At the school level, there are computerised mechanisms for control and audit within the Ministry of Education and controls in schools. Recently, with the desire to increase the regulation that strengthens the policy of the ministry to expand the autonomy of schools, a special unit was created in order to enhance the control and audit processes. This unit inspects a sample of schools and the schools providers of these schools at all levels of education. Primary schools (ISCED 1) have a steering committee in which the school leader presents the school budget and work programme. The committee includes representatives of the inspection, local authorities, teachers and parents.

Kazakhstan:

At the central level, the highest authority for public financial control that implements external control of the republican (central) budget is the Account Committee. The main objective of the Account Committee is to assess and control the execution of the public and emergency governmental budget, strategic documents, the use of governmental loans, vouchers and actives and quasi-governmental sector. The Department for Combating Economic Crimes and Corruption and the General Prosecutor's Office implement inspections in the case of complaints or in the frames of the thematic planned control. Central education authorities control the execution of public transfers.

At the regional level, regional revision committees present the respective regional legislative authorities with an annual report on local budget execution, inspection of financial control, and inspection of the regional budget. Regional legislative authorities are legally free to make suggestions to include object for regional revision committees to control.

At the local level, regional revision committees implement external financial control over local budget execution and present the respective regional legislative authorities with an annual report on local budget execution. Local revision committees implement external financial control over local budget execution. Local legislative authorities are legally free to make suggestions to include object for revision committees to control.

At the school level, departments of the internal control of local and regional education authorities monitor and control schools that are under the respective jurisdiction of local and regional education authorities. Central, regional and local schools are subject to territorial financial inspections from the Ministry of Finance, the General Prosecutor's Office, the Account Committee, the Department for Combating Economic Crimes and Corruption, the Ministry of Finance's committees of financial control, and audit committees.

Portugal:

At the central level, there are also monitoring and evaluation processes for the investment of EU structural funds through the Human Capital Operational Programme (Programme opérationnel – Capital Humain, PO CH).

At the local level, information on the monitoring and evaluation of resource use by municipalities at ISCED level 1 refers to the first four years of education only.

Slovak Republic:

The Ministry of Education, the Ministry of Finance, the Supreme Audit Office and local (ISCED 1-2) and regional authorities (ISCED 3) carry out financial audits of individual schools. The school leadership also evaluates the school budget.

Spain:

The regional education authorities carry out financial audits of individual schools. The education inspectorate verifies schools' compliance with legality. The regional and local education authorities are responsible for supervision and budgetary control of schools.

Sweden:

At the local level, the National School Inspectorate monitors that local education authorities (municipalities) comply with education legislation and regulations.

At the school level, local education authorities (municipalities) are responsible for monitoring and quality control of their schools. Inspection, follow-up and evaluation are often based on administrative and economic reports and the factors examined are expansion, use and allocation of resources and quality. Central education authorities also fulfil functions related to monitoring and evaluation. The National School Inspectorate conducts regular supervision of all schools run by municipalities and can also initiate investigation of a specific school, or investigate complaints from students, parents or other persons. It also monitors that publicly-funded private schools comply with legislation and regulations and monitors the national supervision of upper secondary schools. The National Agency for Education monitors trends in academic results, equality, schools choice, etc.

Uruguay:

The Treasury Divisions of the Education Councils and the Sectorial Infrastructure Directorate of the Central Governing Council of the National Public Education Administration (CODICEN) carry out financial audits of individual school on items allocated directly to the individual school (related to buildings). The Sectorial Programming and Budget Directorate of the CODICEN carries out financial audits of individual schools on items allocated directly to the individual school through The Support Programme for Public Primary Education (Programa de Apoyo a la Escuela Pública Uruguaya, PAEPU) (ISCED 1 only) and the Support

Programme for Secondary Education and Training in Education (*Programa de Apoyo a la Educación Media y Formación en Educación*, PAEMFE) (ISCED 2-3) which are administered by ANEP and allocated largely for capital expenditure.

Table 5.A1.2. Responsibility for evaluating central education programmes/policies

Austria:

The Court of Audit evaluates policies and programmes from the perspective of effective use of public funds.

Belgium (Fl. and Fr.):

State education authorities also evaluate education policies and programmes at the state (Community) level. For example, in the Flemish Community, this includes research commissioned by the Flemish Minister of Education.

Chile:

The Ministry of Social Development evaluates the social impact of educational programmes, e.g. to ensure the proper targeting of financial resources.

Czech Republic:

The Ministry of Education, Youth and Sports monitors and evaluates the school registry.

Portugal:

There are also monitoring and evaluation processes for the investment of EU structural funds through the Human Capital Operational Programme (PO CH).

Slovenia:

The central education inspectorate evaluates education programmes, also for publicly-subsidised private schools.

Sweden:

The central government may at any time in the policy process commission the National Agency for Education or any other government agency to submit evidence in the policy process. The National Agency for Education is regularly asked to provide reports on the state of the education system. Furthermore, the Ministry of Education and Research has a Division for Analysis and International affairs that may evaluate policies and programmes. The Swedish Agency for Public Management (*Statskontoret*) provides the central government and ministries with studies in all areas with the aim of making the public sector more efficient.

Uruguay:

There is no tradition of programme and policy evaluation. The Division for Research, Evaluation and Statistics (*Departamento de Investigación y Estadística Educativa*) of the Central Governing Council of the National Public Education Administration (ANEP) carries out some programme evaluations, typically from a socio-educational perspective. The impact of the Ceibal Plan is also subject to ongoing monitoring and evaluation and the CODICEN has an internal department dedicated to these tasks.

Table 5.A1.3. Public availability of information on education budgets of sub-central authorities (ISCED 1-3)

Austria:

In line with their respective competences sub-central education authorities (states/municipalities) publish their budgets for education (staff, school infrastructure, etc.). Due to the fragmentation of competences there is, however, no comprehensive presentation of total education budgets per state/municipality. According to the Austrian stability pact, municipalities are obliged to publish their annual balance of accounts. The states (provinces) have put in place decrees which provide rules and standards for the financial management by the municipalities, including the closing of accounts. Municipalities have some discretion as to the level of detail the annual balance is published which includes also information on expenditure for schooling as a spending category, but not necessarily for individual schools.

Czech Republic:

General information is published by the concerned education authority (municipalities in the case of ISCED 1-2 and regions in the case of ISCED 3). Detailed information is available upon request from the central financial authorities (Ministry of Finance).

Denmark:

Information about local budgets is available on line through the statistical database of the central statistical office. Available information includes budgetary data on education.

Portugal:

Budgetary information for local education authorities is available upon request from central education authority.

Slovak Republic:

Local and regional authorities are not obliged to publish their budgets, but the general public is entitled to get information about budgets of sub-central authorities based on the right of free access to information. However, all regional and many local authorities do publish their budgets on their website. Also, local authorities report the amount spent on education to regional authorities which summarise the information for the central education authority (Ministry of Education).

Spain:

Information is also available before approval of the budget.

Table 5.A1.4. Public availability of information on budgets for individual schools (ISCED 1-3, public schools)

Belgium (Fl.):

Schools receive their own data and can compare these with other schools according to location and socio-economic profile in an anonymised way through a specific IT tool.

Belgium (Fr.):

Schools receive their own statistical data about students, personnel, outputs or repetition rates, but this does not include financial data.

Chile:

Schools present their annual budgets in terms of expenses to the central financial inspectorate (*Superintendencia de Educación*) which in turn makes them publicly available with some delay. The available information includes expenditure outputs (areas in which budget was actually spent). According to the education legislation, schools should also provide public accountability of resource use to their communities.

Czech Republic:

Information is available upon request from the school.

Denmark:

For the public *Folkeskole* (ISCED 1-2), it is at the discretion of the local authority and the school to make information available. In upper secondary education (ISCED 3), it is at the discretion of schools which function as self-governing institutions.

Estonia:

Information is available upon request from the relevant education authority. The information which is made available varies.

Iceland:

Information is published by the relevant education authority. In basic schools (ISCED 1-2), the type of information provided to the public is at the discretion of local authorities. At ISCED level 3, available information includes schools' own revenues according to source.

Israel:

Information is only available on the budget allocated by the central education authority (Ministry of Education) based on the overall average payments that can be attributed to individual schools. At the time of the data collection, it was at the discretion of local authorities to make information about their contributions to education and the budgets of the schools they administer publicly available. All local authorities, however, publish data for their own budget in practice.

Kazakhstan:

Information is also available on a special website (public procurement portal) which makes information about expenses, such as the cost of purchased food, with the exception of information about salaries, publicly available.

Lithuania:

Information is available upon request from schools. The central government authority approves what information should be publicly available. Information available includes external grants according to source, own revenues according to source, expenditure outputs (areas in which budget was actually spent), and staff salaries.

Portugal:

Information about individual school budgets is available upon request from schools and from the central financial inspectorate (*Instituto de Gestão Financeira da Educação*, IGEFE, IP).

Slovak Republic:

Schools publish an economic report which includes information about revenues by source and expenditures by category.

Slovenia:

Financial data of the closing budget must be reported to the central financial authority and is publicly available. All public entities must use a standard sheet on financial data.

Sweden:

Information is available upon request from the relevant education authority. Information typically includes external grants according to source, own revenues according to source and expenditure outputs (areas in which budget was actually spent).

Uruguay:

All information according to Law No. 18.381 on Access to Public Information is available upon request from the central education authorities.

ANNEX A

Country profiles

This annex presents the approaches of individual OECD review countries for funding early childhood and school education. Country profiles describe national frameworks for the distribution of funding for current and capital expenditure. They illustrate the financial flows across levels of administration and the allocation mechanisms used to determine and distribute funding to school providers and to individual schools. This does not include information on funding targeted at individual students. Country profiles present information for 2016 and draw primarily on the data countries provided for the review's qualitative survey of school funding frameworks as well as country background reports of participating countries and country review reports conducted by the School Resources Review. Annex B provides a glossary of terms and definitions which aid in interpreting the information in the country profiles. Annex C provides further explanations and notes on countries' approaches to funding of early childhood and school education.

The statistical data for Israel are supplied by and under the responsibility of the relevant Israeli authorities. The use of such data by the OECD is without prejudice to the status of the Golan Heights, East Jerusalem and Israeli settlements in the West Bank under the terms of international law.

Austria

Austria is a federal state based on the principle of local self-administration. It is divided into four administrative tiers: the federal (*Bund*), province (*Länder*), district (*Bezirke*) and municipal (*Gemeinden*) levels. For international comparability, the provinces are considered as the state level, the districts as the regional level, and the municipalities as the local level. The "provinces" are therefore referred to as "states" in the tables below. Early childhood education and care (ISCED 0) is the responsibility of the provinces (states). The distribution of governing and financing responsibilities for school education (ISCED 1-3) differs between so-called federal schools (*Bundesschulen*) and provincial schools (state schools, *Landesschulen*). Federal schools at ISCED levels 2-3 comprise academic secondary schools (*Allgemein bildende höhere Schule*, AHS) as well as upper secondary vocational schools and colleges (*Berufsbildende mittlere Schule*, BMS, and *Berufsbildende höhere Schule*, BHS). Provincial schools at ISCED levels 1-2 include primary schools (*Volksschule*, VS), New Secondary Schools (*Neue Mittelschule*, NMS), special needs schools (*Allgemeine Sonderschule*, ASO), and at ISCED level 3 the pre-vocational schools (*Polytechnische Schule*, PTS) and part-time upper secondary vocational schools (*Berufsschule*, BS).

Federal schools receive their funding directly from the federal government via its agencies, the nine provincial school boards (state school boards, *Landesschulräte*), while provincial schools are financed by the provinces and municipalities using funds which are, however, to a significant extent raised at the federal level and transferred to the provinces in accordance with the general Fiscal Adjustment Act (*Finanzausgleichsgesetz*) based on a negotiated distribution coefficient. The provincial school boards are responsible for administering federal schools. The school departments of the offices of the provincial governments (school departments of the offices of the state governments, *Schulabteilungen in den Ämtern der Landesregierung*) are responsible for the administration of provincial schools. Five out of nine provinces have, however, transferred some of their responsibilities for provincial schools to the provincial school board in their province.

For in-depth information on school funding in Austria, see the OECD country review report (*http://dx.doi.org/10.1787/9789264256729-en*) and the country background report (*www.oecd.org/education/schoolresourcesreview.htm*).

Current expenditure

Block grants from the state authorities to municipalities for current expenditure and dedicated grants from the state authorities for teacher salaries and from the municipalities for other current expenditure (early childhood education and care)

Education level	Allocation mechanism	Purpose of grant	Basis to determine the level of the grant
ISCED 0	**Block grant** from state authorities to local authorities	For current expenditure	At the **discretion** of state authorities
ISCED 0	**Earmarked grants** from central authority to state authorities	For federal policy priorities specifically agreed with states	**Negotiated process**
ISCED 0	**Dedicated grant** from state authorities to staff	Mainly for the allocation of teaching resources	At the **discretion** of state authorities
ISCED 0	**Dedicated grant** from local authorities	For current expenditure other than teachers' salaries, such as operating and maintenance costs, including salaries for administrative staff	At the **discretion** of local authorities

Earmarked grant from the central level to the state authorities to cover expenditure for salaries of teachers and dedicated grants from state authorities for teacher salaries and from municipalities for other current expenditure (state schools)

Education level	Allocation mechanism	Purpose of grant	Basis to determine the level of the grant
ISCED 1-3 (state schools)	**Earmarked grant** from central authority to state authorities	For teaching purposes, special needs education and learning support staff	**Funding formula** ● Basic contingent of teachers based on numbers of students and adjusted for type of school ● Profile of student population (students with special educational needs) ● Policy priorities
ISCED 1-3 (state schools)	**Earmarked grant** from central authority to state authorities	For federal policy priorities specifically agreed with states	**Negotiated process**
ISCED 1-3 (state schools)	**Dedicated grant** from state authorities to staff	Mainly for the allocation of teaching resources	**Varies. Basis is decided by state authorities.** Varying funding formulas are used.
ISCED 1-3 (state schools)	**Dedicated grant** from local authorities	For current expenditure other than teachers' salaries, such as operating and maintenance costs, including salaries for administrative staff	At the **discretion** of local authorities

Dedicated grant from central authorities for teacher salaries combined with earmarked grants for supporting special needs students and a restricted block grant from the central level to schools (federal schools)

Education level	Allocation mechanism	Purpose of grant	Basis to determine the level of the grant
ISCED 2-3 (federal schools)	**Dedicated grant** from central authority to staff	For the direct payment of teachers' salaries	**Funding formula** ● Number of students ● Class size ● Central policy priorities ● Administrative discretion
ISCED 2-3 (federal schools)	**Earmarked grant** from central authority to state school boards which determine distribution of teachers to schools	For support for students with SEN	**Funding formula** ● Number of students ● Type of school ● Students with SEN
ISCED 2-3 (federal schools)	**Restricted block grant** from central authority to schools	For some budget autonomy for schools	**Negotiated process**

Capital expenditure: Ad hoc grants and infrastructure investment programmes by individual states and municipalities for state schools and an infrastructure investment programme by central authorities for federal schools

Education level	Allocation mechanism	Purpose of funds	Basis to determine the level of the grant
ISCED 0, ISCED 1-3 (state schools)	**Ad hoc grants** and **Infrastructure investment programme**s from state authorities and local authorities	For the construction and maintenance of school infrastructure	**Administrative discretion**, generally based on an **assessment of needs**
ISCED 0, ISCED 1-3 (state schools)	**Earmarked grant** from central authority to state authorities	For the implementation of federal policy priorities specifically agreed with states	**Negotiated process**
ISCED 2-3 (federal schools	**Infrastructure investment programme** from central authority	For the construction and maintenance of school infrastructure	**Assessment of needs**

Belgium (Flemish and French Communities)

In Belgium, education policy is the responsibility of the three Communities (Flemish, French and German-speaking Communities). For international comparability, the Communities are considered as state authorities. The Flemish and the French Communities participated in the OECD review and information for both Communities is presented in this country profile. Each of the Communities has its own autonomous education system, even though aggregate funding in each of the Communities is partially dependent on a negotiated lump sum transfer from the federal level. Schools are governed by a legally recognised competent authority, typically referred to as school board or school governing body (school provider in the tables below). School providers are responsible for the organisation of the education in accordance with legislation and regulations. School boards can oversee one or several schools and typically administer all resources allocated to their school(s). In each of the two Communities, there are three educational "networks", which are not legal entities but rather classification principles of schools according to legal status: a Community education network; a grant-aided public education network; and a grant-aided private education network. For public schools, the school providers are typically the state educational authority (French Community) or an autonomous public body (Flemish Community Education, *Gemeenschapsonderwijs* GO!), besides – for the case of grant-aided public schools – regional (provincial) and local authorities (cities and municipalities). For government-dependent private-schools, the school providers are private entities such as religious communities or associations. However, the different legal status of schools – whether public or private, municipal or provincial – has no bearing on the funding entitlement for current expenditure and staff. Differences exist for the entitlement for funding for school buildings. Only Community education receives funding for 100% of capital costs, while grant-aided public education and private education can only apply for co-funding from the state authorities. In the country profile presented here, the central level refers to the federal state, the state level to the Community or region, the regional level to the provinces, and the local level to cities and municipalities.

For in-depth information on school funding in the Flemish Community of Belgium, see the OECD country review report (*http://dx.doi.org/10.1787/9789264247598-en*) and the country background report (*www.oecd.org/education/schoolresourcesreview.htm*).

For in-depth information on school funding in the French Community of Belgium, see the country background report (*www.oecd.org/education/schoolresourcesreview.htm*).

Current expenditure in the Flemish and the French Communities of Belgium: lump sum transfer from the central government to the Communities, block grants from the Communities to school providers for operational costs and direct payment of staff by the Communities

Education level	Allocation mechanism	Purpose of grant	Basis to determine the level of the grant
ISCED 0-3	**Lump sum** from central authority to the state authorities (Communities)	For all policy domains, including education	**Negotiated process, Funding formula** (based on demographic criteria): • Size of total population under the age of 18 • Population at the age of compulsory education
ISCED 0-3	**Block grant** from the state level to school providers	To cover operational costs (salaries of technical maintenance staff, instructional materials), work-based learning (as part of vocational programmes) and maintenance of infrastructure	**Funding formula** • Number of students • Student socio-economic characteristics • School size • School location • Level of education provided • Fields of study • General or vocational education • Grade levels offered • Students with special educational needs • Number of apprentices with work-based placements
ISCED 0-3	**Restricted block grant** from the state level to school providers	For extra support for specific student groups: disadvantaged groups, newly arrived immigrants and refugees, children on sick leave and students following specific religion or non-confessional ethics classes	**Funding formula** • Number of students • Number of newly arrived immigrants • Student socio-economic characteristics • School location • Level of education provided • Fields of study • Grade levels offered • Students with SEN
ISCED 0-3	**Dedicated grant** transferred directly from the state level to educational staff	Salaries for teachers, school management and administrative staff	**Funding formula** • Number of teachers • Teacher characteristics (career level, qualification, experience) • Number of students • Student socio-economic characteristics • School size • School location • Level of education provided • Fields of study • General or vocational education • Grade levels offered • Students with SEN • Number of apprentices with work-based placements

Capital expenditure in the Flemish Community of Belgium: ad hoc grants to school providers

Education level	Allocation mechanism	Purpose of funds	Basis to determine the level of the grant
ISCED 0-3	**Infrastructure investment programme** based on public/private partnerships	Infrastructure construction and renovation	**Administrative discretion** • Decision from the Flemish Agency for Educational Infrastructure after investment decision of private partners • Autonomous authority for Flemish Community Education Go! may also choose to transfer a public grant for their own schools
ISCED 0-3	**Ad hoc grant** from autonomous public authority for Flemish Community Education Go! to its own school providers	Infrastructure construction, renovation and maintenance	**Administrative discretion**
ISCED 0-3	**Ad hoc grant** from the Flemish Agency for Educational Infrastructure to school providers (provinces, municipalities, cities and private entities)	Infrastructure construction, renovation and maintenance	**Administrative discretion**: • Based on application dossier • High population density can be a criterion

Capital expenditure in the French Community of Belgium: ad hoc and annual grants to school providers

Education level	Allocation mechanism	Purpose of funds	Basis to determine the level of the grant
ISCED 0-3	**Ad hoc grant** from the state education authority to schools run by the French Community	Infrastructure construction, renovation and maintenance	**Administrative discretion** based on application dossier Criteria that might be considered include: ● Socio-economic characteristics of students ● School location (e.g. densely populated areas)
ISCED 0-3	**Annual grant** from the state level to school providers (provinces, municipalities, cities and private entities)	For instructional and non-instructional equipment bought with the grant for operational expenditures	Not specified

Chile

Schools operate in a fairly decentralised environment, but within a centrally regulated framework. The Ministry of Education (*Ministerio de Educación*, MINEDUC) is responsible for co-ordinating and regulating all aspects regarding education and oversees the implementation of education policy through its regional and local bodies (*Secretarías Regionales Ministeriales* [SEREMI], *Departamentos Provinciales* [DEPROV]). With the implementation of the 2009 General Education Law (*Ley General de Educación*), an Education Quality Assurance System (*Sistema Nacional de Aseguramiento de la Calidad de la Educación Escolar*) was introduced and three further central bodies were created: the National Education Council (*Consejo Nacional de Educación*, CNED), the Agency for Quality Education (*Agencia de Calidad de la Educación*, ACE) and the Education Superintendence (*Superintendencia de Educación*, SIE). Within this central framework, the operation of schools that receive public funding is the responsibility of public and private-subsidised school providers (*sostenedores*). In the public sector, schools are administered by local authorities (municipalities) and their municipal education administration departments (*Departamento Administración de Educación Municipal*, DAEM) or municipally controlled non-profit corporations with delegated authority. In the subsidised private sector, schools are managed individually or as a group of schools. In terms of administration and funding from the central government, public and publicly-subsidised private school providers are treated equivalently. There are also independent private providers that do not receive public funds. These are not considered in this country profile. At the time of the qualitative survey, Chile was planning a reform of its governance arrangements and the recentralisation of public schools through a national system of public education.

For early childhood education and care at ISCED levels 01-02 that is not provided in schools, Chile reported data for publicly-funded provision, specifically for early childhood education and care provided through the central authorities "JUNJI" and "Integra". JUNJI (*Junta Nacional de Jardines Infantiles*) is a specialised institution supervised by the Ministry of Education. It has two modalities to offer early childhood education and care, either by direct administration or through the transfer of funds to partner entities running early childhood education and care centres (known as *via transferencia de fondos*, VTF) based on specific agreements. Integra (*Fundación Nacional para el Desarrollo Integral del Menor*) is an institution which is part of the Networks of Foundations Socio-cultural Office of Presidency of the Republic. Integra has two modalities to offer early childhood education and care, either by direct administration or by "agreement" which consists of transfers of fund to associated entities. The budget for Integra comes from the Ministry of Education.

For in-depth information on school funding in Chile, see the OECD country review report (forthcoming) and the country background report (*www.oecd.org/education/schoolresourcesreview.htm*).

Current expenditure

Block grants from central authorities for early childhood education and care (ECEC)

Education level	Allocation mechanism	Purpose of grant	Basis to determine the level of the grant
ISCED 0	**Block grant** from central authorities to public ECEC centres directly administered by central authorities	For current expenditure	**Funding formula** ● Based on monthly value per child and attendance
ISCED 0	**Block grant** from central authorities to local authorities and publicly-funded private ECEC centres	For current expenditure in public and publicly-subsidised private ECEC centres	**Funding formula** ● Based on monthly value per child and attendance

A mix of block grants and earmarked funding from central authorities to school providers with school providers distributing funding between their individual schools

Education level	Allocation mechanism	Purpose of grant	Basis to determine the level of the grant
ISCED 02-3	**Block grant** from central authority to local authorities and publicly-funded private school providers	General school subsidy Pro-retention Educational Subsidy	**Funding formula** ● Average monthly attendance of children at school ● School student profile (child, youth, adult) ● Educational level provided ● Vocational education ● Special or adult education ● Full day educational provision ● Higher weighting for rural/highly isolated schools ● For pro-retention Educational Subsidy: ● Student from highly disadvantaged socio-economic background ● For schools with delegated administration: ● The main basis is student enrolment
ISCED 02-3	**Block grant** from central authority to local authorities	For the strengthening of public education	**Negotiated process** (the transfer is based on specific agreement with the local authority and depends on the characteristics of the local authority)
ISCED 02-3	**Earmarked grant** from central authority to local authorities and publicly-funded private school providers	Complement for teacher salaries	**Funding formula** ● Education professionals in schools classified as difficult due to geographic location, marginalisation, extreme poverty or other comparable characteristics ● Year of teaching service, teaching advance training, assessed teaching competence
ISCED 02-3	**Earmarked grant** from central authority to local authorities and publicly-funded private school providers	For students with special educational needs and disadvantaged students	**Funding formula** ● Household socio-economic characteristics ● Age/Education level the student attends ● Concentration of socially disadvantaged students in individual schools and historic school performance ● Number of teachers ● Labour market outcomes of graduates
ISCED 02-3	**Earmarked grant** from central authority to local authorities and publicly-funded private schools	Salary incentives for staff in best performing schools (National Performance Evaluation System of Subsidised Schools, SNED)	**Funding formula** ● Monthly value per child and attendance ● Comparison with schools within a comparable group of schools in each region, concentrating up to 35% of the enrolment
ISCED 02-3	**Dedicated grant** from local authorities and publicly-funded private school providers	For salaries and operational costs	**Administrative discretion** within a regulated framework

Capital expenditure: Allocation of funding through discretionary funding, infrastructure investment programmes and annual grants on a competitive basis

Education level	Allocation mechanism	Purpose of funds	Basis to determine the level of the grant
ISCED 0	**Discretionary funding** from central authorities to their regional administrative entities	Infrastructure repairs, construction and maintenance	**Competitive basis**
ISCED 02-3	**Infrastructure investment programme** from central authorities (School Infrastructure Department of the Ministry of Education and the National Fund for Regional Development) to pre-schools and schools	Infrastructure construction, renovation and maintenance; Instructional and non-instructional materials	**Competitive basis**
ISCED 3 (pre-vocational and vocational)	**Annual grant** from the central education authority to delegated administration schools	Construction, renovation and maintenance of school infrastructure	**Competitive basis**

Czech Republic

At the central level, the Ministry of Education, Youth and Sports (MŠMT) establishes the legal framework for the school system and sets parameters for the organisation of schooling. At the regional level, the 14 Czech self-governing regions are responsible for setting long-term development plans for their school systems. They are primarily responsible for organising upper secondary educational provision (ISCED 3) and they distribute the central funding for "teaching costs" to all schools in their region, including those run by local authorities (municipalities). Czech municipalities are the most common public school providers (founders) of basic education schools (ISCED 0 [98%], ISCED 1 [92%], ISCED 2 [80%]). However, less than half (2 560) of the municipalities operate more than one school. On the other hand, regions are the most common public school providers (founders) of ISCED 3 schools (94%). Although municipalities are primarily responsible for providing basic education, in 2013/14, 4.6% of students in the second stage of basic education (lower secondary education) were in schools run by the Czech regions, following either eight-year programmes (4.1%) or six-year programmes in a gymnasium, that is, an academic secondary school. In 1990, an amendment to the Education Act introduced the possibility to establish privately-managed schools. This includes "church schools" and "private schools".

For in-depth information on school funding in the Czech Republic, see the OECD country review report (*http://dx.doi.org/10.1787/9789264262379-en*) and the country background report (*www.oecd.org/education/schoolresourcesreview.htm*).

Current expenditure: Restricted block grants from the central level to regions and from regions to schools and additional discretionary funding at the sub-central levels

Education level	Allocation mechanism	Purpose of grant	Basis to determine the level of the grant
ISCED 0-3	**Restricted block grant** from the central level to regional authorities	For direct costs with school education	**Negotiated process, funding formula** ● Profile of student population ● Characteristics of school network
ISCED 0-3	**Restricted block grant** from regional authorities to schools	To cover direct costs (teacher salaries, learning support staff involved in instructional activities, textbooks and teaching aids, teacher further professional development, support for students with SEN and special needs schools)	**Varies. Negotiated process,** but each region decides the exact **funding formula.** Typically these include: ● Number of students ● School size ● School location ● Specific infrastructure ● Level of education provided ● Fields of education provided ● General or vocational education ● Grade level ● Students with SEN
ISCED 0-3	**Discretionary funding** from regional or local authorities (as school providers) to schools	Additional funds to cover operational costs (maintenance of schools, energy expenditures, communal services and small repairs)	At the **discretion of school providers** which may rely on **funding formulas** ● Based on an assessment of needs

Capital expenditure: infrastructure investment programme and ad hoc decisions at the discretion of the school provider

Education level	Allocation mechanism	Purpose of funds	Basis to determine the level of the grant
ISCED 0-3	**Infrastructure investment programme** at the responsibility of the central education authority and central authority (the Ministry of Regional Development for the investment of EU funds)	For infrastructure construction	**Assessment of needs**
ISCED 0-3	**Annual grants** and **ad hoc decisions**	For infrastructure construction, renovation and maintenance and the provision of instructional and non-instructional equipment	At the **discretion** of the regional and local authorities in their role as **school providers, Assessment of needs**

Denmark

The central government is responsible for the overall framework and objectives of day care, primary and lower secondary education, and upper secondary education. The Ministry for Children and Social Affairs is responsible for the overall national framework for day care. The Ministry of Education is responsible for setting the legal and financial governance framework for primary and lower secondary and upper secondary education. Within these general national frameworks and national legislation, the financial and organisational operation of day care (ISCED level 0) and public primary and lower secondary education, the *Folkeskole*, (ISCED levels 1-2) is the full responsibility of the local authorities (municipalities). Municipalities have full financial and organisational responsibility for the *Folkeskole*. Schools are responsible for providing education in line with the national aims for the *Folkeskole* and the requirements of their municipality, and for planning and organising their education programme. School leaders develop proposals for the activities in their school and for the budget within the financial framework laid down by the municipality. Upper secondary schools (ISCED 3) have the status of self-governing institutions with different histories and academic profiles. Schools finance the implementation of one or more of the upper secondary education programmes by means of grants from the Ministry of Education provided mainly on the basis of the number of students (taximeter system). The school leader answers to a board, the composition of which reflects the school's specific profile.

For in-depth information on school funding in Denmark, see the OECD country review report (*http://dx.doi.org/10.1787/9789264262430-en*) and the country background report (*www.oecd.org/education/schoolresourcesreview.htm*).

Current expenditure

Co-financing through local grants provided by the local authority and parental payments for early childhood education and care (ISCED 0)

Education level	Allocation mechanisms	Purpose of grant	Basis to determine the level of the grant
ISCED 0	**Lump sum** from the central authority to local authorities	For any type of expenditure, including sectors other than education	**Negotiated process, Funding formula** ● Demographic characteristics (municipality's population size, age composition) ● Economic characteristics (index of the socio-economic structure of the municipality)
ISCED 0	**Discretionary funding** from local authorities to public day care centres	For current expenditure	**Varies. Basis is decided by each municipality**

Lump sum from the central to local authorities and various mechanisms for transfers to public schools (ISCED 1-2)

Education level	Allocation mechanisms	Purpose of grant	Basis to determine the level of the grant
ISCED 1-2	**Lump sum** from the central authority to local authorities	For any type of expenditure, including sectors other than education	**Negotiated process, Funding formula** • Demographic characteristics (municipality's population size, age composition) • Economic characteristics (index of the socio-economic structure of the municipality)
ISCED 1-2	**Earmarked grants** from the central authority to local authorities	To promote policy priorities	**Differs across grants**
ISCED 1-2	**Discretionary funding** from local authorities to schools	For current expenditure	**Varies. Basis is decided by each municipality**
ISCED 1-2	**Block grant** from the central authority to private schools	For current expenditure in private schools	**Funding formula** • Demographic characteristics (number of students) • Characteristics of the school network (Education level offered, fields of education offered, type of programme offered, year levels offered)

Funding by a block grant based mostly on an activity-based taximeter system for upper secondary education (ISCED 3)

Education level	Allocation mechanisms	Purpose of grant	Basis to determine the level of the grant
ISCED 3	**Block grant** from the central authority to schools as self-governing institutions	For current expenditure	**Funding formula** • Demographic characteristics (number of students) • Characteristics of the school network (Education level offered, fields of education offered, type of programme offered, year levels offered)
ISCED 3	**Earmarked grants** from the central authority to schools as self-governing schools	To promote policy priorities	**Differs across grants**
ISCED 3	**Block grant** from the central authority to private schools	For current expenditure in private schools	**Funding formula** • Demographic characteristics (number of students) • Characteristics of the school network (Education level offered, fields of education offered, type of programme offered, year levels offered)

Capital expenditure: Discretionary funding from local authorities for public schools (ISCED 0-2) and annual grants from the central authority for self-governing institutions (ISCED 3)

Education level	Allocation mechanisms	Purpose of funds	Basis to determine the level of the grant
ISCED 0-2	**Discretionary funding** from municipalities to schools	For infrastructure construction, renovation and maintenance	**Administrative discretion**
ISCED 3	**Annual grant and Negotiated process** from central authority to self-governing institutions	For capital costs	Not specified

Estonia

The central government and the Ministry of Education and Research are responsible for the national education policy and the overall strategy for the education system. There are three types of school providers: the central state, the local authorities (municipalities) and private providers. Pre-primary education (ISCED 0) is guaranteed by private providers and municipalities. In ISCED 1-3, for general and vocational education, the three types of providers offer competing education services. While municipal provision is dominant in general education, central provision is dominant in vocational education. The central government provides an earmarked grant for general education with the purpose to support the funding of study materials (i.e. textbooks), school lunches, professional development of teachers and school leaders, and salaries of teachers and school leaders. The distribution of funding for current expenditure from the central government to municipalities (in their role of school provider) is further complemented by a set of other earmarked grants for commissioned study places and study allowances in VET schools and different programmes in general education.

For in-depth information on school funding in Estonia, see the OECD country review report (*http://dx.doi.org/10.1787/9789264251731-en*) and the country background report (*www.oecd.org/education/schoolresourcesreview.htm*).

Current expenditure

Earmarked funds from the central level to local authorities (in their role as school providers)

Education level	Recipient	Purpose of funds	Basis to determine the level of the grant
ISCED 0	All local authorities (which are school providers)	For teaching Estonian to pre-school children whose study group's language is not Estonian	**Funding formula** • Number of study groups
ISCED 0	Four largest towns and regional/municipal unions (who allocate the grant to local authorities or organise training directly)	For pre-school teachers' professional training	**Funding formula** • Number of students
ISCED 1-3 (general education)	All local authorities (which are school providers)	For covering teachers and school leaders salaries, teachers and school leaders professional training, students' school lunches and study materials	**Funding formula** • Number of students in municipal schools and regional coefficients • Student's profile (including distinction between stationary [full-time] and non-stationary [part-time] students, and students studying at home) • School size • School location • Type of education offered: mainstream or special education • Students with SEN
ISCED 1-3 (general education)	All local authorities (which are school providers and as appropriate)	For different policy priorities and programmes	**Funding formula** As appropriate: • Mother tongue of student or family migrant background • Type of studies • Family socio-economic background
ISCED 2-3 (pre-vocational and vocational)	Three local authorities that own three VET schools	For state commissioned study places in VET	**Funding formula** • Number of state commissioned places ordered from schools in different study fields • Students with special educational needs
ISCED 2-3 (vocational)	Three local authorities that own three VET schools	For study allowances, including compensating student accommodation and travel costs; school meals	**Funding formula** • Students' place of residence (concerning accommodation and travel costs) • Students' age (concerning school meals)

Restricted block grant from the central authority to schools owned by the central authority

Education level	Allocation mechanism	Purpose of funds	Basis to determine the level of the grant
ISCED 1-3	**Restricted block grant** from the central authority to schools (owned by the central authority)	For general and vocational education	**Funding formula**, using similar principles as for the funding of schools owned by local authorities (both for general education and VET schools)

Discretionary funding and restricted block grants from the local level to schools

Education level	Allocation mechanism	Purpose of funds	Basis to determine the level of the grant
ISCED 0	**Restricted block grant** from local authorities to private pre-schools and/or other local authorities (which are pre-school providers)	For operating costs of private pre-schools, or other local authorities as pre-school providers	**Funding formula** • Number of students in municipalities pre-school whose place of residence is in other municipality • Number of students in private pre-schools
ISCED 0-3	**Discretionary funding** from local authorities to their own schools	Additional funding from municipalities to their schools for covering any type of expenditures	**Administrative discretion**
ISCED 1-3	**Restricted block grant** from local authorities to private schools and/or other local authorities	For operating costs of private general education schools, or other local authorities as school providers	**Negotiated process, Funding formula** • Number of students in private schools or in other municipality schools whose place of residence is the municipality • Type of education offered

Capital expenditure: ad hoc decisions and infrastructure investment programmes

Education level	Allocation mechanism	Purpose of funds	Basis to determine the level of the grant
ISCED 0	**Infrastructure investment programme** from central-level dedicated agencies (EAS, Innove) to local authorities (as pre-school providers)	For the creation of new pre-school places	**Assessment of needs** • Local authorities that require more pre-school places
ISCED 0-3	**Ad hoc decisions** by local authorities (as school providers)	Infrastructure construction, maintenance and renovation	**Assessment of needs**
ISCED 0-3	**Infrastructure investment programme** from central authority to school providers	Infrastructure construction, maintenance and renovation and instructional material	**Competition for funds** • School and pre-school providers compete for funds

Iceland

The 74 local authorities (municipalities) are responsible for setting and governing pre-primary (ISCED 0) and compulsory schools (ISCED 1-2), including the provision of special education. Municipalities allocate funds to schools (ISCED 1-2). Funds are raised through public taxation at the central level and transferred directly to the municipalities. Private schools are funded by the municipalities according to a funding formula defined in the Compulsory School Act. The central authority is responsible for the operation and funding of upper secondary schools (ISCED 3) and textbooks. Publicly accredited private schools at upper secondary level (ISCED 3) receive funds from the central government comparable to public schools. Private schools can also charge school fees to a limited extent at all levels of schooling.

For in-depth information on school funding in Iceland, see the country background report (*www.oecd.org/education/schoolresourcesreview.htm*).

Current expenditure

Block grants combined with earmarked grants from the central level to local authorities which distribute block grants and earmarked grants to pre-primary and compulsory schools (ISCED 0-2)

Education level	Allocation mechanism	Purpose of grant	Basis to determine the level of the grant
ISCED 0	**Block grant** from local authorities to schools	For any type of expenditure	**Administrative discretion**, but based on criteria such as: ● Number of students ● School size ● School location ● Students with special educational needs
ISCED 1-2	**Block grant** from central authorities to local authorities	For any type of expenditure in compulsory education	**Administrative discretion**
ISCED 1-2	**Block grant/Earmarked grant** from central authorities to local authorities	To even out the differences in expenditure and income of local governments with greater needs	**Funding formula** ● Students with special educational needs ● Educational support to new arrivals in the country ● Student transportation costs
ISCED 1-2	**Block grant/Earmarked grant** from local authorities to schools	For salaries and operational costs, extra support for specific student groups. Some local authorities allocate a block grant; others earmark part of the funding for specific purposes	**Varies. The basis is decided by local authorities.** Either a specific **funding formula** developed by the local authority or at the local authority's **discretion**, according to its general budget framework. Criteria primarily include: ● Number of students ● School size ● School location ● Fields of education offered ● Proportion of low achievers

School-specific block grant from central authority to upper secondary schools (ISCED 3)

Education level	Allocation mechanism	Purpose of grant	Basis to determine the level of the grant
ISCED 3	**Block grant** (specific to each school) from the central level to schools	For any type of expenditures	**Funding formula**, including the following criteria: ● Number of students ● School size ● School location ● Fields of education offered ● Type of education offered ● Characteristics of teachers ● Students with special educational needs

Capital expenditure: discretionary funding and negotiated process between central, local authorities and schools

Education level	Allocation mechanism	Purpose of funds	Basis to determine the level of the funds
ISCED 0	**Discretionary funding** from local authorities to pre-schools	Infrastructure construction, maintenance and renovation	**Assessment of needs**
ISCED 1-2	**Negotiated process** between local authorities and schools	Infrastructure construction, maintenance and renovation	**Assessment of needs**
ISCED 3	**Discretionary funding** from central and local authorities to schools	Infrastructure construction, maintenance and renovation	**Administrative discretion**

Israel

The education system is administered by the Ministry of Education and local authorities (municipalities). The Ministry of Economy and Industry is in charge of part of kindergarten for children age 0-2 and a small percentage of vocational education and training in the upper secondary education. Funding for schools is mostly provided by the central and local authorities. The Ministry of Education provides schools with grants for teaching services, either directly or through municipalities, and funds infrastructure investments for all schools. It also provides financial support for transport services for school children. Municipalities are responsible for the direct maintenance of schools at all levels of the education system. They often provide additional funding for the recruitment of supplementary teachers and education and welfare services not covered by the central government. Some reforms have given schools greater autonomy, also for the management of their resources, and increased teachers' salaries and working time. Schools also receive some funding from municipalities and the Ministry of Education to use at their discretion, with a possibility to create new programmes and activities.

Primary to upper secondary education is provided in four main educational streams: two state secular streams (one Hebrew-speaking and one Arabic-speaking), one state religious stream (Hebrew-speaking) and one independent stream (ultra-orthodox Hebrew-speaking). All streams have separate schools, common core subjects and a partially separate curriculum (mainly at upper secondary) and separate management. The ultra-orthodox independent stream, while partially funded by the central state, is less supervised by government policies (but under inspection of the Ministry of Education) and has a partially independent management and curriculum. Funding varies between schools according to the school stream and the local government. This country profile describes the funding framework for the three state streams. The description of publicly-funded private schools mainly refers to schools in the ultra-orthodox independent stream.

Current expenditure

Earmarked grants from the central level to local authorities for non-teachers' salaries and other operational costs at all levels and for teachers' salaries at ISCED 3

Education level	Allocation mechanisms	Purpose of grant	Basis to determine the level of the grant
ISCED 0-3	**Earmarked grant** from central authority to local authorities	For non-teachers' salaries and other operational costs	**Funding formula** ● Number of students ● School size ● Education level offered ● Transportation for students with special educational needs
ISCED 3	**Earmarked grant** from central authority to local authorities	For teachers' salaries	**Funding formula** ● Demographic characteristics ● Profile of student population (students with special educational needs) ● Characteristics of school network ● Economic characteristics

Direct funding of staff salaries through dedicated grants from central and local authorities, and earmarked grants for other operational costs from local authorities to schools

Education level	Allocation mechanisms	Purpose of grant	Basis to determine the level of the grant
ISCED 0-2	**Dedicated grant** from central authority to staff	For staff salaries (teaching staff, principal and deputies)	**Funding formula** ● Number of students ● Socio-economic characteristics ● School location ● Education level offered ● Characteristics of teachers ● Students with SEN **Administrative discretion**
ISCED 3	**Dedicated grant** from local authorities to staff	For staff salaries (teaching staff, principal and deputies)	**Administrative discretion**
ISCED 0-3	**Earmarked grants** from local authorities to schools	For non-teachers' salaries and other operational expenditures	**Administrative discretion**
ISCED 0-1, ISCED 3	**Block grants** from central authority to publicly-funded private schools (principally in the ultra-orthodox stream)	For any type of current expenditure	**Funding formula** ● Number of students ● Teacher characteristics

Capital expenditure: Ad hoc decisions by local and central authorities

Education level	Allocation mechanisms	Purpose of funds	Basis to determine the level of the grant
ISCED 0-3	**Ad hoc decisions** by local and central authorities	Infrastructure construction, renovation and maintenance	**Assessment of needs**

Kazakhstan

The central government and the central education authority (Ministry of Education and Science) are responsible for national education policy and the development of rules and methodologies of education system funding. School resources are distributed by the administration level (authority) that has the jurisdiction over the school/educational organisation. Therefore, funding from the local authority is distributed to ISCED 0-3 educational organisations that are under the local authority jurisdiction. Similarly, funding from the regional authority is distributed to ISCED 0-3 educational organisations that are under their jurisdiction, as well as to ISCED 3 pre-vocational and vocational and educational organisations that meet the needs of students with special educational needs. The major share of financial resources for educational organisations/schools comes from the local and regional budgets (over 70% of all spending on education) due to the fact that most of public schools are under the jurisdiction of local and regional authorities. Finally, funding from the central (republican) authority is distributed to ISCED 0-3 educational organisations that are under central jurisdiction. In terms of transfers across administration levels, general transfers can be transferred from the higher level budgets to the lower level budgets for equalising differences (subventions) in local revenues (per capita) and ensuring that all administration levels have enough resources, whereas targeted transfers are used for the implementation of specific reforms or initiatives, indicated in government programmes.

A proposed reform to school funding, specifically the introduction of a per student funding formula, was postponed and currently the approbation takes place in 73 schools (Years 1-11). The State Programme of Education and Science Development in the Republic of Kazakhstan for 2016-19 states that per student funding formula is to be implemented in 2019. The proposed reform would include a school-specific transfer for current expenditures from the central administrative level to each school via the respective regional and local authority.

For in-depth information on school funding in Kazakhstan, see the OECD country review report (*http://dx.doi.org/10.1787/9789264245891-en*) and the country background report (*www.oecd.org/education/schoolresourcesreview.htm*).

Current expenditure: Earmarked grants and discretionary funding from the central to the regional level, and the regional to the local level, and annual grants and earmarked grants from authorities at each administration level to their own schools

From central to regional authorities

Education level	Allocation mechanism	Purpose of grant	Basis to determine the level of the grant
ISCED 0-3	**Earmarked grant** from central to regional authorities	For equalising differences in regional revenues and implementing specific government programmes and initiatives	**Administrative discretion**, **Negotiated process**, Based on **historical expenditures** and according to differences in regional revenues
ISCED 0-3	**Discretionary funding** from central to regional authorities	For financing school construction and operational costs of specific schools not covered by regional budget	**Administrative discretion**, **Negotiated process**, Based on **historical expenditures**

From regional to local authorities

Education level	Allocation mechanism	Purpose of grant	Basis to determine the level of the grant
ISCED 0-3	**Earmarked grant** from regional to local authorities	For equalising differences in local revenues and implementing specific government programmes and initiatives	**Administrative discretion, Negotiated process,** Based on **historical expenditures** and according to differences in local revenues
ISCED 0-3	**Discretionary funding** from regional to local authorities	For financing school construction and operational costs of specific schools not covered by local budget	**Administrative discretion, Negotiated process,** Based on **historical expenditures**

From authorities at each administration level to their own schools

Education level	Allocation mechanism	Purpose of grant	Basis to determine the level of the grant
ISCED 0-3	**Annual grant** from either central, regional or local authorities (as school providers) to schools (schools receive funding from the administrative level directly responsible for their operation)	For any type of current expenditure	**Administrative discretion** and **negotiations.** In accordance with the schools' annual budget calls, the administrative levels' annual financial plan and based on historical expenditures
ISCED 0-3	**Earmarked grant** from central or regional authorities to regional or local administrations (as school providers) and schools	For equalising differences in regional/local revenues and implementing specific government programmes and initiatives	**Administrative discretion, Negotiated process,** Based on **historical expenditures**

Capital expenditure: discretion from each administrative level based on an assessment of needs

Education level	Allocation mechanism	Purpose of grant	Basis to determine the level of the grant
ISCED 0-3	**Earmarked grant** from the central budget and National Fund (2015-17)	Infrastructure construction, maintenance and renovation Instructional material	**Administrative discretion** based on the **assessment of needs**
ISCED 0-3	**Ad hoc decisions, negotiations and discretionary funding** from either the central, regional or local authority	Infrastructure construction, maintenance and renovation	**Administrative discretion** based on the **assessment of needs**

Lithuania

The school system is divided into three main governance levels: the central level (Ministry of Education and Science), the local level (municipalities) and the school level (at which decisions regarding budget management are usually taken by the school council). The central government is the main source of school resources, although local authorities have a fundamental role by providing additional funding. The central formula-funding scheme, also called "student basket scheme", covers teaching costs, the salaries of school management, administration and professional support staff, as well as textbooks, some school materials and teacher in-service training. The major determinant of funding is the number of students in the school. The grant is calculated as a fixed per-student amount (referred to as the "student basket") multiplied by the number of equivalent students. The grant is made available by the central to local governments, not directly to schools. Municipalities fund salaries of maintenance staff, communal and communication expenses, student transportation and expenditures with materials and repair works, besides having a restricted degree of discretion to reallocate a proportion of the central grant among schools. Municipalities also supplement capital expenditures normally guaranteed by central government and EU structural funds, and manage the student basket share over which authority is granted.

For in-depth information on school funding in Lithuania, see the OECD country review report (*http://dx.doi.org/10.1787/9789264252547-en*) and the country background report (*www.oecd.org/education/schoolresourcesreview.htm*).

Current expenditure: Earmarked grant from the central level to local authorities and discretionary funding from local authorities to schools and pre-schools

Education level	Allocation mechanism	Purpose of grant	Basis to determine the level of the grant
ISCED 0-3	**Earmarked grant** from central authorities to local authorities which have a **restricted degree of discretion** to reallocate a proportion of the grant	Student basket scheme for covering teaching and operational costs	**Funding formula** ● Number of students ● Student characteristics (distinctive minority, migrant status) ● School size ● School location ● Level of education offered ● Fields of study offered ● General or vocational education ● Students with SEN ● Average teacher's salary
ISCED 0	**Discretionary funding** from local authorities to pre-schools	For covering a part of teachers' salaries	**Administrative discretion**
ISCED 0-3	**Discretionary funding** from local authorities to pre-schools and schools	For covering other operational expenditures (salaries of maintenance staff, communal and communication expenses, student transportation and expenditures with materials and repair works)	**Varies. Basis is decided by each local authority**

Capital expenditure: Infrastructure investment programme for school construction and ad hoc decisions and discretionary funding for maintenance and renovation

Education level	Allocation mechanism	Purpose of grant	Basis to determine the level of the grant
ISCED 0-3	**Infrastructure investment programme** from the central level to local authorities	For infrastructure construction	Not specified
ISCED 0-3	**Ad hoc decisions** taken by local authorities	For infrastructure maintenance and renovation	**Assessment of needs**
ISCED 0-3	**Discretionary funding** from local authorities to schools	For maintenance of infrastructure	**Administrative discretion**

Portugal

The central government is the main source of funding for education and the Ministry of Education is responsible for the education budget at all levels of the education system. Portugal has, however, been gradually increasing decision making at sub-central levels while trying to improve the efficiency of public services. Since 2008, local authorities (municipalities) have been given more responsibilities, mostly from pre-primary to lower secondary education. As part of the decentralised approach, local authorities can finance costs for managing educational facilities, transport and extracurricular activities. Furthermore, a pilot project involving some schools has been put in place to provide full municipal autonomy in the distribution of funding for capital and current expenditures – excluding teacher's salaries – to those schools. Portugal has also re-organised its public school network starting in 2005 around school clusters (school providers, in the tables below), aggregating schools from one or more education levels under the same leadership and administration, according to location criteria. School cluster leadership is guaranteed by decision boards composed of representatives – mainly teachers – of the different clustered schools. In terms of funding, schools offering basic education (*Ensino básico* – corresponding to the first four years of ISCED 1) do not have any management responsibilities nor their own budgets. The administrative, budgetary and pedagogical management of these schools is the responsibility of the school cluster the school belongs to. The Ministry of Education directly transfers funds to the school clusters to pay teachers' salaries and non-teaching staff. In some cases, the payment of non-teaching staff salaries is guaranteed through funds transferred from municipalities (raised by the local or central level), namely for pre-schools and schools offering the first four years of ISCED 1. The Ministry of Finance can also transfer funds for capital expenditure, transport and school meals indirectly through municipalities.

Current expenditure: Block grants from the central level to local authorities, and funding from the central and local level to school providers

Education level	Allocation mechanism	Purpose of grant	Basis to determine the level of the grant
ISCED 0-1 (first 4 years), ISCED 2	**Block grant** (municipal social fund) from the central authority to local authorities	For operating costs, extracurricular activities and subsidised meals, excluding teachers' salaries	**Funding formula, Administrative discretion** (based on spending justification by the local authority)
ISCED 0-3	**Block grant** (execution contracts) from the central level to local authorities	For operating and capital costs, excluding teachers' salaries	**Administrative discretion, Negotiated process**
ISCED 0-3	**Earmarked grant** from the central authority to school providers and schools	For covering teachers' salaries	**Administrative discretion** based on **historical trends**
ISCED 2-3	**Restricted block grant** from the central authority to school providers and schools	For covering operating costs	**Administrative discretion** based on **historical trends**
ISCED 3	**Earmarked grant** from the central authority to school providers and schools	For non-teaching staff salaries	**Administrative discretion** based on **historical trends**
ISCED 0-3	**Discretionary funding** from local authorities to school providers and schools	For additional support to any type of current expenditure, except teachers' salaries	**Administrative discretion** based on **historical trends**
ISCED 0-2	**Dedicated grant** from local authorities to non-teaching staff	For covering the salaries of non-teaching staff	**Administrative discretion** based on **historical trends**

Capital expenditure: Ad hoc decisions at the central level and an infrastructure investment programme for upper secondary schools

Education level	Allocation mechanism	Purpose of grant	Basis to determine the level of the grant
ISCED 0-1 (first 4 years)	**Infrastructure investment programme** from local authorities to school providers and schools	For infrastructure construction, maintenance and renovation, provision of non-instructional and instructional equipment	**Assessment of needs**
ISCED 1-2	**Ad hoc decisions** at the central level	For infrastructure construction	**Assessment of needs**
ISCED 1-3	**Ad hoc decisions** at the central level	For infrastructure maintenance and renovation, provision of non-instructional and instructional equipment	**Assessment of needs**
ISCED 3	**Infrastructure investment programme** co-ordinated by a dedicated agency (*Parque Escolar*)	For infrastructure construction	**Assessment of needs**
ISCED 3	**Ad hoc decisions** from a dedicated agency (*Parque Escolar*)	For infrastructure maintenance and renovation, provision of non-instructional and instructional equipment	**Assessment of needs**

Slovak Republic

The Slovak Republic is composed of 8 regional authorities (self-governing regions) and 2 890 local authorities (municipalities). Municipalities are the school providers (founders) of public pre-primary, primary and lower secondary educational institutions (ISCED 0-2). The regional level authorities are the school providers (founders) of public schools providing upper secondary education (ISCED 3). There are also private school providers at all education levels and there are regional state authorities (deconcentrated state administration) as school providers of special schools. The source of funding for primary and secondary school education and its distribution to individual schools is centralised. School providers act as intermediaries and have some scope for reallocation of centrally calculated resources among individual schools. At the school level, there is a considerable degree of financial autonomy. Private school providers receive public funding like public school providers.

For in-depth information on school funding in the Slovak Republic, see the OECD country review report (*http://dx.doi.org/10.1787/9789264247567-en*) and the country background report (*www.oecd.org/education/schoolresourcesreview.htm*).

Current expenditure: block grant from central authorities to school providers for each school, but school providers have some discretion to reallocate a specified proportion

Education level	Allocation mechanisms	Purpose of grant	Basis to determine the level of the grant
ISCED 1-3	**Block grant (school-specific)** from central authority to local authorities (ISCED 1-2), to regional authorities (ISCED 3), and to publicly-funded private school providers	For salaries	**Funding formula** ● Number of students ● Teacher qualification level ● Personal intensity (national average student teacher ratio and other coefficients) special schools ● SEN students integrated in mainstream education ● Language of instruction For ISCED 1-2: ● If Year 0 is offered ● School size ● Sports programmes For ISCED 3: ● Bilingual programmes ● Sports programmes ● Priority VET programmes (with insufficient graduates compared to labour market needs) ● Apprentices in work-based placements
ISCED 1-3	**Block grant (school-specific)** from central authority to local authorities (ISCED 1-2), to regional authorities (ISCED 3), and to publicly-funded private school providers	For operational costs	**Funding formula** ● Number of students ● Students with special educational needs integrated in mainstream education ● Heating intensity requirement (8 different temperature zones) ● Operational intensity requirement other than heating (6 different categories) ● Further education for teachers ● Intensity of educational process (based on personal intensity) ● Language of instruction For ISCED 1-2: ● School size For ISCED 3: ● General or vocational education ● Sports programmes ● Priority VET programmes (with insufficient graduates compared to identified labour market needs) ● Bilingual programmes

Education level	Allocation mechanisms	Purpose of grant	Basis to determine the level of the grant
ISCED 1-3	**Earmarked grant (school-specific)** from central authority to local authorities (ISCED 1-2), regional authorities (ISCED 3) and publicly-funded private school providers	Support to students with special educational needs	**Administrative discretion/at request by the school provider,** typically includes number of students with special educational needs, type of special educational needs and historical trends
ISCED 1-2	**Earmarked grant** from central authority to local authorities	For socially disadvantaged student groups	**Funding formula** • Number of students with poor socio-economic background
ISCED 1-3	**Earmarked grant (school-specific)** from central authority to local authorities (ISCED 1-2), regional authorities (ISCED 3) and publicly-funded private school providers	For student competitions or participation in international projects	**Funding formula** • Number of students placed in the first three positions in the competition, number of international projects the school participates in
ISCED 1-3	**Earmarked grant (school-specific)** from central authority to local authorities (ISCED 1-2), regional authorities (ISCED 3) and publicly-funded private school providers	For development projects in educational areas defined by the central education authorities	**Administrative discretion**
ISCED 1-3	**Earmarked grant (school-specific)** from central authority to local authorities (ISCED 1-2), regional authorities (ISCED 3) and church school providers	For maintenance	**Administrative discretion**, including an **assessment of needs**
ISCED 1-3	**Block grant** from central authority to local authorities (ISCED 1-2), regional authorities (ISCED 3) and private school providers	Top up funding when school-specific grant does not cover staff and operational costs	**Administrative discretion** (based on request and justification)

Capital expenditure

Education level	Allocation mechanisms	Purpose of funds	Basis to determine the level of the grant
ISCED 02-3	**Infrastructure investment programme** from central authority to local authorities (ISCED 02-2) and regional authorities (ISCED 3)	Infrastructure construction	**Administrative discretion**, based on **assessment of needs** and other published criteria
ISCED 1-3	**Earmarked grant** from central authority to local authorities (ISCED 1-2), regional authorities (ISCED 3)	For maintenance and renovation	**Administrative discretion**, based on **assessment of needs**
ISCED 1-3	**Discretionary funding** from local authorities (ISCED 1-2) and regional authorities (ISCED 3) to school providers	Infrastructure construction, maintenance and renovation	**Administrative discretion**

Slovenia

Governance of the education system is mainly shared between the central government and schools. The Ministry of Education, Science and Sport is responsible for drafting, evaluating and implementing regulations and outlining national programmes in education. Pre-school education (ISCED 0) is provided by public and private kindergartens for students aged one to six – the starting age of compulsory basic education. Public kindergartens are founded by local authorities (municipalities). Primary and lower secondary education (ISCED 1-2) is organised in a single-structure nine-year basic school attended by students aged 6 to 15 years. Public basic schools (ISCED 1-2) are established by municipalities, while the system of upper secondary education (ISCED 3) is governed by central education authorities. The central level is the predominant funder in the areas of basic school (ISCED 1-2 [82%]) and upper secondary education (ISCED 3 [99%]), while the municipalities mainly finance pre-school education (ISCED 0 [92%]). For basic and upper secondary schools (ISCED 1-3), the local level can give additional funds for higher standards of education and other additional services.

For in-depth information on school funding in Slovenia, see the country background report (*www.oecd.org/education/schoolresourcesreview.htm*).

Current expenditure

A lump sum from the central to the local level for use at the discretion of local authorities not specifically for education

Education level	Allocation mechanism	Purpose of grant	Basis to determine the level of the grant
ISCED 0-3	**Lump sum** from the central authority to local authorities	Funds not specifically targeted at education	Not specified

A set of earmarked grants to public pre-schools and basic schools

Education level	Allocation mechanism	Purpose of grant	Basis to determine the level of the grant
ISCED 0	**Earmarked grant** from the central authority to pre-schools	For students with special educational needs in kindergartens founded by the central level; extra costs with bilingual classes for Italian and Hungarian national communities and Romani children; 50% of salaries for kindergarten teachers who work in hospital kindergartens	**Administrative discretion**
ISCED 0	**Earmarked grant** from local authorities to pre-schools	For any type of expenditure	**Administrative discretion**
ISCED 1-2	**Restricted block grant** from the central authority to schools	For operating costs directly related with the educational programme	**Funding formula** ● Number of students ● School location (in the case of funds for professional development of teachers) ● Number of teachers ● Characteristics of teachers (e.g. qualification) ● Students with special educational needs ● Students' linguistic background
ISCED 1-2	**Restricted block grant** from local authorities to schools	For operating costs not directly related with the educational programme, and additional funds	**Administrative discretion**
ISCED 1-2	**Earmarked grant** from the central authority to local authorities	For transport of students to schools in areas with brown bears	**Administrative discretion, Historical basis**

A block grant combined with earmarked grants to upper secondary schools

Education level	Allocation mechanism	Purpose of grant	Basis to determine the level of the grant
ISCED 3	**Block grant** from the central authority to schools	For any type of expenditure, except for students with SEN and organisation of the school meals	**Funding formula** • Number of students • Type of education offered
ISCED 3	**Earmarked grant** from the central authority to schools	For funding additional costs with students with SEN and organisation of school meals	**Funding formula** • Number of students with special educational needs • Number of students with supported school meal
ISCED 3	**Earmarked grant** from local authorities to schools	Additional funds for higher standard of education and other additional services	**Administrative discretion**

Capital expenditure

Education level	Allocation mechanism	Purpose of grant	Basis to determine the level of the grant
ISCED 0-3	**Discretionary funding** by local authorities	For infrastructure construction, renovation and maintenance, non-instructional and instructional material	**Administrative discretion**
ISCED 0-2	**Discretionary funding** from the central authority to local authorities	For partial financing of capital investment	**Administrative discretion**
ISCED 3	**Competition for funds and discretionary funding** (for urgent cases) guaranteed by the central authority	For infrastructure construction, renovation and maintenance, non-instructional and instructional material	Schools **compete for funds** In urgent cases that need immediate investment, e.g. leaking roof, leaking pipes, etc.

Spain

In Spain, the management of the school education system is decentralised. The central education authority (Ministry of Education, Culture and Sport) has exclusive competences about basic rules that develop the right to education, but also ensures the development of the legal regime of public teaching and the policy orientation, design and planning of scholarships and study grants. In turn, regional educational authorities (Ministries or Departments of Education of the Autonomous Communities) have exclusive competence over education management in their territory. In general, local authorities (municipalities or groups of municipalities) have no direct governance of schools, even though the Autonomous Communities can agree on the delegation of management competences for certain education services to the local level. Municipalities are also generally responsible for the maintenance of primary school buildings. The organisation of the public financing system is in line with the decentralisation of educational responsibilities - the Autonomous Communities manage public funds in their territory and decide the amounts allocated to school education and their distribution. The funds are guaranteed by tax revenue, transfers from the central level and other forms of income available to the Communities.

For in-depth information on school funding in Spain, see country background report (*www.oecd.org/education/schoolresourcesreview.htm*).

Current expenditure

Lump-sum transfer and earmarked grants from the central government to each Autonomous Community

Education level	Allocation mechanism	Purpose of grant	Basis to determine the level of the grant
ISCED 0-3	**Lump sum** from the central authority to regional authorities (Autonomous Communities)	For any type of public expenditures. Regional authorities decide the percentage allocated to educational purposes	**Negotiated process, Administrative discretion** ● Demographic characteristics (total population, population in school and pre-school age, urban/rural population) ● Characteristics of the school network (number of schools and pre-schools) ● Other needs of educational supply
ISCED 0-3	**Earmarked grants** from the central authority to regional authorities (Autonomous Communities)	For educational support and other several specific purposes	**Negotiated process, Funding formula** ● Demographic characteristics ● Profile of student population ● Characteristics of the school network ● Economic characteristics

Earmarked grants from the central government to municipalities

Education level	Allocation mechanism	Purpose of grant	Basis to determine the level of the grant
ISCED 0	**Earmarked grant** from central authority to local authorities	For early childhood education and care	**Assessment of needs, Negotiated process** ● Demographic characteristics (number of students in ISCED 0)
ISCED 0-3	**Earmarked grants** from the central authority to local authorities	For educational support and other several specific purposes	**Assessment of needs, Negotiated process** ● Demographic characteristics ● Profile of student population

Earmarked grants from the Autonomous Communities to municipalities

Education level	Allocation mechanism	Purpose of grant	Basis to determine the level of the grant
ISCED 0	**Earmarked grant** from regional authorities (Autonomous Communities) to local authorities	For early childhood education and care	**Assessment of needs, Negotiated process** • Demographic characteristics (number of students in ISCED 0)
ISCED 0-3	**Earmarked grants** from regional authorities (Autonomous Communities) to local authorities	For educational support and other several specific purposes	**Assessment of needs, Negotiated process** • Demographic characteristics • Profile of student population

Dedicated grant from Autonomous Communities for salaries at all levels of education and restricted block grant for operating costs in lower and upper secondary schools

Education level	Allocation mechanism	Purpose of grant	Basis to determine the level of the grant
ISCED 0-3	**Dedicated grant** from the regional authorities (Autonomous Communities) to staff	For teacher and non-teacher salaries	**Funding formula** • Number of students • Number and characteristics of teachers and non-teachers • Number of classes • Identified needs of the students • Population projections and other economic indicators
ISCED 2-3	**Restricted block grant** from regional authorities (Autonomous Communities) to schools	For operating costs and maintenance of services	**Funding formula** • Number of classes in each level of education • School size • Levels of education offered • Type of educational programmes • Rural location • Proportion of immigrant students • Proportion of students with curricular delay or with educational support needs.
ISCED 0-3	**Earmarked grant** from regional authorities (Autonomous Communities) to schools	For supporting additional costs with students with SEN	**Funding formula** • Number of students with SEN • Type of SEN • Ages of children • Degree of dependency • Children/professionals ratio • Other specific criteria related to children and schools
ISCED 0-3	**Earmarked grant** from regional authorities (Autonomous Communities) to schools	For teachers' professional development	**Administrative discretion**, based on teachers' working groups or specific development programs in schools

Restricted block grant from municipalities for operating costs in pre-primary and primary schools and earmarked grants for support of special needs education

Education level	Allocation mechanism	Purpose of grant	Basis to determine the level of the grant
ISCED 0-1	**Restricted block grant** from local authorities to schools	For operating costs and maintenance of services	**Administrative discretion** based on schools' specific needs
ISCED 1-2	**Earmarked grant** from local authorities to schools	For supporting additional costs with students with SEN	**Administrative discretion**. Criteria considered include: • Number of students with SEN • Type of special need

Capital expenditure

Education level	Allocation mechanism	Purpose of grant	Basis to determine the level of the grant
ISCED 0-1	**Earmarked grant** (school-specific) from local authorities to schools	For infrastructure construction, maintenance and renovation	**Assessment of needs**
ISCED 0-3	**Ad hoc grant** from regional authorities (Autonomous Communities) to schools	For the provision of instructional material and infrastructure renovation	**Administrative discretion, Assessment of needs**
ISCED 0-3	**Infrastructure investment programme** from regional authorities (Autonomous Communities) to schools	For infrastructure construction, maintenance and renovation	**Assessment of needs**

Sweden

Sweden has a decentralised education system. The central government is in charge of developing the curriculum, national objectives and guidelines for the education system. Within this framework, the local authorities (municipalities) and independent providers are responsible for implementing educational activities, organising and operating school services, allocating resources and ensuring that the national goals for education are met. This includes pre-school, (*förskola*) (ISCED 0), compulsory school (*grundskola*) (ISCED 1-2), and upper secondary school (*gymnasieskola*) (ISCED 3). The Education Act stipulates that the municipal funding mechanism should account for the number of students enrolled and also the "different preconditions and needs of different students". However, the Swedish government believes that it is not possible to further specify a general model for funding allocation, including what proportion of municipal school funding should be reallocated to differentiate for the school's student composition. The major part of funding, including for grant-aided independent schools (*fristående skolor*), comes from municipal tax revenues, although the municipalities also receive funds from the central state budget for their various services.

For in-depth information on school funding in Sweden, see country background report (*www.oecd.org/education/schoolresourcesreview.htm*).

Current expenditure: lump sum to local authorities and various mechanisms (typically a block grant) for local transfers to schools

Education level	Allocation mechanisms	Purpose of grant	Basis to determine the level of the grant
ISCED 0	**Earmarked grant** from central authority to local authorities	Compensation to cover maximum parental fees in early childhood education and care	**Administrative discretion** by the central authorities
ISCED 0-3	**Lump sum** from central authority to local authorities	For any type of expenditure, including sectors other than education	**Administrative discretion**
ISCED 0-3	**Earmarked grants** from central authority to local authorities	To promote policy priorities	**Administrative discretion, Negotiated process**
ISCED 0-3	**Discretionary funding** from local authorities to schools (typically a **block grant**)	For any type of expenditure; typically provides for salaries, buildings, material and equipment	**Varies. Basis is decided by local authorities**, but must account for the number of students and their preconditions and needs

Capital expenditure: Infrastructure investment programmes and ad hoc decisions by individual municipalities

Education level	Allocation mechanisms	Purpose of funds	Basis to determine the level of the grant
ISCED 0-3	**Infrastructure investment programmes** from local authorities to schools	Infrastructure construction, renovation and maintenance	**Varies. Basis is decided by local authorities**.
ISCED 0-3	**Ad hoc decisions** by local authorities	Infrastructure construction, renovation and maintenance	**Assessment of needs** (varies across local authorities)

Uruguay

The school system in Uruguay is highly centralised. The framework for the operation and the organisation of schools is taken at the central level by the Central Governing Council of the National Public Education Administration (*Consejo Directivo Central de la Administración Nacional de Educación Pública*, CODICEN-ANEP) and the individual education councils for the different sub-sectors of the system (*Consejos de Educación*). This includes the Pre-primary and Primary Education Council (*Consejo de Educación Inicial y Primaria*, CEIP), the Secondary Education Council (*Consejo de Educación Secundaria*, CES), the Technical and Professional Education Council (*Consejo de Educación Técnico-Profesional*, CETP), and the Teacher Training Council (*Consejo de Formación en Educación*, CFE). Funds for current expenditure are allocated from the CODICEN to the individual Education Councils based on negotiations and a historical basis. Each education council allocates funding to the schools for which it is responsible via a set of grant transfers at its discretion. However, there are numerous targeted funds administered directly by the central authorities and not via the education councils.

Early childhood education and pre-primary education (ISCED 0) is provided as part of public schools operated by the Pre-Primary and Primary Education Council (CEIP) and through public early childhood care centres (*Centros de Atención a la Primera Infancia*, CAPI) and private Childcare and Family Centres (*Centros de Atención a la Infancia y la Familia*, CAIF) administered and regulated by the Child and Adolescent Institute of Uruguay (*Instituto del Niño y Adolescente del Uruguay*, INAU). Private Childcare and Family Centres are private institutions that are fully publicly funded and provided free of charge for families. They do not cover education for four year-olds.

For in-depth information on school funding in Uruguay, see the OECD country review report (*http://dx.doi.org/10.1787/9789264265530-en*) and the country background report (*www.oecd.org/education/schoolresourcesreview.htm*).

Current expenditure: Annual grant to transfer funds for current expenditure from the Central Governing Council (CODICEN) to individual education councils and a mix of different grants from education councils to individual schools

Education level	Allocation mechanisms	Purpose of grant	Basis to determine the level of the grant
ISCED 0	**Dedicated grant** from central authority (INAU) to private early childhood education providers (CAIF)	For non-teacher salaries	**Administrative discretion**, taking into account type of schools, type of educational programme, enrolment rate
ISCED 0-3	**Annual grant** from central authority (CODICEN) to central authorities (Education Councils)	For current expenditure	**Negotiated process** and **Historical basis**
ISCED 0-3	**Dedicated grant** from central education authorities (CODICEN, Education Councils)	For teacher salaries and teachers' professional development	**Administrative discretion**, taking into account the type of school and the educational programmes provided; the number of teachers is determined also by the enrolment rate
ISCED 0-3	**Restricted block grant** from central education authorities (Education Councils) to schools	For operating costs	**Administrative discretion**, taking into account the type of school and the educational programmes provided
ISCED 0-3	**Dedicated grant** from central authorities (Education Councils)	For instructional materials; telephone expenses	**Administrative discretion**, taking into account the type of school and the educational programmes provided; Allocation of instructional materials based on historical parameters
ISCED 0-3	**Dedicated grant** from central authorities (Education Councils)	For teacher training to support students with special educational needs	**Administrative discretion**, taking into account the type of school and the educational programmes provided Allocation to special primary education accounts for the type of disability, which would have implications for the type of human and material resources required
ISCED 2-3 (only for some specific programmes in general education and for some types of schools in pre-vocational and vocational education [agrarian schools])	**Earmarked grant** from central authorities (Education Councils)	For school meals	**Administrative discretion**, taking into account the type of school and the educational programmes provided

Capital expenditure: A mix of infrastructure investment programmes, ad hoc decisions and discretionary funding

Education level	Allocation mechanisms	Purpose of funds	Basis to determine the level of the grant
ISCED 0-3	**Negotiated process** between Central authorities (CODICEN and Education Councils)	Minor infrastructure construction, maintenance and equipment	**Historical basis**
ISCED 0-3	**Infrastructure investment programme** from central authority (CODICEN) to schools	Infrastructure construction, and major infrastructure works	**Administrative discretion**, including an **assessment of needs**
ISCED 0-3 (pre-vocational and vocational)	**Residual funds** from regular funding for current expenditure from central authorities (Education Councils)	For instructional and non-instructional materials	Not specified
ISCED 0-1	**Negotiated process** (between regional inspectorate, architects teams of Education Council and CODICEN)	Infrastructure renovation, maintenance, and minor infrastructure construction	**Assessment of needs**
ISCED 0-1	**Discretionary funding** from central authorities (Education Council) to schools	Instructional equipment	**Assessment of needs**
ISCED 2-3	**Ad hoc decisions** from central authorities (Education Councils) to schools	Infrastructure renovations and maintenance	**Administrative discretion**, including an **assessment of needs**
ISCED 2-3 (general)	**Discretionary funding** from central authorities (Education Council) to schools	Instructional equipment	**Administrative discretion**

Education level	Allocation mechanisms	Purpose of funds	Basis to determine the level of the grant
ISCED 1 (Full-time primary schools)	**Infrastructure investment programme** from central authority (Education Council, PAEPU)	Extra support for capital expenditures	Not specified
ISCED 2-3	**Infrastructure investment programme** from central authorities (Education Councils, PAEMFE)	Extra support for capital expenditures	Not specified
ISCED 1-3	**Discretionary funding** from a dedicated agency (Ceibal Centre)	For instructional material	**Administrative discretion** (based on need for replacement)

ANNEX B

Glossary

Levels of education according to UNESCO's International Standard Classification of Education (ISCED 2011)

Early childhood education (ISCED 0): Provides learning and educational activities with a holistic approach to support children's early cognitive, physical, social and emotional development and introduce young children to organised instruction outside of the family context to develop some of the skills needed for academic readiness and to prepare them for entry into primary education. ISCED level 0 is further divided into two sub-levels: ISCED 01 and ISCED 02.

Early childhood educational development (ISCED 01): Characterised by a learning environment that is visually stimulating and language-rich. These programmes foster self-expression, with an emphasis on language acquisition and the use of language for meaningful communication. There are opportunities for active play, so that children can exercise their co-ordination and motor skills under supervision and through interaction with staff. Programmes providing only childcare (supervision, nutrition and health) are not covered by ISCED. Early childhood educational development programmes (ISCED level 01) are targeted at children aged 0 to 2 years.

Pre-primary education (ISCED 02): Characterised by interaction with peers and educators, through which children improve their use of language and social skills, start to develop logical and reasoning skills, and talk through their thought processes. They are also introduced to alphabetical and mathematical concepts, and encouraged to explore their surrounding world and environment. Pre-primary education programmes (ISCED level 02) are targeted at children aged 3 until the age to start ISCED 1. The upper age limit for the pre-primary education category depends in each case on the theoretical age of entry into ISCED level 1, i.e. primary education.

Primary education (ISCED 1): Usually begins at age 5, 6 or 7, and has a typical duration of 6 years. Programmes at ISCED level 1 are normally designed to give students a sound basic education in reading, writing and mathematics, along with an elementary understanding of other subjects such as history, geography, natural science, social sciences, art and music. The commencement of reading activities alone is not a sufficient criterion for classification of an education programme at ISCED 1. Programmes classified at ISCED 1 may be referred to in many ways, for example: primary education, elementary education or basic education (stage 1 or lower grades if an education system has one programme that spans ISCED 1 and 2).

Lower secondary education (ISCED 2): Programmes are designed to lay the foundation across a wide range of subjects and to prepare children and young people for more specialised study at upper secondary and higher levels of education. The beginning – or the end – of lower secondary education often involves a change of school for young students and also a change in the style of instruction. Programmes classified at ISCED level 2 may be referred to in many ways, for example: secondary school (stage one/lower grades), junior secondary school, middle school or junior high school. If a programme spans ISCED levels 1 and 2, the terms elementary education or basic school (second stage/upper grades) are often used.

Upper secondary education (ISCED 3): Programmes are more specialised than those at lower secondary and offer students more choices and diverse pathways for completing their secondary education. The range of subjects studied by a single student tends to be narrower than at lower levels of education, but the content is more complex and the study more in depth. Programmes offered are differentiated by orientation and often by broad subject groups. Programmes classified at ISCED level 3 may be referred to in many ways, for example, secondary school (stage 2/upper grades), senior secondary school or (senior) high school.

General, pre-vocational and vocational education: Programmes at ISCED levels 2 and 3 can also be subdivided into two categories based on the degree to which the programme is specifically oriented towards a specific class of occupations or trades and leads to a labour-market relevant qualification: general programmes and pre-vocational/vocational programmes.

General programmes: Refers to programmes that are not designed explicitly to prepare participants for a specific class of occupations or trades or for entry into further vocational or technical education programmes.

Pre-vocational/vocational programmes: This category encompasses both pre-vocational and vocational education. Pre-vocational education is mainly designed to introduce participants to the world of work and to prepare them for entry into further vocational or technical programmes. Successful completion of such programmes does not lead to a labour-market relevant vocational or technical qualification. Vocational programmes prepare participants for direct entry into specific occupations without further training. Successful completion of such programmes leads to a labour-market relevant vocational qualification.

For further details, see:

UNESCO Institute for Statistics (2012), *International Standard Classification of Education ISCED 2011*, UNESCO Institute for Statistics, Montreal, Quebec, *www.uis.unesco.org/Education/ Documents/isced-2011-en.pdf*.

OECD/Eurostat/UNESCO Institute for Statistics (2015), *ISCED 2011 Operational Manual: Guidelines for Classifying National Education Programmes and Related Qualifications*, OECD Publishing, Paris, *http://dx.doi.org/10.1787/9789264228368-en*.

Levels of governance and administration

For international comparability, levels of governance and administration are described following a standard terminology. The report may, however, use the particular terms of a specific national context where country approaches are described in greater detail. For example, for Austria, the report may refer to "states" when information is presented in a comparable format (e.g. for a group of countries with a similar approach or in comparative tables) or to "provinces" when the Austrian funding system is analysed in greater detail.

Central level: The central level specifies authorities that make decisions or participate in different aspects of decision making on a national scale. This includes, among others, the central government, central education, financial and legislative authorities and central auditing services. All authorities below the central level in administrative terms are referred to as sub-central authorities at the sub-central level.

State level: The state level refers to the first territorial unit below the nation in federal countries or countries with similar types of governmental structures. The state level includes, among others, state governments, state education, financial and legislative authorities, and state auditing services. In Austria, for example, the state level refers to the level of the "provinces". In Belgium, the state level refers to the level of the "Communities".

Regional level: The region level is the first territorial unit below the national level in countries that do not have a federal or similar type of governmental structure, and the second territorial unit below the national level in countries with federal or similar types of governmental structures. The regional level includes, among others, regional governments, regional education, financial and legislative authorities, and regional auditing services. In the Czech Republic and the Slovak Republic, for example, the regional level refers to the "self-governing regions". In Spain, the regional level refers to the "Autonomous Communities".

Local level: The local level corresponds to the smallest territorial unit with a governing authority, such as municipalities or communities. This includes local governments, local education, financial and legislative authorities and local auditing services. The local authority may be the education department within a general-purpose local government or it may be a special-purpose government whose sole area of authority is education.

Public and private schools

Public: An educational institution is classified as public if it is controlled and managed by a public education authority or agency, or by a governing body (council, committee, etc.) most of whose members are either appointed by a public authority or elected by public franchise.

Private: An educational institution is classified as private if it is controlled and managed by a non-governmental organisation (e.g. a church, a trade union or a business enterprise, foreign or international agency), or a governing board which consists mostly of members not selected by a public agency. A private institution can receive public funding (publicly-subsidised private schools) or not (independent private schools).

Current and capital expenditure

Current expenditure: Current expenditure describes incurred costs with teaching and learning activities, teachers' and other educational staff's salaries, other operating costs and costs with assets that have a duration of less than one year, except where noted otherwise. Operating costs refer to expenses associated with the maintenance and administration of a school on a day-to-day basis (e.g. heating, electricity, small repairs, perishable instructional materials, etc.).

Capital expenditure: Funding for capital expenditures covers spending on assets that last longer than one year. It includes funds for construction, renovation or major repairs to buildings (immovable) as well as on new or replacement instructional and non-instructional equipment (e.g. furniture, laboratory equipment, computers, etc.).

Allocation mechanisms for current expenditure

Allocation mechanisms describe different approaches to distributing and transferring resources and funds for current expenditure to different levels of governance and administration, to school providers and to individual schools. The mechanisms are primarily based on the level of discretion that the recipient has in deciding on how the funding is used.

Lump sum: Consists of funding for the public sector and leaves discretion to sub-central authorities over the proportion allocated to early childhood and school education.

Block grant: Consists of funds that recipients (sub-central authorities or schools) can use at their own discretion for current expenditure in early childhood or school education.

Restricted block grant: Consists of funds that recipients (sub-central authorities or schools) can use at their own discretion, but within given areas of spending (e.g. operating costs).

Earmarked grant: Consists of funds that recipients (sub-central authorities or schools) are required to use for specific elements/items of current expenditure in early childhood or school education (e.g. teacher professional development, extra funds for special needs education).

School-specific grant: Consists of funds that sub-central authorities are required to use for current expenditure in specific schools (i.e. the grant specifies the amount of funding allocated to each school).

Dedicated grant: Consists of funds which are not administered by the school (e.g. teacher salaries which are directly paid by the relevant authority; operating costs directly paid by the relevant authority). In this case, funds are not transferred to individual schools.

Allocation mechanisms for capital expenditure

Infrastructure investment programme: Refers to a specific, usually central or state-level, initiative targeted at infrastructure investment following medium-term development plans or strategies at the national or sector level for a fixed period of time.

Ad hoc decisions/Ad hoc grant: Refers to an ad hoc agreement between the public funder and the entities receiving the funds.

Competition: Refers to an application process in which individual authorities and/or schools apply for funding for capital expenditure. The authority providing the funding selects the recipients based on the quality of their application as judged against relevant criteria.

Bases for the allocation of funding for current expenditure

The basis for the allocation of funding refers to the method which determines the amount of funding distributed to recipients (sub-central authorities and/or schools).

Administrative discretion: Typically refers to administrators' assessment of the amount of resources that each school needs. It involves decision making about the allocation of funds based on professional judgement and expertise and might involve the use of indicators.

Funding formula: Refers to a universally applied rule using objective criteria to establish the amount of resources that the recipient (sub-central authority or individual school) is entitled to. The relevant authority uses a formally defined procedure (e.g. a mathematical formula with a number of variables and related coefficients) to determine the level of public funds which should be allocated.

Negotiated process: Refers to negotiations and agreements between the funding provider and the funding recipient on the amount of funding (e.g. local authorities making a case for additional resources from relevant authority to respond to short-term needs, bargaining between different levels of governance for regular funding allocation).

ANNEX C

Notes on country profiles

Austria

Current expenditure for early childhood education and care (ISCED 0): Early childhood education and care is the responsibility of the states. Funds for current expenditure are therefore decided at the state level.

Earmarked grants from central authority to state authorities for federal policy priorities specifically agreed with states (ISCED 0, ISCED 1-3 state schools): Specific agreements can be concluded between the federal and the state authorities to foster the implementation of federal government priorities in policy areas under state competence. These agreements are referred to as "Art. 15a agreements" as they are based on article 15a of the federal constitution. The states are usually required to develop a concept for implementation and receive substantial funding from the federal level for implementing this federal policy priority. It is at the discretion of the state to allocate the money to staff costs and/or infrastructure. Agreements are negotiated for a fixed time period only.

For instance, the federal level and the states have agreed on federal co-funding to support the states in offering places in the last year of kindergarten for all children free of charge. Further Art. 15a agreements have been concluded to co-fund the expansion of institutional childcare provision (with a focus on children aged 0-3 years) and the promotion of early language learning for children aged 3-6 in institutionalised childcare. Funding for the Art. 15a agreements on early language support and the expansion of early childhood education and care provision is distributed to the states proportionate to the number of children at the relevant age residing in the respective state. Another example for an Art. 15a agreement is the provision of federal funding for the expansion of all-day schooling which is distributed to the states proportionate to their population size.

Earmarked grant from central authority to state authorities for teaching purposes, special needs education and learning support staff (ISCED 1-3 state schools): The states are almost exclusively funded by a transfer mechanism, the Fiscal Adjustment Act (*Finanzausgleichsgesetz*), which allocates financial means raised by the central government to states and local authorities. The Fiscal Adjustment Act is the key instrument for the distribution of revenues across different levels of administration, that is, from the federal level to the state and local level. This mechanism is based on demographic criteria and negotiated approximately every four to six years between the federal government represented by the Federal Ministry of Finance, the state governments, represented by their governors, and the municipalities represented by the Association of Cities and Towns and the Association of Municipalities. The result of these negotiations is adopted by the Federal Parliament. The agreements according to this redistribution constitute a kind of "automatic" entitlement of the states and municipalities to receive a certain amount of the federal taxes: 21% for the states and 12% for municipalities, as of 2016. Owing to the complex distribution of responsibilities for education, these structures of Austrian federalism are a very important element of education financing.

The Fiscal Adjustment Act also sets out the general principles for the transfer of funds from the federal to the state level for teaching resources for state schools. For Years 1-8, the federal government fully compensates the states for their expenditures on teachers within the limits of staff plans approved by the Federal Minister of Education and the Federal Minister of Finance. The applied funding formula for the establishment of staff plans includes the following parameters: i) Basic contingent of teachers, based on numbers of students and adjusted for type of school, i.e. primary schools – 14.5 students/teacher, general secondary schools – 10 students/teacher, special needs schools – 3.2 students/teacher; ii) To cover the higher resource needs for special needs education, the 3.2 students/teacher formula is flat-rated to 2.7% of all students, who are deduced from the basic contingent; iii) Additional means are earmarked for policy priorities such as language support classes, day care, and class-size reduction to a maximum of 25 students. For example, in 2010/11 there were 10 different priorities for which additional teaching posts had been earmarked.

All monetary transfers for teaching resources from the federal to the state level are earmarked, that is they have to be used by the states for teaching purposes and specified education policy priorities only. The distribution of resources to federal schools is the sole responsibility of the Federal Ministry of Education and is largely administered by the state school boards. Part-time compulsory vocational schools (*Berufsschulen*) are a special case. For this type of school, 50% of personnel costs are funded by the federal authority, the other 50% by the states (out of their overall state budget).

Dedicated grant from state authorities to staff (ISCED 1-3 state schools): There are no national regulations for the distribution of teaching resources to state schools by state governments. State authorities establish their own procedures and principles for the development and implementation of staff plans. While the precise basis for allocation is the decision of the states, states have typically put in place (varying) funding formulas (e.g. sometimes including also socio-economic aspects). The Federal Ministry of Education has no influence on the amount of resources deployed to an individual state school. Funds provided on the basis of the assumed number of students with special needs or language support classes are not earmarked and therefore not subject to controlling by the federal government. During the school year, the Federal Ministry of Education also covers the excess sums of salaries if the states exceed the pre-set staff plans. The amount of the compensation to the federal level is calculated on the basis of the salary level of a beginning teacher. Since the states also hire many experienced teachers at higher levels of the salary scale, the compensation usually falls short of the real cost advanced by the federal ministry.

Dedicated grant from central authority to staff (ISCED 2-3 federal schools): Teaching resources measured as "value units" (*Werteinheiten*) are allocated by the Federal Ministry of Education to the state school boards. A budget plan for current investments has to be elaborated for each school year and requires consultation of the concerned staff members. Federal schools have to deliver data on the numbers of students that are enrolled. Only a very limited share of teaching resources is earmarked for specific schools. The redistribution to individual schools is administered by the individual state school boards. Procedures and criteria to distribute funding for individual schools differ, but formula funding is the predominant mechanism and the distribution usually take into account specificities of schools such as the number of students with a migration background, and language deficits. Administrative discretion is relevant, in particular, to deal with unplanned staff shortages, such as those resulting from the enrolment of refugees and asylum seekers during the school year.

Capital expenditure (ISCED 0-3): For early childhood education and care (ISCED 0), responsibility for capital expenditure lies with the state or the private provider (e.g. associations, churches, etc.). For school education (ISCED 1-3), the main responsibility for capital expenditure lies with the owner of the school. For state schools, most tasks associated with the provision and maintenance of schools have in practice been devolved to the municipal level, including the provision of school buildings, infrastructure and non-teaching staff such as janitors. States typically support municipalities in carrying out these duties by administering allocated funds and have retained their responsibility for vocational, agriculture and forestry schools at upper secondary level (ISCED 3). In the case of federal schools, as a general rule, the Federal Ministry of Education is responsible for providing and maintaining the school infrastructure. A large share of the school infrastructure for federal schools (around 320 school locations) has been outsourced and buildings are administered and maintained by the Federal Real Estate Company (*Bundesimmobiliengesellschaft*) owned by the Federal Republic of Austria. Buildings are rented by the Federal Ministry of Education. Some school buildings of federal schools are owned by other proprietors, mainly municipalities and social partners. Regular funding for current expenditures at all levels of the education system also includes some funds for maintenance and small investments.

Ad hoc grants and infrastructure investment programmes from state and local authorities (ISCED 0, ISCED 1-3 state schools): The municipalities build, maintain and own the school buildings. The state governments have in place programmes to support municipalities in the construction and renovation of schools. The adequacy of school infrastructure in relation to type of school is subject to state legislation and can be further broken down into detailed guidelines for school construction and room equipment. Expert commissions are established to assess the suitability of planned infrastructure.

Infrastructure investment programme from central authority (ISCED 2-3 federal schools): The federal government has adopted a long-term school development programme (*Schulentwicklungsplan*) for the decade 2008-18. The focus is on the modernisation of existing infrastructure and school architecture to provide students and teachers with adequate classrooms and workplaces. Investments are transferred to the owners of the school buildings, i.e. the Federal Real Estate Company and others, mainly municipalities, via (increased) rental payments.

Belgium (Flemish and French Communities)

Lump sum from the central authority to the state authorities for all policy domains (ISCED 0-3): The transfer from the federal budget to the Communities involves some degree of political negotiation on the total amount of the lump sum transferred which cannot be explained by a funding formula only. Moreover, the budget of the Communities entails other (fiscal) sources than the transfer from the federal level, while taxes levied at the local level (provinces, cities and municipalities) may contribute to infrastructure or non-teaching related services. The lump sum can be used for all policy domains at the competence of the Communities, not only for education, and can be distributed across policy domains at the discretion of the Community. There are no transfers from the Communities (state level) to regional or local levels. Funds are transferred rather directly to school providers.

Capital expenditure in the Flemish Community (ISCED 0-3): Access to capital funding is organised through two public agencies. A dedicated public body, GO! Education of the Flemish Community, finances the creation or improvement of buildings in the Flemish Community school network as public assets. The Agency for Educational Infrastructure (*Agentschap voor Infrastructuur in het Onderwijs*, AGIOn) finances building works in schools of other public school providers (municipal and provincial) as well as publicly-subsidised private schools. AGIOn meets 70% of their capital requirements in primary education and 60% in secondary education. The unsubsidised balance, in turn, can be met by a state-guaranteed loan. The asset remains privately owned for publicly-subsidised private schools. For other public school organising bodies, the asset remains owned by the regional and local authorities (municipalities and provinces). In addition, there is the possibility of public-private partnerships.

Capital expenditure in the French Community (ISCED 0-3): The school building fund allocates funds to public schools. Publicly-subsidised private schools do not receive resources from this fund. However, a guarantee fund grants them a capital repayment guarantee for the financing of construction, renovation, modernisation and expansion (Decree 05/02/1990 on school buildings). With regard to emergency works, the priority programme of works (*Programme prioritaire de travaux*, PPT) makes it possible to remedy essential needs by allocating funds to all school providers (under the same funding mechanisms: ISCED level 0-1: 70%, ISCED levels 2-3: 60% by the French Community, the remainder by the school provider) (Decree 16/11/2007 on the priority work programme).

Chile

Block grants from central authorities for early childhood education and care (ISCED 0): These block grants refer to central funding from the central education authority (*Junta Nacional de Jardines Infantiles, JUNJI*) for pre-school providers that operate based on fund transfers (*via transferencia de fondos,* VTF) and from the central education authority (Integra) for pre-school providers that operate based on agreements. Both JUNJI and Integra also transfer funds directly to ECEC centres. The transfers are regulated by specific regulations and agreements with each provider.

Current expenditure for school providers (ISCED 02-3): In addition to the funding allocations in the table, there is also a grant to public schools with delegated administration to non-profit corporations. This, however, only concerns 70 schools, that is, less than 1% of schools (Decree Law No. 3.166). It is, therefore, not presented in this country profile.

General school subsidy (ISCED 02-3): This block grant is paid on equal conditions to all school providers based on average attendance of students at each individual school. The funding follows the student and is spent at the discretion of school providers within a regulated framework.

Pro-Retention Educational Subsidy (Law No. 19,873) (ISCED 02-3): This block grant is paid annually to school providers that have managed to retain their students in schools of highly disadvantaged students in Years 7 to 12.

The Strengthening of Public Education Fund (FAEP, Resolution No. 11, Chilean Ministry of Education) (ISCED 02-3): This block grant aims to support the educational services provided by local authorities as public school providers and is to be used exclusively for initiatives related to such service and their improvement. It is defined by the National Budget Law and regulated by the Ministry of Education (Resolution No. 11, 2016) and transferred to municipal school providers based on specific agreements. Its regulation allows financing a variety of areas such as municipal management improvement, pedagogical resources and student support, infrastructure and equipment improvement, financial restructuring (debt reduction) and educational community participation. In the case of a surplus of resources, central authorities can redistribute funds to local authorities facing extraordinary difficulties which endanger the continuity of educational provision.

Earmarked grants from central authority to local authorities and publicly-funded private providers for students with special educational needs and disadvantaged students (ISCED 02-3): These earmarked grants refer to subsidies for specific purposes, namely, the improvement of schools with a large share of socio-economically disadvantaged students (SEP), the integration of students with special needs education in regular schools (PIE), boarding school operating cost, learning support and maintenance of infrastructure.

Salary incentives for staff in best performing schools (ISCED 02-3): This earmarked grant provides a salary incentive of education professionals (teachers and support staff) of schools with the best performance within a comparable group in each region. It is determined by the National Performance Evaluation System of Subsidised Schools (*Sistema Nacional de Evaluación del Desempeño*, SNED). According to the Law 19.410 (Articles 15-17), the subsidy goes to school providers, but the distribution is decentralised. Every trimester, the school provider distributes 90% of the subsidy among the school`s teachers, and the remaining 10% is used for salary incentives for remarkable teachers. The distribution of these 10% is defined by the teachers, not the school provider.

Dedicated grants from local authorities and publicly-funded private school providers for salaries and operational costs (ISCED 02-3): School providers can only use the school allocation for educational purposes. The Inclusion Law (Law No. 20,845, 2015) specifically allows 11 operations, including salaries for management, teaching staff and teaching assistants; management and operations costs for running the school; services and materials for teaching and learning; maintenance and repair of school property; and improvement of school's educational service. A large share (88%) of publicly-funded private school providers is in charge of one school only.

Infrastructure investment programme from central authorities (ISCED 02-3): The National Fund for Regional Development incorporates provisions which are additional resources detailed in each year's Budget Law. These funds are transferred to the regions in order to promote the investment in priority areas defined at the national level. One of these provisions is the Fund for Educational Infrastructure (*Fondo de Infraestructura Educacional*, FIE).

Czech Republic

Restricted block grant from regional authorities to schools to cover direct costs (ISCED 0-3): Each of the fourteen regions develops a funding formula to allocate funding to regional and municipal schools. There may be negotiations between regional and local authorities regarding the allocation to municipal schools. Regional funding formulas vary, but typically include the criteria presented in the table.

Discretionary funding from regional or local authorities (as school providers) to schools to cover operational costs (ISCED 0-3): Schools at ISCED 1-2 (most managed by local authorities) have several sources of funding. Besides the allocation for direct costs from the regional budget, there are i) additional funding for direct costs (negotiated between the municipal and the regional levels, in their function as school provider [founder]); ii) add-ons to direct costs from the municipal budget; and iii) funding for operational, fully financed from the municipal budget.

Denmark

Current expenditure for early childhood education and care (ISCED 0): Early childhood education and care is partially financed by municipal grants and partially by parental payment. Municipalities can use funds transferred from the central government in the form of a lump sum for the general funding of public services also to finance early childhood education and care. Parental payments must not exceed 25% of the gross operating cost for the individual day care facility or of the average gross operating costs for operating similar day care facilities in the municipality.

Lump sum from the central authority to local authorities for any type of expenditure (ISCED 0, ISCED 1-2): Based on the definitions for the qualitative survey on school funding, the allocation mechanism has been classified as a lump sum. In Denmark, general grants from the central government to municipalities to finance public services are typically referred to as "block grants".

The overall framework for local government service expenditure is determined in the annual negotiations of the municipalities' economy between the central government and Local Government Denmark (LGDK). Within this framework, it is possible to prioritise expenditure partly internally between the municipalities and partly across the sectors in each municipality. The economic agreement between the central government and LGDK is an agreement of the tax and expenditure level for the municipalities collectively. No frames are set for the individual municipality, and the agreement is not binding for the individual municipality. However, in order to keep the collective budgets of the municipalities within the agreed level, LGDK co-ordinates the budget processes of the individual municipalities.

The general grants from the central government are mainly allocated to the individual municipalities according to an equalisation scheme aimed at evening out the differences in the economic situation in the municipalities due to differences in tax base, composition of age groups and social structure. The aim is not to equalise the service levels, as that is a local policy priority, but to give the municipalities approximately the same financial basis on which to solve their tasks.

Current expenditure for the public Folkeskole (ISCED 1-2): In financing the *Folkeskole*, the municipalities are not allowed to finance schools by user fees, but are to finance school expenditures by revenues from local taxes and general grants from the central government. These two sources of revenue account for 71% and 26% of the total municipal revenue respectively in the municipal budgets for 2014. No central funding is directly allocated to the *Folkeskole* and there are no central reimbursements of school expenditures. However, the central level may fund particular programmes additionally through earmarked grants. For instance, DKK 1 billion has been earmarked by the central level for competency development of teachers and school leaders in relation to the 2014 *Folkeskole* reform.

Earmarked grants from the central authority to local authorities to promote policy priorities (ISCED 1-2): The allocation of earmarked grants only happens occasionally, typically in the context of new legislation and always within a limited timeframe. The basis of allocation differs from one grant to another. For example, an earmarked grant for teacher development was negotiated as part of the parliament's agreement on a reform of the *Folkeskole* in 2014. After the reform had passed in parliament, a council was established at a national level to distribute the funds and to monitor and evaluate the use of these funds.

Discretionary funding from local authorities to schools for current expenditure (ISCED 1-2): Funding models for the allocation of current expenditure to schools vary across municipalities. Some municipalities allocate a given amount per student, while most take account of the students' or area's socio-economic characteristics (although with different measures and weightings). School size is typically accounted for. Some municipalities use the number of students, others the required number of classes. Typically, school principals have a high degree of autonomy to use school funding, in consultation with the school board, within the central regulatory framework. Although typically funds for special educational needs are not earmarked, municipalities can apply for additional funding targeted for special needs education.

Block grant from the central authority to private schools for current expenditure (ISCED 1-3): Private basic schools (ISCED 1-2) and continuation schools (private boarding schools that typically offer teaching from Year 8 to Year 10 at ISCED 2) are alternatives to the public *Folkeskole*. Both types are self-governing institutions financed by central subsidies and student contributions. The municipalities are obliged to fund private primary and lower secondary schools. The municipal grant per student in private schools is fixed across municipalities and set each year in the Finance Act of the central government and calculated as a percentage of the average municipal expenditures per student in the *Folkeskole*. The contribution of the municipalities is paid to the central government. The private schools receive their funding from the central government based on the taximeter system. Private upper secondary schools (ISCED 3) have the same public grant system as the private basic schools.

Current expenditure for upper secondary education (ISCED 3): Upper secondary schools are self-governing educational institutions with two sources of revenue for financing their educational programmes: central grants and their own income from income-generating activities. Central grants amount to approximately 80% of the total funding and are thus the primary source of revenue for upper secondary schools. A taximeter system determines the largest share of central grants (92%) according to political priorities. The taximeter system makes funding dependent on the activity level and direct results of the school, measured in terms of the annual number of full-time students or full-time student equivalents. The funds distributed according to the taximeter are not subject to negotiations or administrative redistribution.

These funds are complemented with activity-independent funds. Activity-independent funds include basic grants designed to finance the basic expenditures of the educational institutions, which take into account the distribution of educational opportunities and compensates small schools. Other activity-independent funding includes earmarked grants to supplement the taximeter system and to promote political priorities.

The school-based part of vocational education and training programmes is financed by the central authorities on the basis of the taximeter system. Students receive wages from the company for their work during their internship. The Employers' Reimbursement Fund reimburses the company for the trainees' wages when the student is attending school. All companies, both public and private, contribute with a fixed amount to this fund for each of their employees.

Capital expenditure for early childhood education and care (ISCED 0) and public primary and lower secondary education (ISCED 1-2): The allocation of funding for capital expenditure for public institutions is at the administrative discretion of municipalities. Private schools at ISCED 1-3 receive an activity-based "building/capital" grant from the central authorities.

Capital expenditure for upper secondary education (ISCED 3): Public schools receive an activity-based building/capital grant. The schools own their own buildings so that capital expenditures can be financed by the schools loaning money on the market. If the school board makes capital dispositions for more than DKK 60 million, it has to be approved by the Ministry of Education.

Estonia

School funding in Estonia (ISCED 0-3): The approach to allocating funding for each of the different components of general education has evolved and been contested since the late 1990s. 1998 saw the introduction of a relatively simple per student formula, including initially six and then eight coefficients to adjust per student payments on the basis of differing demographic and socio-economic characteristics among municipalities. Due to a dramatic demographic decline and with a new policy concern to protect rural schools, in 2008 the formula was revised to allocate funding on a per class basis to all schools. In 2012, the formula was revised again to allocate funding on a per student basis.

Earmarked funds from the central level to local authorities (ISCED 0-3): For municipalities which are not school owners (school providers), no grants are provided for general education purposes.

Earmarked funds from the central level to the four largest towns and regional/municipal unions for teachers' professional training (ISCED 0): Regional municipality unions are unions which include municipalities in one county.

Earmarked funds from the central level to all local authorities for different policy priorities and programmes (ISCED 1-3 general education): Policy priorities and programmes include the Language Immersion Programme; the Teaching Estonian for new immigrants and for students whose mother tongue is Russian; and the International Baccalaureate (IB) diploma programme and accommodation costs for children from the most disadvantaged families, among others.

Earmarked funds from the central level to the three local authorities that own VET schools for state commissioned study places in VET (ISCED 2-3 pre-vocational and vocational): The number of state commissioned places ordered from schools in different study fields which is part of the funding formula is based on labour market and social needs.

Restricted block grant from local authorities to private pre-schools and/or other local authorities which are pre-school providers for operating costs (ISCED 0): The grant to private pre-schools is paid only if the municipalities' own pre-school(s) does not have sufficient capacity in terms of pre-school places.

Restricted block grant from local authorities to private schools and/or other local authorities for operating costs (ISCED 1-3): The funding depends on an agreement between the private school owner and the municipality. The government establishes a monthly limit of operational expenses.

Infrastructure investment programme from central-level dedicated agencies to local authorities for the creation of new pre-school places (ISCED 0): Enterprise Estonia (Ettevõtluse Arendamise Sihtasutus, EAS) is an agency responsible for promoting business and regional development and co-ordinates the implementation of EU structural funds. Innove Foundation is responsible for implementing relevant projects in the area of lifelong learning and for mediating EU structural funds.

Iceland

Block grant from central authorities to local authorities for any type of expenditure in compulsory education (ISCED 1-2): A proportion of total income taxation is allocated to education at the local level (2.07%).

Block grant/earmarked grant from central authorities to local authorities to even out the differences in expenditure and income of local governments with greater needs (ISCED 1-2): 71% of the grant are for any type of expenditure, the remaining 29% are for earmarked support. Allocation criteria were under review in 2015 with the intention to make them more general.

Block grant/earmarked grant from local authorities to compulsory schools for salaries and operational costs and extra support for specific student groups (ISCED 1-2): As each local community is an independent financial authority, it determines also the discretion of the individual school leader in deciding the use of the funding received, within the requirements of laws and regulation. Some municipalities allocate a block grant; others earmark part of the funding for specific purposes. Thus some school leaders can use the funding as they see fit as long as they remain within the total budget provided, while others cannot transfer funding between different cost areas without approval from the local community.

School-specific block grant from the central level to upper secondary schools for any type of expenditure (ISCED 3): According to the law, the central education authority funds each school offering upper secondary education individually for teaching and other costs as required, i.e. through a school-specific grant. The proposed funding is based on a comprehensive funding model taking into account general criteria that apply to all schools, as well as specific criteria taking into account the specific circumstances of each school.

Capital expenditure (ISCED 0-3): A portion of block grants for any type of expenditures can be used to cover capital expenditures. In pre-primary and compulsory education (ISCED 0-2), the local authorities are entirely responsible for capital expenditures. For upper secondary schools (ISCED 3), construction costs and initial capital investment for equipment are generally divided between the central government and the relevant municipalities based on a negotiated settlement between central and local authorities. The central government and the relevant municipalities pay 60% and 40% respectively. There are no formal provisions for funding capital expenditure of private schools at any school level.

Israel

Earmarked grants from the central level to local authorities for non-teachers' salaries and other operational costs (ISCED 0-3): The central government allocates funding to local authorities according to to several distribution criteria. Local authorities have certain flexibility to the execution of the budget.

Dedicated grant from central authority (ISCED 0-2) for staff salaries: Public primary and lower secondary schools receive detailed information on the number of instruction hours by categories of subjects at their disposal. The regional administration of the Ministry of Education has a bank of teaching hours to allocate to schools to solve specific problems, such as the completion of study hours, the completion of teachers' salaries, and the provision of support for teachers, at its administrative discretion.

Block grants from central authority to publicly-funded private schools for any type of current expenditure (ISCED 0, ISCED 1-3): Self-managed non-public schools receive a flexible budget for which they give a detailed report. In primary education, funding is distributed according to student numbers, which helps the Ministry of Education to calculate a number of standard classes and the number of learning hours. The ministry also knows the cost of a teaching hour according to the teachers' average profile (experience, diploma, part-time job, etc.). In upper secondary education, the distribution of funds is calculated per student and based on the cost of teaching hours according to the teachers' average profile in a school.

Capital expenditure (ISCED 0-3): Multi-year plans for the construction of schools and classrooms are based on forecasts of student numbers and the lack of existing buildings. The Ministry of Education participates in the planning of the budget. The criterion is the number of classes in accordance to price charts. Local authorities are responsible for the execution and completion of the budget.

Kazakhstan

Earmarked grant from central to regional authorities for equalising differences in regional revenues and implementing specific government programmes and initiatives (ISCED 0-3): The amount of the transfer is provided strictly according to an annual financial plan of the region, which includes a budgetary application with detailed information on the need of funding. Central (republican) funding is directed towards the regions, and then further to the local level. The amount of finances cannot be freely regulated by the regions. In case the budget is not fully spent, the surplus is returned to the regional level, and then further to the central (republican) level.

Capital expenditure (ISCED 0-3): Funding for capital expenditures in schools is mainly guaranteed by ad hoc decisions and discretionary funding. According to the State Programme for Education and Science Development for 2016-19, the top priorities are to decrease the number of schools that provide triple-shift education, to decrease the number of schools that are in state of emergency and to decrease the student place deficit. These are the schools that receive funding first.

Lithuania

School funding in Lithuania (ISCED 0-3): The school council is the self-governing body of the school. The school council collegially discusses issues of school activity and funding and, within the scope of its competence, as defined in the school statutes, adopts decisions.

Earmarked grant from central authorities to local authorities for covering teaching and operational costs (student basket scheme) (ISCED 0-3): Central regulations define an interval of coefficients' variation for teachers' pay, calculated over the basic monthly salary from which the salaries of public servants in Lithuania are calculated. The coefficients vary with the teacher's type (e.g. non-certified, senior, methodologist, expert teacher) and years of experience. The school management then has to adapt the pay-scale to the available number and type of teachers. Municipalities have a restricted degree of discretion to reallocate a proportion of the grant from the central level. The central government grant is calculated taking into account the average teachers' salary, and is defined on an hourly basis. Annual school budgets are then balanced for the actual teacher salary expenses, regulated by a national salary scale.

Capital expenditure (ISCED 0-3): The bulk of funding for investment in school infrastructure comes from specific central government and EU Structural Fund investment grants, supplemented by local government funding. These funds have been mainly allocated to the development of vocational training centres, establishment of multifunctional centres in rural locations, investment in pre-school education and upgrading technology, natural sciences and art facilities in general education.

Portugal

School funding in Portugal (ISCED 0-3): The information contained in the country profile for Portugal mainly refers to the administrative agreements in the continental territory. The autonomous regions of Madeira and Azores have their own government. It is the competence of each regional parliament to legislate on matters related to the education system of each of the regions.

Organisation in school clusters: As of 2015, school clusters represented 83% of the entire school offer, and 98% of primary, lower and upper secondary public schools.

Targeted support: Support to specific groups of students or schools is guaranteed through targeted programmes, such as the National Plan of School Achievement (*Plano Nacional de Sucesso Escolar*) aiming at enhancing student performance and reducing dropout rates or the Education Territories for Priority Intervention programme (*Programa Territórios Educativos de Intervenção Prioritária,* TEIP), directed at schools in socio-economically disadvantaged locations. As of 2016, the TEIP programme involved about 18% of school clusters, which present projects for school and student performance improvement. The approved projects are then funded by the Ministry of Education according to the budgetary needs for implementation of such projects.

Block grant from central authority to local authorities for operating costs, extracurricular activities and subsidised meals, excluding teachers' salaries (ISCED 0-1 first 4 years, ISCED 2): The municipal social fund (*Fundo Social Municipal*) is a central budget block grant to municipalities, aimed at covering current expenses in public pre-schools and public schools offering the first 4 years of ISCED 1, namely non-teaching staff salaries, meals, extracurricular activities, school transport and other operating costs, besides teaching and monitoring staff in extracurricular activities in sports and the arts, student curricular support, health support at school and socio-educational support to students in ISCED 1. Furthermore, it also aims to cover expenses with school transport at ISCED level 2. If the municipality presents expenditure exceeding the budget in a given year, the excess is deducted in the grant of the following year.

Slovak Republic

Block grants from central authorities to school providers (ISCED 1-3): The salary and operational school specific grants are given to school providers (regional authority, local authority, private providers) together as one block grant. The grants are calculated to cover corresponding types of costs, but can be spent on any type of expenditure.

Block grant from central authority to local authorities, regional authorities and private school providers as top up funding when school-specific grant does not cover staff and operational costs (ISCED 1-3): The central education authorities decide the amount of the grant, but do not allocate it for individual schools. The regional and local levels take responsibility, but no mechanism is formally defined.

Infrastructure investment programme from central authority to local and regional authorities for infrastructure construction (ISCED 02-3): The central infrastructure programme focuses on the extension of school capacities in the form of modular schools (construction of new infrastructure or extension of current infrastructure), e.g. in areas where schools have introduced double shifts to respond to demographic changes (e.g. because of people relocating from Bratislava to the suburbs, or in Eastern Slovak Republic). The programme began in 2013 and between 2013 and 2016 new capacities for more than 6 000 students had been built. A similar infrastructure programme was started for kindergartens to extend the capacities by 5 000 places.

Slovenia

Earmarked grant from the central authority to local authorities for transport of students to schools in areas with brown bears (ISCED 1-2): The central level provides funds to municipalities for the transport of students that could be in danger on the way to or from school (if they walked) because of brown bears and other wild animals. These funds are only given to municipalities situated in the area of the habitat of the brown bear. The area is determined in the brown bear management strategy adopted in 2006. The transport is then organised by the municipalities which usually hire a transport company. Funds received by the municipalities are based on the number of students that use this type of transport.

Discretionary funding by local authorities for infrastructure construction, renovation and maintenance, non-instructional and instructional material (ISCED 0-3): Local authorities are mainly responsible for capital expenditure at ISCED 0-2, exceptionally also at ISCED 3.

Discretionary funding from the central authority to local authorities for partial financing of capital investment (ISCED 0-2): In schools of the Italian and Hungarian national communities, the central level covers 100% of the capital investment.

Spain

Lump sum from the central authority to regional authorities for any type of public expenditures (ISCED 0-3): In the basis to determine the level of the grant, other needs of public educational services supply are also generally considered, such as transport, school canteen, school catering, school libraries, school books, school equipment, infrastructure, pedagogical material, school supplies, among others.

Earmarked grants from the central authority to regional authorities for educational support and other several specific purposes (ISCED 0-3): Earmarked grants are allocated for the following purposes: special needs education and special needs schools, operating costs, some especial programs for maintenance of infrastructure, foreign language learning, learning support for disadvantaged students and programs for VET education. These transfers are the result of special agreements with the Autonomous Communities related to the quality of education.

Earmarked grants from the central authority to local authorities for educational support and other several specific purposes (ISCED 0-3): Earmarked grants from central to local authorities are channelled through the Spanish Federation of Municipalities and Provinces (*Federación Española de Municipios y Provincias*, FEMP). These are targeted at the following purposes: dropout, shared school environment, disability and training in educational themes.

Earmarked grant from regional authorities to local authorities for early childhood education and care (ISCED 0): The transfer of these funds is related with the progressive rise of public offer. Regional educational authorities establish the conditions for agreements with local corporations (municipalities) for the provision of ISCED 01, other administrations and private non-profit entities. Transfers are also made from the regional to the local level in order to guarantee a sufficient supply of public offer in public pre-schools or publicly subsidised private pre-schools offering the ISCED 02 level of education.

Earmarked grants from the regional authorities to local authorities for educational support and other several specific purposes (ISCED 0-3): Earmarked grants from regional to local authorities are allocated for the following purposes: special needs education, learning support staff and staff not involved in instructional activities, ICT, school transport and programs against truancy. These are agreed with the municipalities based on the needs of educational supply, and according to regional and local educational planning.

Dedicated grant from regional authorities for teacher and non-teacher salaries (ISCED 0-3): Characteristics of teachers considered in the funding formula include: different professional categories, level of education taught, status as an official (civil servant) or a contracted (no civil servant) teacher.

Earmarked grant from regional authorities to schools for supporting additional costs with students with special educational needs (ISCED 0-3): Regional authorities are responsible for providing funds to cover additional costs with SEN students. These earmarked grants also include funds for co-operative programs with non-profit educational institutions for specific actions with students with SEN. Other specific criteria considered in the basis to determine the level of the grant include: number of teachers required, the curricular level of students with SEN, number of other specialised professionals required, maintenance of supports materials in ordinary schools and maintenance of (medical) support materials in specialised schools.

Sweden

Earmarked grants from the central authority to local authorities to promote policy priorities (ISCED 0-3): The municipalities apply for funding through these earmarked grants from a central education authority, the National Agency for Education.

Discretionary funding from local authorities to schools (ISCED 0-3): The criteria for allocating funds to schools are at the discretion of the municipality or district. The Education Act stipulates that the municipal funding mechanism should account for the number of students enrolled and also the "different precondition and needs of different students".

Uruguay

Capital expenditure (ISCED 0-3): Regular funding of schools for current expenditure includes some funds for maintenance and small investments.

Infrastructure investment programme from the central authorities for extra support for capital expenditure (ISCED 1 full-time primary schools and ISCED 2-3): The Support Programme for Public Primary Education (*Programa de Apoyo a la Escuela Pública Uruguaya*, PAEPU), funded by the World Bank, supports infrastructure and equipment for full-time schools. The Support Programme for Secondary Education and Training in Education (*Programa de Apoyo a la Educación Media y Técnica y a la Formación en Educación*, PAEMFE), funded by the Inter-American Development Bank, supports infrastructure and equipment in secondary education and teacher training institutions. Both PAEMFE and PAEPU are administered by the National Public Education Administration (*Administración Nacional de Educación Pública*, ANEP).

ANNEX D

How the School Resources Review was conducted

Governance of the review

The School Resources Review is overseen by a Group of National Experts (GNE) on School Resources, a subsidiary body of the OECD Education Policy Committee. The GNE on School Resources guides the review and facilitates the exchange of information and experiences concerning school resources among countries. The GNE on School Resources has been chaired by Mr Jørn Skovsgaard, Senior Advisor, Danish Ministry of Education, and vice-chairs Ms Marie-Anne Persoons, Policy advisor, Flemish Ministry of Education and Training and Mr Matej Šiškovič, Director, Education Policy Institute, Ministry of Education, Science, Research and Sport of the Slovak Republic.

Between May 2014 and May 2017, the GNE on School Resources held four official meetings at the OECD Conference Centre in Paris. These were open to all OECD member countries and observers to the Education Policy Committee as well as to the Trade Union Advisory Committee to the OECD (TUAC) and the Business and Industry Advisory Committee to the OECD (BIAC). The project is conducted in co-operation with a range of international organisations to reduce duplication and develop synergies. In particular, within a broader framework of collaboration, a partnership with the European Commission (EC) is established for this project (see below). The review of Kazakhstan was undertaken in co-operation with the World Bank. Other international agencies collaborating with the project include Eurydice, the Inter-American Development Bank (IDB), the Organising Bureau of European School Student Unions (OBESSU), the Standing International Conference of Inspectorates (SICI) and the United Nations Educational, Scientific and Cultural Organization (UNESCO).

National co-ordinators

Each participating country appointed a national co-ordinator, who was responsible for: communications with the OECD Secretariat and within the country about the review; ensuring that the country background report was completed on schedule; liaising with the OECD Secretariat about the organisation of the review team visit, for those countries which opted for a country review; attending meetings of the Group of National Experts on School Resources; co-ordinating country responses to the review's qualitative survey on school funding; co-ordinating country feedback on draft materials; and assisting with dissemination activities. National co-ordinators are listed in Table D.1.

Table D.1. **National co-ordinators in participating countries**

Country	National co-ordinator(s)
Austria	Bernhard Chabera, Austrian Federal Ministry for Education
Belgium (Flemish Community)	Marie-Anne Persoons, Flemish Ministry of Education and Training
Belgium (French Community)	Philippe Dieu, International Relations Directorate of the Federation Wallonia-Brussels
Chile	Eduardo Candia Agusti, Chilean Ministry of Education Carla Guazzini, Chilean Ministry of Education
Czech Republic	Lucie Priknerová, Czech Ministry of Education, Youth and Sports Michael Vlach, Czech Ministry of Education, Youth and Sports
Denmark	Jon Jespersen, Danish Ministry of Education Sigrid Lundetoft Clausen, Danish Ministry of Education
Estonia	Kadi Serbak, Estonian Ministry of Education and Research
Iceland	Sigríður Lára Ásbergsdóttir, Icelandic Ministry of Education, Science and Culture
Kazakhstan	Zhannat Mussina, Information Analytic Center Assem Satmukhambetova, Information Analytic Center
Lithuania	Aidas Aldakauskas, Lithuanian Ministry of Education and Science Vilma Bačkiūtė, Lithuanian Ministry of Education and Science
Luxembourg	Amina Kafai, Luxembourg Ministry of National Education and Vocational Training Charlotte Mahon, Luxembourg Ministry of National Education and Vocational Training
Portugal	Ana Neves, Portuguese Ministry of Education
Slovak Republic	Matej Šiškovič, National Institute for Educational Assessment
Slovenia	Klemen Surk Kokalj, Slovenian Ministry of Education, Science and Sport
Spain	Vicente Alcañiz, National Institute for Educational Assessment Isabel Couso Tapia, Spanish Ministry of Education, Culture and Sport
Sweden	Gunnar Stenberg, Swedish Ministry of Education and Research Merja Strömberg, Swedish Ministry of Education and Research
Uruguay	Cecilia Llambi, National Institute for Educational Evaluation Cecilia Oreiro, National Institute for Educational Evaluation

Collaboration with the European Commission

Within a broader framework of collaboration, a partnership with the European Commission (EC) was established for this project. The support of the EC covers part of the participation costs of countries which are part of the European Union's Erasmus+ programme and contributes significantly to the preparation of the series of thematic comparative reports. Within the EC's Directorate-General for Education and Culture, the collaboration was organised by Unit A.2: *Education and Training in Europe 2020* under the leadership of Michael Teutsch (until December 2016) and Denis Crowley (since January 2017) and deputy leadership of Mónika Képe-Holmberg, and Unit B.2: *Schools and Multilingualism* under the leadership of Sophie Beernaerts (until December 2016) and Michael Teutsch (since January 2017) and deputy leadership of Diana Jablonska. Through its country analysis work the EC contributed to planning individual country reviews in the countries listed in Table D.2, and provided feedback on draft country reviews and the drafts of this thematic comparative report.

Table D.2. **European Commission contribution to country reviews**

Country	EC Country Desk Officer contributing to the planning of the review
Slovak Republic	Christèle Duvieusart, European Commission
Estonia	Krzysztof Kania, European Commission
Belgium (Flemish Community)	Patricia De Smet, European Commission
Denmark	Joanna Basztura, European Commission
Czech Republic	Christèle Duvieusart, European Commission
Lithuania	Joanna Basztura, European Commission
Austria	Klaus Koerner, European Commission

Country background reports

Information on countries' policies and practices was gathered through country background reports (CBRs). The CBRs were prepared in response to a common set of issues and questions, and used a common framework to facilitate comparative analysis and maximise the opportunities for countries to learn from each other. The CBRs were a key source of information for the review's thematic comparative reports. The guidelines for the preparation of CBRs are set out in a dedicated document [EDU/EDPC(2013)11/REV1], also available on the review website (*www.oecd.org/education/schoolresourcesreview.htm*). The CBRs were structured around the following main chapters:

1. The national context

2. The school system

3. Governance of resource use in schools

4. Resource distribution

5. Resource utilisation

6. Resource management

The CBRs were intended for four main audiences: The Secretariat and OECD member and observer countries as an aid to sharing experiences and identifying common problems and policy options; the team of external reviewers who visited the countries which opted for a country review; those interested in the use of school resources in the country concerned; and those interested in the use of school resources at international level and in other countries. All CBRs are available on the review website (*www.oecd.org/education/schoolresourcesreview.htm*).

Qualitative data collection

In addition to the country background reports, the School Resources Review collected information on countries' national approaches to school funding through a qualitative questionnaire prepared by the OECD Secretariat. Seventeen systems participated in this qualitative data collection. The questionnaire focused on formal requirements for funding in terms of laws and regulations for early childhood and school education that were in place in 2016. It did not cover observed practices which can vary considerably. The questionnaire covered the following issues: raising resources for education; the public funding of private providers; budgeting and planning procedures; the distribution of current and capital expenditure; targeted funding; VET funding; the use of funding at the school level; and monitoring and reporting procedures.

The qualitative survey provided crucial information to complement the information available through CBRs and to support the review's analysis. Most of the information gathered through the survey is published in a set of comparative tables included in this report. The review team made every effort to ensure in collaboration with countries that the information available in this report is as valid and robust as possible and reflects specific country contexts while being comparable across countries. However, given the complex nature of school funding and the qualitative nature of this survey, information should be interpreted with care. Country contacts for the qualitative data collection are listed in Table D.3.

Table D.3. **Country contacts for the qualitative data collection**

Country	Country contact(s)
Austria	Bernhard Chabera, Austrian Federal Ministry for Education
Belgium (Flemish Community)	Marie-Anne Persoons, Flemish Ministry of Education and Training
Belgium (French Community)	Philippe Dieu, International Relations Directorate of the Federation Wallonia-Brussels
Chile	Eduardo Candia Agusti, Chilean Ministry of Education Carla Guazzini, Chilean Ministry of Education
Czech Republic	Lucie Priknerová, Czech Ministry of Education, Youth and Sports
Denmark	Jon Jespersen, Danish Ministry of Education
Estonia	Kadi Serbak, Estonian Ministry of Education and Research
Iceland	Gunnar Jóhannes Árnason, Icelandic Ministry of Education, Science and Culture
Israel	Daniel Levi-Mazloum, Israeli Ministry of Education Yoav Azulay, Israeli Ministry of Education
Kazakhstan	Dilyara Tashibaeva, Information Analytic Center Saniya Boranbayeva, Information Analytic Center
Lithuania	Jurga Zacharkienė, Lithuanian Ministry of Education and Science
Portugal	Ana Neves, Portuguese Ministry of Education
Slovak Republic	Ján Toman, National Institute for Educational Assessment
Slovenia	Klemen Surk Kokalj, Slovenian Ministry of Education, Science and Sport
Spain	Isabel Couso Tapia, Spanish Ministry of Education, Culture and Sport José María Gallego, Spanish Ministry of Education, Culture and Sport
Sweden	Gunnar Stenberg, Swedish Ministry of Education and Research
Uruguay	Lucía Castro, National Institute for Educational Evaluation Cecilia Oreiro, National Institute for Educational Evaluation

Country review reports

Another major source of material for this report was the set of country review reports prepared by the external review teams that visited participating countries engaging in a full country review. By providing an external perspective on the use of school resources in the countries concerned, the country review reports were also intended to contribute to national discussions, as well as inform other countries about policy innovations underway. The country review reports were also published as a publication series, *OECD Reviews of School Resources*, in order to enhance the visibility of these country-specific outputs as part of the review.

For each country visited, a team of up to five reviewers (including at least two OECD Secretariat members) analysed the country background report and associated materials and subsequently undertook an intensive case study visit over the course of about seven days. The reviewers were selected in consultation with the country authorities to ensure that they had experience relevant to the main policy issues in the country concerned. The study visit aimed to provide the review team with a variety of perspectives on the governance, distribution, management and utilisation of school resources and included meetings with education and finance authorities at national and sub-national levels; relevant agencies (e.g. audit offices); teacher professional organisations and unions; parents' organisations; representatives of schools and school leaders; students' organisations; teacher educators; researchers; as well as students, teachers and school leaders at the schools visited. The objective was to accumulate sufficient information and understanding on which to base the analysis and policy recommendations.

At the time of publication, 10 review visits were conducted, involving 21 external reviewers with a range of research and policy backgrounds. The reviews involved a planning visit and a main review visit. Details on the composition of the review teams for the main visits can be found in Table D.4. The country review reports are published on the project website (*www.oecd.org/education/schoolresourcesreview.htm*).

Table D.4. **Country reviews and team members**

Country	Review visit team
Kazakhstan 31 March-9 April 2014	Anna Pons, OECD Secretariat (co-ordinator) Jeremie Amoroso, World Bank Jan Herczyński, Institute for Educational Research, Poland Igor Kheyfets, World Bank Marlaine Lockheed, Princeton University, United States Paulo Santiago, OECD Secretariat
Slovak Republic 7-14 October 2014	Paulo Santiago, OECD Secretariat (co-ordinator) Gábor Halász, University Eötvös Loránd, Hungary Rosalind Levačić, Institute of Education - University of London, United Kingdom Claire Shewbridge, OECD Secretariat
Estonia 20-27 October 2014	Paulo Santiago, OECD Secretariat (co-ordinator) Anthony Levitas, Brown University, United States Péter Radó, Education Consultant, Hungary Claire Shewbridge, OECD Secretariat
Belgium (Flemish Community) 3-10 November 2014	Deborah Nusche, OECD Secretariat (co-ordinator) Gary Miron, Western Michigan University, United States Paulo Santiago, OECD Secretariat Richard Teese, University of Melbourne, Australia
Lithuania 2-9 December 2014	Claire Shewbridge, OECD Secretariat (co-ordinator) Katrina Godfrey, Department of Education of Northern Ireland, United Kingdom Zoltán Hermann, Institute of Economics - Academy of Sciences, Hungary Deborah Nusche, OECD Secretariat
Uruguay 17-25 March 2015	Paulo Santiago, OECD Secretariat (co-ordinator) Beatrice Ávalos, Universidad de Chile, Chile Tracey Burns, OECD Secretariat Alejandro Morduchowicz, Inter-American Development Bank Thomas Radinger, OECD Secretariat
Denmark 22-29 April 2015	Deborah Nusche, OECD Secretariat (co-ordinator) Torberg Falch, Norwegian University of Science and Technology, Norway Thomas Radinger, OECD Secretariat Bruce Shaw, Ontario Ministry of Education, Canada
Czech Republic 26 May-2 June 2015	Claire Shewbridge, OECD Secretariat (co-ordinator) Jan Herczyński, Institute for Educational Research, Poland Thomas Radinger, OECD Secretariat Julie Sonnemann, Education Consultant - Learning First, Australia
Austria 24-30 June 2015	Deborah Nusche, OECD Secretariat (co-ordinator) Marius Busemeyer, University of Konstanz, Germany Thomas Radinger, OECD Secretariat Henno Theisens, The Hague University of Applied Sciences, Netherlands
Chile 22-30 September 2015	Paulo Santiago, OECD Secretariat (co-ordinator) Ariel Fiszbein, Inter-American Dialogue, United States Sandra Garcia Jaramillo, Universidad de los Andes, Colombia Thomas Radinger, OECD Secretariat

Analytical background papers

The School Resources Review was also informed by the following analytical background papers and literature reviews prepared in the context of the project:

- Ares Abalde, M. (2014), "School Size Policies: A Literature Review", *OECD Education Working Papers*, No. 106, OECD Publishing, Paris, *http://dx.doi.org/10.1787/5jxt472ddkjl-en*.

- Masdeu Navarro, F. (2015), "Learning support staff: A literature review", *OECD Education Working Papers*, No. 125, OECD Publishing, Paris, *http://dx.doi.org/10.1787/5jrnzm39w45l-en*.

- Gromada, A. and C. Shewbridge (2016), "Student Learning Time: A Literature Review", *OECD Education Working Papers*, No. 127, OECD Publishing, Paris, *http://dx.doi.org/10.1787/5jm409kqqkjh-en*.

- Fakharzadeh, T. (2016), "Budgeting and Accounting in OECD Education Systems: A Literature Review", *OECD Education Working Papers*, No. 128, OECD Publishing, Paris, *http://dx.doi.org/10.1787/5jm3xgsz03kh-en*.

- Boeskens, L. (2016), "Regulating Publicly Funded Private Schools: A Literature Review on Equity and Effectiveness", *OECD Education Working Papers*, No. 147, OECD Publishing, Paris, *http://dx.doi.org/10.1787/5jln6jcg80r4-en*.

- "Targeted School Funding: A Literature Review" by Kerstin Schopohl (under review).

- "Funding Education for Students with Special Educational Needs: A Literature Review" by Oliver Sieweke (under review).

- "The Funding of Vocational Education and Training: A Literature Review" by Antoine Papalia (under review).

- "Conceptualising and Measuring Efficiency and Equity in the Use of School Resources" by Gonçalo Lima (under review).

Dissemination

To facilitate dissemination and encourage feedback, all project documents and outputs were published on the review's website (*www.oecd.org/education/schoolresourcesreview.htm*). Throughout the review, the OECD Secretariat presented the project and its findings at a wide range of internal and external meetings and a significant number of countries organised national events to discuss both the international results from the review and the conclusions of specific country reviews.

ORGANISATION FOR ECONOMIC CO-OPERATION AND DEVELOPMENT

The OECD is a unique forum where governments work together to address the economic, social and environmental challenges of globalisation. The OECD is also at the forefront of efforts to understand and to help governments respond to new developments and concerns, such as corporate governance, the information economy and the challenges of an ageing population. The Organisation provides a setting where governments can compare policy experiences, seek answers to common problems, identify good practice and work to co-ordinate domestic and international policies.

The OECD member countries are: Australia, Austria, Belgium, Canada, Chile, the Czech Republic, Denmark, Estonia, Finland, France, Germany, Greece, Hungary, Iceland, Ireland, Israel, Italy, Japan, Korea, Latvia, Luxembourg, Mexico, the Netherlands, New Zealand, Norway, Poland, Portugal, the Slovak Republic, Slovenia, Spain, Sweden, Switzerland, Turkey, the United Kingdom and the United States. The European Union takes part in the work of the OECD.

OECD Publishing disseminates widely the results of the Organisation's statistics gathering and research on economic, social and environmental issues, as well as the conventions, guidelines and standards agreed by its members.

OECD PUBLISHING, 2, rue André-Pascal, 75775 PARIS CEDEX 16
(91 2017 06 1 P) ISBN 978-92-64-27613-0 – 2017